THE DIARY OF
SAMUEL PEPYS

George Monck, 1st Duke of Albemarle, by Sir Peter Lely

THE DIARY
OF
SAMUEL PEPYS

A new and complete
transcription edited by

ROBERT LATHAM
AND
WILLIAM MATTHEWS

CONTRIBUTING EDITORS

WILLIAM A. ARMSTRONG · MACDONALD EMSLIE
SIR OLIVER MILLAR · the late T. F. REDDAWAY

VOLUME V · 1664

BELL & HYMAN
LONDON

Published by
BELL & HYMAN LIMITED
Denmark House
37–39 Queen Elizabeth Street
London SE1 2QB

First published in 1971 by
G. Bell & Sons Ltd
Reprinted 1974, 1978

© *Bell & Hyman Limited 1971*

ISBN 0 7135 1555 4

Printed in Great Britain by Fletcher & Son Ltd, Norwich

CONTENTS

LIST OF ILLUSTRATIONS

READER'S GUIDE

This section is meant for quick reference.   More detailed information about the editorial methods used in this edition will be found in the Introduction and in the section 'Methods of the Commentary' in vol. I, and also in the statement preceding the Select Glossary at the end of each text volume.

I. THE TEXT

The fact that the MS. is mostly in shorthand makes exact reproduction (e.g. of spelling, capitalisation and punctuation) impossible.

Spelling is in modern British style, except for those longhand words which Pepys spelt differently, and words for which the shorthand indicates a variant pronunciation which is also shown by Pepys's longhand elsewhere.   These latter are given in spellings which reflect Pepys's pronunciations.

Pepys's capitalisation is indicated only in his longhand.

Punctuation is almost all editorial, except for certain full-stops, colons, dashes and parentheses.   Punctuation is almost non-existent in the original since the marks could be confused with shorthand.

Italics are all editorial, but (in e.g. headings to entries) often follow indications given in the MS. (by e.g. the use of larger writing).

The **paragraphing** is that of the MS.

Abbreviations of surnames, titles, place names and ordinary words are expanded.

Single **hyphens** are editorial, and represent Pepys's habit of disjoining the elements of compound words (e.g. Wh. hall/White-hall).   Double hyphens represent Pepys's hyphens.

Single **angle-brackets** mark additions made by Pepys in the body of the MS.; double angle-brackets those made in the margins.

Light **asterisks** are editorial (see below, Section II); heavy asterisks are Pepys's own.

Pepys's **alterations** are indicated by the word 'replacing' ('repl.') in the textual footnotes.

II. THE COMMENTARY

1. Footnotes deal mainly with events and transactions.   They also identify MSS, books, plays, music and quotations, but give only occasional and minimal information about persons and places, words and phrases. The initials which follow certain notes indicate the work of the contributing editors. Light asterisks in the text direct the reader to the Select Glossary for the definition of words whose meanings have changed since the time of the diary. References to the diary are given by volume and page where the text is in page-proof at the time of going to press; in other cases, by entry-dates. In notes to the Introduction, since almost all the references there are to the text, a simpler form of reference (by entry-date only) is used.

2. The **Select List of Persons** is printed unchanged in each text volume. It covers the whole diary and identifies the principal persons, together with those who are described in the MS. by titles or in other ways that make for obscurity.

3. The **Select Glossary** is printed at the end of each text volume. It gives definitions of most recurrent English words and phrases, and identifications of certain recurrent places.

4. The **Companion** (vol. X) is a collection of reference material. It contains maps, genealogical tables, and a Large Glossary, but consists mainly of articles, printed for ease of reference in a single alphabetical series. These give information about matters which are dealt with briefly or not at all in the footnotes and the Select Glossary: i.e. persons, places, words and phrases, food, drink, clothes, the weather etc. They also treat systematically the principal subjects with which the diary is concerned: Pepys's work, interests, health etc. References to the *Companion* are given only rarely in the footnotes. Its principal contents are as follows:

'Bibliography of Works Cited'
'Books' (*General; Catalogues; Book-cases*)
'Christenings'
'Christmas' (*General; Twelfth Night*)
'Clothes'
'Currency' (*Coins etc.*)
'Drink'
'Exchequer'
'Food' (*Meals; Dishes*)
'Funerals'
'Games, Sports and Pastimes'
'Gunpowder Plot Day'
'Health' (*Medical history of Pepys and his wife; Diseases etc.; Medicines*)
'Household' (*General; Servants; Furniture and Furnishings etc.*)
'Language'
'May Day'
'Music' (*General; Dances; Musical Instruments; Songs and Song-Books*)
'Navy' (*Admiralty; Chatham Chest; Dockyards and Dockyard Officers; Navy Board and its Officers; Tickets; Victualling*). See also *Ships*

'Ordnance Office'
Persons (*under names*)
Places (*Buildings, streets, inns etc., under
    names or titles; mainly London;
    other places under place names*)
'Postal Services'
'Privy Seal Office'
'Religion' (*General; Sermons; Sunday
    Observance; Lent, Whitsuntide
    etc.*)
'Royal Fishery'
'St Valentine's Day'
'Science' (*General; Royal Society;
    Scientific Instruments*)
Ships (*Types and individual ships under
    names*)

'Shrove Tuesday'
'Tangier' (*General; the Mole*)
'Theatre' (*General; Theatres: build-
    ings, companies*)
'Toilet' (*Washing, Shaving, Cosmetics
    etc.*)
'Travel' (*By river; By road*)
'Trinity House'
'Wardrobe, the King's Great'
'Wealth'
'Weather'
'Weddings'
'Large Glossary' (*Words; Phrases;
    Proverbs*)

III. DATES

In Pepys's time two reckonings of the calendar year were in use in
Western Europe. Most countries had adopted the New Style – the
revised calendar of Gregory XIII (1582); Britain until 1752 retained the
Old Style – the ancient Roman, or Julian, calendar, which meant that
its dates were ten days behind those of the rest of Western Europe in the
seventeenth century. 1 January in England was therefore 11 January
by the New Style abroad. On the single occasion during the period of
the diary when Pepys was abroad (in Holland in May 1660) he
continued to use the Old Style, thus avoiding a break in the run of his
dates. In the editorial material of the present work dates relating to
countries which had adopted the new reckoning are given in both
styles (e.g. '1/11 January') in order to prevent confusion.

It will be noticed that the shortest and longest days of the year occur
in the diary ten days earlier than in the modern calendar. So, too,
does Lord Mayor's Day in London – on 29 October instead of
9 November.

For most legal purposes (from medieval times until 1752) the new
year in England was held to begin on Lady Day, 25 March. But in
accordance with the general custom, Pepys took it to begin on 1 January,
as in the Julian calendar. He gives to all dates within the overlapping
period between 1 January and 24 March a year-date which comprehends
both styles – e.g. 'January 1 16$\frac{59}{60}$.' In the present commentary a single
year-date, that of the New Style, has been used: e.g. '1 January 1660'.

THE DIARY
1664

$16\frac{63}{64}$. JANUARY.

1. Went to bed between 4 and 5 in the morning with my mind in good temper of satisfaction – and slept till about 8, that many people came to speak with me. Among others, one came with the best New Year's gift that ever I had; namely[a] from Mr. Deering, with a bill of exchange drawn upon himself for the payment of 50l. to Mr. Luellin – it being for my use, with a letter of compliment.[1] I am not resolved what or how to do in this business, but I conclude it is an extraordinary good New Year's gift, though I do not take the whole; or if I do, then give some of it to Luellin. By and by comes Captain Allin and his son Jowles and his wife, who continues pretty still. They would have had me set my hand to a certificate for his Loyalty and I know not what, his ability for any imployment. But I did not think it fit, but did give them a pleasing denial – and after sitting with me an hour, they went away. Several others came to me about business; and then, being to dine at my uncle Wights, I went to the Coffee-house (sending my wife by Will) and there stayed talking an hour with Collonell Middleton and others; and among other things, about a very rich widow, young and handsome, of one Sir Nich. Golds, a merchant lately fallen, and of great Courtiers that already look after her. Her husband not dead a week yet. She is reckoned worth 8000l.[2]

Thence to my Uncle Wights, where Dr.[b]   [3] among others dined, and his wife a seeming proud conceited woman; I know not what to make of her. But the Doctors discourse did please me very well about the disease of the Stone; above all things extolling Turpentine, which he told me how it may be

a l.h. repl. s.h. 'this'   *b* MS. 'Dr. of'

---

1. See above, iv. 415, n. 4.
2. For her marriage to the courtier Thomas Neale, see below, p. 184. The wits thereafter called him 'Golden Neale': *Parl. Hist.*, iv, App. p. xxv.
   3. Supply '[Alexander] Burnet', a friend of Wight.

I

taken in pills with great ease.[1] There was brought to table a hot
pie made of a swan I sent them yesterday, given[a] me by Mr.
Howe; but we did not eat any of it.[2] But my wife and I rise
from table pretending business, and went to the Dukes house, the
first play I have been at these six months, according to my last
vowe;[3] and here saw the so much cried-up play of *Henry the 8th* –
which, though I went with resolution to like it, is so simple a
thing, made up of a great many patches, that, besides the shows
and processions in it, there is nothing in the world good or well
done.[4] Thence, mightily dissatisfied, back at night to my uncle
Wights and supped with them; but against my stomach out of
the offence the sight of my aunts hands gives me; and ending
supper with a mighty laugh (the[b] greatest I have had these many
months) at my uncles being out in his grace after meat, we rise
and broke up and my wife and I home and to bed – being sleepy
since last night.

2. Up and to the office and there sitting all the morning, and
at noon to the Change; in my going met with Luellin and told
him how I had received a letter and bill for 50*l* from Mr. Deering
and delivered it to him; which he told me he would receive
for me. To which I consented, though professed not to desire
it if he doth not think himself sufficiently able by the service I
have done, and that it is rather my desire to have nothing till
he be further sensible of my service. From the Change I brought
him home, and dined with us. And after dinner I took my wife
out (for I do find that I am not able to conquer myself as to
going to plays till I do come to some new vow concerning it

a repl. 'made by'   *b* MS. has the bracket after 'the'

---

1. On 17 July 1664 Burnet showed
Pepys how to take his turpentine pills.
2. The swan probably came by
courtesy of Sandwich, who was
Master of the King's Swans in the
Thames and elsewhere, and Bailiff of
Whittlesea Mere. Will Howe was a
servant of his.
3. A vow of 13 June 1663 to eschew
theatre-going until after Christmas:
above, iv. 182. (A).

4. Davenant's revival of Shakespeare's play (q.v. above, iv. 411 &
n. 5) was so spectacular that it was
talked about for years. In the procession scene (Act V, sc. 5) faces and
figures at windows and balconies
were painted on the backcloth and
wings of the setting. Pepys had not
seen a play since 13 June 1663; this
production was at the LIF. (A).

and*ᵃ* that I am now come: that is to say, that I will not see above one in a month at any of the public theatres till*ᵇ* the sum of 50*s* be spent, and then none before New Year's Day next, unless that I do become worth 1000*l* sooner then then – and then I am free to come to some other terms). And so, leaving him in Lombard Streete, I took her to the King's house and there met with Mr. Nicholson my old colleague[1] – and saw *The Usurper*,[2] which is no good play, though better then what I saw yesterday. However, we rise unsatisfied and took coach and home. And I to the office late, writing letters; and so home to supper and to bed.

3. *Lords day.* Lay long in bed; and then rose and with a fire in my chamber stayed within all day, looking over and settling my accounts in good order – by examining all my books and the kitchen books; and I find that though the proper profit of my last year was but 305*l*, yet I did by other gain make it up 444*l*[3] – which in every part of it was unforeseen of me; and therefore it was a strange oversight for lack of examining my expenses that I should spend 690*l* this year. But for the time to come, I have so distinctly settled all my accounts in writing and the perticulars of all my several layings-out, that I do hope I shall hereafter make a better judgment of my spendings then ever. I dined with my wife in her chamber, she in bed. And then down again and till 11 at night; and broke up and to bed with great content, but could not make an end of writing over my vows as I purposed, but I am agreed in everything how to order myself for the year to come, which I trust in God will be much for my good. So up to prayers and to bed.

This noon Sir W Pen came to invite me and my wife against next Wednesday,*ᶜ* being Twelfth-day, to his usual feast, his wedding day.

a preceded by bracket   *b* repl. 'and that only'
      c MS. 'wedding day'

1. John Nicholson, late of Magdalene College.
2. A tragedy by Edward Howard, first published in 1668. This is the first record of a performance. Hugh Peters is represented as Hugo de Petra, and the references to Damocles the Syracusan are allusions to Oliver Cromwell. (A).
3. The 'proper profit' would be from official fees; the rest from unofficial gifts. For fees in general, see above, i. 223, n. 1.

B

4. Up betimes, and my wife being ready and her maid Besse and the girl, I carried them by coach and set them all down in Covent-garden and there left them, and I to my Lord Sandwich['s] lodgings, but he not being up, I to the Dukes chamber, and there by and by to his closet; where, since his lady was ill, a little red bed of velvet is brought for him to lie alone, which is a very pretty one. After doing business here, I to my Lord's again and there spoke with him, and he seems now almost friends again as he used to be.[1] Here meeting Mr. Pierce the surgeon, he told me, among other Court news, how the Queene is very well again and the King lay with her on Saturday night last. And that she speaks now very pretty English and makes her sense out now and then with pretty phrases – as among others, this is mightily cried up – that meaning to say that she did not like such a horse so well as the rest, he being too prancing and full of tricks, she said he did "make too much vanity." Thence to the Tennice Court[2] (after I had spent a little time in Westminster-hall, thinking to have met with Mrs. Lane, but I could not and am glad of it) and there saw the King play at Tennis and others. But to see how the King's play was extolled without any cause at all, was a loathsome sight, though sometimes endeed he did play very well and deserved to be commended; but such open flattery is beastly. Afterward to St. James's park, being unwilling to go to spend money at the ordinary, and there spent an hour or two, it being a pleasant day, seeing people play at Pell Mell[3] – where it pleased me mightily to hear a gallant, lately come from France, swear at one of his companions for suffering his man (a spruce blade) to be so saucy as to strike a ball while his master was playing on the Mall.

Thence took coach at White-hall and took up my wife, who is mighty sad to think of her father, who is going into Germany against the Turkes. But what will become of her brother I know not; he is so idle, and out of all capacity I think to earn his bread.[4]

Home – and at my office till 12 at night, making my solemn

1. For his recent difference with Pepys over Sandwich's affair with the girl at Chelsea, see above, iv. 386–7.
2. In Whitehall Palace.
3. See above, ii. 64 & n. 2.

4. It seems unlikely that her father went to the war. Her brother Balty soon afterwards decided to seek his fortune in the Dutch army: below, p. 37.

vowes for the next year, which I trust in the Lord I shall keep. But I fear I have a little too severely bound myself in some things and in too many, for I fear I may forget some. But however, I know the worst, and shall by the blessing of God observe to perform or pay my forfeits punctually. So home and to bed – with my mind at rest.

5. Up and to our ⟨office⟩, where we sat all the morning; where my head being willing to take in all business whatever, I am afeared I shall over-clog myself with it. But however, it is my desire to do my duty and shall the willinger bear it. At noon home and to the Change, where I met with Luellin – who went off with me and parted, to meet again at the Coffee-house, but missed. So home and found him there and Mr. Barrow come to speak with me; so they both dined with me alone, my wife not being ready. And after dinner, I up in my chamber with Barrow to discourse about matters of the yard with him and his design of leaving the place, which I am sorry for – and will prevent if I can.[1]

He being gone, then Luellin did give me the 50 pound from Mr. Deering which he doth give me for my pains in his business and which I may hereafter take for him – though there is not the least word or deed I have yet been guilty of in his behalf but what I am sure hath been to the King's advantage and the profit of the service, nor ever will I. And for this money I never did condition with him or expected a farthing at*a* the time when I did do him the service. Nor have given any receipt for it, it being brought me by Luellin. Nor do purpose to give him any

a repl. 'before I had'

---

1. Philip Barrow, Storekeeper at Chatham (for whose disputes with his colleagues see above, iv. 149 & n. 2), was now threatening to resign unless given an extra clerk, and another labourer or two. Mainly through the influence of Pepys and Coventry he had his way. Pepys considered him 'a most well=meaneing man, and one whose aptitude to a little peevish-ness I am soe farr from accompting any ill circumstance in him, that even in that very respect I should preferr him before another of less mettle that might be frightened or flattered to a breach of his trust' (Pepys to Commissioner Pett, 16 February 1664): NMM, LBK/8, p. 96. See below, pp. 50, 88; *Further Corr.*, pp. 14-15.

thanks for it – but will, wherein I can, faithfully endeavour to see him have the privilege of his Patent as the King's merchant.¹ I did give Lue two pieces in gold for a pair of gloves for his kindness herein.

Then he being gone, I to my office, where busy till late at night, that through my mere being over-confounded in business, I could stay there no longer, but went home and, after a little supper, to bed.

6. *Twelfth day.* Up and to my office, where very busy all the morning; being endeed over-loaded with it through my own desire of doing all I can. At noon to the Change but did little, and so home to dinner with my poor wife; and after dinner read a lecture to her in Geography, which she takes very prettily, and with great pleasure to her and me to teach her. And so to the office again, where as busy as ever in my life, one thing after another and answering people's business. Perticularly, drawing up things about Mr. Woods masts, which I expect to have a quarrel about with Sir W. Batten before it be ended – but I care not.² At night home to my wife to supper, discourse, prayers, and to bed.

This morning I begun a practice which I find, by the ease I do it with, that I shall continue, it saving me money and time – that is, to Trimme myself with a Razer³ – which pleases me mightily.

7. Up, putting on my best clothes, and to the office, where all the morning we sat busy; among other things, upon Mr. Wood's performance of his contract for Masts, wherein I was mightily concerned, but I think was found all along in the right and shall have my desire in it, to the King's advantage.⁴

At noon all of us to dinner to Sir W Pens, where a very handsome dinner. Sir J Lawson among others, and his lady

1. Cf. above, iv. 415 & n. 4.
2. Wood's partner William Castle was Batten's son-in-law. For the dispute, see below, n. 4.
3. Pepys was not again shaved by a barber until 20 September 1665.
4. Pepys's notes on this case (7 January etc.) are in NWB, pp. 15,

29, 46. (See esp. his final and fullest note, 30 April, at p. 46.) Wood's masts (delivered in December) were alleged by Pepys to be too short. Wood attended this meeting. The dispute ended with a triumph for Pepys in April.

and his daughter, a very pretty lady and of good deportment – with looking upon whom I was greatly pleased. The rest of the company of the women were all of our own house, of no satisfaction or pleasure at all. My wife was not there, being not well enough nor had any great mind.

But to see how Sir W. Penn imitates me in everything, even in his having of his chimney piece in his dining-room the same with that in my wife's closet – and in everything else, I perceive, wherein he can. But to see again how he was out in one compliment: he lets alone drinking any of the ladies' healths that were there (my Lady Batten and Lawson) till he had begun with my Lady Carteret, who was absent (and that was well enough), and then Mr. Coventry's mistress,[1] at which he was ashamed and would not have had him have drunk it, at least before the ladies present; but his policy,* as he thought, was such that he would do it.

After dinner, by coach with Sir G. Carteret and Sir J. Mennes by appointment to Auditor Beale's[2] in Salsbury-court, and there we did with great content look over some old Leigers to see in what manner they were kept; and endeed it was in an extraordinary good method, and such as (at least out of design to keep them imployed) I do persuade Sir J. Mennes to go upon; which will at least do so much good, it may be, to keep them for want of something to do from envying those that do something.

Thence (calling to see whether Mrs. Turner was returned, which she is and I spoke one word only to her and away again) by coach home and to my office, where late; and then home to supper and bed.

8. Up and all the morning at my office and with Sir J. Mennes, directing him and Mr. Turner[3] about keeping of their books according to yesterday's work – wherein I shall make them work enough. At noon to the Change and there long; and from thence by appointment took Luellin, Mount, and W. Symons and Mr. Pierce the surgeon home to dinner with me, and were merry. But Lord, to hear how W. Symons doth commend and look sadly, and then talk bawdily and merrily,

---

1. Not identified; he never married.
2. Bartholomew Beale, Auditor of the Imprests in the Exchequer.
3. Thomas Turner, Mennes's clerk.

though his wife was dead but the other day, would make a dog laugh. This dinner I did give in further part of kindness to Luellin for his kindness about Deering's fifty pounds which he procured me the other day of him.

We spent all the afternoon together and then they to cards with my wife (who this day put on her Indian blue gown, which is very pretty), where I left them for an hour and to my office and then to them again; and by and by they went away at night and so I again to my office to perfect a letter to Mr. Coventry about Deputy Treasurers;[1] wherein I please myself and hope to give him content and do the King service therein.

So having done, I home and to teach my wife a new lesson in the Globes and to supper and to bed.

We had great pleasure this afternoon, among other things, to talk of our old passages together in Cromwells time. And how W. Symons did make me laugh and wonder today, when he told me how he had made shift to keep in, in good esteem and imployment, through eight governements in one year (the year 1659, which were endeed, and he did name them all)[2] and then failed unhappy in the ninth, *viz.* that of the King's coming in. He made good to me the story which Luellin did tell me the other day, of his wife upon her death-bed – how she dreamt of her uncle Scobell and did foretell, from some discourse she had with him, that she should die four days thence and not sooner, and did all along say so and did so.[3]

Upon the Change, a great talk there was of one Mr. Tryan,

1. BM, Add. 32094, f. 15r, dated this day; copy in NMM, LBK/8, pp. 90-2; printed in *Further Corr.*, 10–14. Pepys recommended the separation of the posts (usually held jointly) of Admiral's secretary and Deputy-Treasurer to the fleet. His views arose mainly from his experience with Creed's accounts during the past year. Cf. also HMC, *Rep.*, 5/1/314*b*.

2. Reckoning by the old calendar year, and counting all changes in the executive, whether or not they were formal changes of the constitution,

the list would be: (1) Protectorate of Richard Cromwell, to 22 April 1659; (2) Council of Officers, 22 April–6 May; (3) Committee of Safety, 7–18 May; (4) Council of State, 19 May–14 October; (5) Council of Officers, 14–27 October; (6) Committee of Safety, 28 October–24 December; (7) Council of State, 2 January 1660–21 February 1660; and (8) reconstituted Council of State, 25 February –1 May 1660.

3. For a similar story (of a parson who preached his own funeral sermon), see below, 20 January 1668 & n.

an old man, a merchant in Lymestreete, robbed last night (his man and maid being gone out after he was a-bed) and gagged and robbed of 1050*l* in money and about 4000*l* in Jewells which he had in his house as security for money. It is believed that his man, by many circumstances, is guilty of confederacy, by their ready going to his secret Till in his desk wherein the key of his cash-chest lay.[1]

9. Up (my underlip being mightily swelled, I know not how but by over-rubbing it, it itching)[2] and to the office, where we sat all the morning; and at noon I home to dinner, and by discourse with my wife thought upon inviting my Lord Sandwich to a dinner shortly. It will cost me at least ten or twelve pound; but however, some arguments of prudence I have, which however I shall think again upon before I proceed to that expense.

After dinner, by coach I carried my wife and Jane to Westminster; left her at Mr. Hunts and I to Westminster-hall and there visited Mrs. Lane and by appointment went out and met her at the Trumpet, Mrs. Hares; but the room being damp, we went to the Bell tavern and there I had her company, but could not do as I used to do (yet nothing but what was honest) for that she told me she had those. So I to talk about her having Hawly; she told me flatly no, she could not love him. I took occasion to enquire of Howletts daughter, with whom I have a mind to meet a little to see what mettle the young wench is made of, being very pretty; but she tells me that she is already betrothed to Mrs. Michells son. And she in discourse tells me more, that Mrs. Michell herself had a daughter before marriage, which is now near 30 year old – a thing I could not have believed.

Thence, leading her to the Hall, I took coach and called my wife and her maid; and so to the New Exchange, where we bought several things of our pretty Mrs. Dorothy Stacy, a pretty woman and hath the modestest look that ever I saw in my life and manner of speech. Thence called at Tom's and saw him

---

1. Francis Tryon was 'a rich usurer and jeweller': HMC, *Rawdon Hastings*, p. 144. Both his man (William Hill) and his maid were out of the house at the time of the burglary, but no collusion was proved. Hill lost some of his own money in the affair. See below, pp. 10–11; *State Trials* (ed. Howell), vi. 566+.

2. Cf. above, iv. 23.

pretty well again, but hath not been currant. So homeward and called at Ludgate at Ashwells uncle's, but she was not within – to have spoke to her to have come to dress my wife at the time when my Lord dines here.[1]   So straight home, calling for Walsingham's *Manuall*[2] at my bookseller, to read but not to buy; recommended for a pretty book by Sir W. Warren, whose warrant however I do not much take till I do read it.

So home to supper and to bed – my wife not being very well since she came home, being troubled with a fainting fit, which she never yet had before since she was my wife.

10.   *Lords day.*   Lay in bed with my wife till 10 or 11 a-clock, having been very sleepy all night. So up, and my brother Tom being come to see me, we to dinner – he telling me how Mrs. Turner found herself discontented with her last bad journey, and not well taken by them in the country, they not desiring her coming down nor the burial of Mr. Edw. Pepys's corps there.[3] After dinner, I to the office, where all the afternoon; and at night my wife and I to my uncle Wight's and there eat some of their swan-pie, which was good, and I invited them to my house to eat a roasted swan on Tuesday next; which after I was come home, did make a quarrel between my wife and I, because she[a] had appointed a wash tomorrow. But however, we were friends again quickly.   So to[b] bed.   All our discourse tonight was about Mr. Tryan's late being robbed and that Collonell Turner (a mad, swearing, confident fellow, well known by all and by me), one much endebted to this man for his very lifelihood, was the man that either did or plotted it;   and the money and things are

a   preceding part of entry crowded into bottom of page
b   repl. 'to prayers and'

---

1. Mary Ashwell had been Mrs Pepys's maid, March–August 1663.
2. *Arcana Aulica: or, Walsingham's manual of prudential maxims for the statesman and the courtier* (1655); a popular guide to success written originally by a French diplomatist, Eustache du Refuge (*Traicté de la*

Cour, etc.) and pirated by Edward Walsingham (fl. 1643–53). Pepys bought it on 11 June 1666; PL 43.
3. Edward Pepys (of Broomsthorpe, Norf.), Jane Turner's brother, had died at her London house on 14 December 1663, but had been buried at Tattersett, Norf.

found in his hand and he and his wife now in Newgate for it – of which we are all glad, so very a known rogue he was.[1]

11. Waked this morning by 4 a-clock by my wife, to call the maids to their wash. And what through my sleeping so long last night and vexation for the lazy sluts lying so long against their great wash, neither my wife nor I could sleep one winke after that time till day; and then I rose and by coach (taking Captain Grove with me and three bottles of Tent, which I sent to Mrs. Lane by my promise on Saturday night last) to White-hall and there with the rest of our company to the Duke and did our business; and thence I to the Tennis Court till noon and there saw several great matches played; and so by invitation to St. James's, where at Mr. Coventry's chamber I dined with my Lord Barkely, Sir G Carteret, Sir Edwd. Turner, Sir Ellis Layton, and one Mr. Seymour, a fine gentleman; where admirable good discourse of all sorts, pleasant and serious.[2]

Thence after dinner to White-hall; where the Duke being busy at the Guinny*a* business – the Duke of Albemarle, Sir W Rider, Povy, Sir J Lawson and I to the Duke of Albemarle's lodgings and there did some business;[3] and so to the Court again

a MS. 'Guimy'

---

1. See below, pp. 18–19. James Turner (self-styled colonel; an ex-Cavalier, son of a parson, and said to be a solicitor) had been employed by Tryon on several occasions: *State Trials* (ed. Howell), vi. 572, 607, 621. He was arrested this day. It was people of this sort who earned for ex-Cavaliers their raffish reputation: cf. above, iv. 374 & n. 1. When about to be hanged, and engaged in his confession, he put swearing as the first and foremost of his sins; for the legal charges now preferred against him, see HMC, *Rawdon Hastings*, ii. 145. He is there said to have had 28 children, counting only those born in wedlock. His case became a *cause*

célèbre. At least two pamphlet lives of him were published in the early months of 1664.

2. The guests named here were Lord Berkeley of Stratton (a Navy Commissioner), Carteret (Navy Treasurer), Turnor (Speaker of the House of Commons and Attorney-General to the Duke of York), Sir Ellis Leighton (Secretary to the Royal African Company), and (probably) Edward Seymour (M.P., later Speaker of the Commons and Navy Treasurer).

3. This was a meeting of the Tangier Committee; Lawson was in command of the Mediterranean squadron.

and I to the Duke of Yorkes lodgings, where the Guinny Company are choosing their Assistants for the next year by balletting. Thence by coach with Sir J. Robinson, Lieutenant of the Tower; he set me down at Cornhill; but Lord, the simple discourse that all the way we had, he magnifying his great undertakings and cares that have been upon him for these last two years,[1] and how he commanded the city to the content of all parties, when the loggerhead knows nothing almost that is sense.

Thence to the Coffee-house, whither comes Sir W. Petty and Captain Grant,[2] and we fell in talk (besides a young gentleman I suppose a merchant, his name Mr. Hill, that hath travelled and I perceive is a master in most sorts of Musique and other things)[3] of Musique, the Universall Character[4] – art of Memory – Granger's counterfeiting of hands[5] – and other most excellent discourses, to my great content, having not been in so good company a great while. And had I time I should covett the acquaintance of that Mr. Hill.

⟨This morning I stood by the King, arguing with a pretty Quaker woman that delivered to him a desire of hers in writing. The King showed her Sir J Minnes, as a man the fittest for her quaking religion, saying that his beard was the stiffest thing about him. And again merrily said, looking upon the length of her paper, that if all she desired was of that length, she might lose her desires. She modestly saying nothing till he begun seriously to discourse with her, arguing the truth of his spirit against hers.

1. He had also been Lord Mayor, 1662–3.
2. John Graunt, friend of Petty and, like him, a statistician.
3. Thomas Hill, merchant, became a close friend of Pepys later. He was several times to tell Pepys about music in Italy from personal knowledge: e.g. below, 12 October 1668. (E).
4. The attempt to produce a non-mathematical system of characters or symbols which could represent words in any language – a favourite project of the virtuosi of the time. The signs would represent not sounds (as in shorthand), but ideas. Bacon and Comenius were interested in it; for Bishop Wilkins's book on the subject, see below, 11 January 1666.
5. Abraham Gowrie Granger (alias Hill, alias Browne, etc.), a notorious forger, was alleged in the recent trial of Col. Turner to have plotted to counterfeit Tryon's will and his signature: *State Trials* (ed. Howell), vi. 580. A warrant for his arrest was issued on 14 February: *CSPD 1663–4*, p. 480. He had also recently been accused of forging a deed in the case of Lord Gerard v. Fitton: below, 21 February 1668 & n.

She replying still with these words, "O King!" and thou'd him all along.⟩*a*1

The general talk of the towne still is of Collonell Turner, about the robbery; who it is thought will be hanged.

I heard the Duke of Yorke tell tonight how letters are come that fifteen are condemned for the last plot by the judges at Yorke;2 and among others, Captain Otes, against whom it was proved that he drow his sword at his going out; and flinging away the Scabbard, said that he would either return victor or be hanged.

So home, where I find the house full of the washing and my wife mighty angry about Will's being here today talking with her maids, which she overheard, idling of their time, and he telling what a good maid my old Jane3 was and that she would never have her like again – at which I was angry; and after directing her to beat at least the little girl – I went to the office and there reproved Will, who told me that he went thither by my wife's order, she having commanded him to come thither on Monday morning. Now God forgive me how apt I am to be jealous of her as to this fellow, and that she must need take this time, when she knows I must be gone out to the Duke; though methinks, had she that mind, she would never think it discretion to tell me this story of him, to let me know that he was there; much less to make me offended with him, to forbid him coming again. But this cursed humour I cannot kill in myself by all the reason I have; which God forgive me for and convince me of the folly of it – and the disquiet it brings me.

So home – where, God be thanked, when I came to speak to my wife my trouble of mind soon vanished, and to bed. The

a   paragraph crowded into bottom of the page

---

1. Cf. Clarendon, *Life*, ii. 124: 'The king had always admitted the quakers for his divertisement and mirth, because he thought, that of all the factions they were the most innocent, and had least of malice . . . against his person and his government.' For a guess at the identity of the Quakeress, see Bryant, ii. 204 n.

2. On 2 January, 15 of the conspirators in the Derwentdale Plot (see above, iv. 347 & n. 4) were convicted. One of the letters is probably that from Col. J. Freschville to Williamson, York, 5 January: *CSPD 1663-4*, p. 431.

3. Jane Birch.

house foul with the washing and quite out of order against tomorrow's dinner.

12. Up and to the office, where we sat all the morning; and at noon to the Change awhile and so home – getting things against dinner ready. And anon comes my uncle Wight and my aunt with their Cozen Mary and Robert, and by chance my Uncle Tho.*a* Pepys. We had a good dinner, the chief dish a swan roasted, and that excellent meat. At dinner and all day very merry. After dinner to Cards, where till evening; then to the office a little and to cards again with them – and lost half-a-Crowne. They*b* being gone, my wife did tell me how my Uncle did this*c* day accost her alone and spoke of his hopings she was with child; and kissing her earnestly, told her he should be very glad of it; and from all circumstances, methinks he doth seem to have some intention of good to us,[1] which I shall endeavour to continue more then ever I did yet. So to my office till late and then home to bed – after being at prayers, which is the first time after my late vow to say prayers in my family twice in every week.[2]

13. Up and to my office a little, and then abroad to many several places about business; among others, to the Geometrical Instrument makers,[3] and then through Bedlam (calling by the way at a old bookseller's, and there fell into looking over Spanish books and pitched upon some, till I thought of my oath when I was going to agree for them and so with much ado got myself out of the shop, glad at my heart, and so away) to the Affrican-house to look upon their book of contracts for several commodities for my information in the prizes* we give in the Navy. So to the Coffee,* where extraordinary good discourse of Dr. Whist[l]ers[4] upon my Question concerning the keeping of Masts,

a l.h. repl. l.h. 'Wigh'-
b rest of paragraph crowded into bottom of page
c repl. 'try'

1. Uncle Wight's intentions were not what they seemed: below, pp. 145–6.
2. A New-Year resolution; it was not kept for long.
3. Probably John Browne of the Minories: see below, p. 17.
4. Physician and fellow of the Royal Society.

he arguing against keeping them dry, by showing the nature of Corrupcion in bodies and the several ways thereof.[1]

So to the Change and thence with Sir W. Rider to the Trinity-house to dinner; and then home and to my office till night, and then with Mr. Bland to Sir T. Viners about pieces-of-eight ⟨for Sir J Lawson⟩, and so back to my office and there late upon business; and so home to supper and to bed.

14. Up and to the office, where all the morning; and at noon all of us, *viz.*, Sir G. Carteret and Sir W. Batten at one end and Mr. Coventry, Sir J. Mennes and I (in the middle at the other end, being taught how to sit there all three by my sitting so[a] much the backwarder) at the other end, to Sir G. Carteret and there dined well. Here I saw Mr. Scott, the bastard, that married his youngest daughter.[2] Much pleasant talk at table; and then up and to the office, where we sat long upon our design of dividing the Controllers work into some of the rest of our hands for the better doing of it;[3] but he would not yield to it, though the simple man knows in his heart that he doth not do one part of it. So he taking upon him to do it all, we rose, I vexed at the heart to see the King's service run after this manner; but it cannot be helped.

Thence to the Old James to the reference about Mr. Blands business,[4] Sir W Rider being now added to us, and I believe we shall soon come to some determination in it. So home and to my office. Did business and then up to Sir W. Penn and did express my trouble about this day's business, he not being there, and plainly told him what[b] I thought of it. And though I know

a repl. 'in'   *b* repl. 'that'

---

1. Pepys's questions probably arose from his recent disputes with William Wood: above, p. 6 & n. 4. Oak and other timber was kept dry in circulating air, but the storage of fir and pine masts required the exclusion of air. They were usually kept in water in mast-docks to preserve the soundness and resilience which derived from their resin. The sticks were floated in at various stages of the tide and fastened, in vertical ties, between heavy horizontal timbers at either end. Locks kept the water at high-tide level. R. G. Albion, *Forests and sea power*, pp. 70–1.

2. See above, iv. 254.

3. See above, iv. 62 & n. 3.

4. The dispute about charges for freightage: see above, iv. 404.

him a false fellow, yet I adventured, as I have done often, to tell him clearly my opinion of Sir W. Batten and his design in this business, which is very bad.

Thence home; and after a lecture to my wife in her Globes, to prayers and to bed.

15. Up and to my office, where all the morning; and among other things, Mr. Turner with me, and I did tell him my mind freely about the Controller his maister and all the office, and my mind touching himself too, as he did carry himself either well or ill to me and my clerks[1] – which I doubt not but it will operate well.

Thence to the Change and there met my uncle Wight, who was very kind to me and would have had me home with him. And so kind that I begin to wonder and think something of it of good to me.

Thence home to dinner; and after dinner with Mr. Hater by water, and walked thither*a* and back again from*b* Deptford, where I did do something, checking the Iron business. But my chief business was my discourse with Mr. Hater about what hath passed last night and today about the office business, and my resolutions to do him all the good I can therein.

So home; and my wife tells me with my Uncle Wight hath been with her and played at cards with her, and is mighty inquisitive to know whether she is with child or no – which makes me wonder what his meaning is; and after all my thoughts, I cannot think, unless it be in order to the making his Will, that he might know how to do by me. And I would to God my wife had told him that she was.

So to my office late doing business, and then home; where after a lecture upon the globes to my wife – to bed.

16. Up; and having paid some money in the morning to my Uncle Tho. on his yearly annuity[2] – to the office, where we sat

a repl. 'back'   *b* repl. 'to'

---

1. Cf. above, iii. 25 & n. 3.   2. See above, ii. 133, n. 1.

all the morning. At noon I to the Change about some pieces-of-eight for Sir J Lawson.[1] And there I hear that Collonell Turner is found guilty of Felony at the Sessions in Mr. Tryan's business, which will save his life.[2] So home and met there James Harper, come to see his kinswoman, our Jane: I made much of him and made him dine with us – he talking after the old simple manner that he used to do. He being gone, I by water to Westminster-hall and there did see Mrs. Lane, and de là, elle and I to the cabaret at the Cloche in the street du roy; and there, after some caresses, je l'ay foutée sous de la chaise deux times, and the last to my great pleasure; mais j'ai grand peur que je l'ay fait faire aussi elle même. Mais after I had done, elle commençait parler as before and I did perceive that je n'avais fait rien de danger à elle. Et avec ça, I came away; and though I did make grand promises à la contraire, nonobstant je ne la verrai pas long time. So by coach home and to my office, where Browne of the Minerys brought me an instrument made of a Spyrall line, very pretty for all Questions in Arithmetique almost.[3] But it must be some use that must make me perfect in it.

So home to supper and to bed – with my mind un peu troublé pour ce que j'ai fait today. But I hope it will be la dernière de toute ma vie.

17. *Lords day.* Up, and I and my wife to church, where Pembleton appeared; which God forgive me, did vex me – but I made nothing of it. So home to dinner; and betimes my wife and I to the French church[4] and there heard a good sermon – the

1. On 16 and 18 January Lawson agreed with the Board to bring over from Calais 20,000 pieces-of-eight (half at 4s. 6d. each, half at 4s. 7d.) to be used in paying seamen: PRO, Adm. 106/3520, f. 17r (memo. in Pepys's hand).

2. A mistake; in fact, Turner was this day found guilty of both felony and burglary. Sentence of execution was passed on the 19th and he was executed on the 21st. (See *State Trials*, ed. Howell, vi. 615, 619.) If he had been convicted of felony alone,

he could have pleaded his clergy (as a literate man), and perhaps have escaped with his life. But burglary was non-clergiable.

3. A variety of slide-rule consisting of a logarithmic scale marked along a spiral line; attributed to Milburne (1650). See A. Wolf, *Hist. science in 16th and 17th centuries*, pp. 559–60. Pepys had ordered it on 26 December 1663.

4. The Huguenot church in Threadneedle St.

first time my wife and I were there ever together. We sat by three sisters,[1] all pretty women. It was pleasant to hear the reader give notice to them that the children to be catechized the next Sunday were them of Hounsditch and Blanche Chapiton.[2] Thence home and there find Ashwell come to see my wife (we having called at her lodging the other day to speak with her about dressing my wife when my Lord Sandwich dines here); and is as merry as ever, and speaks as unconcerned for any difference between us or her going away as ever. She being gone, my wife and I to see Sir W Penn and there supped with him, much against my stomach, for the dishes were so deadly foul that I could not endure to look upon them.

So after supper, home to prayers and to bed.

18. Up, being troubled to find my wife so ready to have me go out of doors; God forgive me for my jealousy, that I cannot forbear, though God knows that I have no reason to do so or to expect her being so true to me as I would[a] have her. I abroad to White-hall, where the Court all in mourning for the Duchesse of Savoy;[3] we did our business with the Duke, and so I to W. Howe at my Lord's lodgings, not seeing my Lord, he being abroad; and there I advised with W. Howe about my having my Lord to dinner at my house; who likes of it well, though it troubles me that I should come to need the advice of such a boy, but for the present it is necessary.[4] Here I found Mr. Mallard and had from him a common Tune set by my desire to the Lyra Vyall,[5] which goes most admirably. Thence home by coach to the Change, after [having] been at the Coffee-house, where I hear Turner is found guilty of Felony and Burglary; and strange

a repl. 'could'

---

1. Sisters of the parson: below, p. 342.

2. Blanch Appleton in Aldgate Ward. (R).

3. Christina of Bourbon, Dowager-Duchess of Savoy, second daughter of Henry IV of France and aunt of Charles II of England, had died in December. The English court had gone into short mourning on 17 January: HMC, *Ormonde*, n.s., iii. 140.

4. Because of the recent coolness between Pepys and Sandwich: above, iv. 386–7.

5. Mallard was a professional musician. For 'Lyra Vyall', see above, i. 295, n. 4. (E).

stories of his confidence at the Barr, but yet great indiscretion in his argueing. All desirous of his being hanged.[1]

So home and found that Will had been with my wife there; but Lord, why should I think any evil of that, and yet I cannot forbear it. But upon enquiry, though I found no reason of doubtfulness, yet I could not bring my nature to any quiet or content in my wife all day and night – nay, though I went with her to divert myself at my Uncle Wights and there we played at Cards till 12 at night and went home in a great shower of rain, it having not rained a great while before. Here was one Mr. Benson a Dutchman played and supped with us, that pretends to sing well; and I expected great matters but found nothing to be pleased with at all. So home and to bed, yet troubled in my mind.

19. Up, without any kindness to my wife; and so to the office, where we sat all the morning; and at noon I to the Change, and thence to Mr. Cutlers with Sir W Rider to dinner. And after dinner, with him to the Old James upon our reference of Mr. Blands; and having sot there upon that business half an hour, broke up; and I home and there find Madam Turner and her sister Dike come to see us, and stayed chatting till night and so away; and I to my office till very late, and my eyes begin to fail me and be in pain, which I never felt to nowadays, which I impute to sitting up late writing and reading by candlelight. So home to supper and to bed.

20. Up and by coach to my Lord Sandwiches; and after long staying till his coming down (he not sending for me up, but it may be he did not know I was there), he came down and I walked with him to the Tennis Court, and there left him seeing the King play. At his lodgings this morning there came to him Mr. W. Mountagu's fine lady, which occasioned my Lord's calling me to her about some business for a friend of her, pro-ferred to be a midshipman at sea. My Lord recommended the whole matter to me. She is a fine confident lady I think, but not so pretty as I once thought her. My Lord did also seal a

---

1. He was hanged on the 21st at the end of Lime St, the scene of his crime. The Lord Mayor and Aldermen are reported to have petitioned the King against a reprieve. For his arrogant conduct of his case, see *State Trials* (ed. Howell), vi. 565+.

lease for the house he is now taking in Lincoln's-Inn-fields, which stands him in 250*l* per annum Rent.[1]

Thence by water to my brother's, whom I find not well in bed – sick they think of a consumption. And I fear he is not well; but doth not complain nor desire to take anything. From him I visited Mr. Honiwood, who is lame, and to thank him for his visit to me the other day, but we were both abroad. So to Mr. Comanders in Warwicke-lane to speak to him about drawing up my Will, which he will meet me about in a day or two.[2] So to the Change and walked home thence with Sir Rd. Ford,[3] who told me that Turner is to be hanged tomorrow and with what impudence he hath carried out his trial; but that last night, when he brought him news of his death, he begin to be sober and shed some tears, and he hopes will die a penitent, he having already confessed all the thing; but says it was partly done for a Joco, and partly to get an occasion of obliging the old man by his care in getting him his things again, he having some hopes of being the better by him in his estate at his death.

Home to dinner; and after dinner my wife and I by water (which we have not been together many a day; that is, not since last summer, but the weather*a* is now very warm) and left her at Axe-yard and I to White-hall; and meeting Mr. Pierce, walked with him an hour in the matted gallery. Among other things, he tells me that my Lady Castlemaine is not at all set by by the King, but that he doth dote upon Mrs. Stuart only – and that to the leaving off all business in the world – and to the open slighting of the Queen. That he values not who sees him or stands by him while he dallies with her openly – and then privately in her chamber below, where the very sentries observe his going in and out – and that so commonly that the Duke or any of the nobles, when they would ask where the King is,

a MS. 'well'

---

1. The house is now nos 57–8, Lincoln's Inn Fields (built c. 1640; rebuilt c. 1730): LCC, *Survey of London, Parish of St Giles-in-the-Fields*, i. 90+. Clarendon paid £400 p.a. in rent for Worcester House (*CSPClar.*, v. 305); Carteret's official residence in Broad St cost £70 p.a.

(below, p. 278); the Navy Commissioners, displaced from their official residences in 1674 and 1686, were each allowed £80 p.a.: *Cat.*, i. 80; iv. 7.

2. For Pepys's wills, see above, i. 90 & n. 1. His wife had suggested his making this one: above, iv. 433.

3. A Sheriff of the city.

they will ordinarily say, "Is the King above or below?" meaning with Mrs. Stuart.

That the King doth not openly disown my Lady Castlemaine, but that she comes to Court; but that my Lord Fitzharding and the Hambletons,[1] and sometimes my Lord Sandwich they say, have their snaps at her. But he says my Lord Sandwich will lead her from her lodgings in the darkest and obscurest manner and leave her at the entrance into the Queens lodgings, that he might be the least observed.

That the Duke of Monmouth the King doth still dote on beyond measure, insomuch that the King only, and the Duke of Yorke and Prince Robt. and the Duke of Monmouth, do now wear deep mourning, that is, long cloaks, for the Duchesse of Savoy; so that he mourns as a Prince of the Blood, while the Duke of Yorke doth no more and all the nobles of the land not so much – which gives great offence, and he says the Duke of Yorke doth consider. But that the Duke of Yorke doth give himself up to business and is like to prove a noble prince; and so endeed I do from my heart think he will.[2]

He says that it is believed, as well as hoped, that care is taken to lay up a hidden treasure of money by the King against a bad day. I pray God it be so. But I should be more glad that the King himself would look after business, which it seems he doth not in the least.

By and by came by Mr. Coventry, and so we broke off, and he and I took a turn or two and so parted; and then my Lord Sandwich came upon me to speak,*ᵃ* with whom my business of

a MS. 'spoke'

1. The Hamiltons. The three brothers, James, George and Anthony, grandsons of the 1st Earl of Abercorn, were all prominent at the court of Charles II. Anthony Hamilton wrote the *histoire amoureuse* of the court (under the name of his brother-in-law) – the *Mémoires du Comte de Grammont*, published in 1713 – which refers to James Hamilton's being cured (by Lady Chesterfield) 'of all that yet remained to him of tenderness for Lady Castlemaine' (1930 ed., p. 156).

2. Pepys had a high, though not uncritical, regard for the Duke's work as Admiral, and expressed it both in the diary and elsewhere: e.g. below, pp. 185–6; *Naval Minutes*, pp. 90–1, 159, 338, 418. The Duke had technical knowledge, and a taste for reform.

coming again tonight to this end of the town chiefly was – in order to the seeing in what manner he received me, in order to my inviting him to dinner to my house. But as well in the morning as now, though I did wait upon him home and there offered occasion of talk with him, yet he treats me, though with respect, yet as a stranger, without any of the intimacy or friendship which he used to do; and which I fear he will never, through his consciousness of his faults, he ever will again – which I must confess doth trouble me above anything in the world almost, though I neither do need at present or fear to need to be so troubled; nay and more, though I do not think that he would deny me any friendship now if I did need it; but only that he hath not the face to be free with me, but doth look upon me as a remembrancer of his former vanity and an espy upon his present practices. For I perceive that Pickering today is great with him again,[1] and that he hath done a great courtesy for Mr. Pierce the surgeon, to a good value, though both these and none but these did I mention by name to my Lord in the business which hath caused all this difference between my Lord and me. However, I am resolved to forbear my laying out my money upon a dinner till I see him in a better posture, and by grave and humble though high deportment to make him think I do not want him; and that will make him the readier to admit me to his friendship again I believe, the soonest of anything but downright impudence and thrusting myself, as others do, upon him; and imposing upon him which yet I cannot do, nor will not endeavour.

So home, calling with my wife to see my brother again, who was up and walks up and down the house pretty well; but I do think he is in a consumption.

Home – troubled in mind for these passages with my Lord. But am resolved to better my care in my business, to make me stand upon my own legs the better and to lay up as well as to get money; and among other ways, I will have a good fleece out of Creeds coat[2] ere it be long, or I will have a fall.

So to my office and did some business; and then home to supper and to bed – after I had by candlelight shaved myself

1. They had quarrelled over Sandwich's love-affair: above, iv. 301, 303.

2. Sc. 'a good coat out of Creed's fleece': a share of the booty. Pepys expected a reward for helping Creed to his commission for the despatch of Spanish coins to Tangier: below, pp. 39, 45–7 etc.

and cut off all my beard clear,[1] which will make my work a great deal the less in shaving.

21. Up; and after sending my wife to my aunt Wight's to get a place to see Turner hanged, I to the office, where we sat all the morning. And at noon, going to the Change and seeing people flock in that, I enquired and found that Turner was not yet hanged; and so I went among them to Leadenhall-street at the end of Lyme-street, near where the robbery was done, and to St. Mary Axe, where he lived; and there I got for a shilling to stand upon the wheel of a Cart, in great pain, above an hour before the execution was done – he delaying the time by long discourses and prayers one after another, in hopes of a reprieve; but none came, and at last was flung off the lather[2] in his cloak. A comely-looked man he was, and kept his countenance to the end – I was sorry to see him. It was believed there was at least 12 or 14000 people in the street. So I home all in a sweat, and dined by myself; and after dinner to the Old James and there found Sir W Rider and Mr. Cutler at dinner and made a second dinner with them; and anon came Mr. Bland and Custos and Clerke and so we fell to the business of reference;[3] and upon a letter from Mr. Povey to Sir W Rider and I, telling us that the King is concerned in it, we took occasion to fling off the business from off our shoulders and would have nothing to do with it unless we had power from the King or Comissioners of Tanger. And I think it will be best for us to continue of that mind and to have no hand, it being likely to go against the King.

Thence to the Coffee-house and heard the full of Turner's discourse on the Cart,[4] which was chiefly to clear himself of all things laid to his charge but this fault for which he now suffers, which he confesses. He deplored the condition of his family. But his chief design was to lengthen time, believing still a reprieve would come, though the Sheriffe advised him to expect no such

1. Pepys seems to have had a lightly grown moustache at this time: cf. above, iii. 97.

2. After the later part of the century ladders were no longer used (at Tyburn at any rate) for the 'drop'. The noose was tied round the victim's neck as he stood in the cart in which he had travelled from prison, and the hangman then drove the cart away, leaving him suspended.

3. Cf. above, iv. 404.

4. Cf. *The speech and deportment of Col. James Turner at his execution in Leaden-Hall street . . .* (1663).

thing, for the King was resolved to grant none.   After that, I had good discourse with a pretty young merchant, with mighty content.   So to my office and did a little business; and then to my aunt Wights to fetch my wife home, where Dr. Burnett did tell me how poorly the Sheriffes did endeavour to get one Jewell returned by Turner after he was convicted, as a due to them, and not to give to Mr. Tryan the true owner; but ruled against them, to their great*a* dishonour – though they plead it might be another's Jewell for ought they knew and not Tryan's. After supper, home; and my wife tells me mighty stories of my uncles fond and kind discourses to her today, which makes me confident that he hath thoughts of kindness for us, he repeating his desire for her to be with child – for it cannot enter into my head that he should have any unworthy thoughts concerning her.   After doing some business at my office, I home to supper, prayers, and to bed.

22.   Up; and it being a brave morning, by water with a galley to Woolwich and there, both at the ropeyard and the other yard, did much business; and thence to Greenwich to see Mr. Pett and others value the Carved work of the *Henrietta* (God knows in an ill manner for the King);[1] and so to Deptford and there viewed Sir W. Petty's vessel, which hath an odd appearance but not such as people do make of it, for I am of the opinion that he would

---

a   repl. same symbol badly formed

---

1. The *Henrietta* was the King's latest and favourite yacht. The carvings were inside the cabins and the Navy Board had some time before objected to their cost. (Later, by the King's order, they were gilded: *CSPD 1663–4*, pp. 290, 161, 623.) Pepys has another note on this occasion in NWB (p. 20) which runs: 'I found them standing upon the shore looking upon the vessel, which lay upon the shore also, and in my view did set their prices upon everything distinct. I coming, demanded by what rule they valued any piece; they answered . . . by the prices formerly given for the work done upon the other boats. And this I found was their only rule – which shows the great consequence of bad Precedents. But by and by, I suppose upon hearing that I was there, came out of a Taverne to me Mr. Leadman the Carver, Capt. Pett, Mr Cowly, and several other officers, all very fine in their best clothes; and upon a little enquiry, I found that Leadman makes a dinner for them today; and at dinner, there the rates are concluded upon – which answers with what I have formerly bin told of the same nature at Chatham.'   For similar complaints later, see *Cat.*, iv, pp. ciii, 519, 520 etc.

never have discoursed so much of it if it were not better then other vessels, and so I believe that he was abused the other day, as he is now, by tongues that I am sure speak before they know anything good or bad of her.[1] I am sorry to find his ingenuity discouraged so.

So home, reading all the way a good book; and so home to dinner, and after dinner a lesson on the globes to my wife; and so to my office, where till 10 or 11 a-clock at night; and so home to supper and to bed.

23. Up and to the office, where we sat all the morning. At noon home to dinner, where Hawly came to see us and dined with us. And after we had dined came Mr. Mallard; and after he had eat something, I brought down my vyall, which he played on – the first Maister that ever touched her yet, and she proves very well and will be, I think, an admirable instrument. He played some very fine things of his own, but I was afeared to enter too far in their commendation for fear he should offer to copy them for me out, and so I be forced to give or lend him something. So to the office in the evening, whither Mr. Comander came to me and we discoursed about my Will, which I am resolved to perfect the next week by the grace of God. He being gone, I to write letters and other business late. And so home to supper and to bed.

24. *Lords day.* Lay long in bed. And then up; and being desirous to perform my vows that I lately made, among others to be performed this month, I[a] did go to my office and there fell on entering out of a by-book part of my second Journall-book,[2] which hath lay these two years and more unentered. Upon this work till dinner; and after dinner, to it again till night and then home to supper; and after supper, to read a lecture to my wife

a MS. 'and'

---

1. De Cominges, the French Ambassador, in a despatch to Louis XIV of 25 January/4 February, referred to Petty's double-bottomed ship as 'la plus ridicule et inutile machine que l'esprit de l'homme puisse concevoir':

PRO, PRO 31/3/113, f. 27r. For the ship, see above, iv. 256 & n. 3.

2. PL 1837; covering 1 July 1661– 30 June 1663. The 'by-book' has not survived.

upon the globes, and so to prayers and to bed. This evening also, I drow up a rough draught of my last Will – to my mind.

25. Up and by coach to Whitehall to my Lord's lodgings; and seeing that, knowing that I was in the house, my Lord did not nevertheless send for me up, I did go to the Duke's lodgings and there stayed while he was making ready; in which time my Lord Sandwich came, and so all into his closet and did our common business. And so broke up and I homeward by coach with Sir W. Batten and stayed at Warwicke-lane; and there called upon Mr. Commander and did give him my last Will and testament to write over in form, and so to the Change, where I did several businesses. So home to dinner; and after I had dined, Luellin came and we set him something to eat, and I left him there with my wife and to the office upon a perticular meeting of the East India Company, where I think I did the King good service against the Company in the business of their sending our ships home empty from the Indys, contrary to their contract.[1] And yet, God forgive me, I find that I could be willing to receive a bribe if it were offered me to conceal my arguments that I find against them, in consideration that none of my fellow-officers, whose duty it is more then mine, had ever studied the case or at this hour do understand it, and myself alone must do it.

That being done, Mr. Povy and Bland came to speak with me about their business of the reference,[2] wherein I shall have some more trouble, but cannot help it; besides, I hope to make some good use of Mr. Povy to my advantage.

So home, after business done at my office, to supper; then to the globes with my wife and to bed – troubled a little in mind to think that my Lord Sandwich should continue this strangeness to me that methinks he shows me nowadays, more then while the thing[3] was fresh.

26. Up and to the office, where we sat all the*a* morning. At noon to the Change, after being at the Coffee-house, where I sat

a   repl. 'that'

---

1. See above, iv. 368, n. 2.   Sandwich's affair with Betty Becke:
2. See above, iv. 404, n. 2.   above, iv. 386–7.
3. The   estrangement   following

by Tom Killigrew; who told us of a fire last night in my Lady Castlemaynes lodging, where she bid 40*l* for one to adventure the fetching of a cabinet out, which at last was got to be done – and the fire at last quenched without doing much wrong.[1] To Change and there did much business; so home to dinner and then to the office all the afternoon. And so at night my aunt Wight and Mrs. Buggins came to sit with my wife, and I in to them all the evening, my uncle coming afterward, and after him Mr. Benson the Duchman, a frank, merry man. We were very merry and played at cards till late and so broke up. And to bed in good hopes that this my friendship with my uncle and aunt will end well.

27. Up and to the office; and at noon to the Coffee-house, where I sat with Sir G Asckue and Sir Wm. Petty, who in discourse is methinks one of the most rational men that ever I heard speak with a tongue, having all his notions the most distinct and clear; and did among other things (saying that in all his life these three books were the most esteemed and[a] generally cried up for wit in the world – *Religio Medici*, Osborne's *Advice to a Son*, and *Hudibras*)[2] did say that in these, in the two first principally, the wit lie in[b] confirming some pretty sayings, which are generally like paradoxes, by some argument smartly and pleasantly urged – which takes with people who do not trouble themselfs to examine the force of an argument which pleases them in the delivery, upon a subject which they like; whereas (as by many perticular instances of mine and others out of Osborne) he did really find fault and weaken the strength of many of Osbornes arguments, so as that in downright disputation they would not bear weight; at least, so far but that they might be weakened, and better found in their rooms to confirm what is there said. He showed finely

a repl. 'for'   *b* MS. 'and'

1. On the 27th Sandwich wrote to Legge, Master of the Ordnance, ordering, on the King's behalf, the provision of leather buckets, crows and hatchets at Whitehall 'to be kept for the prevention of danger by fire': HMC, *Eliot Hodgkin*, p. 301.

2. Pepys retained a copy of Sir Thomas Browne's *Religio Medici* (first published in 1642) in the 1686 edition of his *Works*: PL 2368. For the Osborne and *Hudibras*, see above, ii. 22 & n. 2; iii. 294 & n. 2.

whence it happens that good writers are not admired by the present age;[a] because there are but few in any age that do mind anything that is abstruce and curious; and so, longer before anybody doth put the true praise and set it on foot in the world – the generality of mankind pleasing themselfs in the easy delights of the world, as eating, drinking, dancing, hunting, fencing, which we see the meanest men do the best, those that profess it. A gentleman never dances so well as the dancing-master and an ordinary fiddler makes better music for a shilling then a gentleman will do after spending forty. And so in all the delights of the world almost.

Thence to the Change; and after doing much business, home, taking Comissioner Pett thence with me, and all alone dined together. He told me many stories of the yard; but I do know him so well and had his character given me this morning by Hempson, as well as my own knowledge of him before, that I shall know how to value anything he says either of friendship or other businesses.[1] He was mighty serious with me in discourse about the consequence of Sir W. Petty's boat, as the most dangerous thing in the world if it should be practised in the world, by endangering our loss of the command of the seas and our trade while the Turkes and others shall get the use of them, which, without doubt, by bearing more sail will go faster then any other ships; and not being of burden, our Merchants cannot have the use of them and so will be at the mercy of their enemies – so that I perceive he is afeared that the Honour of his trade[2] will down, though (which is a truth) he pretends this consideration to hinder the growth of this invention. He being gone, my wife and I took coach and to Covent-garden to buy a mask at the French house, Madam Charett's, for my wife – in the way observing the street full of coaches at the new play, *The Indian*

<hr>

a l.h. repl. s.h. 'age'

<hr>

1. Pepys made a note of Hempson's views in NWB, p. 11. According to Hempson, Pett was a miser, prone to charge all expenses to the King (even for the banquet he gave to the King at his restoration), and disliked by the gentry of the county as 'false-hearted'.

2. Shipbuilding. Pepys has a similar note on this conversation (with a cross-reference to the diary) in NWB, p. 20.

Queene; which for show, they say, exceeds *Henry the 8th*.[1] Thence back to Mrs. Turners and sat a while with them, talking of plays and I know not what; and so called to see Tom, but not at home, though they say he is in a deep consumption, and Mrs. Turner and Dike and they say he will not live two[a] months to an end.[2]

So home and to the office, and then to supper and to bed.

28. Up and to the office, where all the morning sitting; and at noon upon several things to the Change, and thence to Sir G. Carteret's to dinner, of my own accord; and after dinner with Mr. Wayth down to Deptford doing several businesses and by land back again, it being very cold, the boat meeting me after my staying a while for him at an alehouse by Redriffe stairs; so home and took Will coming out of my doors, at which I was a little moved and told my wife of her keeping him from the office (though God knows my base jealous head was the cause of it); which she seemed troubled at; and that it was only to discourse with him about finding a place for her brother. So I to my[b] office late – Mr. Comander coming to read over my Will, in order to the engrossing it; and so he being gone, I to other business; among others, chiefly upon preparing matters against Creed for my profit; and so home to supper and bed, being mightily troubled with my left eye all this evening from some dirt that is got into it.

29. Up, and after shaving myself (wherein twice now, one after another, I have cut myself much, but I think it is from the bluntness of the rasor) there came Mr. Deane to me and stayed with me a while talking about Masts; wherein he prepared me in

a repl. 'these'　　　　*b* repl. 'the'

---

1. See above, iv. 411; above, p. 2. *The Indian Queen* was a rhymed heroic tragedy by Sir Robert Howard and John Dryden; now at the TR, Drury Lane, where it had its first performance on 25 January; published in 1665. This production was notable for its scenery; according to

Evelyn (5 February 1664) it was 'so beautiful with rich scenes as the like had never been seen here, or haply (except rarely) elsewhere on a mercenary theatre'. (A).

2. Pepys's brother Tom died on 15 March.

several things against Mr. Wood[1] and also about Sir W. Pettys boat, which he says must needs prove a folly – though I do not think so, unless it be that the King will not have it encouraged.

At noon by appointment comes Mr. Hartlib and his wife, and a little before them Mr. Langly and Bostocke (old acquaintances of mine at Westminster, Clerkes); and after showing them my house and drinking, they set out by water, my wife and I with them, down to Wapping on board the *Crowne*, a merchantman, Captain Floyd – a civil person. Here was Vice-Admirall Goodson, whom the more I know the more I value for a serious man and staunch. Here was Whisler the flagmaker; which vexed me,[2] but it mattered not. Here was other sorry company and the discourse poor, so that we had no pleasure there at all but only to see, and bless God to find, the difference that is now between our condition and that heretofore, when we were not only much below Hartlibb in all respects, but even these two fellows above named, of whom I am now quite ashamed that ever my education should lead me to such low company. But it is God's goodness only, for which let him be praised.

After dinner I broke up and with my wife home; and thence to the Fleece in Cornhill by appointment to meet my Lord Marlbrough (a serious and worthy gentleman); who, after doing our business about the company and Captain Browne,[3] he and they begun to talk of the state of the Duch in India, which is like to be in a little time without any control; for we are lost there, and the Portugois as bad.[4]

Thence to the Coffee-house, where good discourse, especially of Lieutenant Collonell Baron touching the manners of the Turkes government, among whom he lived long. So to my uncle Wights, where late playing at Cards, and so home.

30. **Up, and a sorry sermon of a young fellow I knew at**

1. Cf. above, p. 6 & n. 4.
2. Perhaps because of the dispute of 1662–3 about his flags; above, iv. 151.
3. I.e. the dispute with the E. India Company: see above, iv. 368 & n. 2. Marlborough had commanded the expedition to Bombay, 1662–3.
4. The Dutch had control of the sea from their bases in the E. Indies, and had between 1655 and 1663 wrested control of Ceylon and the Malabar coast from the Portuguese.

Cambrige. But the day kept solemnly for the King's murther,[1] and I all day within doors making up my Brampton papers; and in the evening Mr. Comander came and we made perfect and signed and sealed my last Will and Testament, which is so to my mind, and I hope to the liking of God Almighty, that I take great joy in myself that it is done, and by that means my mind in a good condition of quiet. At night, to supper and to bed. ⟨This evening, being in an humour of making all things even and clear in the world, I tore some old papers; among others, a Romance which (under the title of *Love a Cheate*) I begun ten year ago at Cambrige; and at this time, reading it over tonight, I liked it very well and wondered a little at myself at my vein at that time when I wrote it, doubting that I cannot do so well now if I would try.⟩[a]

31. *Lords day.* Up, and in my chamber all day long (but a little at dinner) settling all my Brampton Accounts to this day in very good order, I having obliged myself by oath to do that and some other things within this month. I did also perfectly prepare a state of my Estate and annexed it to my last Will and Testament, which now is perfect.[2] And lastly, I did make up my month's accounts and find that I have gained above 50*l* this month clear, and so am worth 858*l* clear, which is the greatest sum I ever yet was maister of. And also read over my usual vowes, as I do every Lord's day, but with greater seriousness then ordinary, and I do hope that every day I shall see more and more the pleasure of looking after my business and laying up of money. And blessed be God for what I have already been enabled by his grace to do. So to supper and to bed, with my mind in mighty great ease and content,[b] but my head very full of thoughts and business to despatch this next month also; and among others, to provide for answering to the Exchequer for my Uncles being Generall-Receiver in the yeare 1647,[3] which I am at present wholly unable to do. But I must find time to look over all his papers.

a addition crowded into bottom of page   *b* MS. 'contempt'

---

1. For the service, see above, ii. 26, n. 1.

2. Neither the will nor the note of his estate has survived. For his wills, see above, i. 90 & n. 1.

3. Robert Pepys of Brampton had been receiver for Huntingdonshire of the monthly assessments: below, p. 39.

FEBRUARY.

1. Up (my maids rising early this morning to washing) and being ready, I find Mr. Strutt the purser below with 12 bottles of sack – and tells me (what from Sir W. Batten I had heard before) how young Jack Davis[1] hath railed against Sir W. Batten for his endeavouring to turn him out of his place. At which for the fellow's sake, because it will likely prove his ruin, I am sorry, though I do believe he is a very arch rogue.

I took Strutt by coach with me to White-hall, where I set him down; and I to my Lord's, but find him gone out betimes to the Wardrobe; which I am glad to see that he so attends his business, though it troubles me that my counsel to my prejudice must be the cause of it. They tell me that he goes into the country next week – and that the young ladies come up this week before my old Lady.[2] Here I hear how two men[a] the last night, justling for the wall about the New Exchange, did kill one another, each thrusting the other through – one of them of the King's Chappell, one Cave, and the other a retayner of my Lord Generall Middleton's.[3]

Thence to White-hall, where in the Dukes chamber the King came and stayed an hour or two, laughing at Sir W Petty, who was there[b] about his boat, and at Gresham College in general. At which poor Petty was I perceive at some loss, but did argue discreetly and bear the unreasonable follies of the King's objec-

a   MS. 'mind'   b   blot above symbol

---

1. Clerk in the Navy Office.
2. His two daughters, Lady Jemima and Lady Paulina Mountagu, and his niece Elizabeth Pickering, were coming to town ahead of his wife ('my old Lady'): below, p. 53.
3. 'Mr. John Cave, one of the Gentlemen of his Majesties Chappell Royall, goeing home to his lodging upon the 30th of January about 7 or

8 of the clock in the evening, about the new Exchange, was by one James Elliott, a Scott, run through the body, of which wound he departed this life the 16th day of February following 1663 . . .': E. F. Rimbault (ed.), *Old cheque-book*, pp. 12, 212. For disputes about who should 'take the wall', see above, i. 46, n. 4. (E).

tions and other bystanders with great discretion – and offered to take oddes against the King's best boats; but the King would not lay, but cried him down with words only.[1] Gresham College he mightily laughed at for spending time only in weighing of ayre, and doing nothing else since they sat.[2]

Thence to Westminster-hall and there met with diverse people, it being term-time. Among others, I spoke with Mrs. Lane, of whom I doubted to hear something of the effects of our last meeting about a fortnight or three weeks ago, but to my content did not. Here I met with Mr. Pierce, who tells me of several passages at Court; among others, how the King, coming the other day to his Theatre to see *The Indian Queene* (which he commends for a very fine thing),[3] my Lady Castlemaine was in the next box before he came; and leaning over other ladies a while to whisper with the King, she ris out of that box and went into the King's and sat herself on the King's[a] right hand between the King and the Duke of Yorke – which he swears put the King himself, as well as everybody else, out of countenance, and believes that she did it only to show the world that she is not out of favour yet – as was believed.

Thence with Alderman Maynell by his coach to the Change, and there with several people busy; and so home to dinner and took my wife out immediately to the King's Theatre, it being a new month (and once a month I may go) and there saw *The Indian Queen* acted, which endeed is a most pleasant show and beyond my expectation; the play good but spoiled with the Ryme, which breaks the sense. But above my expectation most,

a repl. 'r'-

---

1. For Petty's vessel, see above, iv. 256, n. 3. Pepys has a similar note of this conversation in NWB, p. 20, but under 2 February. The King launched the vessel on the following 22 December.

2. The gibe was of course untrue, and in any case this laughable weighing of air did in fact lead (by way of Newcomen's steam-engine in Anne's reign) to the development of steam-power. Cf. the similar complaint of a pamphleteer in 1680: 'We prize our selves in fruitless Curiosities; we turn our Lice and Fleas into Bulls and Pigs by our *Magnifying-glasses*; we are searching for the World in the Moon with our *Telescopes*; we send to weigh the Air on the top of *Teneriffe* ... which are voted ingenuities, whilst the Notions of Trade are turned into Ridicule, or much out of fashion' (qu. J. R. McCulloch, ed., *Select coll. early Engl. tracts on commerce*, p. 357).

3. See above, p. 29 , n. 1. (A).

the eldest Marshall did do her part most excellently well as ever I heard woman in my life, but her voice not so sweet as Ianthes – but however, we came home mightily contented.[1] Here we met Mr. Pickering and his mistress, Mrs. Doll. Wilde. He tells me that the business runs high between the Chancellor and my Lord Bristoll against the Parliament.[2] And that my Lord Lauderdale and Cooper[3] open high against the Chancellor – which I am sorry for. In my way home I light*a* and to the Coffee-house, where I heard Lieutenant Collonell Baron tell very good stories of his travels over the high hills in Asia above the Cloudes. How clear the heaven is above them. How thick, like a mist, the way is through the cloud, that wets like a sponge one's clothes. The ground above the clouds all dry and parched, nothing in the world growing, it being only a dry earth. Yet not so hot above as below the clouds. The stars at night most delicate bright and a fine clear blue sky. But cannot see the earth at any time through the clouds, but the clouds look like a world below you.

Thence home and to supper, being hungry; and so to the office, did business, especially about Creed,[4] for whom I am now pretty well fitted – and so home to bed.

This day in Westminster-hall, W. Bowyer told me that his father is dead lately and died by*b* being drowned in the River, coming over in the night; but he says he had not been drinking. He was take with his stick in his hand and cloak over his shoulder, as ruddy as before he died. His horse was taken overnight in the water, hampered in the bridle; but they were so silly as not to look for his*c* master till the next morning that he was found drowned.[5]

a repl. 'to'   *b* repl. 'of'   *c* repl. 'is'

---

1. Anne Marshall was the elder of two sisters who played at the Theatre Royal and was at this time the principal actress in the King's Company. In this production she played the title-role of Zemboalla. 'Ianthe' was Pepys's name for Mrs Betterton (after her role in *The siege of Rhodes*); a leading actress at the LIF. (A).

2. See below, p. 60 & n. 4.

3. Anthony Ashley Cooper, Lord Ashley (cr. 1st Earl of Shaftesbury, 1672).

4. See below, p. 39.

5. Robert Bowyer ('father Bowyer'), now aged 70, had often befriended Pepys. He had presumably been trying to ford the Thames near his home at Huntsmore, Bucks.

2. Up and to the office; where, though Candlemas=day, Mr. Coventry, Sir W. Penn and I all the morning, the others being at a Survey at Deptford; at noon by coach to the Change with Mr. Coventry. Thence to the Coffee-house with Captain Cocke, who discoursed well of the good effects in some kind of a Duch war and conquest (which I did not consider before but the contrary); that is, that the trade of the world is too little for us two, therefore one must down.[1] Secondly, that though our merchants will not be the better husbands by all this, yet our Wool will bear a better prize* by vaunting of our cloths, and by that our tenants will be better able to pay rents and our lands will be more worth, and all our own manufactures – which now the Dutch out-vie us in. ⟨That he thinks the Duch are not in so good a condition as heretofore, because of want of men always, and now from the wars against the Turke more then ever.⟩[a2]

Thence to the Change again, and thence off to the Sun taverne with Sir W Warren and with him discoursed long and had good advice and hints from him; and among [other] things, he did give me a pair of gloves for my wife, wrapped up in paper; which I would not open, feeling it hard, but did tell him my wife should thank him, and so went on in discourse. When I came home, Lord, in what pain I was to get my wife out of the room without bidding her go, that I might see what these gloves were; and by and by, she being gone, it proves a pair of white gloves for her and 40 pieces in good gold: which did so cheer my heart that I could eat no victuals almost for dinner for joy to think how God doth bless us every day more and more – and more yet I hope he will upon the encrease of my duty and endeavours. I was at great loss what to do, whether tell my wife of it or no; which I could hardly forbear, but yet I did and will think of it first before I do, for fear of making her think me to be in a better condition or in a better way of getting money then yet I am.

a addition crowded in between paragraphs

1. It was a common idea that the total amount of trade in the world was a fixed quantity.

2. The Dutch were not directly involved in these wars, but being largely dependent on mercenaries for their army, would have to compete for recruits with the Empire and France who were preparing for the summer's campaign on the Danube.

D

After dinner to the office, where doing infinite of business till past 10 at night to the comfort of my mind; and so home with joy to supper and to bed.

This evening Mr. Hempson came and told me how Sir W. Batten his master will not hear of continuing him in his imploy-ment as Clerk of the Survey at Chatham, from whence of a sudden he hath removed him without any new or extraordinary cause, and I believe (as he himself doth in part write and J Norman doth confess) for nothing but for that he was twice with me the other day and did not wait upon him – so much he fears me and all that have to do with me.   Of this more in my Memorandum Book of my office – upon this day, there I shall find it.[1]

3.   Up; and after long discourse with my Cosen Tho. Pepys the Executor, I with my wife by coach to Holborne, where I light and she to her father's.   I to the Temple and several places and so to the Change, where much business; and then home to dinner alone, and so to the Miter tavern by appointment (and there by chance met with W Howe, come to buy wine for my Lord against his going down to Hinchingbrooke; and I private with him a great while, discoursing of my Lord's strangeness to me; but he answers that I have no reason to think any such thing, but that my Lord is only in general a more reserved man then he was before) to meet Sir W Rider and Mr. Clerke; and there after much ado made an end, giving Mr. Custos 202*l* against Mr Bland; which I endeavoured to bring down but could not, and think it is well enough ended for Mr. Bland for all that.[2]   Thence by coach to fetch my wife from her brother's, and find her gone home.   Called at Sir Robt. Bernards about surrendering my estate in reversion to the use of my life,[3] which will be done.   And at Rog. Pepys, who was gone to bed in pain

1. ? NWB, p. 11 (or later copied into it: see below, p. 116 & n. 1). According to Commissioner Pett, Hempson was dismissed because of his repeated absences: *CSPD 1663-4*, p. 449.
2. This was the dispute about freight charges: see above, iv. 404.

3. This was his reversionary interest in the estate of his uncle Robert Pepys. Pepys was now arranging the succes-sion to his land but retaining his life income.

of a boyle, that he could not sit or stand. So home, where my wife is full of sad stories of her good-natured father and roguish brother, who is going for Holland, and his wife, to be a soldier;[1] and so after a little at the office, to bed. This night late, coming in my coach coming up Ludgate hill, I saw two gallants and their footmen taking a pretty wench which I have much eyed lately, set up shop upon the hill, a seller of ribband and gloves. They seem to drag her by some force, but the wench went and I believe had her turn served; but God forgive me, what thoughts and wishes I had of being in their place.

In Covent-garden tonight, going to fetch home my wife, I stopped at the great Coffee-house there, where I never was before – where Draydon the poet (I knew at Cambrige) and all the wits of the town, and Harris the player and Mr. Hoole of our college;[2] and had I had time then, or could at other times, it will be good coming thither, for there I perceive is very witty and pleasant discourse. But I could not tarry and it was late; they were all ready to go away.

4. Up and to the office, where after a while setting, I left the board upon pretence of serious business and by coach to Paul's schoole, where I heard some good speeches of the boys that were to be elected this year.[3] Thence by and by with Mr. Pullen and Banes[4] (a great nonconformist) with several other of my old acquaintance to the Nags-head tavern and there did give them a bottle of sack; and away again and I to the school and up to hear the upper-form examined; and there was kept by very many of the Mercers, Clutterbucke, Barker, Harrington, and others, and with great respect used by them all and had a noble

---

1. Balty appears to have stayed in Holland for about a year: below, vi. 169.

2. The coffee-house was probably the one later known as Will's, on the corner of Bow St and Russell St; established at about this time, it was by the 1690s the favourite resort of literary London. Dryden had been a scholar of Trinity College, Cambridge, 1650-4, and William Hoole

(Howell), a historian, had been a Fellow of Magdalene from 1652.

3. Sc. elected to leaving exhibitions. This was Apposition Day at the school: q.v. above, iv. 33, n. 1.

4. Old Paulines. Benjamin Pullen was a Fellow of Trinity College, Cambridge, and later (1674-86) Regius Professor of Greek. Jeremy Baines had just (1663) taken his B.A. from St John's, Cambridge.

dinner.[1] Here they tell me that in Dr. Colett's Will he says that he would have a master found for the school that hath good skill in Latin and (if it could be) one that had some knowledge of the Greeke; so little was Greek known here at that time.[2] Dr. Wilkins and one Mr. Smallwood, posers.[3] After great pleasure there, and especially to [hear] Mr. Crumlum[4] so often to tell of my being a benefactor to the school – I to my booksellers and there spent an hour looking over *Theatrum Urbium*[5] and *Flandria illustrata*,[6] with excellent cuts, with great content. So homewards and called at my little Millener's,[7] where I chatted with her, her husband out of the way, and a mad merry soul she is. So home to the office; and by and by comes my wife home from the burial of Captain Groves wife at Wapping (she telling me a story how her maid Jane, going into the boat, did fall down and show her arse*a* in the boat) and all; and comes my Uncle Wight and Mr. Maes with the state of their case,[8] which he told me very discreetly and I believe is a very hard one. And so after drinking a bottle of ale or two, they gone and I a little more to the office; and so home to prayers and to bed.

a s.h. repl. l.h. 'ar'——

---

1. The meeting of the Apposition Court of the Mercers' Company, held annually this day at the school, was by custom accompanied by a feast.

2. The phrase ('Yf suyche may be gotten') occurs not in Colet's will but in the statutes he made in 1518 when founding the school. William Lily, first High Master, was one of the few Englishmen so qualified; Colet would himself have had difficulty in fulfilling this requirement. See Sir M. McDonnell, *Hist. St Paul's School*, ch. iii; M. L. Clarke, *Classical educ. in Britain, 1500–1900*, p. 17.

3. Examiners. Dr John Wilkins, one of the founders of the Royal Society (later Bishop of Chester) and Dr Matthew Smallwood, Canon of St Paul's (later Dean of Lichfield).

4. Samuel Cromleholme, High Master.

5. Either J. Blaeu, *Theatrum civitatum . . . Italiae* (Amsterdam, 1663; PL 2993), or *Urbium praecipuarum mundi theatrum quintum*; one of the six volumes of engravings of cities published at Cologne, 1572–1618, by G. Braun & F. Hogenberg. The series had no general title. There is no copy in the PL, but Pepys kept a copy of the frontispiece in his collection of title-pages etc.; PL 2977 (69).

6. By Antonius Sanderus (Amsterdam, 1641–4); not in the PL.

7. Cf. below, p. 105.

8. A dispute about customs duties: below, p. 43 & n. 2.

This evening I made an end of my letter to Creed about his pieces-of-eight and sent it away to him: I pray God give good end to it, to bring me some money and that duly as from him.[1]

5. Up; and down by water, a brave morning, to Woolwich and there spent an hour or two to good purpose; and so walked to Greenwich and thence to Deptford, where I find (with Sir W. Batten upon the survey) Sir J. Mennes, Sir W. Penn and my Lady Batten come down and going to dinner. I dined with them, and so after dinner by water home, all the way going and coming reading *Faber fortunæ*,[2] which I can never read too often. At home a while with my wife; and so to my office, where till 8 a-clock, and then home to look after some Brampton papers and perticularly those of my uncles accounts as Generall-Receiver of the county for the year 1647 of our Monthly Assessement;[3] which, contrary to my expectation, I found in such good order and so thoroughly that I did not expect nor could have thought; and that being done, having seen discharges for every farthing of money he received, I went to bed late with great quiet.

6. Up and to the office, where we sat all the morning; and so at noon to the Change, where I met Mr. Coventry, the first time I ever saw him there. And after a little talk with him and other merchants, I up and down about several businesses and so home; whither came one Father Fogourdy, an[a] Irish priest of my wife's and her mother's acquaintance in France – a sober, discreet person, but one that I would not have converse with my wife, for fear of meddling with her religion.[4] But I like the man well. Thence with my wife abroad, and left her at Toms while I abroad about several businesses; and so back to her, myself being vexed to find Tom at my first coming, abroad, and all his

a repl. 'the'

---

1. See below, p. 46 & n. 1.
2. Bacon's Latin essay: q.v. above, ii. 102, n. 1.
3. See below, vi. 65 & n. 2.
4. Fogarty had presumably been known to them during their stay in Paris, c. 1652–3. Irish Catholic priests were normally educated in France in this period. Pepys was often frightened that his wife would turn Catholic, despite her Huguenot upbringing: see esp. below, p. 92 & n. 2.

books, papers and bills loose upon the open table in the parlour, and he abroad – which I ranted at him for when he came in. Then by coach home, calling at my Cosen Scotts, who (she) lies dying, they say upon a miscarriage. My wife could not be admitted to see her, nor anybody. At home to the office late writing letters, and then home – to supper and to bed. Father Fogourdy confirms to me the news that for certain there is peace made between the pope and King of France.[1]

7. *Lords day.* Up and to church and thence home; my wife, being ill of those, kept her bed all day and I up and dined by her bedside; and then all the afternoon, till late at night, writing some letters of business to my father, stating of matters to him in general of great import, and other letters to ease my mind in the week-days that I have not time to think of; and so up to my wife and with great mirth read Sir W Davenents two speeches in dispraise of London and Paris, by way of reproach one to the other,[2] and so to prayers and to bed.

8. Up, and by coach called upon Mr. Phillips and after a little talk with him, away to my Lord Sandwiches; but he being gone abroad, I stayed a little and talked with W Howe; and so to Westminster in term-time. And there met Mr. Pierce, who told me largely how the King still doth dote upon his women, even beyond all shame. And that the good Queen will of herself stop before she goes sometimes into her dressing-room, till she know whether the King be there, for fear he should be, as she hath sometimes taken him, with Mrs. Stuart.

And that some of the best parts of the Queenes Joynture is, contrary to faith and against the opinion of my Lord Treasurer and his Council, bestowed or rented, I know not how, to my Lord Fitzharding and Mrs. Stuart and others of that crew.[3]

1. The Peace of Pisa, 2/12 February; for the dispute, see above, iii. 253 & n. 3.

2. From the second part of *The first day's entertainment at Rutland House, by declamations and music, after the manner of the ancients,* which Davenant wrote and presented in 1656, when he began his shrewd efforts to revive the theatre during the Commonwealth. The *Entertainment* was published in 1657; PL 2347 (*Works,* 1673). (A).

3. On 4 February three warrants had passed for the grant to Fitzharding of leases of land in Northamptonshire: *CSPD 1663–4*, p. 468.

That the King doth dote infinitely upon the Duke of Monmouth, apparently as one that he entends to have succeed him.[1] God knows what will be the end of it.

After he was gone, I went and talked with Mrs. Lane about persuading her to Hawly, and I think she will come on, which I wish were done. And so to Mr. Howlett and his wife and talked about the same, and they are mightily for it and I bid them promote it, for I think it will be for both their goods – and my content. But I was much pleased to look upon their pretty daughter, which is grown a pretty maid and will make a fine modest woman.

Thence to the Change by coach; and after some business done, home to dinner and thence to Guild[a] hall, thinking to have heard some pleading, but there was no Courts; and so to Cades the stationer and there did look upon some pictures which he promised to give me the buying of,[2] but I found he would have played the Jacke with me; but at last he did proffer me what I expected, and I have laid aside 10 or 12*l* worth and will think of it; but I am loath to lay out so much money upon them.

So home, a little vexed in my mind to think how today I was forced to compliment W. Howe and admit myself to an equality with Mr. Moore, which is come to challenge in his discourse with me; but I will admit it no more, but let me stand or fall, I will show myself as strange to them as my Lord doth himself to me.

After at the office till 9 a-clock, I home, in fear of some pain by taking cold; and so to supper and to bed.

9. Up and to the office, where sat all the morning. At noon by coach with Mr. Coventry to the Change, where busy with several people. Great talk of the Duch proclaiming themselfs in India lords of the Southern Seas and deny traffique there to all ships but their own, upon pain of confiscation[3] – which makes our merchants mad. Great doubt of two ships of ours, the *Greyhound* and another very rich, coming from the Streights, for

a MS. 'Guield'

---

1. See above, iii. 238, n. 4.
2. See above, iv. 434.
3. See below, pp. 49–50, & n.

fear of the Turkes.[1] Matters are made up between the Pope and the King of France; so that now all the doubt is what the French will do with his armies.

Thence home and there find Captain Grove, in mourning for his wife, and Hawly, and they dined with me. After dinner and Grove gone, Hawly and I talked of his mistress Mrs. Lane, and I seriously advising him and enquiring his condition – and do believe that I shall bring them together.

By and by comes Mr. Moore, with whom much good discourse of my Lord; and among other things, told me that my Lord is mightily altered, that is, grown very high and stately and doth not admit of any to come into his chamber to him as heretofore; and that I must not think much of his strangeness to me, for it was the same he doth to everybody. And that he would not have me to be solicitous in the matter, but keep off and give him now and then a visit and no more, for he says he himself doth not go to him nowadays but when he sends[a] for him, nor then doth not stay for him if he be not there at the hour appointed; "For," says he, "I do find that I can stand upon my own legs and I will not by an over-submission make myself cheap to anybody and contemptible" – which was the doctrine of the world that I lacked most – and shall fallow it. I discoursed with him about my money that my Lord hath and the 1000*l* that I stand bound with him in to my Cosen Tho. Pepys,[2] in both which I will get myself at liberty as soon as I can – for I do not like his being angry and in debt both together to me; and besides, I do not perceive he looks after paying his debts, but runs farther and farther in.

He being gone, my wife and I did walk an hour or two above in our chamber, seriously talking of businesses. I told her my Lord owed me 700*l* and showed her the bond – and how I entended to carry myself to my Lord. She and I did cast about how to get Captain Grove for my sister, in which we are mighty

a repl. 'says'

1. The other ship was the *Concord*; both were merchantmen of the Levant Company. The *Greyhound*'s cargo was valued by the Customs House at £150,000: HMC, *Heath-* cote, p. 145. For their safe arrival, see below, p. 49; cf. newsletter in Tanner 47, f. 68*r*.

2. See above, iii. 17; iv. 285.

earnest at present; and I think it will be a good match – and will endeavour it. So to my office a while; then home to supper and to bed.

10. Up, and by coach to my Lord Sandwich to his new house (a fine house, but deadly dear)[1] in Lincoln's Inne fields – where I found and spoke a little to him. He is high and strange still, but did ask me how my wife did and at parting remembered him to his Cosen – which I thought was pretty well, being willing to flatter myself that in time he will be well again.

Thence home straight and busy all the forenoon; and at noon with Mr. Bland to Mr. Povy's, but he being at dinner and full of company, we retreated and went into Fleet-street to a friend's of his; and after long stay, he telling me the long and most perplexed story of Coronell and Bushells business of Sugars, wherein Parke and Greene and Mr. Bland and 40 more have been so concerned about the King of Portugalls duties, wherein every party hath laboured to cheat another.[2] A most pleasant and profitable story to hear. And in the close made me understand Mr. Maes's business[3] better then I did before. By and by dinner came; and after dinner and good discourse, that and such as I was willing for improvement sake to hear, I went away too to White-hall to a Committee of Tanger – where I took occasion to demand of Creed whether he had received my letter,[4] and he told me yes, "aye", that he would answer it – which makes me much wonder what he means to do with me. But I will be even with him before I have done, let him make as light of it as he will.

---

1. See above, p. 20 & n. 1.

2. In 1662 certain English ships were alleged to have sailed from Brazil to London without paying duties at Lisbon, and the Portuguese government had tried to have this claim off-set against the unpaid part of the Queen's dowry. (Cf. above, iii. 91 & n. 1.) The best short account of the matter is in the letters in HMC, *Heathcote*, pp. 34, 46–7; see also PRO, PC 2/56 (Index, 'Portugal'); *CTB*, i. 385; *CSPD 1664–5*, p. 61; *CSPVen. 1661–4*, pp. 120, 123. Sir

Augustine Coronel was a Spanish–Jewish financier, an agent of the King of Portugal, involved in the dowry arrangements, who had allegedly cheated his creditors by going bankrupt. The merchants here named (all of London) were Edward Bushell, John Packer, John Green and John Bland.

3. Iudoco Maes, a Portuguese Jew, imprisoned for evasion of the duties, had tried to escape from England in December 1663.

4. See above, p. 39 & n. 1.

Thence to the Temple, where my Cosen Roger Pepys did show me a letter my father wrote to him last term to show me – proposing such things about Sturtlow*ᵃ* and a portion for Pall and I know not what,[1] that vexes me to see him plotting how to put me to trouble and charge and not thinking to pay our debts and legacies. But I will write him a letter will persuade him to be wiser.

So home; and finding my wife abroad (after her coming home from being with my aunt Wight today to buy Lent provisions)[2] gone with Will to my brother's, I fallowed them by coach but found them not, for they were newly gone home from thence; which troubled me. I to Sir Robt. Bernards chamber and there did Surrender my Reversions in Brampton lands to the use of my Will[3] – which I was glad to have done, my Will being now good in all points. Thence homewards, calling a little at the Coffeehouse, where a little merry discourse; and so home, where I find my wife, who says she went to her father's to be satisfied about her brother – who I find at my house with her. He is going this next tide with his wife into Holland to seek his fortune. He had taken his leave of us in the morning. I did give my wife x*s* to give him and a coat that I had by me, a close-bodied light-coloured cloth coat with a gold edgeing*ᵇ* in each seam that was the lace of my wife's best*ᶜ* petticoat that she had when I married*ᵈ* her. I stayed not there, but to my office, where Stanes the Glazier was with me till 10 at night making up his Contract; and poor man, I made him almost mad through a mistake of mine, but did afterward reconcile all – for I would not have the man that labours to serve the King so cheap above others, suffer too much.[4]

He gone, I did a little business more and so home to supper and to bed – being now pretty well again, the weather being warm. My pain doth leave me, without coming to any great excess·

a repl. 'a'   *b* repl. 'l'-
c repl. 'first'   *d* repl. 'h'-

---

1. Cf. above, iv. 308.
2. Her husband was a fishmonger.
3. See above, p. 36 & n. 3.
4. The Board had recently awarded Thomas Stanes a contract for poop lanterns etc., in return for his information about the extortionate prices of other contractors and his undertaking to do the work 'best and cheapest': *CSPD 1663–4*, p. 395.

But my cold that I had got I suppose was not very great, it being only the leaving of my waste-coat unbuttoned one morning.

11. Up, and after much pleasant discourse with my wife, and to the office, where we sat all the morning and did much business, and some much to my content, by prevailing against Sir W. Batten for the King's profit. At noon home to dinner my wife and I, hand-to-fist to a very fine pig. This noon Mr. Falconer came and visited my wife and brought her a present, a silver state-cup and cover, value about 3 or 4*l* – for the courtesy I did him the other day.[1] He did not stay dinner with me. I am almost sorry for this present, because I would have reserved him for a place to go in summer a-visiting at Woolwich with my wife.

After dinner my wife and I up to her closet, and saw a new parcel of fine shells of her brother's giving;[2] and then to the office, where till 11 at night and then home after I had writ an angry letter to my father upon the letter my Cosen Roger showed me yesterday. So home and to bed, my mind disturbed about the letter I am forced to write tonight to my father,[3] it being very severe; but it is convenient I should do it.

12. Up and ready; did find below Mr. Creedes boy with a letter from his maister for me. So I fell to reading it, and it is by way of stating the case between S: Pepys and J: Creed, most excellently writ, both showing his stoutness yet willingness to peace, reproaching me yet flattering me again; and in a word, in as good a manner as I think the world could have wrote; and endeed, put me to a greater stand then ever I thought I could have been in this matter. All the morning thinking how to behave myself in that business; and at noon to the Coffee-house and thence by his appointment met him upon the Change and with him back to the Coffee-house, where with great seriousness and strangeness on both sides he said his part and I mine – he some-times owning my favour and assistance, yet endeavouring to lessen it; as, that the success of his business was not wholly or

1. Presumably during Pepys's visit on 22 January to the Woolwich ropeyard, of which Falconer was in charge.

2. For shell-work, see above, i. 148 & n. 2.

3. See below, p. 48.

very much to be imputed to that assistance. I to allege the contrary and plainly to tell him that from the beginning I never had it in my mind to do him all that kindness for nothing; but he gaining 5 or 600*l*, I did expect a share of it; at least, a real and not a complimentary*a* acknowledgment of him.[1] In Fine, I said nothing all the while that I need fear he can do me more hurt with then before I spoke them.   The most I told him was after we were come to a peace, when he asked me whether he should answer the Boards letter or no – I told him he might forbear it awhile and no more.   Then he asked how the letter could be signed by them without their much enquiry: I told him*b* it was as I ordered it and nothing at all else of any moment, whether my words be ever hereafter spoken of again or no. So that I have the same, neither better nor worse, force over him that I had before, if he should not do his part.   And the peace between us was this.   Says he, "After all; well," says he, "I know you will expect, since there must be some condescension, that it doth become me to begin it; and therefore," says he, "I do propose (just like the interstice between the death of the old and coming in of the present king, all that time is swallowed up as if it hath never been), so our breach of friendship may be as if it hath never been."   That I should lay aside all misapprehensions of him or his first letter, and that he would reckon himself obliged to show the same ingenuous knowledge of my love and service to him as at the beginning he ought to have done, before by my first letter I did (as he well observed) put him out of a capacity of doing it without seeming to do it servilely.   And so it rests and I shall expect* how he will deal by me.

After that I begin to be free, and both of us to discourse of other things, and he went home with me and dined with me and

a MS. 'complentative'   *b* repl. 'them'

---

1. For the dispute, see above, iii. 279 & n. 1.   It concerned the reward Creed was to give to Pepys for his assistance in aiding the passing of his accounts as Muster-Master and Deputy-Treasurer of the fleet, 1660–2, for which he claimed £521, and which included some undeclared profits from exchanging sterling into pieces-of-eight. See his letter to Pepys, with Pepys's endorsement, 14 July 1664, PRO, SP 29/100, no. 59. He gave £20 to Pepys on the following 18 July – less than Pepys expected but 'better than nothing'.

my wife, and very pleasant, having a good dinner and the opening
of my Lampry (cutting a notch on one side), which proved very
good.

After dinner he and I to Deptford, walking all the way; where
we met Sir W Petty and I*a* took him back and I got him to go
with me to his vessel and discourse it over to me; which he did
very well and then walked back together to the waterside at
Redriffe, with good discourse all the way. So Creede and I by
boat to my house; and thence took coach with my wife and called
at Alderman Backewells, and there changed Mr. Falconers state-
cup that he did give us the other day for a fair Tankard. The
cup weighed with the fashion 5*l*–16*s*. And another little cup
that Joyce Norton did give us 17*s* – both 6*l*. 13*s*. – for which we
had the tankard, which came to 6*l*. 10*s*., at 5*s*. 7*d*. per oz., and 3*s*
in money. And with great content away thence to my brother's
– Creed going away there and my brother bringing me the old
silk Standard that I lodged there long ago;[1] and then back again
home. And thence, hearing that my uncle Wight had been at
my house, I went to him to the Miter; and there with*b* him and
Maes, Norbury and Mr. Rawlinson till late, eating some pot
venison (where the Crowne earthen-pot pleased me mightily);
and then homewards and met Mr. Barrow, so back with him to
the Miter and sat talking about his business of his discontent in
the yard,[2] wherein sometimes he was very foolish and pettish, till
12 at night; and so went away, and I home and up to my wife
a-bed – with my mind ill at ease whether I should think that I had
by this made myself a bad end, by missing the certainty of 100*l*
which I proposed to myself so much; or a good one, by easing
myself of the uncertain good effect but the certain trouble and
reflection which must have fallen on me if we had proceeded to a
public dispute endeed, besides imbarquing myself against my
Lord, who (which I had forgot) had given him[3] his hand for the
value of the pieces-of-eight at his rates, which were all false –
which, by the way, I shall take heed to the giving my Lord notice
of it hereafter, whenever he goes out again.[4]

a repl. 'did'   *b* repl. 'then'

---

1. Perhaps the flag Pepys found on
20 July 1662.
2. See above, p. 5 & n. 1.

3. Creed.
4. Sc. whenever he sails again
(to the Mediterranean).

13.ᵃ Up; · and after I had told my wife in the morning in bed the passages yesterday with Creed, my head and heart was mightily lighter then they were before; and so up and to the Office; and thence, after sitting, at 11 a-clock with Mr. Coventry to the Affrican-house and there with Sir W Rider, by agreement we looked over part of my Lord Peterborough's accounts there, being by Mr. Creed and Vernatz.¹ Anon down to dinner (to a table which Mr. Coventry keeps here, out of his 300*l* per annum as one of the Assistants to the Royall Company);² a very pretty dinner and good company and excellent discourse. And so up again to our work for an hour till the Company came too, having a meeting of their own;ᵇ and so we broke up and Creed and I took coach and to Reeves's the perspective-glass maker; and there did endeed see very excellent Microscopes, which did discover a louse or mite or sand most perfectly and largely.³ Being sated with that, we went away (yet with a good will, were it not for my obligations, to have bought one) and walked to the New Exchange; and after a turn or two and talked, I took coach and home and so to my office (after I had been with my wife and saw herᶜ day's work in ripping the silk standard which we brought home last night; and it will serve to line a bed or for twenty uses, to our great content); and there wrote fair my angry letter to my father upon that that he wrote to my Cosen Roger Pepys; which I hope will make him the more careful to trust to my advice for the time to come, without so many needless complaints and Jealousys, which are troublesome to me, because without reason.

a repl. '14'; blot in upper margin   *b* repl. 'our'   *c* repl. 'here'

---

1. Philibert Vernatty was a clerk or accountant at Tangier in the service of Peterborough (Governor, 1661–3). Disputes over the accounts continued for several months, principally between Peterborough and Thomas Povey, Treasurer of the Tangier Committee. Pepys was involved not only as a member of the committee but also as Sandwich's agent. A report on them was made on 19 May 1664: below, p. 153. For an abstract of the final figures, as declared in the Exchequer on 19 January 1666 and 9 December 1679, see Routh, pp. 365–6.

2. For the Royal African Company, see above, iv. 152–3 & n.

3. Microscopes were novelties. Pepys bought one on the following 26 July. Richard Reeves was selling them as early as 1662; Hooke's demonstrations before the Royal Society date from April 1663.

14. *Lords day.* Up and to church alone, where a lazy sermon of Mr. Mills upon a text to introduce catechizing in his parish, which I perceive he entends to begin.[1] So home and very pleasant with my wife at dinner. All the afternoon at my office alone, doing business; and then in the evening, after a walk with my wife in the garden, she and I to my Uncle Wight's to supper, where Mr. Norbury; but my Uncle out of tune. And after supper he seemed displeased mightily at my aunts desiring [to] put off a Copper kettle, which it seems with great study he had provided to boil meat in and now she is put in the head that it is not wholesome – which vexed him, but we were very merry about it; and by and by home, and after prayers to bed.[a]

15. Up; and carrying my wife to my Lord's lodgings, left her and I to White-hall to the Duke; where he first put on a periwigg today[2] but methought his hair, cut short in order thereto, did look very prettily of itself before he put on his periwig. Thence to his closet and did our business. And thence Mr. Coventry and I down to his chamber and spent a little time; and so parted and I took my wife homeward, I stopping at the Coffee-house and thence a while to the Change (where great news of the arrivall of two rich ships, the *Greyhound* and another, which they were mightily afeared of and great insurance given);[3] and so home to dinner and after an hour with my wife at her globes, I to the office, where very busy till 11 at night; and so home to supper and to bed.

This afternoon Sir Tho Chamberlin came to the office to me and showed me several letters from the East Indys, showing the heighth that the Dutch are come to there; showing scorn to all the English even in our only Factory there of Surratt, beating several men and hanging the English Standard St. George under the Duch flag in scorn; saying that whatever their masters do or say at home, they will do what they list and will be masters of all

a blot in upper margin

---

1. This was another sign of Milles's conversion from Puritanism. He had begun 'to nibble at the Common Prayer' on 4 November 1660 and was first seen in a surplice on 26 October 1662. .

2. For this fashion, see above, iv. 358, n. 1.

3. See above, pp. 41–2 & n.

the world there, and have so proclaimed themselfs Soveraigne of all the South Seas[1] – which certainly our King cannot endure, if the parliament will give him money. But I doubt and yet do hope they will not yet, till we are more ready for it.

16. Up and to the office, where very busy all the morning; and most with Mr. Wood, I vexing him about his masts. At noon to the Change a little, and thence brought Mr. Barrow to dinner with me – where I had a haunch of venison roasted, given me yesterday,[a] and so had a pretty dinner. Full of discourse of his business, wherein the poor man is mightily troubled; and I pity him in it but hope to get[b] him some ease.[2] He being gone, I to the office, where very busy till night that my Uncle Wight and Mr. Maes came to me; and after discourse about Maes's business,[3] to supper, very merry but my mind upon my business; and so, they being gone – I to my vyall a little, which I have not done some months I think before, and then a little to my office at 11 at night, and so home and to bed.

17. Up, and with my wife, setting her down by her father's in Long-acre, in so ill-looked a place, among all the bawdy-houses, that I was troubled at it to see her go thither. Thence I to White-hall and there walked up and down, talking with Mr. Pierce, who tells me of the King's giving of my Lord Fitzharding two leases, which belongs endeed to the Queene, worth 20000*l* to him,[4] and how people do talk of it – and other things of that nature, which I am sorry to hear. He and I walked round the parke with great pleasure and back again; and finding no time to speak with my Lord of Albemarle, I walked to the Change

a repl. 'the other'   *b* repl. 'to'

---

1. There is no reference to this incident at Surat in Sir W. Foster's *Engl. factories in India, 1661–64*, which is based on the records both of Surat and of the Dutch E. India Company. Surat was the principal centre of English trade in India (Pepys's 'East Indys'). The Dutch had recently taken control of the Cochin coast, and had by this time completely displaced the Portuguese as the dominant power of the Indian Ocean. Chamberlain was Governor of the E. India Company.

2. See above, p. 5 & n. 1. On this day Pepys wrote to Commissioner Pett supporting Barrow's case: *Further Corr.*, pp. 14–15.

3. See above, p. 43 & n. 2.

4. See above, p. 40 & n. 3.

and there met my wife at our pretty Dolls[1] and so took her home, and Creed also, whom I met there, and sent her home while Creed and I stayed on the Change; and by and by home and dined – where I found an excellent Mastiffe, his name Towzer, sent me by a surgeon.[2] After dinner I took my wife again by coach (leaving Creed by the way, going to Gresham College, of which he is now become one of the Virtuosos)[3] and to White-hall, where I delivered a paper about Tanger to my Lord Duke of Albemarle in the council-chamber; and so to Mrs. Hunts to call my wife, and so by coach straight home and at my office till 3 a-clock in the morning – having spent much time this evening in discourse with Mr. Cutler, who tells me how the Dutch deal with us abroad and do not value us anywhere. And how he and Sir W Rider have found reason to lay aside Captain Cocke in their company, he having played some indiscreet and unfair tricks with them, and hath lost himself everywhere by his im-posing upon all the world with the conceit he hath of his own wit*. And so hath, he tells me, Sir Rd. Ford also, both of whom are very witty men.

He being gone, Sir W Rider come and stayed with me till about 12 at night, having found ourselfs work till that time about understanding the measuring of Mr. Woods masts; which though I did so well before as to be thought to deal very hardly against Wood, yet I am ashamed I understood it no better and do hope yet, whatever be thought of me, to save the King some more money.[4] And out of an impatience to break up with my head full of confused confounded notions but nothing brought to a clear comprehension, I was resolved to set up, and did, till now it is ready to strike 4 a-clock, all alone, cold, and my candle not enough left to light me to my own house; and so, with my business however brought to some good understanding and set it down pretty clear, I went home to bed, with my mind at good quiet and the girle setting up for me (the rest all a-bed); I eat and drank a little and to bed, weary, sleepy, cold, and my head akeing.

---

1. Dorothy Stacey of the New Exchange, Strand.

2. A ship's surgeon.

3. He was elected F.R.S. on 16 December 1663: Birch, i. 345.

4. Pepys has some notes on this (22 February) in NWB, p. 15. The Board had discussed the matter inconclusively on 11 February, when Pepys had argued that they were too short. See above, p. 6, n. 4.

18. Called up to the office; and much against my will, I rose, my head akeing mightily – and to the office, where I did argue to good purpose for the King what I have been fitting myself for the last night against Mr. Wood, about his masts; but brought it to no issue. Very full of business till noon, and then with Mr. Coventry to the Affrican-house and there fell to my Lord Peterborough's accounts; and by and by to dinner, where excellent discourse – Sir G. Carteret and other of the Affrican Company with us. And then up to the accounts again, which were by and by done; and then I straight home, my head in great pain and drowzy; so after doing a little business at the office and wrote to my father about sending him the mastiffe was given me yesterday, I home and by daylight to bed, about 6 a-clock, and fell to sleep. Wakened about 12 when my wife came to bed, and then to sleep again and so till morning, and then up in good
《19.》 order in my head again; and shaved myself and then to the office, whither Mr. Cutler came and walked and talked with me a great while, and then to the Change together; and it being early, did tell me several excellent examples of men raised upon the Change by their great diligence and saving – as also his own fortune and how Credit grew upon him; that when he was not really worth 1100*l.*, he had credit for 100000*l* – of Sir W Rider, how he ris*a* – and others. By and by joyned with us Sir John Bankes, who told us several passages of the East India Company and how in his very case, when there was due to him and Alderman Mico 64000*l* from the Dutch for injury done to them in the East Indys, Oliver presently after the peace, they delaying to pay them the money, he sent them word that if they*b* did not pay them by such a day, he would grant letters of Mart to these merchants against them – by which they were so fearful of him, they did presently pay the money, every farding.[1]

By and by, the Change filling, I did many businesses; and

a repl. 'ris'   *b* MS. 'he'

1. Pepys seems here to have confused the payment of £85,000 to the E. India Company made after the Treaty of 1654, with the payment of £50,000 to Banks and others made in 1659 for their losses from three trading ventures. Banks himself made a profit of only £465. See D. C. Coleman, *Sir John Banks*, pp. 18–19; *Cal. court mins E. India Co. 1650–4* (ed. E. B. Sainsbury), p. xxi; ib., *1655–9*, pp. v, vi; Thurloe, *State Papers*, iii. 21.

about 2 a-clock went off with my uncle Wight to his house,
whence by appointment we took our wifes (they by coach with
Mr. Mawes) and we on foot to Mr. Jaggard, a Salter in Thames-
street, for whom I did a courtesy among the poor victuallers. His
wife, whom long ago I had seen, being daughter to old Day,
my uncle Wights master,[1] is a very plain woman, but pretty
children they have. They live, methought at first, in but a plain
way; but afterward I saw their dinner, all fish, brought in very
neatly. But the company being but bad, I had no great pleasure
in it. After dinner I to the office, where we should have met
upon business extraordinary; but business not coming, we broke
up and I thither again and took my wife; and taking a coach,
went to visit my Ladies Jem. and Paul. Mountagu and Mrs. Eliz.
Pickering, whom we find at their father's new house in Lincolnes
fields; but the house all in dirt. They received us well enough
but[a] I did not endeavour to carry myself over familiarly with
them; and so after a little stay, there coming[b] in presently after
us my Lady Aberguemy[2] and other ladies, we back again by
coach and visited, my wife did, my she-Cosen Scott, who is very
ill still; and thence to Jaggards again, where a very good supper
and great store of plate; and above all, after supper Mrs. Jaggard
did at my entreaty play on the vyall; but so well as I did not
think any woman in England could, and but few Maisters; I must
confess it did mightily surprize me, though I knew heretofore that
she could play, but little thought so well. After her, I set Maes
to singing; but he did it so like a coxcomb that I was sick of him.

About 11 at night I carried my aunt home by coach, and then
home myself, having set my wife down at home by the way.
My aunt tells me they are counted very rich people, worth at
least 10 or 12000*l*. And their country house[3] all the year long
and all things answerable – which mightily surprizes [me] to think
for how poor a man I took him when I did him that courtesy at
our office.

a repl. 'and'   *b* repl. same symbol badly formed

1. William Wight had been
apprenticed to John Day, fishmonger,
in 1632.

2. Lady Abergavenny, wife of the
11th Baron; not apparently a relative

of the Sandwichs. This day was
Lady Paulina's birthday.

3. Probably at Rickmansworth,
Herts. Jaggard's Billingsgate proper-
ties are referred to below, 19 March
1668.

So after prayers, to bed – pleased at nothing all this day but Mrs. Jaggerd playing on the vyall, and that was enough to make me bear with all the rest that did not content me.

20. Up and to the office, where we sat all the morning; and at noon to the Change with Mr. Coventry and thence home to dinner; and after dinner, by a Gally down to Woolwich, where with Mr. Falconer, and then at the other yard,[1] doing some business to my content; and so walked to Greenwich, it being a very fine evening, and brought night home with me by water. And so to my office, where late doing business; and then home to supper and to bed.

21. *Lords day.* Up; and having many businesses at the office today, I spent all the morning there, drawing up a letter to Mr. Coventry about preserving of Masts, being collections of my own.[2] And at noon home to dinner, whither my brother Tom comes. And after dinner I took him up and read my letter lately of discontent to my father; and he is seemingly pleased at it – and cries out on my sister's ill-nature and lazy life there.

He being gone, I to my office again and there made an end of my morning's work; and then after reading my vowes of Course* – home; and back again with Mr. Maes and walked with him, talking of his business in the garden; and he being gone, my wife and I walked a turn or two also; and then my Uncle Wight fetching of us,*a* she and I to his house to supper, I by the way calling on Sir G Carteret to desire his consent to my bringing Maes to him, which he agreed to. So I to my uncle's but stayed a great while, vexed both of us for Maes's not coming in; and anon he came, and I with him from supper to Sir G. Carteret and there did largely discourse of the business; and I believe he

a repl. 'me'

---

1. Deptford.
2. Dated Shrove Tuesday (23 February); copy in Hewer's hand: NMM, LBK/8, pp. 97–9, printed (together with the accompanying memorandum in Pepys's hand, pp. 99–100) in *Further Corr.*, pp. 15–19.

Pepys argued, largely on the advice of Warren, that the best method would be to submerge the masts in the water of creeks. He opposed the building of a mast-house at Deptford, and the suggestion of keeping them in the proposed new dock at Chatham.

may expect as much favour as he can do him, though I fear that will not be much.   So back and after setting there a good while – we home; and going, my wife told me how my uncle, when he had her alone, did tell her that he did love her as well as ever he did, though he did not find it convenient to show it publicly for reasons on both sides; seeming to mean, as well to prevent my jealousy as his wife's.   But I am apt to think that he doth mean us well, and to give us something if he should die without children.

So home to prayers and to bed.

My wife called up the people to washing by 4 a-clock in the morning.   And our little girl Su is a most admirable slut* and pleases us mightily, doing more service than both the other and deserves wages better.*a*

22.   Up and shaved myself.   And then my wife and I by coach out and I set her down by her father's, being vexed in my mind and angry with her for the ill-favoured place, among or near the bawdy-houses, that she is forced to come to him.   So left her there, and I to Sir Ph. Warwickes but did not speak with him.   Thence to take a turn in St. James park; and meeting Anth. Joyce, walked with him a turn*b* in the Pell Mell and so parted, he St. Jame-ward and I out to*c* White-hall-ward and so to a picture-sellers by the Half-Moon in the Strand over against the Exchange, and there looked over the maps of several cities and did buy two books of cities stitched together,[1] cost me 9*s.* 6*d.*; and when I came home, thought of my vowe and paid 5*s.* into my poor-box for it, hoping in God that I shall forfeit no more in that kind.

Thence, meeting Mr. Moore, to the Exchange and there find my wife at pretty Doll's; and thence by coach set her [at] my uncle Wights to go with my aunt to market once more against Lent, and I to the Coffee-house and thence to the Change[2] – my chief business being to enquire about the manner of other countries' keeping of their Masts wet or dry – and got good advice about it; and so home and alone eat a bad, cold dinner,

a blot below symbol   *b* repl. 'little'   *c* repl. 'at'

---

1. Not retained in the PL. The Exchange in this case was the New Exchange, Strand.

2. The Royal Exchange, in the city.

my people being at their washing all day; and so to the office and all the afternoon upon my letter to Mr. Coventry about keeping of Masts; and ended it very well at night and wrote it fair over.

This evening came Mr. Alsopp the King's Brewer, with whom I spent an hour talking and bewailing the posture of things at present. The King led away by half a dozen men, that none of his serious servants and friends can come at him. These are Lodderdale, Buckingham, Hamilton, Fitzharding, to whom he hath it seems given 12000*l.* per annum too, in the best part of the King's estate[1] and that that the old Duke of Buckingham[2] could never get of the King. Projers is another ⟨and Sir H. Bennett⟩. He loves not the Queen at all, but is rather sullen to her; and she by all reports incapable of children. He is so fond of the Duke of Monmouth that everybody admires* it; and he says the Duke hath said that he would be the death of any man that says the King was not married to her[3] – though Alsopp says it is well known that she was a common whore when the King lay with her. But it seems, he says, that the King is mighty kind to these his bastard children and at this day will go at midnight to my Lady Castlemaynes nurses and take the child and dance it in his arms.[a]

That he is not likely to have his tables up again in his house,[4] for the crew that are about him will not have him come to common view again, but keep him obscurely among themselfs.

He hath this night, it seems, ordered that the hall (which there is a ball to be in tonight before the King) be guarded, as the Queen-mother's is, by his Horse-Guards; whereas heretofore they were by the Lord Chamberlin or Steward and their people. But it is feared they will reduce all to the soldiery, and all other places taken away. And which is worst of all, that he will alter the present militia and bring all to a flying army.[5]

a repl. 'knee'

---

1. See above, p. 40, n. 3.
2. The first Duke (d. 1628).
3. Lucy Walter, Monmouth's mother: for the supposed marriage, see above, iii. 238 & n. 4.
4. See above, iv. 407 & n. 3.

5. Sc. abolish the part-time militia officered by the gentry (recently re-established in 1662), and rely on a small professional mobile army similar to that established by an act of 1663 in Scotland.

That my Lord Lodderdale, being middleton's enemy and one that scores[a] the Chancellor, even to open affronts before the King, hath got the whole power of Scottland into his hand; whereas the other day he was in a fair way to have had his whole estate and honour and life voted away from him.[1]

That the King hath done himself all imaginable[b] wrong in that business of my Lord Antrim in Ireland; who, though he was the head of rebels, yet he[2] by his letter owns to have acted by his fathers and mothers and his commissions.[3] But it seems the truth is, he hath obliged himself, upon the clearing of his estate, to

---

a possibly a mistake for 'scorns'   *b* repl. 'im'-

---

1. On 5 January Middleton had been forced to resign from the captain-generalship and the keepership of Edinburgh Castle – Rothes, Lauderdale's agent, succeeding him in both offices. Lauderdale, Secretary to the Scottish Privy Council, was now supreme, after a rivalry which had been fierce and open since the Restoration. In August 1663 Middleton had had Lauderdale included in a bill of incapacity, but the King had refused his assent to that part of the bill. Clarendon had supported Middleton because, for all his militarism, he had, unlike his rival, been strongly in favour of a restoration of episcopacy in Scotland.
2. The King.
3. Antrim (a leader of the Irish Catholic royalists) had given valuable aid to Montrose in Scotland during the civil war, but had also opposed Ormond (leader of the Irish Protestant royalists in Ireland), and in 1650 had made his peace with the parliamentarians. He was briefly imprisoned in 1660, was excluded from the Act of Oblivion, and under the terms of the Act of Settlement was made liable to the confiscation of his

estates (which were heavily encumbered with debts). But principally because of his services to Montrose, the King agreed to support him, and sent a letter (10 July 1663) to Ormond, the Lord-Lieutenant, a copy of which was also sent to the commissioners administering the land settlement. The letter had the effect of saving Antrim's estates, despite the terms of the act. It had been published illegally in the autumn of 1663 (with critical observations attributed to Ludlow) as *Murder will out ... or The king's letter justifying the Marquess of Antrim* (repr. *Somers Tracts*, ed. Scott, v. 624–8). Criticism of the King was widespread, and arose from distrust of the Catholics, from dislike of Antrim (which was general) and from suspicion of this use of the royal authority. Antrim had been implicated in the Catholic rebellion of 1641, but it was wrong to speak of him as 'the head of rebels'. HMC, *Ormonde*, n.s., iii. 62, 93, 96–7; Clarendon, *Life*, ii. 75+; T. Carte, *Ormond*, iv. 153+; George Hill, *Macdonnells of Antrim*, ch. vi and app. xi; R. Bagwell, *Ireland under Stuarts*, iii. 39+.

settle it upon a daughter of the Queen-mother's (by my Lord Germin, I suppose) in marriage, be it to whom the Queen pleases – which is a sad story.[1] It seems a daughter of the Duke of Lenox's was by force going to be married the other day at Summersett-house to Harry Germin, but she got away and run to the King, and he says he will protect her. She is it seems very near akin to the King.[2] Such mad doings there is every day among them.

The rape upon a woman at Turnstile the other day, her husband being bound in his shirt, they both being in bed together, it being night, by two Frenchmen, who did not only lie with her but abused her with a Linke, is hushed up for 300*l* – being the Queen-mother's servants.[3]

There was a French book in verse[4] the other day translated and presented to the Duke of Monmouth, in such a high style that the Duke of Yorke, he tells me, was mightily offended at it. The Duke of Monmouth's mother's brother[5] hath a place at Court; and being a Welchman, I think he told me, will talk very broad of the King's being married to his sister.

The King did the other day at the Council commit my[a] Lord Digby's Chaplin and Steward and another servant, who went upon the process begun there against their lord, to swear that they saw him at church and receive the Sacrament as a protestant (which the Judges said was sufficient to prove him such in the eye of the law); the King, I say, did commit them all to the Gatehouse, notwithstanding their pleading their dependence upon him and the faith they owed him as their lord whose bread they

a repl. 'the'

1. There is no truth in this story: it was inspired by the fact that Henrietta-Maria and Jermyn (and court Catholics generally) supported Antrim.

2. Esmé Stuart, 1st Duke of Lennox (d. 1583) was a cousin of James I. The incident has not been traced. The young woman may have been Miss Lawson, a court beauty and a niece of the 4th Duke.

3. They were in fact condemned at the April sessions. The link was said to be lit. Newsletter, 26 April: Tanner 47, f. 131*v*.

4. Not traced.

5. Not identified. See *Comp.*: 'Walter, Lucy'.

eat.[1] And that the King should say that he would soon see whether he was King, or Digby.

That the Queene-mother hath outrun herself in her expenses and is now come to pay very ill and run in debt, the money being spent that she received for leases.[2]

He believes there is not any money laid up in bank, as I told him some did hope. But he says, from the best informers he can assure me there is no such thing, nor anybody that should look after such a thing – and that there is not now above 80000*l* of the Dunkircke money[3] left in stock.

That Oliver, in the year when he spent 1400000*l* in the Navy, did spend in the whole expense of the kingdom 2600000*l*.[4]

That all the Court are mad for a Dutch war; but both he and I did concur that it was a thing rather to be dreaded then hoped for – unless, by the French King's falling upon Flanders, they and the Dutch should be divided.[5]

That our Embassador[6] had, it is true, an Audience; but in the most dishonourable way that could be, for the Princes of the Blood (though invited by our Imbassador, which was the greatest

1. George Digby (2nd Earl of Bristol) had been in disgrace since July 1663 (see above, iv. 271 & n. 1); a proclamation for his arrest had been issued on 25 August, but he had fled into hiding. In October the King had ordered his prosecution as a catholic recusant. On Sunday, 17 January 1664, he had suddenly presented himself at Wimbledon parish church and there, in the presence of a notary and witnesses, renounced Catholicism. Later he took the minister and others home to dinner. Now (on 17 February) the minister, Thomas Luckin, and three of Bristol's servants (Abraham Doucett, William Martin and Robert Taylor) were committed, together with the two churchwardens and a constable, for failing to arrest him or give notice of his presence. All were released (except the minister) on the 24th. PRO, PC 2/57, ff. 12r, 15r; de Cominges to Louis XIV, 23 January/4 February (*Pepysiana*, pp. 298-9); HMC, *Ormonde*, n.s., iii. 81, 141; ib., *Heathcote*, pp. 144-7.

2. In common with all landowners restored to their estates in 1660, the Queen Mother had reaped a good harvest by selling new leases.

3. See above, iii. 229.

4. The year referred to was probably 1652, when, according to figures given to Pepys by Carteret, the navy charge (1 January–31 December) was £1,410,312: Rawl. A 195a, f. 241r. Cf. M. P. Ashley, *Fin. and comm. policy under Protect.*, pp. 47-8.

5. The French claims on the Spanish Netherlands were in fact enforced after the death of Philip IV in the War of Devolution (1667-8). At the moment France and Holland were bound together by a treaty of 1662.

6. To France: Lord Holles.

absurdity that ever embassador committed these 400 years) were not there, and so were not said to give place to our King's imbassador.[1]   And that our King did openly say the other day in the privy chamber, that he would not be hector'd out of his right and preeminency's by the King of France, as great as he was.

That the pope is glad to yield to a peace with the French (as the newsbook says) upon the basest terms that ever was.[2]

That the talk which these people about our King that I named before ⟨have, is to tell him how neither privileges of Parliament nor City is anything; but his will is all and ought to be so; and their discourse, it seems⟩[a] when they are alone, is so base and sordid that it makes the eares of the very gentlemen of the back-stairs, I think he called them, to tingle to hear it spoke in the King's hearing – and that must be very bad endeed.   That my Lord Digby did send to Lisbon a[b] couple of priests to search out what they could against the Chancellor concerning the match, as to the point of his knowing beforehand that she[3] was not capable of bearing children and that something was given her to make her so;[4] but as private as they were, when they came thither they were clapped up prisoners.   That my Lord Digby endeavours what he can to bring the business into the House of Commons, hoping there to master the Chancellor, there being many enemies of his there – but I hope the contrary.   That

a addition crowded in between paragraphs   *b* repl. 'to'

1. A canard; Holles was not received in audience by Louis XIV until 10 March: see his despatch, 12/22 March, in PRO, SP 78/118, f. 110r; Venetian despatch in *CSPVen. 1664-6*, p. 1; HMC, *Heathcote*, p. 147. For this dispute over precedency, see above, iv. 420 & n. 1.

2. See above, p. 40 & n. 1. The terms were not yet published in detail, but *The Intelligencer* (22 February, p. 122) reported the conclusion of the peace, and Louis XIV's announcement that the Pope had granted him more than he had

demanded. Part of the treaty was published in *The Intelligencer* of 14 March. For the terms, see C. Gérin, *Louis XIV et le Saint-Siège*, vol. i, ch. ix.

3. The Queen.

4. Bristol had in July 1663 impeached Clarendon before the House of Lords, charging him, *inter alia*, with having planned a barren marriage for the King so that the line of succession should run, as it ultimately did, through his own daughter. The story about Bristol's priests has not been traced elsewhere.

whereas the late King did morgage Clarendon to somebody for 20000*l*, and this*ᵃ* King hath given it to the Duke of Albemarle and he sold it to my Lord Chancellor, whose title of Earldome is fetched from thence, the King hath this day sent his order to the Privy Seal for the payment of this 20000*l* to my Lord Chancellor, to clear the morgage.¹

Ireland in a very distracted condition about the hard usage which the protestants meet with, and the too good which the catholiques. And from all together, God knows my heart, I expect nothing but ruin can fallow, unless things are better ordered in a little time.

He being gone, my wife came and told me how kind my uncle Wight*ᵇ* hath been to her today also; and that though she sees*ᶜ* that all his kindness to us comes from respect to her, she discovers nothing but great civility from him; yet by*ᵈ* what she says, he otherwise will tell me. But today he told her plainly that had she a child it should be his heire; and that should I or she want, he would be a good friend to us, and did give my wife instructions to consent to all his wife says at any time, she being a pettish woman; which argues a design he hath I think of keeping us in with his wife, in order to our good, sure – and he declaring her jealousy of him, that so he dares not come to see my wife as otherwise he would do and will endeavour to do. It looks strange, putting all together; but yet I am in hopes he means well. My aunt also is mighty opened to my wife, and tells her mighty plain how her husband did entend to double her portion to her at his death as a joynture. That he will give presently 100*l* to her niece Mary and a good legacy at his death. And it seems did as much to the other sister – which vexes to think that he should bestow so much upon his wife's friend daily as he doth.

---

a repl. 'hath s'- *b* MS. 'Wright' *c* or 'says'
d MS. 'but'

---

1. The warrant issued for this purpose is dated 19 December 1663; the mortgage of Clarendon Park (Wilts.) was held by Christopher Lord Hatton, Viscount Fanshaw and others. Charles I had borrowed £27,400 on the security of this and other lands: *CTB*, i. 47, 564. Clarendon never obtained the ownership of the estate, which reverted to Albemarle on Clarendon's disgrace in 1667. Cf. *CSPD 1660–1*, pp. 127, 285, 286; below, p. 203 & n. 1.

But it cannot be helped for the time past, and I will endeavour to remedy it for the time to come.[1]

After all this discourse with my wife at my office alone, she home to see how the wash goes on and I to make an end of my work; and so home to supper and to bed.

23ᵈ. Up, it being *Shrove Tuseday*, and at the office sat all the morning. At noon to the Change and there met with Sir W Rider; and of a sudden, knowing what I had at home, brought him and Mr. Cutler and Mr. Cooke, clerk to Mr. Secretary Morrice, a sober and learned man and one I knew heretofore when he was my Lord   secretary at Dunkirke.[2] I made much of them and had a pretty dinner for a sudden; we talked very pleasantly, and they many good discourses of their travels abroad. After dinner, they gone and I to my office, where doing many businesses very late; but to my good content, to see how I grow in estimation, every day more and more, and have things given more oftener then I used to have formerly; as, to have a case of very pretty knifes with agate hafts by Mrs. Russell.[3] So home and to bed.

This day, by the blessing of God, I have lived 31 years in the world; and by the grace of God I find myself not only in good health in everything, and perticularly [as] to the stone, but only pain upon taking cold; and also in a fair way of coming to a better esteem and estate in the world then ever I expected; but I pray God give me a heart to fear a fall and to prepare for it.

24. *Ashwendesday*. Up and by water, it being a very fine morning, to White-hall and there to speak with Sir Ph.ᵃ Warr-

a repl. 'W'

---

1. William Wight, a rich man, did not die until 1672. His will has not been traced. The nieces here referred to were Mary and Katherine Norbury, daughters of his wife's sister. His 'wife's friend' was possibly the Dr Venner on whom she was said to dote: below, p. 340.

2. John Cooke had been secretary to Col. Sir William Lockhart, Governor of Dunkirk, 1658–60. The latter was a 'Lord' in that he had served as ambassador to France and as a Scottish privy councillor during the Interregnum.

3. A ship's chandler.

wicke, but he was gone out to Chappell. So I spent much of the morning walking in the park and going to the Queen's chapel, where I stayed and saw their masse till a man came and bid me go out or kneel down; so I did go*a* out. And thence to Somersett-house and there into the chapel, where Monsieur Despagne used to preach.[1] But now it is made very fine and was ten times more crowded then the Queen's chapel at St. James's – which I wonder at. Thence down to the garden of Somersett-house and up and down the new building, which in every respect will be mighty magnificent and costly.[2] I stayed a great while talking with a man in the garden that was sawing of a piece of marble – and did give him 6*d* to drink. He told me much of the nature and labour of that work; how he could not saw above 4 inch. of the stone in a day; and of a greater, not above one or two. And after it is sawed, then it is rubbed with coarse and then with finer and finer sand till they come to putty, and so polish it as smooth as glass. Their saws have no teeth, but it is the sand only which the saw rubs up and down that doth the thing.

Thence by water to the Coffee-house and there sat long with Alderman Barker, talking of Hemp and that trade. And thence to the Change a little; and so home and dined with my wife, and then to the office till the evening, and then walked a while merrily with my wife in the garden; and so she gone, I to work again*b* till late; and so home to supper and to bed.

a repl. 'but kneel d'-   *b* MS. 'a again'

---

1. This was the Queen Mother's chapel, served by French Capuchins. During the Protectorate, Jean d'Espagne had been minister of a French Protestant congregation there, which was much favoured by Anglicans; for their expulsion in 1661, see *CSPD 1660-1*, p. 277. Pepys kept in his library a copy of d'Espagne's *Shibbóleth, ou Reformation de quelques passages . . . de la Bible* (London, 1653): PL 413(1).

2. The extent of the work now carried out is obscure, but it seems to have included the New or Great Gallery (demolished c. 1776), whose design has been attributed both to Inigo Jones and to John Webb: C. Campbell, *Vitruvius Britannicus* (1717), i. 4; R. Needham and A. Webster, *Somerset House*, pp. 142+; Whinney and Millar, p. 35, n. 1, p. 137, n. 2; *Country Life*, 1967, p. 1249. Both Campbell and Sir John Summerson (*Archit. in Brit. 1530-1830*, pl. 68*a*) have given the date 1661-2 to this building. By 18 October 1664 (see below) the Queen Mother's new rooms were finished.

25. Up and to the office, where we sat, and thence with[a] Mr. Coventry by coach to the Glass-house and there dined, and both before and after did my Lord Peterborough's accounts.[1] Thence home to the office and there did business till called by Creed; and with him by coach (setting my wife at my brother's) to my Lord's and saw the young ladies and talked a little with them; and thence to White-hall a while, talking but doing no business; but resolved of going to meet my Lord tomorrow, having got a horse of Mr. Coventry today. So home, taking up my wife. And after doing something at my office, home, God forgive me, disturbed in mind out of my jealousy of my wife tomorrow when I am out of town, which is a hell to my mind and yet without all reason. God forgive me for it and mend me. So home, and getting my things ready for my journey, to bed.

26. Up; and after dressing myself handsomely for riding, I out and by water to Westminster to Mr. Creeds chamber; and after drinking some Chocolatte and playing on the vyall, Mr. Mallard being there, upon Creeds new vyall, which proves methinks much worse then mine,[2] and looking upon his new contrivance of a desk and shelves for books, we set out from an Inne hard by, whither Mr. Coventrys horse was carried – and round about the bush through bad ways to Highgate; good discourse in the way had between us and it being all day a most admirable pleasant day. We, upon consultation, had stopped at the Cocke, a mile a-this-side Barnett,[3] being unwilling to put ourselfs to the charge or doubtful acceptance of any provision against my Lord's coming by, and there got something and dined, setting a boy to look towards Barnett-hill against their coming. And after two or three false alarms they came, and we met the coach very gracefully, and I had a kind receipt from both Lord and Lady as I could wish and some kind discourse; and then rode by the coach a good way and so fell to discoursing with several of the people there, being a dozen attending the coach and another coach for the maids and parson. Among others, talking with

1. See above, p. 48, n. 1.
2. For the new viol, see above, iv.
282. Mallard was probably a professional musician. (E).
3. At Whetstone, Mdx.

W. Howe, he told me how my Lord in his hearing the other day did largely tell my Lord Peterburgh and Povy (who went with them down to Hinchingbrooke) how and when he discarded Creed and took me to him;[1] and that since, the Duke of Yorke hath several times thanked him for me – which did not a little please me. And anon, I desiring Mr. Howe*a* to tell me upon [what] occasion this discourse happened, he desired me to say nothing of it now, for he would not have my Lord to take notice of our being together, but he would tell me another time – which put me into some trouble to think what he meant by it; but when*b* we came to my Lord's house, I went in; and whether it was my Lord's neglect or general indifference I know not, but he made me no kind of compliment there and methinks the young ladies look somewhat highly upon me. So I went away without bidding adieu to anybody, being desirous not to be thought too servile; but I do hope and believe that my Lord doth yet value me as high as ever, though he dares not admit me to the freedom he once did – and that my Lady is still the same woman. So rode home and there found my uncle Wight. Tis an odd thing, as my wife tells me, his caressing* her and coming on purpose to give her visitts; but I do not trouble myself for him at all, but hope the best and very good effects of it. He being gone, I eat something and my wife – I told all this day's passages, and she to give me very good and rationall advice how to behave myself to my Lord and his family, by slighting everybody but my Lord and Lady and not to seem to have the least society or fellowship with them; which I am resolved to do, knowing that it is my high carriage that must do me good there, and to appear in good clothes and garbe.

To the office a little; and being weary, early home and to bed.

27. Up, but weary, and to the office, where we sat all the morning. Before I*c* went to the office there came Bagwell's wife to me to speak for her husband. I liked the woman very well and stroked her under the chin, but could not find in my

a repl. 'Creed'   *b* repl. 'when'   *c* repl. 'that'

---

1. For the Restoration voyage: above, i. 83, 84. Howe and Pepys were soon plotting to displace Creed again: below, p. 119.

heart to offer anything uncivil to her, she being I believe a very modest woman. At noon with Mr. Coventry to the affrican-house, and to my Lord Peterborough's business again; and then to dinner, where before dinner we had the best oysters I have seen this year, and I think as good in all respects as ever I eat in my life. I eat a great many. Great good company at dinner. Among others, Sir Martin Noell, who told us the dispute between him, as Farmer of the Addicionall Duty, and the East India Company, whether Callico's be Linnen or no;[1] which he says it is, having been ever esteemed so; they say that[a] it is made of Cotton-woole and grows upon trees, not like Flax or hemp. But it was carried against the Company, though they stand out against the verdict.

Thence home and to the office, where late; and so home to supper and to bed. I had a very pleasing and condescending answer from my poor father today, in answer to my angry discontentful letter to him the other day, which pleases me mightily.

28. *Lords day.* Up and walked to Pauls; and by chance it was an extraordinary day for the Readers of the Inns of Court and all the students to come to church, it being an old ceremony not used these 25 years – upon the first Sunday in Lent.[2] Abundance there was of students, more then there was room to seat but upon forms, and the Church mighty full. One Hawkins

a MS. 'they'

---

1. Linen paid 5% less duty than calico. The dispute about the rating of calico dated from at least 1649, and this case of Noell's was still unsettled in 1667, Parliament encouraging the Company's resistance to the judgment of the Court of Exchequer: *Cal. court mins E. India Co. 1644-9* (ed. E. B. Sainsbury), p. 343; ib., *1660-3*, pp. 290, 332; ib., *1664-7*, pp. 2, 45.

2. By direction of the judges, readers on the first Sunday of their Lenten readings took their students to the Paul's Cross sermons. The first orders date from at least 1627. They were repeated on 29 April 1642. No readers were appointed during the revolutionary period, and Paul's Cross was pulled down: *Cal. Inner Temple rec.* (ed. F. A. Inderwick), vol. ii, p. xc; John B. Williamson, *Hist. Temple, London*, pp. 339, 469. For a short time after the Restoration the observance was revived, but c. 1677 public readings were abolished: Sir W. Holdsworth, *Hist. Engl. law*, vi. 489.

preached, an Oxford man – a good sermon upon these words:
"But the wisdom from above is first pure, then peaceable."[1]

Both before and after sermon I was most impatiently troubled
at the Quire, the worst that ever I heard. But what was extraordinary, the Bishop of London, who sat there in a pew made
a-purpose for him by the pulpitt, doth give the last blessing to the
congregation[a] – which was, he being a comely old man, a very
decent thing methought.[2]

The lieutenant of the Tower, Sir J Robinson, would needs
have me by coach home with him; and sending word home to
my house, I did go and dine with him, his ordinary table being
very good – and his Lady a very high-carriaged but comely[b] big
woman; I was mightily pleased with her. His officers of his
Regiment dined with him. No discourse at table to any purpose.
Only, after dinner my Lady would needs see a boy which was
represented to her to be an innocent country boy, brought up to
town a day or two ago and left here to the wide world, and he
losing his way, fell into the Tower; and which my Lady believes
and takes pity of him and will keep him; but though a little boy
and but young, yet he tells his tale so readily and answers all
Que[s]tions so wittily, that for certain he is an arch rogue and
bred in this town. But my Lady will not believe it, but ordered
victuals to be given him – and I think will keep him as a foot-boy
for their eldest son.

After dinner to Chappell in the Tower with the Lieutenant,
with the Keyes carried before us and the Warders and gentleman
Porter going before us. And I sat with the Lieutenant in his pew
in great state, but slept all the sermon. None, it seems, of the
prisoners in the Tower that are there now, though they may,
will come to prayers there.[3]

Church being done, I back to Sir Johns house, and there left
him and home; and by and by to Sir Wm. Pen and stayed a
while talking with him about Sir J. Mennes his folly in his office,

a repl. 'people'   *b* repl. 'comel'-

1. A loose recollection of Jas, iii.
17. The preacher was Dr William
Hawkyns, Fellow of Magdalen College and Canon of Winchester.
2. Humphrey Henchman (Bishop
of London since 1663) was now 71;
he died in 1675 in his 83rd year.
3. The implication is that they
were nonconformists.

of which I am sick and weary to speak of it; and how the King
is abused in it – though Pen, I know, offers the discourse only
like a rogue to get it out of me; but I am very free to tell my
mind to him in the case, being not unwilling he should tell him
again if he will, or anybody else.

Thence home and walked in the garden by brave Mooneshine
with my wife above two hours, till past 8 a'-clock; then to supper,
and after prayers to bed.

29.   Up and by coach with Sir W Pen to Charing-cross, and
there I light and to Sir Ph. Warwicke to visit him and discourse
with him about*a* navy business, which I did at large – and he
most largely with me, not only about*b* the navy but about the
general Revenue of England, above two hours I think, many
staying all the while without; but he seemed to take pains to let
me either understand the affairs of the Revenue or else to be a
wittnesse of his pains and care in stating of it.[1]

He showed me endeed many excellent collections of the state
of the Revenue in former Kings and the late times and the present.
He showed me how the very Assessements between 1643 and
1659, which was taxes (besides Excize, Customes, Sequestracions,
Decimacions,[2] King and Queenes and Church lands, or anything
else but just the assessements) come to above 15 Millions.[3] He
showed me a discourse of his concerning the Revenues of this and
foreign States.[4]   How that of Spayne was great, but divided with
his kingdoms and so came to little.   How that of France did and
doth much exceed ours before for quantity; and that it is at the
will of the Prince to tax what he will upon his people; which is
not here.   That the Hollanders have the best manner of tax,

a repl. 'above'   *b* repl. 'but'

---

1. Warwick was secretary to the
Lord Treasurer: his summaries of the
revenue for this period are in BM,
Harl. 1223, ff. 200–32.

2. The latter two were levies
made on Royalists.

3. The 'assessment' introduced by
the Long Parliament in 1643 was
much more efficient than any previous direct tax.   Its total yield over the
period 1644–60 has been calculated at
£16¼ m.: M. P. Ashley, *Fin. and
comm. policy under Protect.*, pp. 79–80.

4. Untraced;   Warwick's only
published work on politics (*Discourse
of Government*, 1694) has very little on
finance.

which is only upon the expense of provisions, by an excize; and doth conclude that no other tax is proper for England but a pound=rate or excize upon the expense of provisions.[1]

He showed me every perticular sort of payment away of money since the King's coming in to this day; and told me, from one to one, how little he hath received of profit from most of them, and I believe him truly. That the 1200000*l* which the parliament with so much ado did first vote to give the King, and since hath been re-examined by several committees of the present parliament, is yet above 300000*l* short of making up really to the King the 1200000*l* – as by perticulars he showed me.[2] And in my Lord Treasurer's excellent letter to the King upon this subject,[3] he tells the King how it was the spending more then the revenue that did give the first occasion of his father's ruine, and did since to the Rebells; who he says, just like Henry the 8, had great and sudden encrease of wealth, but yet by over-spending both died poor. And further tells the King*a* how much of this 1200000*l* depends upon the life of the Prince* and so must*b* be renewed by parliament

a MS. 'thing'   *b* MS. 'much'

---

1. Introduced into England in 1643 and covering over half a dozen commodities, the excise after the Restoration was reduced to a charge on drinks (including coffee and tea but excluding wine). In Holland it was a small charge levied on a wide variety of goods. In 1673 Sir William Temple reckoned that the consumption of a single dish in a Dutch tavern might involve 30 separate excises: *Observations upon the . . . Netherlands* (1932 ed.), p. 153. Many English commentators argued that a general excise was the most productive and least painful of taxes.

2. In September 1660 the Commons had decided on £1,200,000 as the sum to be raised as settled peace-time revenue, basing their estimate on the figures of income and expenditure for 1637–41: *CJ*, viii. 150. In June 1661

Coventry had reported a deficit of £275,000 to a committee of the House (ib., pp. 273–4), and as a result the Hearth Tax was added to the sources of settled revenue in May 1662. Even so, the deficit continued: in June 1663 it was almost £200,000 (ib., p. 498); in March 1665, £363,700 (BM, Harl. 1223, f. 223*r*). Revenue continually fell short of the sums on which parliament's calculations had been based. It was this shortage, and not the King's extravagance, which was the main cause of the government's financial weakness.

3. Warwick had been responsible for the representations on this subject made by Southampton in July and November 1663; BM, Harl. 1223, ff. 200–46. This letter of Southampton has not been traced.

again to his Successor; which is seldom done without parting with some of the prerogatives of the Crown; or, if denied and he persists to take it of the people, it gives occasion to a Civill war, which may, as it did in the late business of Tonnage and Poundage, prove fatal to the Crowne.[1]

He showed me how many ways the Lord Treasurer did take before he moved the King to Farme the Customes in the manner he doth, and the reasons that moved him to do it.[2]

He showed me a very excellent argument to prove that our Importing lesse then we export doth not impoverish the kingdom, according to the received opinion – which though it be a paradox and that I do not remember the argument,[3] yet methought there was a great deal in what he said; and upon the whole, I find him a most exact and methodicall man and of great*a* industry. And very glad that he thought fit to show me all this, though I cannot easily guess the reason why he should do it to me – unless from the plainness that he sees I use to him in telling him how much the King may suffer for our want of understanding the case of our Treasury.

Thence to White-hall (where my Lord Sandwich was, and gave me a good countenance I thought) and before the Duke did our usual business; and so I about several businesses in the House[4] and then out to the Mewes[5] with Sir W Pen. But in my way, first did meet with W Howe, who did of himself advise me to appear more free with my Lord and to come to him; for my own strangeness, he tells me, he thinks doth make my Lord the worse. At the Mewes, Sir W Pen and Mr. Baxter[6]

a repl. 'distinct'

---

1. Parliament refused to give Charles I the customary grant for life of tonnage and poundage (customs dues), both in 1625 at the beginning of the reign and in 1641 on the eve of the Civil War.

2. In 1660–2 the customs had been collected directly by royal commissioners and others in much the same way as in 1643–60. In September 1662 they were put to farm – a method lasting till 1671 – costs of collection having been abnormally high since the Restoration. One of Southampton's plans for combining farming and direct collection is summarised in *CSPD 1661–2*, p. 452.

3. The argument here presumably concerned the import and export of bullion, not trade in general. Cf. below, vi. 23.

4. Whitehall Palace.

5. The royal stables, Charing Cross.

6. Nicholas Baxter, 'escuyer of the great horses' to the Duke of York.

did show me several good horses; but "Pen", which Sir W. Penn did give the Duke of Yorke, was given away by the Duke the other day to a Frenchman; which Baxter is cruelly vexed at, saying indeed that he was the best horse that he expects a great while to have to do with.

Thence I to the Change and thence to a Coffe-house with Sir W Warren – and did talk much about his and Woods business;[1] and thence homewards and in my way did stay to look upon a house on Fire in an Inne-yard in Lombardstreete. But Lord, how the mercers and Merchants who had warehouses there did carry away their cloths and silks. But at last it was quenched, and I home to dinner; and after dinner carried my wife and set her and her two maids down in Fleetestreete to buy things and I to White-hall to little purpose. And so to Westminster-hall and there talked with Mrs. Lane and Howlett; but the match with Hawly,[2] I perceive, will not take – and so I am resolved wholly to avoid occasion of farther trouble with her.

Thence by water to Salsbury Court and find my wife by agreement at Mrs. Turners; and after a little stay and chat set her and young Armiger down in Cheapeside, and so my wife and I home. Got home before our maids, who by and by came with a great cry and fright that they had like to have been killed by a coach; but Lord, to see how Jane did tell the story like a fool and a dissembling fanatic, like her grandmother,[3] but so like a changeling,* would make a man laugh to death almost and yet be vexed to hear her.

By and by to the office to make up my monthly accounts; which I made up tonight and find, to my great content, myself worth 890 and odd pounds, the greatest sum I ever yet knew. And so with a heart at good ease, to bed.*a*

a   followed by one blank page

---

1. See above, p. 6 & n. 4.
2. Hawley had been wooing Betty Lane for four years.

3. Possibly old Mrs Harper: cf. above, iv. 276. The maid was Jane Gentleman.

MARCH.

1. Up and to the office, where we sat all the morning; and at noon to the Change and after much business and meeting my uncle Wight, who told me how Mr. Maes had like to have been trapanned yesterday but was forced to run for it[1] – so with Creed and Mr. Hunt home to dinner; and after a good and pleasant dinner, Mr. Hunt parted and I took Mr. Creed and my wife and down to Deptford, it being most pleasant weather. And there till night, discoursing with the officers there about several things; and so walked home by moonshine, it being mighty pleasant; and so home and I to my office, where late about getting myself a thorough understanding in the business of masts; and so home to bed – my left eye being mightily troubled with Rhume.

2. Up, my eye mightily out of order with the Rhume that is fallen down into it. However, I by coach endeavoured to have waited on my Lord Sandwich, but meeting him in Chancery-lane going toward the City, I stopped and so fairly* walked home again – calling at Pauls churchyard and there looked upon a pretty Burlesque poem called *Scarronides, or Virgile Travesty*[2] – extraordinary good. At home to the office till dinner; and after dinner, my wife to cut my hair short, which is grown pretty long again. And then to the office and there till 9 at night doing business. This afternoon we had a good present of tongues and Bacon from Mr. Shales of Portsmouth.[3] So at night home to supper; and being troubled with my eye, to bed. This morning Mr. Burgby, one of the writing clerks belonging to the Council,

1. Maes, involved in the dispute over Portuguese customs dues, had already been imprisoned once. See above, p. 43 & n. 2.
2. Published anonymously by Charles Cotton: The licence to publish was issued only on this day (*Trans. Stat. Reg.*, ii. 339). Witty and ob-

scene, with a strong appeal to all who had been put through Virgil at school: G. Kitchin, *Survey of burlesque and parody in English*, p. 91. Not in the PL.

3. John Shales, navy victualling agent.

was with me about business, a knowing man. He complains
how most of the Lords of the Council do look after themselfs
and their own ends and none the public, unless Sir Edw. Nicholas. [1]
Sir G Carteret is diligent, but all for his own ends and profit.
My Lord Privy Seale, a destroyer of everybody's business and
doth no good at all to the public. [2] The Archbishop of Canterbury[3] speaks very little nor doth much, being now come to the
highest pitch that he can expect. He tells me he believes that
things will go very high against the Chancellor by Digby, and
that bad things will be proved. [4] Talks much of his neglecting
the King and making the King to trot every day to him, [5] when
he is well enough to go to visit his Cosen, Chief-Justice Hide,
but not to the Council or King. He commends my Lord of
Ormond mightily in Ireland; but cries out cruelly of Sir G. Lane
for his corruption and that he hath done my Lord great dishonour
by selling of places here, which are now all taken away and the
poor wretches ready to starve. [6] That nobody almost understands or judges of business better then the King, if he would
not be guilty of his father's fault, to be doubtful of himself and
easily be removed from his own opinion. That my Lord
Lauderdale is never from the King's eare nor counsel and that
he is a most cunning fellow. Upon the whole, that he finds
things go very bad everywhere; and even in the Council, nobody
minds the public.

3. Up pretty early and so to the office, where we sat all the
morning making a very great contract with Sir W. Warren for
provision for the year coming. [7] And so home to dinner, and

1. Nicholas had resigned as Secretary of State in October 1662, but
continued to serve as Privy Councillor.
Both Clarendon (*Hist.*, ii. 535–6) and
Burnet (i. 180) attest to his probity.

2. Clarendon (*Life*, i. 463–4) and
Burnet (i. 176) also held low views of
Robartes's ability. He was proud
and pedantic.

3. Gilbert Sheldon.

4. Digby (Bristol) had unsuccess-
fully impeached Clarendon in July
1663 and was now planning a

renewed attack. See below, p. 85.

5. 'trotting' cf. below, p. 89.

6. Lane was secretary to Ormond
(the Lord Lieutenant), and a notorious
pluralist. At Michaelmas 1663 econ-
omies in the royal household (of
which Ormond was Lord Steward)
resulted in the dismissal of about 300
officers. Many had bought their
places, but there was no compensation.
See HMC, *Ormonde*, n.s., iii. 35, 43,
78, 91, 177–8.

7. See below, pp. 215–16 & n.

there was W. Howe come to dine with me.   And before dinner
he and I walked in the garden, and we did discourse together; he
assuring me of what he told me the other day of my Lord's speaking so highly in my commendation to my Lord Peterborough
and Povy, which speaks my Lord's having yet a good opinion
of me; and also how well my Lord and Lady both are pleased
with their children's being at my father's and when the bigger
ladies were there a little while ago,[1] at which I am very glad.
After dinner he went away, I having discoursed with him about
his own proceedings in his studies; and I observe him to be very
considerate and to mind*a* his book, in order to preferring himself
by my Lord's favour to something and, I hope, to the outing of
Creed in his Secretary-ship[2] – for he tells me that he is confident
my Lord doth not love him nor will trust him in any secret
matter, he is so cunning and crafty in all he doth.

So my wife and I out of doors, thinking to have gone to have
seen a play; but when we came to take coach, they tell us there
are none, this week being the first of Lent; but Lord, to see how
impatient I find myself within to see a play, I being at Liberty
once a month to see one,[3] and I think it is the best method I could
have taken.

But to my office; did very much business with several people
till night*b* and so home, being unwilling to stay late because of
my eye, which is not yet well of the rheum that is fallen down
into it.   But to supper and to bed.

4.   Up, my eye being pretty well; and then by coach to my
Lord Sandwich, with whom I spoke, walking a good while with
him in his garden, which and the house is very fine – talking of
my Lord Peterburgh's accounts,[4] wherein he is concerned both
for the foolery as also inconvenience which may happen upon my
Lord Peterborough's ill-stating of his matters, so as to have his

a repl. 'my'   b repl. 'late at'

---

1. Sandwich's two elder daughters
(Lady Jemima and Lady Paulina)
had spent the winter at the Pepys
house at Brampton.

2. Howe hoped to displace Creed

as secretary to Sandwich when he
sailed as Admiral.

3. Cf. his oath, above, p. 33. (A).

4. See above, p. 48, n. 1.

gain discovered unnecessarily. We did talk long and friendly, that I hope the worst is past – and all will be well. There were several people by, trying a new-fashion gun brought my Lord this morning to shoot off often, one after another, without trouble or danger – very pretty.[1]

Thence to the Temple; and there, taking White's boat, down to Woolwich, taking Mr. Shish[2] at Deptford in my way, with whom I had some good discourse of the Navy business. At Woolwich discoursed with him and Mr. Pett about Ironworke and other businesses and then walked home; and at Greenwich did observe the foundacion laying of a very great house for the King, which will cost a great deal of money.[3] So home to dinner; and my Uncle Wight coming in, he along with my wife and I by coach; and setting him down by the way going to Mr. Maes, we two to my Lord Sandwich's to visit my Lady, with whom I left my wife discoursing and I to White-hall, and there being met by the Duke of Yorke, he called me to him and discoursed a pretty while with me about the new ship's despatch building at Woolwich;[4] and talking of the charge, did say that he finds alway the best the best cheap[5] – instancing in French guns, which in France you may buy for 4 pistoles, as good to look to as others of 16, but not the service.

I never had so much discourse with the Duke before, and till now did ever fear to meet him. He found me and Mr. Prin

1. A repeating gun: possibly the one patented by Abraham Hill on 3 March: PRO, Signet index 1660–1737, f. 118r. Cf. above, iii. 130 & n. 4.

2. Jonas Shish, Assistant-Shipwright, Deptford yard.

3. The old palace by the riverside, dating from the 15th and 16th centuries, had been pulled down c. 1662, and a new one begun. The design (attributed to John Webb) was in the form of three sides of a square, of which the e. side was now being constructed. Work on it ended in 1669 or 1670. The palace was converted by William III (following an idea of James II's) into a naval hospital, and the building to which Pepys refers is probably the e. half of the present King Charles's block of the Royal Naval College. See *Pub. Walpole Soc.*, 31/45–107; *Journ. R. Inst. Brit. Archit.* (ser. 3), 18/317+; E. Hasted, *Hist. Kent* (ed. Drake), i. 65. Views in G. H. Chettle, *The Queen's House, Greenwich* (LCC, *Survey of London*, monograph 14), pl. 6; *Drawings of Engl. in 17th cent.* (ed. P. H. Hulton), pl. 9.

4. The *Royal Catherine*; for her launch, see below, p. 306 & n. 3.

5. The ship cost £4357: Rawl. A 174, ff. 6–7.

together, talking of the Chest=mony,[1] which we are to blame
not to look after.

Thence to my Lord's and took up my wife, whom my Lady
hath received with her old good-nature and kindness; and so
homeward and she home, I lighting by the way; and upon the
Change met my uncle Wight and told him my discourse this
afternoon with Sir G Carteret in Maes business, but much to his
discomfort. And after a dish of Coffee, home and I at my office
a good while with Sir W Warren, talking with great pleasure of
many businesses, and then home to supper; my wife and I had
a good fowle to supper, and then I to the office again and so home,
my mind in great ease to think of our coming to so good a
respect with my Lord again and Lady, and that my Lady doth
so much cry up my father's usage of her children and the goodness of the ayre there, found in the young ladies' faces at their
return thence as she says – as also my being put into the commission of the Fishery,[2] for which I must give my Lord thanks;
and so home to bed – having a great cold in my head and throat
tonight from my late cutting my hair[a] so close to my head; but
I hope it will be soon gone again.

5. Up and to the office; where though I had a great cold, I
was[b] forced to speak much, upon a public meeting of the East
India Company at our office – where our own company was
full; and there was also my Lord George Barkely in behalfe of
the company of Merchants (I suppose he is on[c] the company);
who hearing my name, took notice of me and condoled my Cosen
Edwd. Pepys's death, not knowing whose son I was nor did
demand it of me.[3] We broke up without coming to any conclusion, for want of my Lord Marlbrough.

We broke up and to the Change, where with several people

a MS. 'heart'   b repl. 'did'   c ? 'one [of]'

1. Both William Prynne and Pepys
were members of the commission
enquiring into the Chatham Chest.
See below, p. 105 & n. 2.
2. See below, p. 79.
3. The meeting was held at 9 a.m.
to end the dispute about freightage:
above, iv. 368, n. 2; *Cal. court mins*

E. India Co. 1664-7 (ed. E. B. Sainsbury), p. 18. Lord Berkeley (of
Berkeley, the 9th baron) was a
member of the Committee of the
Company, and became Governor of
the Levant Company in 1673. For
Edward Pepys's death, see above, iv.
421 & n. 1.

and my Uncle Wight to drink a dish of Coffee. And so home to dinner and then to the office all the afternoon, my eye and my throat being very bad, and my cold increasing so as I could not speak almost at all at night. So at night home to supper, that is, a posset, and to bed.

6. *Lords day.* Up; and my cold continuing in great extremity, I could not go out to church but sat all day (a little time at dinner excepted) in my closet at the office till night, drawing up a second letter to Mr. Coventry about the measure of Masts,[1] to my great satisfaction; and so in the evening home, and my Uncle and Aunt Wight came to us and supped with us; where pretty merry, but that my cold put me out of Humour. At night, with my cold and my eye also sore still, to bed.

7. Up betimes; and the Duke being gone abroad today, as we heard by a messenger, I spent the morning at my office, writing fair my yesterday's work till almost 2 a-clock (only, Sir G. Carteret coming, I went down a little way by water towards Deptford; but having more mind to have my business done, I pretended business at the Change and so went into another boat); and then eating a bit, my wife and I by coach to the Dukes house, where we saw *The Unfortunate Lovers*;[2] but I know not whether I am grown more curious* then I was or no, but I was not much pleased with it; though I know not where to lay the fault – unless it was that the house was very empty, by reason of a new play at the other house.[3] Yet here was my Lady Castlemayne in a box, and it was pleasant to hear an ordinary lady hard by us, that it seems did not know her before, say, being told who she was, that she was well enough. Thence home, and I ended and sent away my letter to Mr. Coventry (having first

1. Dated 6 March; copies in NMM, LBK/8, pp. 100-4 (mostly in Hewer's hand, with conclusion in Pepys's, partially printed in *Further Corr.*, pp. 20-5); BM, Add. 11602, ff. 132+ (in Hewer's hand). A long and detailed comparison (with statistical table) of the measurements, prices and value of Scandinavian masts (supplied by Warren) and New England masts (supplied by Wood), concluding in favour of the former. For the dispute over Wood's masts (from which all this arose), see above, p. 6, n. 4.

2. A tragedy by Davenant, licensed in 1638, and published in 1643; now at the LIF. (A).

3. The TR, Drury Lane. (A).

read it and had the opinion of Sir W. Warren in the case); and
so home to supper and to bed – my cold being pretty well gone
but my eye remaining still soare and rhumey, which I wonder
at, my right eye ayling nothing.

8. Up, with some little discontent with my wife upon her
saying that she had got and used some puppy-dog water, being
put upon it by a desire of my aunt Wight to get some for her;
who hath a mind, unknown to her husband, to get some for her
ugly face. I to the office, where we sat all the morning; doing
not much business through the multitude of counsellors, one
hindering another – it was Mr. Coventry's own saying to me in
his coach going to the Change. But I wonder that he did give
me no thanks for my letter last night – but I believe he did only
forget it. Thence home, whither Luellin came and dined with
me; but we made no long stay at dinner, for *Heraclius*[1] being
acted, which my wife and I have a mighty mind to see, we do
resolve, though not exactly agreeing with the letter of my vowe,[2]
yet altogether with the sense, to see another this month – by
going hither instead of that at Court, there having been none
conveniently since I made my vow for us to see there, nor like
to be this Lent; and besides, we did walk home on purpose to
make this going as cheap as that would have been to have seen
one at Court; and my conscience knows that it is only the
saving of money and the time also that I entend by my oaths,
and this hath cost no more of either – so that my conscience
before God doth, after good consultation and resolution of paying
my forfeit did my conscience accuse me of breaking my vow,
I do not find myself in the least apprehensive that I have done any
vyolence to my oaths. The play hath[a] one very good passage
well managed in it; about two persons pretending and yet
denying themselfs to be son to the Tyrant Phocas and yet heire
of Mauricius to the Crowne. The guarments like Romans
very well. The little guirle[3] is come to act very prettily and

a MS. 'is hath'

---

1. A version of Pierre Corneille's
tragedy of that name by an unknown
translator, performed at the LIF.
(A).

2. Cf. above, p. 33. (A).
3. Possibly Ann Gibbs, afterwards
the wife of Thomas Shadwell: see
above, iv. 56, n. 2. (A).

spoke the epilogue most admirably. But at the beginning, at the drawing up of the Curtaine, there was the finest Scene of the Emperor and his people about him, standing in their fixed and different postures in their Roman habits, above all that ever I yet saw at any of the Theatres.[1] Walked home, calling to see my brother Tom, who is in bed and I doubt very ill – of a consumption. To my office a while; and so home to supper and to bed.

9. Up pretty betimes to my office, where all day long, but a little at home at dinner, at my office finishing all things about Mr. Wood's contract for Masts; wherein I am sure I shall save the King 400*l* before I have done. At night home to supper and to bed.

10. Up and to the office, where all the morning doing business. And at noon to the Change and there very busy; and so home to dinner with my wife to a good hog's harslet,[*a*] a piece of meat I love but have not eat of I think this seven year. And after dinner abroad by coach, set her at Mrs. Hunts and I to White-hall; and at the Privy Seale office enquired and found the Bill[2] come for the Corporacion of the Royall Fishery; whereof the Duke of Yorke is made present Governor and several other very great persons, to the number of 32, made his assistants for their lives: whereof, by my Lord Sandwichs favour, I am one and take it not only as a matter of honour but that that may come to be of profit to me.[3] And so with great content went and called my wife; and so home and to the office, where busy late; and so home to supper and to bed.

11. Up and by coach to my[*b*] Lord Sandwiches; who not

         a MS. 'harsnet'   *b* repl. 'see'

---

1. Tableau effects of this kind were frequently introduced in Restoration productions. The 'Roman habits' were probably tunics or cuirasses, buskins, cloaks, gauntlets, perukes and plumed helmets. Loose mantles were sometimes worn by Roman characters, but the toga was not used until much later in the history of the English theatre. (A).

2. The royal warrant authorising the issue of a charter.

3. The Royal Fishery Council of 1661 was now replaced by a corporation on the Dutch model by a charter (8 April). '32' should be 36.

being up, I stayed talking with Mr. Moore till my Lord was ready, and come down and went directly out, without calling for me or seeing anybody. I know not whether he knew I was there, but I am apt to think not; because if he would have given me that slighting, yet he would not have done it to others that were there. So I went back again, doing nothing but discoursing with Mr. Moore – who I find by discourse to be grown rich; and endeed not to use me at all with the respect he used to do, but as his equal. He made me known to their*a* Chaplin,[1] who is a worthy, able man. Thence home; and by and by to the Coffee-house and thence to the Change and so home to dinner; and after a little chat with my wife, to the office, where all the afternoon till very late at the office busy. And so home to supper and to bed – hoping in God that my diligence, as it is really very useful for the King, so it will end in profit to myself. In the meantime I have good content in mind to see myself improve every day in knowledge and being known.

12. Lay long, pleasantly entertaining myself with my wife; and then up and to the office – where busy till noon, vexed to see how Sir J. Mennes deserves rather to be pitied for his dotage and folly then imployed at a great salary[2] to ruin the King's business. At noon to the Change and thence*b* home to dinner; and then down to Deptford, where busy a while; and then walking home, it fell hard a-raining. So at Halfway-house put in; and there meeting Mr. Stacy with some company of pretty women – I took him aside to a room by ourselfs and there talked with him about the several sorts of Tarrs;[3] and so by and by parted and I walked home, and there late at the office; and so home to supper and to bed.

13. *Lords day.* I lay long in bed, talking with my wife; and

a repl. 'his'   *b* repl. 'there'

---

1. At his death in 1672, Sandwich had two chaplains, John Turner and Gervase Fulwood.

2. The Comptroller's official salary was £500 p.a. as against Pepys's £350.

3. Cf. Pepys's notes on the subject (23, 26 March) in NWB, p. 25. John Stacey was a tar merchant.

then up, in great doubt whether I should not go see Mr. Coventry or no, who hath not been well these two or three days; but it being foul weather, I stayed within; and so to my office and there all the morning reading some Common law, to which I will allot a little time now and then, for I much want it. At noon home to dinner; and then after some discourse with my wife, to the office again; and by and by Sir W Pen came to me after sermon and walked with me in the garden, and then one comes to tell me that Anth. and Will Joyce were come to see me; so I in to them and made mighty much of them, and very pleasant we were. And most of their business I find to be to advise about getting some woman to attend my Brother Tom, whom they say is very ill and seems much to want one – to which I agreed, and desired them to get their wifes to enquire out one. By and by they bid me good-night; but immediately as they were gone out of doors comes Mrs. Turner's boy with a note to me, to tell me that my brother Tom was so ill as they feared he could not long live and that it would be fit I should come and see him. So I sent for them back, and they came; and Will Joyce desiring to speak with me alone, I took him up and there he did plainly tell me, to my great astonishment, that my brother is deadly ill and that their chief business of coming was to tell me so; and which is worse, that his disease is the pox, which he hath heretofore got and hath not been cured, but is come to this; and that this is certain, though a secret told his father Fenner by the Doctor which he helped my brother to.

This troubled me mightily; but however, I thought fit to go see him for speech of people's sake, and so walked along with them, and in our way called on my Uncle Fenner (where I have not been this 12 months and more) and advised with him; and then to my brother, who lies in bed talking idle. He could only say that he knew me and then fell to other discourse, and his face like a dying man – which Mrs. Turner, who was here, and others conclude he is.

The company being gone, I took the mayde, which seems a very grave and serious woman, and in W. Joyces company did enquire how things are with her*a* master. She told me many things very discreetly and said she had all his papers and books and key of his cutting-house. And showed me a bag which I

a repl. 'his'

and Wm: Joyce told, coming to 5*l* 14*s* – which we left with
her again.

After giving her good counsel, and the boys, and seeing a
nurse there of Mrs. Holden's[1] choosing, I left them and so walked
home, greatly troubled to think of my brother's condition and
the trouble that would arise to me by his death or continuing sick.

So at home, my mind troubled, to bed.

14. Up, and walked to my brother's, where I find he hath
continued talking idle all night and now knows me not – which
troubles me mightily. So I walked down and discoursed a great
while alone with the mayde, who tells me many passages of her
master's practices and how she concludes that he hath run behind-
hand a great while and owes money and hath been dunned by
several people; among others, by one Cave, both husband and
wife, but whether it was for money or something worse she
knows not. But there is one Cranburne, I think she called him,
in Fleete-lane with whom he hath many times been mighty
private, but what their dealings have been she knows not, but
believes they[a] were naught*. And then his sitting up two Saturday nights, one after another, when all were a-bed, doing something to himself; which she now suspects what it was but did not
before. But tells me that he hath been a very bad husband* as to
spending his time, and hath often told him of it. So that upon
the whole, I do find he is, whether he lives or dies, a ruined man.
And what trouble will befall me by it, I know not.

Thence to White-hall; and in the Dukes chamber, while he
was dressing, two persons of quality that were there did tell his
Royal Highness how the other night in Holborne about midnight, being at cards, a link-boy came by and run into the house
and told the people the house was a-falling; upon this, the whole
family was frighted, concluding that the boy had said that the
house was a-fire; so they left their cards above, and one would
have got out of the balcone, but it was not open; the other
went up to fetch down his children that were in bed. So all got

a MS. 'there'. Possibly this passage is incomplete and should read: 'there
were not' . . .

---

1. A neighbour; wife of Joseph Holden, haberdasher.

clear out of the house; and no sooner so, but the house fell down indeed, from top to bottom. It seems my Lord Southamptons canaille[1] did come too near their foundation and so weakened the house, and down it came – which in every respect is a most extraordinary passage.[2]

By and by into his closet and did our business with him. But I did not speed as I expected, in a business about the manner of buying hemp for this year; which troubled me. But it proceeds only from my pride, that I must need expect everything to be ordered just as I apprehend. Though it was not, I think, from my error, but their not being willing to hear and consider all that I had to propose.

Being broke up, I fallowed my Lord Sandwich and thanked him for his putting me into the Fishery; which I perceive he expected, and cried "Oh!" says he, "in the Fishery you mean. I told you I would remember you in it" – but offered no other discourse; but demanding whether he had any commands for me – methought he cried "No," as if he had no more mind to discourse with me, which still troubles me and hath done all the day, though I think I am a fool for it, in not pursuing my resolution of going handsome in clothes and looking high – for that must do it when all is done with my Lord. Thence by coach with Sir Wm. Batten to the City and his son Castle, who talks mighty[a] highly against Captain Taylor, calling him knave;[3] and I find that the old doting father is led and talks just as the son do, or the son as the father would have him.

Light, and to Mr. Moxons and there saw our office globes in doing, which will be very handsome – but cost money. So to the Coffee-house; and there very fine discourse with Mr. Hill the merchant, a pretty gentile, young, and sober man.

a MS. 'my'

---

1. Probably the sewer from old Southampton House on the s. side of Holborn, east of Chancery Lane. The house was pulled down c. 1652; Southampton Buildings now occupy the site. (R).

2. The incident occurred on 9 March and is reported (more briefly than here) in *The Intelligencer*, 14 March, p. 175.

3. John Taylor, shipbuilder, was associated with Batten's friend Wood in the supply of New England masts over which there was now dispute, but was prepared to accept Pepys's verdict: below, pp. 123–4.

So to the Change and thence home, where my wife and I fell out about my not being willing to have her have her*a* gown laced, but would lay out the same money and more on a plain new one. At this she flounced away in a manner I never saw her, nor which I could ever endure. So I away to the office, though she had dressed herself to go see my Lady Sandwich. She by and by in a rage fallows me; and coming to me, tells me in spiteful manner, like a vixen and with a look full of rancour, that she would go buy a new one and lace it and make me pay for it, and then let me burn it if I would after she had done it – and so went away in fury. This vexed me cruelly; but being very busy, I had not hand[1] to give myself up to consult what to do in it. But anon, I suppose after she saw that I did not fallow her, she came again to the office; where I made her stay, being busy with another, half an hour; and her stomach coming down, we were presently friends. And so after my business being over at the office, we out and by coach to my Lady Sandwiches, with whom I left my wife; and I to White-hall, where I met Mr. De Cretz;[2] and after an hour's discourse with him, met with nobody to do other business with, but back again to my Lady and after half an hour's discourse with her, to my brother's, who I find in the same or worse condition. The Doctors give him over and so do all that see him. He talks no sense two words together now. And I confess it made me weep to see that he should not be able when I asked him, to say who I was.

I went to Mrs. Turners, and by her discourse with my brother's Doctor, Mr. Powell, I find that she is full now of the disease*b* which my brother is troubled with, and talks of it mightily; which I am sorry for – there being other company; but methinks it should be for her honour to forbear talking of it. The shame of this very thing, I confess, troubles me as much as anything.

Back to my brother's, and took my wife and carried her to my uncle Fenners and there had much private discourse with him. He tells me the Doctor's thoughts of my brother's little hopes of recovery; and from that, to tell me his thoughts long of my brother's bad husbandry; and from that, to say that he believes

a repl. 'a laced'   *b* repl. 'dis'-

---

1. Sc. 'free hand', time.   2. Emanuel de Critz, painter. (OM).

he owes a great deal of money – as, to my Cozen Scott, I know not how much – and Dr Tho. Pepys, 30*l*; but that the Doctor confesses that he is paid 20*l* of it. And what with that and what he owes my father and me, I doubt he is in a very sad condition; that if he lives, he will not be able to show his head – which will be a very great shame to me.[1]

After this I went in to my*a* aunt and my wife and Anth. Joyce and his wife, who were by chance there, and drank; and so home, my mind and head troubled, but I hope it will over in a little time, one way or other.

After doing a little at my office of business, I home to supper and to bed.

From notice that my uncle Fenner did give my father the last week of my brother's condition, my mother is coming up to Towne, which also doth trouble me.

The business between my Lords Chancellor and Bristoll, they say, is hushed up, and the latter gone or going by the King's licence to France.[2]

15. Up and to the office, where we sat all the morning; and at noon comes Madam Turner and her daughter The – her chief errand to tell me that she had got Dr. Wiverly her Doctor to search my brother's mouth, where Mr. Powell says there is an Ulcer; from whence he concludes that he hath had the pox. But the Doctor swears there is not, nor ever was any. And my brother being very sensible, which I was glad to hear, he did talk with him about it; and he did wholly disclaim that ever he had that disease or that ever he said to Powell*b* that he had it – all which did put me into great comfort as to that reproach which was spread against him. So I sent for a barrel of oysters and they dined, and we were very merry, I being willing to be

a repl. 'them'   *b* repl. 'the other two'

1. Tom's debts (c. £307 all told) are set out in the papers Pepys collected on his brother's death: Rawl. A 182, esp. ff. 301+. Benjamin Scott was an attorney and administered the estate, but does not appear as a creditor. Dr Thomas Pepys was owed £8, Pepys himself £87 (which probably includes the debt of his father). Cf. below, p. 97, n. 3; *Family Letters*, pp. 7–11.

2. Bristol, who had attempted to impeach Clarendon, was now in hiding in Wimbledon, not in France. Cf. below, p. 89 & n. 3.

so upon this news. After dinner we took coach and to my brother's; where, contrary to my expectation, he continues as bad or worse, talking idle and now not at all knowing any of us as before. Here we stayed a great while, I going up and down the house looking after things. In the evening Dr. Wiverley came again and I sent for Mr. Powell (the Doctor and I having first by ourselfs searched my brother again at his privities; where he was as clear as ever he was born, and in the Doctor's opinion had been ever so). And we three alone discoursed that business, where the Coxcomb did give us his simple reasons for what he had said; which the Doctor fully confuted and left the fellow, only saying that he should cease to report any such thing and that what he had said was the best of his judgment, from my brother's words and ulcer, as he supposed, in his mouth. I threatened him that I would have satisfaction if I heard any more such discourse. And so good night to them two, giving the Doctor a piece for his fee but the other nothing.

I to my brother again, where Madam Turner and her company, and Mrs. Croxton, my wife, and Mrs. Holding. About 8 a-clock my brother begun to fetch his spittle with more pain and to speak as much, but not so distinctly; till at last, the phlegm getting the maistery of him and he beginning as we thought to rattle, I had no mind to see him die, as we thought he presently would, and so withdrew and led Mrs. Turner home. But before I came back, which was in a quarter^a of an hour, my brother was dead. I went up and found the nurse holding his eyes shut; and he, poor wretch, lying with his chops fallen, a most sad sight and that which put me into a present very great transport of grief and cries. And endeed, it was a most sad sight to see the poor wretch lie now still and dead and pale like a stone. I stayed till he was almost cold, while Mrs. Croxton, Holden, and the rest did strip and lay him out – they observing his corps, as they told me afterwards, to be as clear as any they ever saw. And so this was the end of my poor brother, continuing talking idle and his lips working^b even to his last, that his phlegm hindered his breathing; and at last his breath broke out, bringing a flood of phlegm and stuff out with it, and so he died.

This evening he talked among other talk a great deal of French, very plain and good; as among others – "*quand un homme*

a MS. 'half a quarter'   *b* MS. 'walking'

boit quand il n'a poynt d'inclinacion a boire il ne luy fait jamais de bien." I once begun to tell him something of his condition and asked him*ª* whither he thought he should go. He in distracted manner answered me – "Why, whither should I go? there are but two ways. If I go to the bad way, I must give God thanks for it. And if I go the other way, I must give God the more thanks for it; and I hope I have not been so undutiful and unthankful in my life but I hope I shall go that way." This was all the sense, good or bad, I could get of him this day.

I left my wife to see him laid out, and I by coach home, carrying my brother's papers, all I could find, with me. And having wrote a letter to my father, telling him what hath been said, I returned by coach, it being very late and dark, to my brother's. But all being gone, the Corps laid out and my wife at Mrs. Turners, I thither; and there, after an hour's talk, we up to bed – my wife and I in the little blue chamber. And I lay close to my wife, being full of disorder and grief for my brother, that I could not sleep nor wake with satisfaction; at last I slept till 5 or 6 a-clock. And then I rose and up, leaving my wife in 《16.》 bed, and to my brother's, where I set them on cleaning the house. And my wife coming anon to look after things, I up and down to my Cosen Stradwickes and uncle Fenners about discoursing for the funeral, which I am resolved to put off till Friday next. Thence home and trimmed myself; and then to the Change and told my uncle Wight of my brother's death; and so by coach to my Cosen Turners and there dined very well. But my wife having those upon her today and in great pain, we were forced to rise in some disorder and in Mrs.*ᵇ* Turners coach carried her home and put her to bed. Then back again with my Cosen Norton to Mrs. Turners and there stayed a while talking with Dr Pepys,[1] that puppy, whom I had no patience to hear. So I left them, and to my brother's to look after things – and saw the Coffin brought; and by and by Mrs. Holden came and saw him nailed up. Then came W. Joyce to me half-drunk, and much ado I had to tell him the story of my brother's being found clear of what was said, but he would interrupt me by

a repl. 'me'   *b* repl. 'her'

---

1. Thomas Pepys, physician; Pepys's cousin.

some idle discourse or other, of his crying what a good man and a good speaker[1] my brother was and God knows what. At last, weary of him, I got him away and I to Mrs. Turner's; and there, though my heart is still heavy to think of my poor brother, yet I could give way to my fancy to hear Mrs. The play upon the Harpsicon – though the Musique did not please me neither. Thence to my brother's and found them with my maid Elizabeth, taking an Inventory of the goods of the house; which I was well pleased at, and am much beholding to Mr. Honywoods man in doing of it.[2] His name is Herbert, one that says he knew me when he lived with Sir Samuel Morland[3] – but I have forgot him. So I left them at it and by coach home and to my office, there to do a little business; but God knows, my heart and head is so full of my brother's death and the consequences of it, that I can do very little or understand it.

So home to supper; and after looking over[a] some business in my chamber, to bed to my wife, who continues in bed in some pain still. This day I have a great barrel of Oysters given me by Mr. Barrow,[4] as big as 16 of others, and[b] I took it in the coach with me to Mrs. Turner's and gave them her.

This day the Parliament met again after a long prorogation – but what they have done I have not been in the way to hear.

17. Up and to my brother's, where all the morning doing business against tomorrow; and so to my Cosen Stradwickes[5] about the same business and to the Change; and thence home to dinner – where my wife in bed, sick still but not so bad as yesterday. I dined by her and so to the office, where we sat this afternoon – having changed this day our settings from morning to afternoons because of the parliament which returned yesterday

a　blot above symbol　　　　*b*　repl. 'were but'

---

1. Sc. one who spoke well of others. Tom had an impediment in his speech.

2. The inventory is now in Rawl. A 182, ff. 311+. Peter Honywood lodged at Tom Pepys's.

3. Pepys's tutor at Cambridge, and, like Pepys, a government servant under the Protectorate.

4. Storekeeper, Chatham. Pepys had intervened on his behalf in recent disputes at the dockyard: see above, p. 5 & n. 1.

5. Provision merchant; he supplied the funeral biscuit.

– but was adjourned till Monday next upon pretence that many of
the members were said to be upon the road and also the King
had other affairs and so desired them to adjourn till then.[1] But
the truth is, the King is offended at my Lord of Bristoll as they
say, whom he hath found to have been all this while (pretending
a desire of leave to go into France and to have all the difference
between him and the Chancellor made up) endeavouring to make
factions in both Houses to[2] the Chancellor's. So the King did
this to keep the Houses from meeting; and in the meanwhile sent
a guard and a herald last night to have taken him at Wimbleton,
where he was in the morning; but could not find him – at
which the King was and is still mightily concerned and runs up
and down to and from the Chancellor's like a boy – and it seems
would make Digbys articles against the Chancellor to be treason-
able reflection against his Majesty.[3] So that the King is very high
as they say; and God knows what will fallow upon it.

   After office I to my brother's again, and thence to Madam
Turners, in both places preparing things against tomorrow. And
this night I have altered my resolution of burying him in the

1. *CJ*, viii. 534; parliament had
not met since 27 July 1663. Office
days were now (15 March) fixed for
Monday and Thursday afternoons and
Saturday mornings: PRO, Adm.
106/3520, f. 18*v*.
   2. Sc. in opposition to.
   3. After Bristol's impeachment of
Clarendon in July 1663 the King had
issued a proclamation for his arrest
for 'crimes of a high nature against
the King's person and government'
(25 August; Steele, no. 3386); it was
now believed possible that a charge
of treason could be sustained. Bristol,
in hiding, wrote letters from addresses
in Flanders and France to give the
impression he was out of reach:
HMC, *Ormonde*, n.s., iii. 73. On
16 March the King, judging he might
be in town for the opening of parliament, made a determined attempt to
catch him both at his Queen St house
and at his country house in Wimble-

don. It was said that he was about
to have dinner at Wimbledon when
the guards came for him. But he
escaped: HMC, op. cit., iii. 73, 152.
For his intrigues with members of
parliament, see ib., pp. 134, 159; de
Cominges to Louis XIV, 25 January,
4 February 1664 (*Pepysiana*, pp. 298–
9). He sent a letter to the House of
Lords by his wife, which the house
refused to open when it met on the
21st: HMC, op. cit., iii. 154. There
are two angry references to him in
Charles II's letters to his sister,
Henrietta, of 24 and 28 March: C. H.
Hartmann, *The King my brother*, pp.
91–2. The story that the King had
persuaded parliament to adjourn in
order to be able to arrest him is not
proved, but likely, and was commonly repeated: e.g. *CSPD 1663–4*,
p. 522. Bristol did not emerge from
hiding until Clarendon's fall in 1667.
See also Clarendon, *Life*, ii. 259–63.

churchyard among my young brothers and sisters; and bury him in the church in the middle Isle, as near as I can to my mother's pew – this costs me 20*s* more.[1] This being all, home by coach, bringing my brother's silver tankard*ᵃ* for safety along with me; and so to supper after writing to my father, and so to bed.

18. Up betimes and walked to my brother's, where a great while putting things in order against anon. Then to Madam Turners and eat a breakfast there. And so to Wotton my shoe-maker and there got a pair of shoes blacked on the soles, against anon for me. So to my brother's, and to the church and with the grave-maker chose a place for my brother to lie in, just under my mother's pew. But to see how a man's tombes are at the mercy of such a fellow, that for 6*d* he would (as his own words were) "I will justle them together but I will make room for him" – speaking of the fullness of the middle Isle where he was to lie. And that he would for my father's sake do my brother that is dead all the civility he can; which was to disturb other corps that are not quite rotten*ᵇ* to make room for him. And methought his manner of speaking it was very remarkable – as of a thing that now was in his power to do a man a courtesy or not.

At noon my wife, though in pain, comes; but I being forced to go home, she went back with me – where I dressed myself and so did Besse; and so to my brother's again – whither, though invited as the custom is at 1 or 2 a-clock, they came not till 4 or 5. But at last, one after another they came – many more then I bid; and my reckoning that I bid was 120, but I believe there was nearer 150. Their service was six biscuits a-piece and what they pleased of burnt claret – my Cosen Joyce Norton kept the wine and cakes above – and did give out to them that served, who had white gloves given them.[2] But above all, I am beholden to

a blot below symbol   *b* repl. 'ready'

---

1. The church was St Bride's, Fleet St. 'Church dutyes' totalled £2 8*s*.; the gravemaker received 1*s*. 6*d*.: Rawl. A 182, f. 335*r*.

2. According to the funeral accounts (in Pepys's hand), the gloves (of white kid) cost 9*s*.; the claret £2 2*s*. 6*d*.; the biscuit £4 11*s*. 0*d*.; the coffin £1 9*s*. 0*d*.; and the ringers 5*s*.: Rawl. A. 182, ff. 305*r*, 336*r*, printed in *Family Letters*, p. 7.

Mrs. Holding,[1] who was most kind and did take mighty pains, not only in getting the house and everything else ready, but this day in going up and down to see the house filled and served, in order to mine and their great content I think – the men setting by themselfs in some rooms, and women by themselfs in others – very close, but yet room enough. Anon to church, walking out into the street to the Conduict and so across the street, and had a very good company along with the Corps. And being come to the grave as above, Dr. Pierson, the Minister of the parish, did read the service for buriall and so I saw my poor brother laid into the grave; and so all broke up and I and my wife and Madam Turner and her family to my brother's, and by and by fell to a barrell of oysters, Cake, and cheese of Mr. Honiwoods, with him in his chamber and below – being too merry for so late a sad work; but Lord, to see how the world makes nothing of the memory of a man an hour after he is dead. And endeed, I must blame myself; for though at the sight of him, dead and dying, I had real grief for a while, while he was in my sight, yet presently after and ever since, I have had very little grief endeed for him.

By and by, it beginning to be late, I put things in some order in the house and so took my wife and Besse (who hath done me very good service in cleaning and getting ready everything and serving the wine and things today, and is endeed a most excellent good-natured and faithful wench and I love her mightily) by coach home; and so after being at the office to set down this day's work, home to supper and to bed.

19.   Up and to the office, where all the morning; and at noon my wife and I alone, having a good hen with eggs to dinner, with great content. Then by coach to my brother's, where I spent the afternoon in paying some of the charges of the buriall and in looking over his papers; among which I find several letters of my brother John's to him, speaking very foul words of me and my deportment to him here, and very crafty designs about Sturtlow land and God knows what – which I am very glad to know and shall make him repent them. Anon my father and my brother John came to town by coach. I sat till night

1. Holden: see above, p. 82 & n. 1.

with him, giving him an account^a of things. He, poor man, very sad and sickly. I in great pain through a simple squeezing of my cods today, by putting one leg over another as I have formerly done,[1] which made me hasten home; and after a little at the office, in great disorder home to bed.

20. *Lords day.* Kept my bed all the morning, having laid a poultice to my cods last night to take down the tumour there which I got yesterday; which it did do, being applied pretty warm and soon after the beginning of the swelling – and the pain was gone also. We lay talking all the while; among other things, of religion, wherein I am sorry so often to hear my wife talk^b of her being and resolving to die a Catholique; and endeed, a small matter I believe would absolutely turn her, which I am sorry for.[2] Up at noon to dinner; and then to my chamber with a fire till late at night, looking over my brother Tho's papers, sorting of them – among which I find many base letters of my brother John's to him against me and carrying on plots against me to promote Tom's having of his Banbury Mistress,[3] in base slighting terms and in worse of my sister Pall – such as I shall take a convenient time to make my father know, and him also, to his sorrow.

---

a MS. 'accounts'   *b* MS. 'take'

---

1. Cf. above, ii. 194 & n. 4.
2. Cf. above, p. 39. She made a similar avowal on 25 October 1668, and the diary for August 1666 reveals her painting a Virgin's head. Before her marriage her penchant towards Popery had caused some distress to her Huguenot family. Her brother, Balty, attributed it to the short period of about two weeks which she had spent in a Paris convent at the age of 12 or 13: *Family Letters*, p. 28. But she was never received into the Catholic church, and Balty, writing to Pepys on 8 February 1674, as-

serted that from the time of her marriage until her death she never had 'the least thoughts of Popery': ib., p. 26. Dr Milles, Rector of St Olave's, certified in 1681 that she received the sacrament from his hands shortly before her death in 1669: Rawl. A 175, f. 266r. It was one of the charges brought against Pepys in 1674 by the parliamentary enemies of the Duke of York that he himself was a Papist and had tried without success to convert his wife: *CJ*, ix. 306, 309, 310; Grey, ii. 426+.
3. See above, iii. 210.

So after supper to bed – our people rising to wash tomorrow.

21. Up; and it snowing this morning a little, which from the mildness of the winter and the weather beginning to be hot and the summer to come on apace is a little strange to us – I did not go abroad, because of my tumour, for fear it shall rise again; but stayed within and by and by my father came, poor man, to me, and my brother John; after much talk and taking them up to my chamber, I did there after some discourse bring in my business of anger with John and did before my father read all his roguish letters; which troubled my father mightily, especially to hear me say what I did, against my allowing anything for the time to come to him out of my own purse, and other words very severe – while he, like a simple rogue, made very silly and churlish answers to me, not like a man of any goodness or wit – at which I was as much disturbed as the other. And*ᵃ* will be as good as my word, in making him to his cost know that I will remember his carriage to me in this perticular the longest day I live. It troubled me to see my poor father so troubled, whose good nature did make him, poor wretch, to yield; I believe to comply with my brother Tom and him in part*ᵇ* of their designs, but without any ill intent to me or doubt of me or my good intentions to him or them – though it doth trouble me a little that he should in any manner do it.

They dined with me; and after dinner, abroad with my wife to buy some things for her; and I to the office, where we sat till*ᶜ* night; and then after doing some business at my closet, I home and to supper and to bed.

This day the House of Parliament met and the King met them, with the Queene with him – and he made a speech to them; among other things, discoursing largely of the plots abroad against him and the peace of the kingdom. And among other things, that the dissatisfied party had great hopes upon the effect of the act for a Trienniall parliament granted by his father – which he desired them to peruse, and I think repeal. So the House did retire to their own House and did order that act to be read tomorrow before them. And I suppose will be repealed, though I believe much against the will of a good many that sit there.[1]

22.[a] Up, and spent the whole morning and afternoon at my office. Only in the evening, my wife being at my aunt Wights, I went thither; calling at my own house, going out found the parlour curtains drawn; and enquiring the reason of it, they told me that their mistress had got Mrs. Buggin's fine little dog and our little bitch – which is proud at this time – and I am apt to think that she was helping him to lime her – for going afterwards to my uncle Wights and supping there with her, where very merry with Mr. Woolly's drollery, and going home, I found the little dog so little that of himself he could not reach our bitch; which I am sorry for – for it is the finest dog that ever I saw in my life – as if he were painted, the colours are so finely mixed and shaded. God forgive me, it went against me to have my wife and servants look upon them while they endeavoured to do something, and yet it provoked me to pleasure with my wife more then usual tonight.

23. Up; and going out saw Mrs. Buggins's dog, which proves, as I thought last night, so pretty that I took him and the bitch into my closet below and, by holding down the bitch, help him to lime her; which he did very stoutly, so as I hope it will take – for it is the prettiest dog that ever I saw.

So to the office, where very busy all the morning; and so to the Change and off thence with Sir W Ryder to the Trinity-house and there dined very well. And good discourse among the old men – of Islands now and then rising and falling again in the

a repl. '21'

---

1. The Triennial Act of 1641 was repealed on 5 April 1664. The King now said, 'I pray, Mr Speaker, and you, gentlemen of the House of Commons, give that Triennial Bill Once a Reading in your House; and then, in God's name, do what you think fit for Me, and yourselves, and the whole Kingdom': *LJ*, xi. 582. The act was an offence to his prerogative, since it required and provided for the summons of a new parliament every three years whether the King wanted it or not. Writing to his sister Henrietta on 24 March, he referred to it as 'that wild act': C. H. Hartmann, *The King my brother*, p. 91.

sea; and that there is many dangers of grounds and rocks that come just up to the edge almost of the sea, that is never discovered and ships perish without the world's knowing the reason of it.

Among other things, they observed that there are but two seamen in*ª* the Parliament house, *viz.*, Sir W Batten and Sir W Pen – and not above 20 or 30 merchants; which is a strange thing in an Island, and no wonder that things of trade go no better nor are better understood.[1]

Thence home and all the afternoon at the office; only, for an hour in the evening my Lady Jemimah, Paulina, and Madam Pickering came to see us; but my wife would not be seen, being unready.* Very merry with them, they mightily talking of their thrifty living for a fortnight before their mother came to town and other such simple talk, and of their merry life at Brampton at my father's this winter. So they being gone, to the office again till late; and so home and to supper and bed.

24. Called up by my father, poor man, coming to advise with me about Tom's house and other matters. And he being gone, I down by water to Greenwich, it being*ᵇ* very foggy; and I walked very finely to Woolwich and there did very much business at both yards. And thence walked back, Captain Grove with me, talking; and so to Deptford and did the like there; and then walked to Redriffe (calling and eating a bit of collops and eggs at Halfway-house) and so home to the office, where we sat late; and then home weary to supper and to bed.

a MS. 'is'   *b* repl. same symbol badly formed

---

1. These remarks, both about wrecks and about M.P.s, may have been inspired by the business of the day, for Trinity House decided at this meeting to petition the King against the impressment of sailors for land service: HMC, *Rep.*, 8/1/sect. i. 252*a*. There were in fact c. 20–24 merchants in the House of Commons, and 7 members who had formerly been merchants. (Inf. from Prof. B. D. Henning.) Pepys in his *Naval Minutes* (p. 53) has a query (written in the 1680s) which raises the same point in a different way: 'Consider what proportion of burgesses in Parliament we have relating to sea-ports' – but gives no answer.

25. *Lady=day.* Up and by water to White-hall, and there to Chappell, where it was most infinite full to hear Dr. Critton.[1] Being not known, some great person in the pew I pretended to and went in did question my coming in; I told them my pretence,[2] so they turned to the orders of the chapel which hung behind upon the wall, and read it and were satisfied – but they did not demand whether I was in waiting or no.   And so I was in some fear lest he that was in waiting might come and betray me.

The Doctor preached upon the 31 *Jeremy* and the 21 and 22 verses – about a woman compassing a man; meaning the Virgin conceiving and bearing our Saviour.   It was the worst sermon I ever heard him make, I must confess, and yet it was good. And in two places very bitter, advising the King to do as the Emperor Severus did, to hang up a Presbyter John (a[a] short coat and a long gowne interchangeably[)] in all the Courts of England.[3] But the story of Severus was pretty: that he hanged up 40 Senators before the Senate-house and then made a speech presently to the Senate in praise of his own lenity, and then decreed that never any Senatour after that time should suffer in the same manner without consent of the Senate;[4] which he compared to the proceeding of the Long Parliament against my Lord Strafford.[5]   He said the greatest part of the Lay=Magistrates

a repl. 'or'

---

1. Robert Creighton, Dean of Wells, the most outspoken of court preachers: cf. above, iii. 42 & n. 5.

2. Pepys must have pretended that he was on duty as a deputy to Sandwich as Clerk of the Privy Seal: see above, iii. 67, n. 3.

3. 'Presbyter John' and 'short coat' here signify puritan parsons; the 'long gowne' signifies lawyers – i.e. the magistracy, to judge by Pepys's report of a later passage in this sermon. Cf. J. Howell, *Epist. Ho-Elianae* (ed. Jacobs), ii. 625 (9 November [1653]): 'The soldiers have a great spleen to the Lawyers, insomuch that they threaten to hang up their *Gowns* among the *Scots Colours* in *Westminster-hall.*'

4. This appears to be a conflation of two stories about Severus (Emperor, A.D. 193–211): one is of his speech to the Senate in June 193, in which he promised this immunity to the senators; the other relates to June 197, when, after the war against Albinus, he executed 41 senators by his own authority alone, and after a speech in which he praised his own clemency. See *Scriptores historiae Augustae* (*Severus*), VII, v, and ib., XII, ix.

5. Strafford, Charles I's strong minister, had been executed by act of attainder in 1641, after a failure to secure his conviction by impeachment.

in England were puritans and would not do justice; and the Bishops, their powers were so taken away and lessened, that they could not exercise the power they ought.¹ He told the King and the ladies, plainly speaking of death and of the skulls and bones of dead men and women, how there is no difference – that nobody could tell that of the great Marius or Alexander from a pyoneer; nor, for all the pains the ladies take with their faces, he that should look in a Charnell-house could not distinguish which was Cleopatras or fair Rosamonds or Jane Shoares.²

Thence by water home. After dinner to the office. Thence with my wife to see my father and discourse how he finds Tom's matters, which he doth very ill, and that he finds him to have been so negligent that he used to trust his servants with cutting out of clothes, never hardly cutting out anything himself. And by the abstract of his accounts, we find him to [owe] about above 290*l* and to be coming to him under 200*l*.³

Thence home with my wife, it being very durty on foot, and bought some fowl in Gracious-street and some oysters against our feast tomorrow. So home; and after at the office a while, home to supper and to bed.

26. Up very betimes, and to my*ᵃ* office and there read over some papers against a meeting by and by at this office of Mr. Povy, Sir W Rider, Creed, Vernatz and Mr. Gauden about my Lord Peterborough's accounts for Tanger⁴ – wherein we proceeded a good way; but Lord, to see how ridiculous Mr. Povy is in all he says or doth; not like a man nor*ᵇ* fit for to be in*ᶜ* such imployments as he is, and perticularly that of a Treasurer

---

a repl. 'the'   *b* MS. 'more'   *c* repl. 'a'

---

1. Neither the lay nor the ecclesiastical courts were able to suppress conventicles at this time, and Creighton's explanation, although exaggerated, has some truth in it. His remarks applied particularly to the town magistrates.

2. Fair Rosamund (Rosamund Clifford, mistress of Henry II) and Jane Shore (mistress of Edward IV) were familiar figures of English history and ballad.

3. Cf. above, p. 85, n. 1. Some of the debts were still giving trouble 13 years later: *Family Letters*, p. 54.

4. See above, p. 48 & n. 1.

(paying many and very great sums without the least written order), as he is to be King of England. And seems but this day, after much discourse of mine, to be sensible of that part of his folly, besides a great deal more in other things. ⟨This morning in discourse, Sir W. Rider [said] that he hath kept a*ᵃ* journall of his life for almost these 40 years, even to this day, and still doth – which pleased me mightily.⟩*ᵇ*

That being done – Sir J. Mennes and I sat all the morning; and then I to the Change and there got a way, by pretence of business with my Uncle Wight, to put off Creed, whom I had invited to dinner; and so home and there find Madam Turner, her Daughter The, Joyce Norton, my father and Mr. Honywood, and by and by comes my uncle Wight and aunt – this being my solemn feast for my cutting of the stone, it being now, blessed be God, this day six yeares since*ᶜ* that time.¹ And I bless God I do in all respects find myself free from that disease or any signs of it, more then that upon the least cold I continue to have pain in making water, by gathering of wind and growing costive – till which be removed I am at no ease; but without that, I am very well. One evil more I have, which is that upon the least squeeze almost, my cods begin*ᵈ* to swell and come to great pain, which is very strange and troublesome to me; though upon the speedy applying of a poultice, it goes down again and in two days I am well again.

Dinner not being presently ready, I spent some time myself and showed them a map of Tanger, left this morning at my house by Creed, cut by our order, the Comissioners, new drawn by Jonas Moore² – which is very pleasant and I purpose to have it finely set out and hung up.

Mrs. Hunt coming to see my wife by chance, dined here with us.

After dinner Sir W Batten sent to speak with me and told

a repl. 'hath'   *b* addition crowded in between paragraphs
        c repl. 'then'   *d* MS. 'being'

---

1. See above, i. 97, n. 3.
2. *A mapp of the citty of Tanger; with the Straits of Gibraltar* (engraved by Hollar), 1664; a copy is now in the BM (K. Top. cxvii, 79, 11, TAB). Moore was surveyor to the Duke of York.

me that he had proffered our bill today in the House; and that it was read without any dissenters and he fears not but will pass very well – which I shall be glad of.[1] He told me also how Sir [2] Temple hath spoke very discontentful words in the House about the Tryenniall bill, but it hath been read the second time today and committed[3] – and he believes will go on without more ado, though there are many in the House are displeased at it, though they dare not say much. But above all expectation, Mr. Prin is the man against it,[4] comparing it to the Idoll whose head was of gold and his body and legs and feet of different metal; so this bill had several degrees of calling of parliaments, in case the King and then the Council and then the Lord Chancellor and then the Sheriffes should fail to do it.

He tells me also how, upon occasion of some prentices being put in the pillory today for beating of their master, or some such-like thing, in Cheapeside – a company of prentices came and rescued them and pulled down the Pillory; and they being set up again, did the like again. So that the Lord Mayor and Major-Generall Browne was fain to come and stay there to keep the peace; and drums all up and down the City was beat to raise the train-bands for to quiet the town.[5] And by and by going

1. 'A Bill for enabling the principal officers and commissioners of his Majesty's Navy Royal, for the Performance of their Duties in the service thereof' (*CJ*, viii. 537); passed at the end of this session on 17 May (16 Car. II c. 5). See above, iv. 81, 82 & n. 1.

2. Supply 'Richard'.

3. A mistake: it was given a second reading and committed on the 24th. On this day it was debated in the Committee of the Whole: *CJ*, viii. 536–7. Temple opposed the new Triennial bill because, while it promised regular parliaments, it lacked safeguards.

4. I.e. against the act of 1641, with its strict safeguards (now repealed by the present measure). He had supported it in 1641, but now opposed it

in the belief that it was unconstitutional and would justify the summons of parliament, e.g. by any 12 peers, even if they were a minority. Cf. the report of the debate of the 24th in *Verney Mem.*, ii. 201. The evidence generally is discussed by Professor C. Robbins in *Hunt. Lib. Quart.*, 12/121+. Pepys's evidence both here and at 28 March is valuable.

5. Two apprentices, convicted of an assault on their master (Ireland, a cooper on Breadstreet Hill), had been sentenced to stand in the pillory and to be whipped from there to their master's house. For the riot, see *The Intelligencer*, 28 March, p. 208; Tanner 47, f. 107r (newsletter, 29 March). The sentence was eventually carried out.

out with my Uncle and Aunt Wight by coach with my wife through Cheapside (the rest of the company, after much content and mirth, being broke up), we saw a trained-band stand in Cheapside upon their guard. We went much against my uncles will as far almost*a* as Hyde-park, he and my aunt falling out all the way about it, which vexed me. But by this I understand my uncle more then ever I did, for he was mighty soon angry and wished a pox take her – which I was sorry to hear. The weather,*b* I confess, turning on a sudden to rain, did make it very unpleasant; but yet there was no occasion in the world for his being so angry. But she bore herself very discreetly, and I must confess she proves to me much another woman then I thought her. But all was peace again presently. And so it raining very fast, we met many brave coaches coming from the park, and so we turned and set them down at home; and so home ourselfs and ended the day with great content – to think how it hath pleased the Lord in six years time to raise me from a condition of constant and dangerous and most painful sickness and low condition and poverty to a state of constant health almost – great honour and plenty, for which the Lord God of Heaven make me truly thankful.

My wife found her gown come home laced; which is indeed very handsome but will cost me a great deal of money, more than ever I intended – but it is but for once. So to the office and did business; and then home and to bed.

27. *Lords day.* Lay long in bed, wrangling with my wife about the charge she puts me to at this time for clothes, more then I intended; and very angry we were – but quitly*c* friends again. And so rising and ready, I to my office and there fell upon business; and then to dinner and then to my office again to my business. And by and by in the afternoon walked forth towards my father's; but it being church-time, walked to St. Jones's[1] to try if I could see the *belle* Butler, but could not; only

a repl. 'as'   *b* MS. 'well'
c cf. 'letters of mart' (marque): above, p. 52

1. *Recte* St James's (Clerkenwell). (R).

saw her sister, who endeed is pretty, with a fine Roman nose. Thence walked through the ducking-pond fields;[1] but they are so altered since my father used to carry us to Islington to the old man's at the Kings-head to eat cakes and ale (his name was Pitts) that I did not know which was the ducking-pond nor where I was. So through Fee=lane[2] to my father's and there met Mr. Moore and discoursed with him and my father about who should administer for my brother Tom; and I find we shall have trouble in it – but I will clear my hands of it. And which vexed me, my father seemed troubled that I should seem to rely so wholly upon the advice of Mr. Moore and take nobody else – but I satisfied him, and so home; and in Cheapeside, both coming and going, it was full of apprentices, who have been here all this day and have done violence I think to the master of the boys that were put in the pillory yesterday. But Lord, to see how the train-bands are raised upon this; the drums beating everywhere as if an enemy were upon them – so much is this city subject to be put into a disarray upon very small occasions. But it was pleasant to hear the boys, and perticularly one little one that I demanded the business: he told me that that had never been done in the City since it was a city, two prentices put in the pillory, and that it ought not to be so.

So I walked home; and then it being fine moonshine, with my wife an hour in the garden, talking of her clothes against Easter and about her maids; Jane being to be gone and the great dispute whether Besse, whom we both love, should be raised to be chamber-maid or no. We have both a mind to it, but know not whether we should venture the making her proud and so make a bad chamber-maid of a very good-natured and sufficient cook-maid.

So to my office a little and then to supper – prayers and to bed.

28. This is the first morning that I have begin, and I hope shall continue, to rise betimes in the morning; and so up and to

---

1. Both Clerkenwell and Islington had ducking-ponds. The sport of setting dogs to chase ducks was a popular one: W. J. Pinks, *Hist.* *Clerkenwell*, pp. 543–4. Cf. Ben Jonson, *Every man in his humour*, Act I, sc. 1.

2. Fleet Lane. (R).

my office and thence about 7 a-clock to T. Trice and advised
with him about our administering to my brother Tom; and I
went to my father and told him what to do, which was to
administer and to let my Cosen Scott have a letter of Atturny
to fallow the business here in his absence for him – who by
that means will have the power of paying himself (which we
cannot however hinder) and do us a kindness we think too.[1]
But Lord, what a shame methinks to me, that in this condition
and at this age I should know no better the laws of my own
country.

Thence to Westminster-hall and spent till noon, it being
parliament; and at noon walked with Creed into St. James's
parke, talking of many things; perticularly of the poor parts and
great unfitness for business of Mr. Povy and yet what a show he
makes in the world. Mr. Coventry not being come to his
chamber, I walked through the house[2] with him for an hour in
St. James's fields, talking of the same subject. And then parted
and back, and with great impatience, sometimes reading, sometimes walking, sometimes thinking that Mr. Coventry, though
he invited us to dinner with him, was gone with the rest to the
office without a dinner. At last, at past 4 a-clock, I heard that
the Parliament was not up yet, and so walked to Westminster-
hall and there find it so; and meeting with Sir J. Mennes and
being very hungry, went over with him to the Leg, and before
we had cut a bit, the House rises; however, we eat a bit and
away to St. James's and there eat a second part of our dinner
with Mr. Coventry and his brother Harry, Sir W. Batten, and
Sir W. Penn.

The great matter today in the House hath been that Mr.
Vaughan, the great speaker, is this day come to town and hath
declared himself in a speech of an hour and a half, with great
reason and eloquence, against the repealing of the bill for Trienniall parliaments – but with no successe; but the House hath
carried it that there shall be such Parliaments, but without any

---

1. Letters of administration were
granted to John Pepys, sen., who in
turn made over his powers by letter
of attorney to Benjamin Scott on

2 April: *Family Letters*, p. 10. But
Pepys did all the business for his
father.

2. St James's Palace.

coercive*ᵃ* power upon the King if he will bring this act.¹ But Lord, to see how the best things are not done without some design; for I perceive all these gentlemen that I was with today were against it² (though there was reason enough on their side); yet purely, I could perceive, because it was the King's mind to have it; and should he demand anything else, I believe they*ᵇ* would give it him.

But this the discontented presbyters and that faction of the House will be highly displeased [with]; but it was carried clearly against them in the House.

We had excellent good table-talk, some of which I have entered in my book of stories.³ So with them by coach home and there find [by] my wife that Father Fogourdy hath been with her today and she is mightily for our going to hear a famous Reulé preach at the French Embassadors house;⁴ I pray God he do not tempt her in any matters of religion – which troubles*ᶜ* me. And also, she had messages from her mother today, who sent for her old morning-gown; which was almost past wearing and I used to call it her Kingdome, from the ease and content she used to have in the wearing of it.⁵ I am glad I do not hear of her begging anything of more value. But I do not like that these

a l.h. repl. l.h. 'coerv'- *b* repl. 'he' *c* repl. 'though'

---

1. *CJ*, viii. 538. John Vaughan (M.P. for Cardiganshire) was a leading critic of the government. His speech is in *CSPD 1661–2*, p. 330, erroneously calendared under '3 April (?) 1662'.
2. I.e. against the act of 1641, and in favour of the bill repealing it. For the court's efforts to mobilise votes, see J. R. Jones in *Bull. Inst. Hist. Res.*, 34/81+.
3. This book has not been traced.
4. The preacher was probably Pierre Roulles (Roulès), curé of Saint-Barthélemy, Paris, a court preacher. He had preached the funeral sermon on Louis XIII, and, as a leader of the *cabale des dévots*,

published in August 1664 an attack on Molière's *Tartuffe*. The house of the French Ambassador (de Cominges) was Exeter House, Strand. For Father Fogarty, see above, p. 39, n. 4.
5. Possibly an allusion to the opening line (by now proverbial) of the ballad by Sir Edward Dyer (d. 1607): 'My minde to me a Kingdome is,/ Such perfect joyes therein I finde' – one of the most popular ballads of the time. Cf. John Clarke, *Parœmiologia* (1639), p. 16. It was set to music by Byrd. Pepys had a copy (c. 1624) in his collection of ballads: H. E. Rollins (ed.), *Pepys Ballads*, i, no. 37. (E.)

messages should now come all upon Monday mornings, when my wife expects of course* I should be abroad at the Dukes.

To the office, where Mr. Norman came and showed me a design of his for the Storekeepers books, for the keeping of them reguler in order to a balance[1] – which I am mightily satisfied to see and shall love the fellow the better; as he is in all things sober, so perticularly for his endeavour to do something in this thing, so much wanted.

So late home to supper and to bed, weary with walking so long to no purpose in the park today.

29. Was called up this morning by a messenger from Sir G. Carteret to come to him to Sir W. Batten's; and so I rose and thither to him, and with him[a] and Sir J. Mennes[b] to Sir G. Carteret to examine his accounts and there we sat at it all the morning.[2] About noon Sir W. Batten came from the House of Parliament and told us our bill for our office was read the second time today with great applause, and is committed.[3] By and by to dinner, where good cheer; and Sir G. Carteret in his humour a very good man, and the most kind father and pleased father in his children that ever I saw. Here is now hung up a picture of my Lady Carteret, drawn by Lilly;[4] a very fine picture, but yet not so good as I have seen of his doing. After dinner to the business again, without any intermission till almost night; and then home and took coach and to my father to see and discourse with him; and so home again and to my office, where late, and then home and to bed.

a repl. 'them'   *b* repl. 'Sir G. Carteret'

---

1. James Norman was either now or soon afterwards Clerk of the Survey, Chatham. Until then he had been clerk to Batten in the Navy Office. His scheme was put into operation in April: *CSPD Add. 1660-85*, p. 101.

2. The accounts ran to December 1663. Cf. Pepys's comments on them: NWB, pp. 52-3.

3. For the bill, see above, p. 99

& n. 1. Batten, Penn, Coventry and Carteret were put on the committee: *CJ*, viii. 538.

4. Probably the very good three-quarter length which, with an equally good companion piece of Sir George (q.v. below, opp. vi. 167), now belongs to Mr G. Malet de Carteret, St Ouen's Manor, Jersey: N. V. L. Rybot, *The Islet of St Helier and Elizabeth Castle* (1947 ed.), pls II, III. (OM).

30. Up very betimes to my office; and thence at 7 a-clock to Sir G. Carteret and there with Sir J. Mennes made an end of his accounts. But stayed not dinner, my Lady having made us drink our morning draught there – of several wines. But I drank nothing but some of her Coffee; which was purely* made, with a little sugar in it.

Thence to the Change a great while and had good discourse with Captain Cocke at the Coffee-house about a Dutch war. And it seems the King's design is, by getting under-hand the merchants to bring in their complaints to the parliament, to make them in honour begin a war – which he cannot in honour declare first, for fear they should not second him with money.[1]   Thence homewards, staying a pretty while with my little she-Millener at the end of Burchin-lane – talking and buying gloves of her. And then home to dinner and in the afternoon had a meeting upon the Chest business; but I fear, unless I have time to look after it, nothing will ever be done, and that I fear I shall not.[2]

In the evening comes Sir W. Batten, who tells us that the Committee hath approved of our bill, with very few amendments in words, not in matter.

So to my office, where late with Sir W Warren; and so home to supper and to bed.

31. Up betimes and to my office, where by and by comes Povy, Sir Wm. Rider, Mr Bland, Creed, and Vernatz about my Lord Peterborough's accounts;[3] which we now went through, but with great difficulty and many high words between Mr. Povey and I; for I could not endure to see so many things extraordinary put in, against truth and reason. He was very angry, but I endeavoured all I could to profess my satisfaction in my Lord's part of the accounts, but not in those foolish idle things (they say I said) that others had put in.

Anon we rose and parted, both of us angry but I contented

1. See below, p. 107 & n. 1.
2. Cf. above, iii. 257 & n. 2. The Commission for the Chatham Chest now entered on its most vigorous period. At this meeting, attended by Mennes, Penn and Pepys (a bare quorum), they read the commission of 1617, and gathered together all the available records kept by the clerk: BM, Add. 9317, ff. 2*v*, 3*r*. Pepys was unable to attend the following meeting on 1 April: ib., f. 3*v*.
3. See above, p. 48 & n. 1.

because I knew all of them must know I was in the right.   Then
with Creed to Deptford, where I did a great deal of business, enquiring into the business of Canvas[1] and other things with great
content.   And so walked back again, good discourse between
Creed and I by the way, but most upon the folly of Povy.   And
at home found Luellin, and so we to dinner; and thence I to the
office, where we sat all the afternoon late; and being up and my
head mightily crowded with business, I took my wife by coach
to see my father.   I left her at his house and went to him to an
ale-house hard by, where my Cosen Scott was and my father's
new Tenant, Langford, a tailor, whom I have promised my
custom and he seems a[a] very modest, careful young man.[2]
Thence, my wife coming with the coach to the alley-end, I
home; and after supper to the making up my monthly accounts
and to my great content find myself worth above 900*l.*, the greatest
sum I ever yet had.   Having done my accounts, late to bed.

My head of late mighty full of business, and with good content
to myself in it;   though sometimes it troubles me that nobody
else but I should bend themselfs to serve the King with that
diligence, whereby much of my pains proves ineffectual.[b]

a   MS. 'he'   *b*   followed by one blank page

---

1. Pepys's notes on this subject
(dated this day) are in NWB, p. 21.
Cf. below, p. 157 & n. 3.
2. William Langford was now to
occupy Pepys's old home in Salisbury Court, recently made vacant by
Tom Pepys's death.   Langford was a
sub-tenant of Pepys's father, and
after the house was destroyed in the
Fire made a new lease with the landlord: below, 23 December 1668.

APRILL.

1. Up and to my office, where busy till noon; and then to the Change – where I find all the merchants concerned with the presenting their complaints to the committee of Parliament appointed to receive them this afternoon against the Dutch.[1] So home to dinner and thence by coach, setting my wife down at the New Exchange; I to White-hall and coming too soon for the Tanger Committee, walked to Mr. Blagrave for a song I left long ago there; and here I spoke with his kinswoman, he not being within, but did not hear her sing,[a] being not enough acquainted with her – but would be glad to have her to come and be at my house a week now and then.[2]

Back to White-hall and in the Gallery met the Duke of Yorke (I also saw the Queene going to the parke and her maids of honour; she herself look ill, and methinks Mrs. Stewart is grown fatter and not so fair as she was) and he called me to[b] him and discourse a good while with me; and after he was gone twice or thrice, stayed and called me again to him the whole length of the Howse. And at last talked of the Dutch; and I perceive doth much wish that the Parliament will find reason to fall out with them. He gone, I by and by find that the Comissioners of Tanger met at the Duke of Albemarles, and so I have lost my labour. So with Creed to the Change and there took up my wife and left him, and we two home, and I to walk in the garden with W. Howe, whom we took up, he having been to see us. He tells me how Creede hath been questioned before the Council about a letter that hath been met with, wherein he is mentioned by some fanatiques as a serviceable friend to them; but he says

<hr>

a repl. same symbol badly formed   *b* repl. 'to'

<hr>

1. The committee had been constituted on 26 March: for its report, see below, p. 129 & n. 2.

2. She was Blagrave's pretty niece,

but proved 'too melancholy' to be employed in this way: above, iii. 67; below, p. 242.

he acquitted himself well in it.[1]   But however, something sticks against him, he says, with my Lord; at which I am not very sorry, for I believe he is a false fellow.   I walked with him to Pauls, he telling me how my Lord is little at home – minds his carding and little else – takes little notice of anybody; but that he doth not think that he is displeased, as I fear, with me; but is strange to all – which makes me the less troubled.   So walked back home, and late at the office; so home and to bed.   This day Mrs. Turner did lend me, as a rarity, a manuscript of one Mr. Wells, writ long ago, teaching the method of building a ship;[2] which pleases me mightily.   I was at it tonight but durst not stay long at it, I being come to have a great pain and water in my eyes after candle-light.

2.   Up and to my office, and afterwards sat – where great contest with Sir W. Batten and Mr. Wood and that doting fool Sir J. Mennes, that says whatever Sir W. Batten says, though never minding whether to the King's profit or not.   At noon to the Coffee-house, where excellent discourse with Sir W Petty; who proposed it, as a thing that is truly questionable, whether there really be any difference between waking and dreaming – that it is hard not only to tell how we know when we do a thing really or in a dream, but also to know what the difference between one and the other.

Thence to the Change; but hearing[a] at this discourse and afterward with Sir Tho. Chamberlin,[3] who tells me what I heard from others, that the complaints of most Companies were yesterday presented to the committee of Parliament against the Dutch, excepting that of the East India, which he tells me was because they would not be said to be the first and only cause of a

a   MS. 'having'

---

1. There appears to be no trace of the examination (presumably before a committee) or of the letter in the records of the Council and of the Secretary of State. Creed's puritanism led to the same suspicion later: below, vi. 15.

2. John Wells was Storekeeper at Deptford yard in the 1630s and one of the experts then consulted on the building of the *Royal Sovereign*. He was author of one important memorandum on methods of measuring ships, and part-author of another: Oppenheim, pp. 266–7. Pepys did not retain any of his memoranda, or copies of them, in the PL.

3. Governor, E. India Company.

war with Holland, and that it is very probable[a] as well as most necessary that we fall out with that people – I went to the Change and there found most people gone; and so home to dinner, and thence to Sir W Warren's and with him passed the whole afternoon; first looking over two ships of Captain Taylors and Phin Pett's[1] now in building, and am resolved to learn something of that art, for I find it is not hard, and very useful. And thence to Woolwich; and after seeing Mr. Falconer, who is very ill, I to the yard and there heard Mr. Pett tell me several things of Sir W. Batten's ill managements;[2] and so with Sir W. Warren walked to Greenwich, having good discourse; and thence by water, it being now moonshine and 9 or 10 a-clock at night, and landed at Wapping and by him and his man safely brought to my door; and so he home – having spent the day with him very well. So home and eat something and then to my office a while; and so home to prayers[b] and to bed.

3. *Lords day.* Being weary last night, lay long – and called up by W. Joyce; so I rose and his business was to ask advice of me – he being summoned to the House of Lords tomorrow for endeavouring to arrest my Lady Peters for a debt.[3] I did give

a l.h. repl. 'S'-   *b* repl. 'bed'

---

1. John Taylor's yard (like Warren's) was at Wapping. Phineas Pett (son of John Pett) was now building merchantmen at one of the yards in which the Petts had an interest. He wrote to Pepys in September 1664 from Limehouse. *Mar. Mirr.*, 12/431–2.

2. This was Christopher Pett, Master-Shipwright of Woolwich Dockyard, uncle of the above-mentioned Phineas. Pepys made a note of this conversation in NWB, p. 41.

3. Elizabeth, wife of the 4th Baron Petre, was a disorderly character, who had in 1655 already served a term of imprisonment: GEC, iii. 87, n.(*e*). She had owed money for several years to Joyce, who was a chandler in Covent Garden. About

five months previously he had obtained a warrant against her, but she had escaped arrest by pleading privilege as a peeress. (Wives and widows of peers, as well as peers themselves, were at this time exempt from corporal arrest on charges of debt or trespass: Sir E. Coke, *Reports*, 1738, pt vi, 52*b*–54*b*. The privilege was reduced in the reign of William III: D. Ogg, *Engl. in reigns of James II and William III*, p. 502). The case was referred to the committee of privileges of the House of Lords, and Joyce, after one day's imprisonment and a period on bail, was forced to apologise both to the House and to her ladyship. For the papers in the case, see *LJ*, xi. 590, 592, 594, 598; HMC, *Rep.*, 7/176.

him advice and will assist him. He stayed all the morning, but would not dine with me. So to my office and did business. At noon home to dinner; and being set with my wife in the kitchen, my father comes and sat down there and dined with us. After dinner gives me an account what he had done in his*a* business of his house and goods;*b* which is almost finished and he the next week expects to be going down to Brampton again; which I am glad of, because I fear the children of my Lord's that are there, for fear of any discontent.

He being gone, I to my office and there very busy setting papers in order till late at night. Only, in the afternoon my wife sent for me home to see her new laced gown, that is, her gown that is new laced; and endeed, it becomes her very nobly and is well made. I am much pleased with it.

At night to supper, prayers, and to bed.

4. Up, and walked to my Lord Sandwiches and there spoke with him about W. Joyce, who told me he would do what was fit in so tender a point. I can yet discern a coldness in him to admit me to any discourse with him. Thence to Westminster to the painted-chamber[1] and there met the two Joyces – Will in a very melancholy taking. After a little discourse, I to the Lords' House before they sat, and stood within it a good while, while the Duke of Yorke came to me and spoke to me a good while about*c* the new ship at Woolwich[2] – afterward I spoke with my Lord Barkely and my Lord Peterburgh about it. And so stayed without a good while*d* and saw my Lady Peters, an impudent jade, soliciting all the Lords on her behalf; and at last W. Joyce was called in, and by the consequence and what my Lord Peterborough told me, I find that he did speak all he said to his disadvantage and so was committed to the Black Rod[3] – which is

a symbol re-formed   *b* followed by two small smudges
                    repl. 'of'   *d* repl. 't'-

1. See   *Comp.*:   'Westminster Palace'. (R).

2. Probably the *Royal Catherine*; see below, p. 306.

3. He was ordered to be im-prisoned during the pleasure of the House: *LJ*, xi. 592. Peterborough was chairman of the Committee of Privileges: ib., p. 598.

very hard, he doing what he did by the advice of my Lord Peters's own steward. But the Serjeant of the Black Rod did direct one of his messengers to take him in custody, and so he was peaceably conducted to the Swan-with-Two-Necks in Tuttle-street, to a handsome dining-room, and there was most civilly used – my uncle Fenner and his Brother Anthony and some other friends being with him. But who would have thought that that fellow, that I should have sworn could have spoke before all the world, should in this be so daunted as not to know what he said, and now to cry like a child. I protest it is very strange to observe.

I left them*a* providing of his staying there tonight and getting a petition against tomorrow; and so away to Westminster-hall, and meeting Mr. Coventry, he took me to his chamber with Sir Wm. Hickeman, a member of their House and a very civil gentleman. Here we dined very plentifully, and thence to White-hall to the Dukes, where we all met; and after some discourse of the condition of the fleet in order to a Duch war, for that I perceive the Duke hath a mind it should come to, we away to the office, where we sat; and I took care to rise betimes, and so by water to Halfway-house, talking all the way good discourse with Mr. Wayth. And there found my wife,*b* who was gone with her maid Besse to have a walk. But Lord, how my jealous mind did make me suspect that she might have some appointment to meet somebody. But I found the poor souls coming away thence, so I took them back and eat and drank; and then home and after at the office a while, I home to supper and to bed. It was a sad sight methought today, to see my Lord Peters, coming out of the House, fall out with his lady (from whom he is parted) about this business, saying that she disgraced him. But she hath been a handsome woman and is, it seems, not only a lewd woman but very high-spirited.

5. Up very betimes and walked to my Cosen Anth. Joyces, and thence with him to his Brother Will in Tuttle-street, where I find him pretty cheery over he was yesterday (like a coxcomb), his wife being come to him and having had his boy with him last night. Here I stayed an hour or two and writ over a fresh

a repl. 'him'   *b* MS. 'way'

petition,[1] that which was drawn by their solicitor not pleasing me. And thence to the painted-chamber, and by and by away by coach to my Lord Peterburgh's and there delivered the petition into his hand; which he promised most readily to deliver to the House today. Thence back and there spoke to several Lords, and so did his Sollicitor (one that W. Joyce hath promised 5*l* to if he be released); and a great dispute we hear there was in the House for and against it. At last it was carried that he should be bayled till the House meets again[a] after Easter, he giving bond for his appearance. This was not so good as we hoped, but as good as we could well expect.

Anon comes the King and passed the bill[b] for repealing the Triennial act[2] – and another about writts of Errour.[3] I crowded in and heard the King's speech to them; but he speaks the worst that ever I heard man in my life – worse then if he read it all, and he had it in writing in his hand.[4]

Thence, after the House was up and I enquired what the order of the House was, I to W. Joyce with his Brother and told them all. Here was Kate come, and is a comely fat woman. I would not stay dinner, thinking to go home to dinner; and did go by water as far as the bridge, but thinking that they would take it kindly my being there to be bailed for him if there was need, I returned. But finding them gone out to look after it, only Will and his wife and sister left and some friends that came to visit him – I to Westminster-hall; and by and by, by agreement to Mrs. Lanes lodging, whither I sent for a lobster and with Mr. Swayne and his wife eat it, and argued before them mightily for

a repl. 'to'   *b* s.h. repl. l.h. 'Tr'-

1. Dated this day; summarised (with two later petitions) in HMC, *Rep.*, 7/176.

2. *LJ*, xi. 593; 16 Car. II c. 1. See above, p. 94, n. 1.

3. 'An Act for preventing of Abatements of Writts of Error upon Judgements in the Exchequer'; 16 Car. II c. 2.

4. For this speech, see *LJ*, loc. cit.; for Charles's poor elocution, see above, iv. 250 & n. 4, 251. Pepys had no right to be present, but members of the public did sometimes crowd in on these occasions. At both the opening and closing of sessions it was difficult to exclude strangers: cf. Sir J. Neale, *Eliz. House of Commons*, p. 353.

Hawly.[1] But all would not do, though I made her angry in calling her old and making her know what herself is. Her body was out of temper for any dalliance; and so after staying there three or four hours, but yet taking care to have my oath safe of not staying a quarter of an hour together with her, I went to W. Joyce, where I find the order come and Bayle (his father and brother) given and he paying his fees, which come to above 12*l*, besides 5*l* he is to give one man and his charges of eating and drinking here, and 10*s* a day as many days as he stands under Bayle – which I hope will teach him hereafter to hold his tongue better then he used to do. Thence with Anth. Joyces wife alone home, talking of Will's folly. And having set her down, home myself, where I find my wife dressed as if she had been abroad, but I think she was not. But she answering me some way that I did not like, I pulled her by the nose; indeed, to offend her, though afterward, to appease her,[a] I denied it, but only it was done in jest. The poor wretch took it mighty ill; and I believe, besides wringing her nose, she did feel pain and so cried a great while. But by and by I made her friends. And so after supper to my office a while, and then home to bed.

This day great numbers of merchants came to a grand committee of the House to bring in their Claymes against the Dutch. I pray God guide the issue to our good.

6. Up and to my office – whither by and by came John Noble, my father's old servant, to speak with me. I smelling the business, took him home; and there all alone he told me how he had been serviceable to my brother Tom in the business of his getting his servant, an ugly jade, Margeret, with child. She was brought to bed in St. Sepulchers parish of two children. One is dead, the other is alive; her name Elizabeth and goes by the name of Taylor, daughter to John Taylor. It seems Tom did a

a MS. 'here'

---

1. I.e. for the match between Hawley and Betty Lane which had been hanging fire for some years. Pepys had vowed on the previous 29 February to make no more attempts to overcome the girl's reluctance, for fear of offending her. The Swaines were probably William Swaine and his wife, victuallers, who lived next door but one to the Dog Tavern in New Palace Yard.

great while trust one Crawly with the business, who daily got money of him; and at last, finding himself abused, he broke the matter to J. Noble – upon a vow of secrecy. Toms first plot was to go on the other side the water and give a beggar-woman something to take the child. They did once go, but did nothing, J. Noble saying that seven year hence the mother might come to demand the child and force him to produce it, or to be suspected of murther. Then, I think it was, that they consulted and got one Cave, a poor pensioner in St. Brides parish, to take it, giving him 5*l*; he thereby promising to keep it for ever, without more charge to them. The parish hereupon indite the man Cave for bringing this child upon the parish, and by Sir Rd. Browne is sent to the Counter. Cave thence writes to Tom to get him out. Tom answers him in a letter of his own hand, which J Noble showed me, but not signed by him, wherein he speaks of freeing him and getting security for him, but nothing as to the business of the child or anything like it. So that for as much as I could guess, there is nothing therein to my brother's prejudice as to the main point; and therefore I did not labour to tear or take away the paper.

Cave being released, demands 5*l* more to secure my brother for ever against the child. And he was forced to give it him – and took bond of Cave in 100*l*, made at a Scrivener's, one Hudson I think in the Old Bayly, to secure John Taylor and his assigns &c. (in consideration of 10*l* paid him) from all trouble or charge of meat, drink, clothes and breeding of Elizabeth Taylor. And it seems, in the doing of it, J Noble was looked upon as the assigns of this John Taylor. Noble says that he furnished Tom with this money, and is also bound by another bond to pay him 20*s* more this next Easter Monday. But nothing for either sum appears under Toms hand. I told him how I am like to lose a great sum by his death and would not pay any more myself, but I would speak to my father about it against the afternoon. So away he went. And I all the morning in my office busy and at noon home to dinner – mightily oppressed with wind. And after dinner took coach and to Paternoster-Row and there bought a pretty silk for a petticoat for my wife, and thence set her down at the New Exchange; and I leaving the coat at Unthankes, went to White-hall; but the Councell meeting at Worcester-house, I went thither and there delivered to the Duke of Albemarle a paper touching some Tanger business. And thence to the Change for my wife and walked to my father's, who was packing up some things for the country. I took him up and told him this business of Tom; at which the poor wretch was much troubled and desired me that I would speak with J Noble and do what I could and thought fit in it, without concerning him in it. So I went to Noble and saw the bond that Cave did give and also Toms letter which I mention above. And upon the whole, I think some shame may come but*a* that it will be hard, from anything I see there, to prove the child to be his. Thence to my father and told what I had done and how I had quieted Noble by telling him that though we are resolved to part with no more money out of our own purses, yet if he can make it appear a true*b* debt, that it may be justifiable for us to pay it, we will do our parts to get it paid, and said that I would have it paid before my own debt.

So my father and I both a little satisfied, though vexed to think what a rogue my brother was in all respects. I took my wife by coach home; and to my office, where late with Sir Wm. Warren, and so home to supper and to bed.

I heard today that the Dutch have begun with us by granting letters of mart against us. But I believe it not.

7. Up and to my office, where busy; and by and by comes Sir W Warren and old Mr. Bond in order to the resolving me some questions about*c* masts and their proportions; but he could say little to me to my satisfaction and so I held him not long but parted. So to my office, busy till noon, and then to the Change, where high talk of the Duch's protest against our Royall*d* Company in Guinny[1] and their granting letters of Marke against us there. And everybody expects a war, but I hope it will not yet be so nor that this is true. Thence to dinner, where my wife got me a pleasant French Fricasse of veale for dinner. And thence to the office, where vexed to see how Sir W. Batten ordered things

a repl. 'and'   *b* repl. 'due'   *c* repl. 'against'   *d* repl. 'g'

---

1. Probably the protest (7 June 1663) from the Director-General of the Dutch W. Africa Company to Francis Selwyn, agent of the English Royal African Company. A translation was sent from Holland to the Secretary of State on 21/31 March: PRO, SP 84/169, n.f.

this afternoon (*vide* my office book; for about this time I have begun, my notions and informations increasing now greatly every day, to enter all occurrences extraordinary in my office in a book by themselfs);[1] and so in the evening, after long discourse and eased my mind by discourse with Sir W. Warren, I to my business late; and so home to supper and to bed.

8. Up betimes and to the office; and anon it begin to be fair, after a great shower this morning; Sir W. Batten and I by water (calling his son Castle by the way, between whom and I no notice at all of his letter the other day to me) to Deptford; and after a turn in the yard, I went with him to the Almes-house to see the new building which[a] he with some ambition is building of there, during his being Maister of Trinity-house.[2] And a good work it is; but to see how simply he answered somebody concerning

a repl. 'what'

---

1. Presumably his 'Navy White Book', PL 2581 (incorporated in the PL, according to Pepys's catalogue, between 1700 and 1703). On p. 43 is a note about Batten's unreasonable severity against Warren. The first entry is dated 6 October 1663, but may well have been made later, as this passage implies. Pepys first mentions the need for a personal memorandum book at 20 June 1662, and it appears that he then began to keep a book of reference which has now disappeared. (Cf. above, iv. 11 & n. 1; ib., p. 241, n. 3.) The 'Navy White Book' was of a different nature – a reformer's handbook of abuses, of things that went wrong. The last entry is dated December 1672; before completion it was bound in white vellum and entitled on the spine 'Navy White Book': below, 9 April 1669. It seems to have been this book to which Pepys refers in a letter to Coventry of 28 July 1667, where it is described as 'observations I have (I hope usefully) made on

points wherein want of order, industry, and foresight in matters within the disposal of this Office has not (to tell truth) smally contributed to what his Majesty has suffered in the pursuit of this war – which project, though calculated chiefly for the service of a war, yet will it (I doubt not) administer considerations of use in peace': *Further Corr.*, p. 180.

2. Since the 15th century the corporation had maintained a hospital of 21 almshouses adjoining their hall. C. R. B. Barrett (*Trin. House*, p. 113) believes that Batten was now rebuilding some of these old houses; and this view may be not incompatible with the corporation's minute of 18 May 1664 that six persons were to be appointed to occupy the 'new houses': HMC, *Rep.*, 8/1/sect. i. 252*b*. Another group of almshouses was later built in Church St, Deptford, for which Pepys himself, as an Elder Brother, drafted regulations. See N. Dews, *Hist. Deptford*, p. 246; J. R. Tanner in *EHR*, 44/581.

setting up the arms of the corporation upon the door, that[a] and anything else; he did not deny it but said he would leave that to the Maister that comes after him.

There I left him and to the King's yard again and there made good enquiry into the business of the poop lanterns; wherein I find occasion to correct myself mightily for what I have done in the contract with the platerer and am resolved, though I know not how, to make them to alter it, though they signed it last night. And so I took Stanes home with me by boat and discoursed it; and he will come to reason when I can make him to understand it.[1]

No sooner landed but it fell a mighty storm of rain and hayle; so I put into a Cane-shop and bought one to walk with, cost me 4s-6d – all of one Joynt.

So home to dinner, and had an excellent Good friday dinner of pease porridge – and apple pie.

So to the office all the afternoon, preparing a new book for my contracts.[2] And this afternoon came home the office globes, done to my great content. In the evening, a little to visit Sir W Pen, who hath a feeling this day or two of his old pain.[3] Then to walk in the garden with my wife, and so to my office a while, and then home to the only Lenten supper I have had of wiggs and ale. And so to[b] bed. This morning betimes came to my office to me Boatswain Smith of Woolwich, telling me a notable piece of knavery of the officers of that yard and Mr. Gold, in behalf of a contract made for some old ropes by Mr. Wood. And I believe I shall find Sir W. Batten of the plot – (*vide* my office daybook).[4]

a repl. 'he'   *b* repl. 'to prayers and'

---

1. Thomas Stanes was the glazier. For the contract (31 March; for four poop lanterns), see *CSPD 1664–5*, pp. 132, 136. Pepys had commended it to the Board and to the Duke as cheaper by 40% than previous contracts, but Batten had refused to sign it on 7 April because he had not read it: NWB, p. 45.

2. For Pepys's contract-books, see above, iii. 65, n. 2.

3. Gout, from which he had suffered much in 1663.

4. No day-books have been traced, and none were listed among the books remaining in the office in October 1688: BM, Add. 9303, ff. 52–3, 124–5. Batten was an old friend of Wood. There is no note of the 'plot' in the NWB.

9.   The last night, whether it was from cold I got today upon
《 *Sicke.* 》 the water I know not – or whether it was from my
mind being over-concerned with Stanes's business of
the platery of the navy, for my minde was mighty troubled with
that business all night long – I did wake about one a-clock in the
morning, a thing I most rarely do – and pissed a little with great
pain.   Continued sleepy, but in a high fever all night, fiery hot
and in some pain.   Toward morning I slept a little.   And
waking, found myself better – but pissed with some pain.   And
rose, I confess, with my clothes sweating, and it was somewhat
cold too;   which I believe might do me more hurt – for I continued cold and apt to shake all the morning, but that some
trouble with Sir J. Mennes and Sir W. Batten kept me warm.
At noon home to dinner upon tripes.   And so though not well,
abroad with my wife by coach to her tailor's and the New
Exchange;   and thence to my father's and spoke one word with
him;   and thence home, where I find myself sick in my stomach
and vomited, which I do not use to do.   Then I drank a glass or
two of Hypocras, and to the office to despatch some business
necessary.   And so home and to bed – and by the help of
Mithrydate slept very well.

10.   *Lords* [*d*]*ay.*   Lay long in bed; and then up and my wife
dressed herself,[a] it being Easterday.   But I not being so well
as to go out, she (though much against her will) stayed at home
with me – for she had put on her new best gown, which endeed
is very fine now with the lace.*   And this morning her tailor
brought home her other new laced silk gown, with a smaller
lace and new petticoat I bought the other day – both very pretty.
We spent the day in pleasant talk and company one with another ⟨reading in Dr. Fullers book what he says of the family of
the cliffords and Kingsmils⟩[1] and at night, being myself better
then I was, by taking a glister which did carry away a great deal
of wind – I, after supper at night, went to bed and slept well.

a   MS. 'himself'

---

1. Elizabeth Pepys through her maternal grandmother, Dorothea, daughter of Sir Conyers Clifford, claimed relationship with the Clif-fords, Earls of Cumberland.   Fuller's *Worthies* has a section on the Clif-fords, but omits both the Kingsmills and the Pepyses.   Cf. above, iii. 26.

11. Lay long, talking with my wife. Then up and to my chamber, preparing papers against my father comes to lie here for discourse about country business. Dined well with my wife at home, being myself not yet thorough well, making water with some pain; but better then I was and all my fear of an ague gone away.

In the afternoon my father came to see us. And he gone, I up to my morning's work again; and so in the evening a little to the office and to see Sir W. Batten, who is ill again. And so home to supper and to bed.

12. Up; and after my wife had dressed herself very fine in her new laced gown, and very handsome endeed – W. Howe also coming to see us – I carried her by coach to my uncle Wights and set her down there; and W. Howe and I to the Coffee-house, where we sat talking about getting of him some place under my Lord of advantage, if he should go to sea. And I would be glad to get him secretary and to out Creed if I can – for he is a crafty and false rogue.[1]

Thence a little to the Change, and thence took him to my Uncle Wight – where dined my father, poor melancholy man, that used to be as full of life as anybody – and also my aunts brother Mr. Sutton, a merchant in Flanders, a very sober, fine[a] man – and Mr. Cole and his lady. But Lord, how I used to adore that man's talk,[2] and now methinks he is but an ordinary man. His son a pretty boy endeed, but his nose unhappily awry. Other good company and an indifferent, and but indifferent, dinner for so much company. And after dinner got a coach, very dear, it being Easter time and very foul weather, to my Lord's and there visited my Lady. And leaving my wife there, I and W. Howe to Mr. Pagets and there heard some musique, not very good – but only one Dr. Walgrave, an Englishman bred at Rome, who plays the best upon the lute that I ever heard man.

a   repl. 'pretty'

---

1. See below, p. 210, n. 2.
2. I.e. Mr Cole's. He was probably the lawyer of that name who appears to have been a friend of the Wights. But possibly Jack Cole, an old schoolfellow of Pepys whose conversation he valued.

Here I also met Mr. Hill, the little merchant. And after all was done, we sung. I did well enough a psalm or two of Lawes;[1] he I perceive hath good skill and sings well – and a friend of his[2] sings a good bass.

Thence late; walked with them two as far as my Lord's, thinking to take up my wife and carry them home. But there being no coach to be got, away they went. And I stayed a great while, it being very late, about 10 a-clock, before a coach could be got. I found my Lord and ladies and my wife at supper. My Lord seems very kind. But I am apt to think still the worst, and that it is only in show, my wife and Lady being there.

So home and find my father come to lie at our house; and so supped and saw him, poor man, to bed – my heart never being fuller of love to him, nor admiration of his prudence and pains heretofore in the world then now, to see how Tom hath carried himself in his trade – and how the poor man hath his thoughts going to provide for his younger children and my mother. But I hope they shall never want. So myself and wife to bed.

13. Though late, past 12, before we went to bed – yet I heard my poor father up; and so I rung up my people and I rose and got something to eat and drink for him; and so abroad – it being a mighty foul day, by coach, setting my father down at Fleetstreet; and I to St. James – where I found Mr. Coventry (the Duke being now come thither for the summer) with a gold-smith, sorting out his old plate to change for new; but Lord, what a deal he hath. I stayed and had two or three hours dis-course with him – talking about the disorders of our office, and I largely to tell how things are carried by Sir W. Batten and Sir J. Mennes to my great grief. He seems much concerned also, and for all the King's matters that are done after the same rate everywhere else, and even the Dukes household matters too – generally with corruption, but most endeed*a* with neglect and indifference. I spoke very loud and clear to him my thoughts of

a MS. 'an end'

---

1. See above, i. 285, n. 5. (E).   2. Possibly Thomas Andrews. (E).

Sir J. Mennes and the other, and trust him with the using of them.

Then to talk of our business with the Dutch; he tells me fully that he believes it will not come to a warr. For first he showed me a letter from Sir George Downing,[1] his own hand, where he assures him that the Dutch themselfs do not desire but above all things fear it. And that they neither have given letters of Mart against our ships in Guinny, nor doth De Ruyter stay at home with his fleet with an eye to any such thing, but for want of a wind, and is now come out and is going to the Streights.[2]

He tells me also that the most he expects is that upon the merchants' complaints, the parliament will represent them to the King, desiring his securing of his subjects against them. And though perhaps they may not directly see fit, yet even this will be enough to let the Dutch know that the Parliament do not oppose the King; and by that means take away their hopes, which was that the King of England could not get money or do anything towards a war with them. And so thought themselfs free from making any restitution – which by this they will be deceived in.

He tells me also that the Dutch States are in no good order themselfs, differing one with another. And that for certain none but the States of Holland and Zealand will contribute towards a war, the other reckoning themselfs, being inland, not concerned in the profits of war or[a] peace.

But it is pretty to see what he says. That those here that are

a repl. 'of'

---

1. Envoy-extraordinary to the United Provinces.

2. This letter has not been traced. But cf. Downing's similar letters from The Hague to Arlington (29 March/8 April; PRO, SP 29/176, ff. 35–7), and to Clarendon (8/18 April, *CSPClar.*, v. 389–90). Downing was deceived. De Ruyter was in fact about to begin one of his most remarkable voyages. After cruising in the Mediterranean he suddenly and secretly sailed for W. Africa, captured all but one of the re-cent British acquisitions on the Guinea Coast and then crossed the Atlantic to raid Barbados and Newfoundland. Laden with plunder, he returned by the north of Scotland, evading the guard of the English fleet, and re-gained harbour in July 1665. His departure now was further delayed by the weather and he did not put to sea until 28 April/8 May: Lister, iii. 305 (Downing to Clarendon, 6/16 May).

forward for a war at Court, they*ᵃ* are reported in the world to be
only designers of getting money into the King's hands. They
that elsewhere are for it have a design to trouble the kingdom and
to give the fanatics an opportunity of doing hurt. And lastly,
those that are against it (as he himself for one is very cold therein)
are said to be bribed by the Dutch.[1]

After all this discourse he carried me in his coach, it raining
still, to Charing-cross and there put me into another; and I
calling my father and brother, carried them to my house to
dinner – my wife keeping bed all day, she having those upon her.

All the afternoon at the office with W. Boddam, looking over
his perticulars about the Chest of Chatham, which show enough
what a knave Commissioner Pett hath been all along, and how
Sir W. Batten hath gone*ᵇ* on in getting good allowances to
himself and others out of the poor's money.[2] Time will show all.

So in the evening to see Sir W. Penn and then home to my
father to keep him company, he being to go out of town. And
up late with him and my brother John, till past 12 at night, to
make up papers of Tom's accounts fit to leave with my Cosen
Scott.[3] At last we did make an end of them, and so after supper
all to bed.

14. Up betimes. And after my father's eating something, I
walked out with him as far as Milk-street, he turning down to
Cripplegate to take coach. And at the end of the street I took

a repl. 'says'   *b* repl. 'received'

---

1. Although Clarendon (writing
several years later) bracketed his
enemy Coventry with Arlington as
one of those who had favoured war
(*Life*, ii. 303+), this report of
Pepys's is a much better indication of
his attitude. It confirms the memoranda Coventry wrote on the subject
in 1665 and later: Longleat, Coventry
MSS, 102; BM, Add. 32094, ff. 50+.

2. For the commission of enquiry
into the Chest, see above, p. 105 &
n. 2. William Bodham was clerk
to the commission; he was now

working on a summary of the
Chest's accounts, 1660–3. Pett
should have attended this meeting,
but excused himself. He and Batten
were on the 20th ordered to bring in
their accounts. BM, Add. 9317, ff.
3r, 4r, 5r, 5v.

3. Pepys retained the accounts he
drew up of Tom's estate (dated this
day), together with the papers on
which they were based, and also the
papers concerning his father's administration of the state: Rawl. A 182, ff.
290–351.

leave, being much afeared I shall not see him here any more, he doth decay so much every day. And so I walked on, there being never a coach to be had till I came to Charing-cross; and there Collonell Froud[1] took me up and carried me to St. James's – where with Mr. Coventry and Povy &c. about my Lord Peterborough's accounts;[2] but Lord, to see still what a puppy that Povy is with all his show is very strange. Thence to Whitehall and W. Coventry and I and Sir W Rider resolved upon a day to meet and make an end of all that business.

Thence walked with Creed to the Coffee-house in Covent garden, where no company. But he told me many fine experiments at Gresham College, and some demonstrating that the heat and cold of the weather doth rarify and condense the very body of glasse; as, in a Bolt head with cold water in it, put into hot water, shall first, by rarifying the glass, make the water sink, and then when the heat comes to the water, makes that rise again. And then put into cold water, makes the water, by condensing the glass, to rise; and then when the Cold[a] comes to the water, makes it sink – which is very pretty, and true; he saw it tried.[3]

Thence by coach home and dined above with my wife by her bedside – she keeping her bed, those being upon her. So to the office, where a great conflict with Wood and Castle about their New England masts.[4]

So in the evening, my mind a little vexed but yet without reason, for I shall prevail, I[b] hope, for the King's profit. And so home to supper and to bed.

15. Up; and all the morning with[c] Captain Taylor at my house, talking about things of the Navy; and among other things, I showed him my letters to Mr. Coventry, wherein he acknowledges that nobody to this day did ever understand so much as I have done. And I believe him, for I perceive he did

a l.h. repl. s.h. ? 'heat'   *b* repl. 'as'   *c* repl. 'I was'

---

1. Philip Frowde, secretary to the Duchess of York.

2. See above, p. 48, n. 1.

3. See Robert Hooke's description of this demonstration in Birch, i. 411; he had conducted the experiment on 6 April. Creed was now a fellow of the Royal Society.

4. See above, p. 6, n. 4.

very much listen to every article, as things new to him – and is contented to abide by my opinion therein in his great contest with us about his and Mr. Woods masts. At noon to the Change, where I met with Mr. Hill the little merchant, with whom I perceive I shall contract a musicall acquaintance.[1] But I will make it as little troublesome as I can.

Home and dined; and then with my wife by coach to the Duke's house and there saw *The German Princesse* acted – by the woman herself.[2] But never was anything, so well done in earnest, worse performed in Jest upon the stage. And endeed, the whole play, abating the drollery of him that acts her husband, is very simple, unless here and there a witty sprankle or two. We met and sat by Dr. Clerke. Thence homewards, calling at Madam Turner's. And thence set my wife down at my aunt Wight's and I to my office till late and then at 10 at night fetched her home; and so again to my office a little and then to supper and to bed.

16. Up and to the office, where all the morning upon the dispute of Mr. Wood's masts. And at noon with Mr. Coventry to the Affrican-house. And after a good and pleasant dinner, up with him, Sir W Rider, simple Povy (of all, the most ridiculous fool that ever I knew to pretend to business) and Creed and Vernatty, about my Lord Peterborough's accounts; but the more we look into them, the more we see of them that makes dispute – which made us break off; and so I home and there find my wife and Besse gone over the water to Halfway-house; and I after them, thinking to have gone to Woolwich, but it was too late; so eat a cake and home, and thence by coach to have spoke with Tom Trice about a letter I met with this afternoon from my Cosen Scott, wherein he seems to deny proceeding as my father's atturney in administring for him in my Brother Tom's estate. But I find him gone out of town and so

1. Thomas Hill remained a close friend until his death in Lisbon in 1675. It was he who later introduced the musician Cesare Morelli into Pepys's service as an amanuensis. (E).
2. Mary Moders, the impostor:

see above, iv. 163 & n. 4. The play is ascribed to John Holden in 'The session of the poets': *Poems on affairs of State, 1660–1714*, vol. i (ed. G. deF. Lord), p. 336. It was not printed. This is the first record of a performance. (A).

returned vexed home and to the office, where late writing a letter to him.[1]   And so home and to bed.

17. *Lords day.*   Up; and I put on my best cloth black suit and my velvet cloak, and with my wife, in her best laced suit, to church – where we have not been these nine or ten weeks.   The truth is, my jealousy hath hindered it, for fear she should see Pembleton.   He was here today, but I think sat so as he could not see her; which did please me, God help me, mightily – though I know well enough that in reason this is nothing but my ridiculous folly.   Home to dinner; and in the afternoon, after long consulting whether to go to Woolwich or no to see Mr. Falconer, but endeed to prevent my wife going to church, I did however go to church with her, where a young simple fellow did preach – I slept soundly all the sermon; and thence to Sir W Pens, my wife and I, and there sat talking with him and his daughter; and thence with my wife walked to my[a] Uncle Wights and there supped; where very merry, but I vexed to see what charges the vanity of my aunt puts her husband to among her friends,* and nothing at all among ours.[2]   Home and to bed.

Our parson Mr. Mills his own mistake in reading of the service was very remarkable; that instead of saying "We beseech thee to preserve to our use the kindly fruits of the earth"[b] – he cries, "Preserve to our use our gracious Queene Katherine."[3]

18.   Up; and by coach to Westminster and there solicited W. Joyces business again.[4]   And did speak to the Duke of Yorke about it – who did understand it very well.   I afterward did without the House fall in company with my Lady Peters and

a repl. 'Sir'   *b* repl. symbol rendered illegible

---

1. Cf. the draft letter from Pepys to Benjamin Scott (20 April) in Rawl. A 182, f. 312r (printed in *Family Letters*, pp. 7–8). Pepys regretted Scott's decision and pointed out that his father would never have undertaken the administration had it not been for Scott's promise to act as his attorney.

2. Pepys is perhaps thinking of her large dinner party on 12 April.

3. The passage is from the Litany. Pepys himself misquotes it: the phrase is 'to give and preserve'.

4. See above, p. 109, n. 3.

endeavoured to mollify her; but she told me she would not, to redeem her from hell, do anything to release him, but would be revenged while she lived, if she lived the age of Methusalem.

I made many friends, and so did others. At last it was ordered by the Lords that it[a] should be referred to the Committee of Privileges to consider. So I, after discoursing with the Joyces, away by coach to the Change – and there, among other things, do hear that a Jew hath put in a policy of 4 per cent to any man to insure against a Dutch warr for four months.[1] I could find in my heart to take him at this offer, but however will advise first; and to that end took coach to St. James, but Mr. Coventry was gone forth; and I thence to Westminster, where Mrs. Lane was gone forth and so I missed of my intent to be with her this afternoon. And therefore, meeting Mr. Blagrave, went home with him and there he and his Kinswoman sang but I was not pleased with it, they singing methought very ill, or else I am grown worse to please then heretofore. Thence to the hall again; and after meeting with several persons and talking there, I to Mrs. Hunts (where I knew my wife and my aunt Wight were about business); and they being gone to walk in the park, I went after them with Mrs. Hunt, who stayed at home for me; and finding them, did by coach, which I had agreed to wait for me, go with them all and Mr. Hunt and a kinswoman of theirs, Mrs. Steward, to Hide-park, where I have not been since last year – where I saw the King with his periwigg, but not altered at all.[2] And my Lady Castlemayne in a coach by herself, in Yellow satin and a pinner on. And many brave persons. And myself, being in a hackney and full of people, was ashamed to be seen by the world, many of them knowing me.

Thence in the evening home, setting my aunt at home; and thence we and sent for a Joynt of meat to supper, and thence to the office at 11 a-clock at night, and so home to bed.

a MS. 'I'

---

1. Three months, according to a newsletter of this day: HMC, *Heathcote*, p. 148.

2. This was the first occasion on which Pepys had seen him wear one. For the fashion, see above, iv. 358, n. 1.

19. Up and to St. James's, where long with Mr. Coventry, Povy &c. in their Tanger accounts; but such the folly of that coxcomb Povy that we could do little in it. And so parted for that time, and I to walk with Creed and Vernatz in the physique garden in St. James park, where I first saw Orange-trees – and other fine trees.[1] So to Westminster-hall and thence by water to the Temple; and so walked to the Change and there find the Change full of news from Guiny; some say the Dutch have sunk our ships and taken our fort and others say we have done the same to them.[2] But I find by our merchants that something is done, but is yet a secret among them. So home to dinner and then to the office; and at night with Captain Taylor, consulting how to get a little money by letting him the *Elias* to fetch masts from New England.[3] So home to supper and to bed.*a*

20. Up; and by coach to Westminster and there solicited W. Joyces business all the morning. And meeting in the Hall with Mr. Coventry, he told me how the Committee for Trade have received now all the complaints of the merchants against the Dutch, and were resolved to report*b* very highly the wrongs they have done us (when God knows, it is only our own negligence and laziness that hath done us the wrong); and this to be made to the House tomorrow. I went also out of the hall with Mrs.

a entry crowded into bottom of page   *b* repl. 'reported'

---

1. The Physic Garden lay, apparently, between the palace and the Spring Garden Wall, and had been constructed by the Molletts: *CTB*, i. 280. John Rose had in 1661 been put in charge of it and 'of all the orange trees and other trees and greens therein to be planted': ib., p. 294. Orange trees are said to have been introduced into English gardens in the reign of Henry VIII: Evelyn, i. 9 & n. 2; v. 427. For methods of cultivation at this time, see *Garden Book of Sir Thomas Hanmer* (ed. Rohde), pp. 129–32.

2. Cf. HMC, *Heathcote*, p. 149

(similar conflicting news in a newsletter, The Hague, 15 April). In fact, Capt. Robert Holmes had taken Goree and most of the Dutch settlements on the Gold Coast in the early part of this year. In the autumn de Ruyter recovered these conquests and destroyed every English settlement except Cape Coast Castle. Open war followed in March 1665.

3. This was a frigate. She sank on the return voyage: below, p. 321. The trade was mostly carried by large mast ships built in New England.

Lane to the Swan at Mr Herberts in the Palace-yard to try a couple of bands. And did (though I had a mind to be playing the fool with her) purposely stay but a little while and kept the door open and called the maister and mistress of the house one after another to drink and talk with me, and showed them both my old and the new bands. So that as I did nothing, so they are able to bear witness that I had no opportunity there to do anything.[1]

Thence by coach[a] with Sir W Pen home, calling at the Temple for Lawes's Psalms[2] – which I did not so much (by being against my oath[b]) buy, as only lay down money till others be bound better for me; and by that time I hope to get money of the Treasurer of the Navy by bill; which according to my oath, shall make me able to do it.

At home dined, and all the afternoon at a Comittee of the Chest. And at night comes my aunt and Uncle Wight and Nan Ferrers and supped merrily with me – my uncle coming in an hour after them, almost foxed. Great pleasure by discourse with them. And so they gone, late to bed.

21. Up pretty betimes and to my office, and thither came by and by Mr. Vernatz and stayed two hours with me; but Mr. Gauden did not come and so he went away to meet again anon. Then comes Mr. Creed; and after some discourse, he and I and my wife by coach to Westminster (leaving her at Unthankes her tailors) hall and there at the Lords House heard that it is ordered that upon submission upon the knee, both to the House and my Lady Peters, W. Joyce shall be released. I forthwith made him submit and ask pardon upon his knees; which he did before several Lords. But my Lady would not hear it, but swore she would post the Lords, that the world might know what pitiful Lords the King hath – and that Revenge was sweeter to her then milk – and that she would never be satisfied unless he stood in a

---

    a repl. 'water he'   *b* l.h. repl. same word badly written

---

1. Cf. his resolution of the pre-   2. See above, i. 285, n. 5. There
ceding 29 February.   is no copy in the PL. (E).

pillory and demand pardon there.[1]   But I perceive the Lords are ashamed of her.   And so I away, calling with my wife at a place or two to enquire after a couple of maids recommended to us; but[a] we find both of them bad.   So set my wife at my Uncle Wights, and I home and presently to the Change, where I did some business.   And thence to my Uncles and there dined very well; and so to the office; we sat all the afternoon but no sooner sat but news comes my Lady Sandwich was come to see us; so I went out, and running up (her friend however before me) I perceive by my dear Lady's blushing that in my dining-room she was doing something upon the pott; which I also was ashamed of and so fell to some discourse, but without pleasure, through very pity to my Lady.   She tells me, and I find true since, that the House this day hath voted that the King be desired to demand right for the wrong done us by the Dutch, and that they will stand[b] by him with their lives and fortunes[2] – which is a very high vote, and more then I expected.   What the issue will be, God knows.   My Lady, my wife not being at home, did not stay but, poor good woman, went away, I being mightily taken with her dear visitt.   And so to the office, where all the afternoon till late; and so to my office and then to supper and to bed – thinking to rise betimes tomorrow.

22.   Having directed it last night, I was called up this morning before 4 a-clock.   It was full light, enough to dress myself; and so by water against tide, it being a little coole, to Greenewich and thence (only that[c] it was somewhat foggy till the sun got to some

a repl. 'for'   *b* repl. 'stam'   *c* repl. 'for'

---

1. In a petition of 20 April, Joyce told the Committee of Privileges that Lady Petre was demanding a large sum of money as compensation from him: HMC, *Rep.*, 7/176. For the case, see above, p. 109, n 3.

2. *CJ*, viii. 548. The committee appointed to consider 'how the Trade of the Nation may be improved and advanced' reported *nem. con.* that 'the several and respective Wrongs, Dishonours and Indignities, done to his Majesty by the Subjects of the United Provinces, by invading of his Rights in *India*, *Africa*, and elsewhere ... [are] the greatest Obstruction of our Foreign Trade'. The House resolved *nem. con.* to present an address to this effect to the King, and assured him 'that they will, with their Lives and Fortunes, assist his Majesty against all Opposition whatsoever'. See also *CSPD 1663-4*, p. 562.

heighth) walked with great pleasure to Woolwich, in my way
staying several times to listen to the nightingales. I did much
business both at the Ropeyard and the other and one Floate.[1]
I discovered[a] a plain cheat, which in time I shall publish, of Mr.
Ackeworths.[2] Thence, having visited Mr. Falconer also, who
lies still sick but hopes to be better, I walked to Greenwich, Mr.
Deane with me. Much good discourse, and I think him a very
just man; only, a little conceited, but yet very able in his way.
And so he by water with me also to town. I home, and
immediately dressing myself, by coach with my wife to my Lord
Sandwiches; but they having dined, we would not light but went
to Mrs. Turners and there got something to eat; and thence,
after reading part of a good play, Mrs. The, my wife and I in
their coach to Hide parke, where great plenty of gallants. And
pleasant it was, only for the dust.[3] Here I saw Mrs. Bendy, my
Lady Spillman's fair daughter that was, who continues yet very
handsome. Many others I saw, with great content. And so
back again to Mrs. Turners, and then took a coach and home.
I did also carry them into St. James's park and showed them the
garden.[4]

   To my office awhile while supper was making ready, and so
home to supper and to bed.

   23. *Coronacion day*.[5] Up; and after doing something at my
office, and it being a holiday, no sitting likely to be, I down by
water to Sir W Warren's, who hath been ill, and there talked

            a l.h. repl. s.h. 'discor' –

---

1. The other yard was either the
main dockyard or the timber yard.
The float was a raft or stage (usually
made of old masts): NWB, p. 83.
   2. William Ackworth (Storekeeper at Woolwich) was now
accused of embezzling a cable: Rawl.
A 174, ff. 4–5. Pepys had already
noticed the faultiness of his book-
keeping: above, iii. 136. Cf. also

below, p. 156; 18 March 1668 etc.
   3. A common complaint: cf.
Shadwell's *The Answer*: 'And then
in Hide-Park do repair/To make a
dust and take no Air.' Cf. also below,
p. 139; vi. 77.
   4. The Physic Garden: see above,
p. 127 & n. 1.
   5. Cf. above, ii. 83.

long with him; good discourse, especially about Sir W. Batten's knaveries and his son Castle['s] ill language of me behind my back, saying that I favour my fellow-Traytours[1] – but I shall be even with him. So home and to the Change, where I met with Mr. Coventry – who himself is now full of talk of a Dutch war, for it seems the Lords have concurred in the Commons' vote about it[2] and so the next week it will be presented to the King. Insomuch that he doth desire we would look about to see what stores we lack, and buy what we can. Home to dinner, where I and my wife much troubled about my money that is in my Lord Sandwiches hand,[3] for fear of his going to sea and be killed. But I will get what of it out I can.

All the afternoon, not being well, at my office and there did much business, my thoughts still running upon a warr and my money.

At night home to supper and to bed.

24. *Lords day.* Up; and all the morning in my chamber setting some of my private papers in order[4] – for I perceive that now public business takes up so much of my time that I must get time a-Sundays or a-nights to look after my own matters.

Dined and spent all the afternoon talking with my wife. At night, a little to the office and so home to supper and to bed.

25. Up; and with Sir W Pen by coach to St. James's; and there up to the Duke, and after he was ready, to his closet – where most of our talk about a Dutch war, and discoursing of things endeed now for it. The Duke (which gives me great good hope) doth talk of setting up a good discipline in the fleet.

In the Duke's chamber there is a bird, given him by Mr. Pierce the surgeon, comes from the East Indys – black the greatest part,

---

1. Probably Warren in particular; both Pepys and Warren had served the Protectorate governments.
2. *LJ*, xi. 600; see below, p. 135 & n. 6.
3. See above, iv. 286.
4. On this day 'layd up' his Brampton papers in his 'high presse' in his chamber: see Sotheby's *Catalogue*, 30 November 1970, no. 223.

with the finest coller of white about the neck. But talks many things, and neyes like the horse and other things, the best almost that ever I heard bird in my life.[1]

Thence down with Mr. Coventry and Sir W Rider, who was there (going along with us from the East Indya-house today) to discourse of my Lord Peterborough's accounts.[2] And then walked over the parke and in Mr. Cutler's coach with him and Rider as far as the Strand; and thence I walked to my Lord Sandwiches, where by agreement I met my wife and there dined with the young ladies; my Lady being not well, kept her chamber. Much simple discourse at table among the young ladies. After dinner walked in the garden, talking with Mr. Moore about my Lord's business. He told me my Lord runs in debt every day more and more, and takes little care how to come out of it. He counted to me how my Lord pays use now for above 9000*l*[3] – which is a sad thing, especially considering the probability of his going to sea in great danger of his life – and his children, many of them, to provide for.

Thence, the young ladies going out to visit, I took my wife by coach out through the City, discoursing how to spend the afternoon – and conquered, with much ado, a desire of going to a play. But took her out at White-chapel and to Bednell-green; so to Hackny, where I have not been many a year, since a little child I boarded there. Thence to Kingsland by my nurse's house, Goody Lawrence, where my brother Tom and I was kept when young.[4] Then to Newington-green and saw the outside of Mrs. Herberts house where she lived, and my aunt Ellen[5] with her. But Lord, how in every point I find myself to over-value things when a child. Thence to Islington, and so to St. John's to

---

1. Almost certainly a mina from Bengal. Many were imported by the E. India Company later in the century, but this appears to be the earliest known specimen to have arrived: Sir W. Foster, *John Company*, pp. 88–9. For two early drawings, see E. Albin, *Nat. hist. birds* (1734), ii, pl. 38; George Edwards, *Nat. hist. uncommon birds* (1743), i, pl. 17.

2. See above, p. 48, n. 1.
3. For Sandwich's finances, see below, p. 206 & n. 1.
4. Pepys and his brother were the fifth and sixth in a succession of eleven children born to their parents between 1627 and 1641. Only four survived childhood. See below, p. 361 & n. 1.
5. Ellen Kite, sister of Pepys's mother.

the Red bull and there saw the latter part of a rude Prize fight*a**1 –
but with good pleasure enough. And thence back to Islington
and at the Kings-head, where Pitts lived, we light and eat and
drunk for remembrance of the old house sake. And so through
Kingsland again and so to Bishopsgate, and so home with great
pleasure – the country mighty pleasant; and we with great content home, and after supper to bed. Only, a little*b* troubled at
the young ladies leaving my wife so today, and from some
passages fearing my Lady might be offended. But I hope the
best.

26. Up, and to my Lord Sandwiches; and coming a little too
early, I went and saw W. Joyce, and by and by comes in Anthony
– they both owning a great deal of kindness received*c* from me
in their late business. And endeed, I did what I could, and yet
less I could not well do. It hath cost the poor man above 40*l*,
besides he is likely to lose his debt. Thence to my Lord's;
and by and by he comes down, and with him (Creed with us)
I rode in his coach to St. James, talking about W. Joyces business.
My [Lord] merry; and my Lady Peters, he says, is a drunken Jade,
he himself having seen her drunk in the Lobby of their house.
I went up with him to the Duke, where methought the Duke
did not show him any so great fondness as he was wont; and
methought my Lord was not pleased that I should see the Duke
made no more of him – not that I know anything of any unkindness, but I think verily he is not as he was with him in his esteem.
By and by the Duke went out and we with him through the
park; and there I left him going into White-hall and Creed and
I walked round the park, a pleasant walk, observing the birds,*2*
which is very pleasant; and so walked to the ⟨New⟩ Exchange

a MS. 'fought'   *b* repl. 'trouble'   *c* repl. 'to me'

---

1. The Red Bull, an open-air
theatre in St John's St, Clerkenwell,
was used for this purpose after it fell
into disuse as a playhouse. Cf. Act I,
sc. I, of Davenant's play, *The playhouse
to be let* (acted late in the summer of
1663), in which the Player says:

'Tell 'em the Red Bull stands empty
for fencers:/There are no tenants in
it but old spiders./Go, bid the men
of wrath allay their heat/With prizes
there.' (A).

2. See above, ii. 157 & n. 1.

and there had a most delicate dish of curds and cream, and discourse with the good woman of the house, a discreet well-bred
woman and a place of great delight; I shall make it now and
then to go thither.

Thence up; and after a turn or two in the Change, home to the
Old Exchange by coach, where great news and true I saw by
written letters, of strange fires seen at Amsterdam in the ayre; and
not only there, but in other places thereabouts.[1]

The talk of a Duch war is not so hot, but yet I fear it will
come to it at last. So home and to the office, where we sat late.

My wife gone this afternoon to the buriall of my she-Cosen
Scott – a good woman.[2] And it is a sad consideration how the
pepys's decay, and nobody almost that I know in a present way
of encreasing them.[3] At night, late at my office; and so home
to my wife to supper and bed.

27. Up, and all the morning very busy with multitude of
clients, till my head begin to be overloaded. Toward noon I
took coach and to the Parliament-house's door; and there stayed
the rising of the House and with Sir G. Carteret and Mr. Coventry
discoursed of some tar that I have been endeavouring to buy – for
the market begins apace to rise upon us. And I would be glad
first to serve the King well, and next, if I could, I find myself now
begin to cast how to get a penny myself. Home by coach with
Alderman Backewell in his coach, whose opinion is that the
Dutch will not give over that business without putting us to
some trouble to set out a fleet; and then if they see we go on well,
will seek to salve up the matter. Upon the Change, busy.
Thence home to dinner and thence to the office, till my head
was ready to burst with business, and so with my wife by coach;

---

1. Dr D. J. Schove writes: 'Cf.
The Newes, 28 April, p. 275. A
comet was said to have "passed over
the *Hague* like a Pillar of Fire, with a
great Light, and in the passage
seem'd to scatter some sparks . . .".
The phenomenon was probably
auroral: see D. J. Schove in *Journ.
Brit. Astron. Ass.*, 62/38+, 62+; ib.,
63/266+, 321+.'

2. Judith, wife of Benjamin Scott,
buried at St Sepulchre's, Holborn.
She was the daughter of Richard
Pepys, Lord Chief Justice of Ireland
(first cousin of Pepys's father), and
died childless.

3. But Uncle Wight had thought
of a method: below, pp. 145-6.

I sent her to my Lady Sandwich and myself to my Cosen Roger Pepys's chamber. And there he did advise me about our Exchequer business[1] – and also about my brother John; he is put by my father upon interceding for him, but I will not yet seem the least to pardon him, nor can I in my heart.[2] However, he and I did talk how to get him a Mandamus for a fellowship, which I will endeavour.[3]

Thence to my Lady's; and in my way met Mr. Sanchy of Cambrige, whom I have not met a great while. He seems a simple fellow – and tells me their Master, Dr Raynbow, is newly made Bishop of Carlisle.[4]

To my Lady's, and she not being well, did not see her; but straight home with my wife and late to my office, concluding in the business of Woods masts; which I have now done and I believe taken more pains in it then ever any Principall Officer in this world ever did in anything to no profit to this day.[5]

So, weary, sleepy and hungry, home and to bed.

This day the Houses attended the King and delivered their votes to him upon the business of the Dutch; and he thanks them and promises an answer in writing.[6]

28. Up and close at my office all the morning. To the Change, busy, at noon and so home to dinner; and then I to the afternoon at the office till night; and so late home, quite tired with business and without joy in myself, otherwise then that I am by God's grace enabled to go through it and one day hope to have benefit by it. So home to supper and to bed.

29. Up betimes, and with Sir W Rider and Cutler to Whitehall. Rider and I to St. James and there with Mr. Coventry did proceed strictly upon some fooleries of Mr. Povys in my Lord Peterborough's accounts; which will touch him home. And I

1. Robert Pepys's accounts as receiver of assessments for Huntingdonshire: see above, p. 31 & n. 3.

2. For the coolness between them, see above, p. 91.

3. Nothing came of the proposal. The King could order appointment to fellowships in this way.

4. Dr Edward Rainbowe, Master of Magdalene College, 1642–50 and 1660–4, was nominated Bishop of Carlisle in this month.

5. See above, p. 6, n. 4. Pepys's final memorandum on the dispute (30 April) is in NWB, p. 46.

6. *LJ*, xi. 601, 603.

am glad of it, for he is the most troublesome impertinent man
that ever I met with.   Thence to*a* the Change and there, after
some business – home to dinner, where Luellin and Mount came
to me and dined; and after dinner my wife and I by coach to see
my Lady Sandwich, where we find all the children and my Lord
removed, and the house so melancholy that I thought my Lady
had been dead, knowing that she was not well.   But it
seems she hath the mezles, and I fear the small pox – poor lady;
it grieves me mightily, for it will be a sad hour to that family
should she miscarry.   Thence straight home and to the office;
and in the evening comes Mr. Hill the merchant and another with
him that sings well, and we sung some things and good Musique
it seemed to me; only, my mind too full of business to have much
pleasure in it.   But I will have more of it.   They gone, and I
having paid Mr. Moxon for the work he hath done for the
office upon the King's globes,[1] I to my office, where very late,
busy upon Captain Taylors bills for his masts, which I think will
never off of my hand.[2]   Home to supper and to bed.

30.   Up, and all the morning at the office.   At noon to the
Change; where after business done, Sir W Rider and Cutler
took me to the Old James and there did give me a good dish of
Mackrell, the first I have seen this year, very good – and good
discourse.   After dinner we fell to business about their contract
for Tarr, in which and in another business of Sir W. Rider's
Canvas, wherein I got him to contract with me, I hold them to
some terms, against their Wills, to the King's advantage, which I
believe they will take notice of to my credit.[3]

Thence home and by water by a gally down to Woolwich
and there a good while with Mr. Pett upon the new ship[4] –

a repl. 'to'

---

1. On this day a bill for over £20
was registered in the Navy Treasury
for 'new covering' a pair of globes
at the Navy Office: PRO, Adm.
20/5, p. 281. For their purchase, see
above, p. 83.
2. The masts had been delivered
to Chatham yard in January, and
the bills had been sent to Pepys on
21 January: *CSPD 1663–4*, pp. 447,
449.
3. The draft contract for the tar is
dated 28 April; the canvas contract
seems to have gone to Col. Reymes:
CSPD 1664–5, p. 132.
4. The *Royal Catherine*: see below,
p. 306.

discoursing and learning of him.   Thence with Mr. Deane to see
Mr. Falconer, and there find him in a way to be well.

So to the water (after much discourse with great content with
Mr. Deane) and home*ᵃ* late and so to the office;   wrote to my
father, among other things, my continued displeasure against my
brother John, so that I will give him nothing more out of my
own purse;   which will trouble the poor man, but however, it is
fit I should take notice of my brother's ill carriage to me.
Then home and till 12 at night about my monthly accounts,
wherein I have just kept within compass, this having been a
spending month.

So my people being all abed, I put myself to bed very sleepy.

All the news now is what will become of the Dutch business,
whether war or peace.   We all seem to desire it, as thinking
ourselfs to have advantages at present over them;   but for my
part I dread it.   The Parliament promises to assist the King
with lives and fortunes.   And he receives it with thanks, and
promises to demand satisfaction of the Dutch.

My poor Lady Sandwich is fallen sick three days since of the
Mezles.

My Lord Digby's business[1] is hushed up, and nothing made of
it – he gone and the discourse quite ended.

Never more quiet in my family all days of my life then now,
there being only my wife and I and Besse and the little girl
Susan;   the best wenches, to our content, that we can ever expect.

a   MS. 'love'

1. See above, p. 60 & n. 4.

MAY.

1. *Lords day.* Lay long in bed. Went not to church, but stayed at home to examine my last night's accounts, which I find right – and that I am 908*l* Creditor in the world – the same I was last month.

Dined; and after dinner – down by water with my wife and Besse with great pleasure, as low as Greenwich, and so back again, playing as it were leisurely upon the water to Deptford, where I landed and sent my wife up higher, to land below Half-way-house. I to the King's yard and there spoke about several businesses with the officers; and so with Mr. Wayth, consulting about Canvas, to Halfway-house where my wife was; and after eating there we broke and walked home before quite dark. So to supper, prayers, and to bed.

2. Lay pretty long in bed. So up and by water[a] to St. James and there attended the Duke with Sir W. Batten and Sir J. Mennes. And having done our work with him, walked to Westminster-hall; and after walking there and talking of business, met Mr. Rawlinson and by coach to the Change – where I did some business; and home to dinner and presently by coach to the King's play-house to see *The Labarynth*,[1] but coming too soon, walked to my Lord's to hear how my Lady doth; who is pretty well, at least past all fear. There, by Captain Ferrers meeting with a opportunity of my Lord's coach to carry us to the parke anon – we directed it to come to the play-house door, and so we walked, my wife and I and Madamoiselle.[2]

a repl. 'coach'

---

1. ? an English version of Thomas Corneille's *Ariane* (though no translation of it appeared under the title *The Labyrinth* until 1795 in Dublin); or possibly Thomas Forde's tragicomedy, *Love's Labyrinth*, published in his *Virtus Rediviva* (1660) or possibly an adaptation of Walter Hawkes-worth's Latin comedy *Labyrinthus* (first acted at Trinity College, Cambridge, in March 1603), which it resembles in some respects. Played at the TR, Drury Lane. (A).

2. Mlle Leblanc, governess to Sandwich's daughters.

I paid for her going in, and there saw *The Labarinth*, the poorest play methinks that ever I saw, there being nothing in it but the odd accidents that fell out by a lady's being bred up in man's apparel and a man in a woman's. Here was Mrs. Stewart, who is endeed very pretty, but not like my Lady Castlemaine for all that. Thence in the coach to the parke, where no pleasure – there being much dust.[1] Little company. And one of horses almost spoiled by falling down and getting his legs over the pole. But all mended presently; and after riding up and down, home, set Madamoiselle at home, and we home – and to my office, whither comes Mr. Bland and pays me the debt he acknow-ledged he owed me for my service in his business of the *Tanger= Merchant*[2] – twenty pieces of new gold, a pleasant sight – it cheered my heart; and he being gone, I home to supper and showed them her and she poor wretch would fain have kept them to look on, without any other design but a simple love to them; but I thought it not convenient and so took them into my own hand. So after supper to bed.

3. Up; and being ready, went by agreement to Mr. Blands and there drank my morning draught in good Chocolatte, and slabbering my band sent home for another. And so he and I by water to White-hall and walked to St. James, where met Creed and Vernatty and by and by Sir W Rider; and so to Mr. Coventry's chamber and there upon my Lord Peterburgh's accounts,[3] where I endeavoured to show the folly and punish it as much as I could of Mr. Povy, for of all the men in the world, I never knew any man of his degree so great a coxcomb in such imployments. I see I have lost him for ever, but I value it not; for he is a coxcomb and I doubt not over-honest by some things which I see. And yet for all his folly, he hath the good luck now and then to speak his follies in so good words and with as good a show as if it were reason and to the purpose – which is really one of the wonders of my life.

Thence walked to Westminster hall and there in the Lords' House did in a great crowd, from 10 a-clock till almost 3, hear

---

1. Cf. above, p. 130 & n. 3.   3. See above, p. 48 & n. 1.
2. See above, iv. 20 & n. 2.

the cause of Mr. Roberts, my Lord Privy Seales son, against Win,
who by false ways did get the father of Mr. Roberts's wife (Mr.
Brodvill) to give him the estate and disinherit his daughter.[1]
The cause was managed for my Lord Privy Seale by Finch the
Sollicitor. But I do really think*a* that he is truly a man of as
great eloquence as ever I heard, or ever hope to hear in all my
life.[2]

Thence, after long staying to speak with my Lord Sandwich,
at last he coming out to me and speaking with me about business
of my Lord Peterborough, I by coach home to the office, where
all the afternoon. Only stepped home to eat one bit and to the
office again, having eaten nothing before today. My wife
abroad with my aunt Wight and Norbury.

I in the evening to my Uncle Wight's; and not finding them
come home, they being gone to the parke and the Mullbury-
garden, I went to the Change, and there meeting with Mr.
Hempson, whom Sir W. Batten hath lately turned out of his

a repl. 'thing'

---

1. Robert Robartes, son and heir
apparent of Lord Robartes, Lord
Privy Seal, had married Sarah,
daughter of John Bodvile, who had
bequeathed to his daughter and her
son Charles an estate in Wales, in
return for which Lord Robartes had
settled £3000 p.a. on his son and
daughter-in-law. A later will in
favour of Thomas Wynn had been
adjudged fraudulent by a Chancery
decree of 21 January 1664, but the
court had declared its inability to
provide relief in this case and gave
Robartes a year's time in which to
seek relief elsewhere. On 21 March
he had addressed a petition to the
House of Lords, the upshot of which
was the hearing which Pepys here
describes, and an order of 28 November to the Chancellor 'to make

speedy decree ... according to
Equity and Justice'. *LJ*, xi. 606,
608, 609, 630–1; HMC, *Rep.*, 7/175–
6; *CSPD 1663–4*, p. 450; cf. ib.,
1662–3, p. 354.

2. The eloquence of Sir Heneage
Finch, Solicitor-General, was remarkable, but (according to Roger
North) was apt to run away with his
judgement: *Lives of Norths* (ed.
Jessopp), iii. 198. Burnet's comment
(ii. 43) was that his manner was
'laboured and affected: and he saw
it ... despised before he died'.
Pepys seems always to have admired
his style: below, 21 April 1669; PL
2874, p. 432 (an entry in the Brooke
House journal, in which Pepys refers
to his own eloquence in speeches
before the Committee, 1669–70, as
inferior to that of Finch).

place, merely because of his coming to me when he came to town before he went to him.[a1]   And there he told me many rogueries of Sir W. Batten.   How he knows and is able to prove that Captain Cox of Chatham did give him 10*l* in gold to get him to certify for him at the King's coming in.   And that Tom Newborne did make poor men give him 3*l* to get Sir W. Batten to cause them to be entered in the yard; and that Sir W. Batten hath oftentimes said – "By God, Tom, you shall get something and I will have some on't."[2]   His present Clerke[3] that is come in Norman's room hath given him something for his place.   That they live high and (as Sir Frances Clerkes Lady told his wife) do lack money as well as other people, and have bribes of a piece of Sattin and cabinetts and other things from people that deal with him; and that hardly anybody goes to sea or hath anything done by Sir W. Batten but it comes with a bribe; and that this is publicly true – that his wife was a whore and that he had Libells flung within his doors for a cuckold as soon as he was married. That he received 100*l* in money and in other things, to the value of 50 more of Hempson and that he entends to give him back but 50*l*.   That he hath abused the Chest and hath now some 1000*l* by him of it.

I met also upon the Change with Mr. Cutler.   And he told me how for certain Lawson hath proclaimed Warr again with Argiers – though they had at his first coming given back the ships which they had taken, and all their men; though they refused afterward to make him restitution for the goods which they had taken out of them.[4]

a MS. 'home'

---

1. See above, p. 36 & n. 1. William Hempson was Clerk of the Survey at Chatham.

2. John Cox was Master-Attendant at Chatham; Newborne a solicitor.   Pepys has a note of both these stories in NWB, p. 11 (3 May), with a cross-reference (referring to the rest of the stories in this entry): '*vide* my Journall this day', and a variation in Batten's words ('By God, Tom, we must share; thou must have some, and I must some of it').

3. Probably Gilsthropp (Gilsthorpe): below, vi. 244.

4. Eighteen ships were involved: see newsletter (5 May, reporting news from Marseilles) in Tanner 47, f. 135r. This led to the imposition of another treaty on Algiers (below, p. 332 & n. 3), but there was no formal declaration of war: cf. *CSPD Add. 1660–85*, p. 103.

Thence to my Uncle Wights; and he not being at home, I went with Mr. Norbury near hand to the Fleece, a Mum-house in Leaden-hall, and there drank Mum; and by and by broke up, it being about 11 a-clock at night. And so leaving them also at home, went home myself and to bed.

4. Up; and my new Taylor, Langford,[1] comes and takes measure of me for a new black cloth suit and cloak. And I think he will prove a very careful fellow and will please me well. Thence to attend my Lord Peterborough in bed and give him an account of yesterday's proceeding with Povey. I perceive I labour in a business will bring me little pleasure; but no matter, I shall do the King some service. To my Lord's lodgings, where during my Lady's sickness he is. There spoke with him about the same business; back – and by water to my Cosen Scotts; there condoled with him the loss of my Cosen his wife and talked about his matters as atturny to my father in his Administring to my Brother Tom. He tells me we are like to receive some shame about the business of his bastard with Jacke Noble; but no matter, so it cost us no money.

Thence to the Coffee-house and to the Change a while. News uncertain how the Dutch proceed; some say for, some say against a warr. The plague encreases at Amsterdam.[2] So home to dinner; and after dinner to my office, where very late, till my eyes (which begin to fail me nowadays by candle-light) begin to trouble me. Only, in the afternoon comes Mr. Peter Honiwood to see me and gave me 20s, his and his friends'* allowance for my brother John;[3] which, God forgive my pride, methinks I think myself too high to take of him; but it is an ungrateful point of pride in me, which God forgive.

Home at night to supper and to bed.

5. Up betimes to my office, busy; and so abroad to change some plate for my father to send today by the carrier to Bramp-

---

1. His father's new tenant: above, p. 106.

2. It had now reached several of the principal streets: Downing to Clarendon, The Hague, 12/22 April (Lister, iii. 308). See above, iv. 340, n. 2.

3. This is referred to at 3 March 1665 as 'quarterage', and seems to have been an allowance made to John while he was at Cambridge. The Honywoods rented rooms at the Pepys house in Salisbury Court.

ton; but I observe and do fear it may be to my wrong that I change spoons of my uncle Robert's into new and set a *P* upon them – that thereby I cannot claim them hereafter – as it was my brother Tom's practice. However, the matter of this is not great, and so I did it. So to the Change; and meeting*a* Sir W Warren, with him to a tavern and there talked as we used to do, of the evils the King suffers in our ordering of business in the Navy, as Sir W. Batten now forces us by his knavery.

So home to dinner and to the office, where all the afternoon; and thence betimes*b* home, my eyes beginning every day to grow less and less able to bear with long reading or writing – though it be by daylight, which I never observed till*c* now.

So home to my wife – and after supper to bed.

6. This morning up and to my office, where Sympson my Joyner came to work upon altering my closet, which I alter by setting the door in another place, and several other things to my great content.[1] Busy at it all day; only, in the afternoon home and there, my books at the office being out of order, wrote letters and other businesses. So at night, with my head full of the business of my closet, home to bed. And strange it is to think how building doth fill my mind and put out all other things out of my thoughts.

7. Betimes at my office with the Joyners, and giving order for other things about it. By and by we sat all the morning. At noon to dinner; and after dinner comes Deane of Woolwich,[2] and I spent, as I had appointed, all the afternoon with him about

a repl. 'to'   *b* repl. 'late'   *c* repl. 'to'

---

1. For the cost of this and other work in the office, see PRO, Adm. 20/5, p. 308. 'Conveniences and accommodacions for placeing of Papers and Records' were provided. Thomas Simpson was Master-Joiner at Deptford and Woolwich yards, and later made bookcases for Pepys: below, 23 July 1666.

2. Anthony Deane, Assistant-Shipwright, Woolwich.

instructions which he gives me to understand the building of a ship, and I think I shall soon understand it. In the evening a little to my office to see how my work goes forward there. And then home and spent the evening also with Mr. Deane, and had a good supper; and then he [to] bed, he lying at my house.

8. *Lords day.* This day my new tailor, Mr. Langford, brought me home a new*a* black cloth suit and cloak, lined with silk Moyre. And he being gone, who pleases me very well with his work and I hope will use me pretty well – then Deane and I to my chamber, and there we repeated my yesterday's lesson about ships all the morning, and I hope I shall soon understand it. At noon to dinner; and strange how in discourse he cries up Chymistry[1] from some talk he hath had with an acquaintance of his, a Chymist, when, poor man, he understands not one word of it – but I discern very well that it is only his good nature; but in this of building of ships he hath taken great pains, more then most builders I believe have.

After dinner he went away, and my wife and I to church; and after church to Sir W. Penn and there sat and talked with him; and the perfidious rogue seems, as he doth always, mightily civil to us, though I know he hates and envies us.

So home to supper – prayers, and to bed.

9. Up and to my office all the morning, and there saw several things done in my work, to my great content. And at [noon] home to dinner, and after dinner in Sir W. Penn's coach; he set my wife and I down at the New Exchange, and after buying something we walked to my Lady Sandwich, who, good lady, is now, thanks be to God, so well as to sit up and sent to us, if we

---

a MS. 'newt'. Hereabout Pepys makes more s.h. errors than hitherto, and occasionally writes sprawlingly – perhaps an effect of his eye trouble.

---

1. Deane was perhaps talking about the controversy between the apothecaries and the physicians which Pepys had heard discussed on 3 November 1663.

were not afeared, to come up to her; so we did, but she was mightily against my wife's coming so near her – though, poor wretch, she is as well as ever she was as to the mezles, and nothing can I see upon her face. There we sat talking with her above three hours, till 6 a-clock, of several things with great pleasure; and so away – and home by coach, buying several things for my wife in our way home; and so after looking what had been done in my office today with good content, home to supper and to bed – but strange how I cannot get anything to take place in my mind while my work lasts at my office.

This*a* day my wife and I, in our way to paternoster-row to buy things, called upon Mr. Hollyard to advise upon her drying up her issue in her leg, which inclines of it[self] to dry up, and he admits of it that it should be dried up.

10. Up and at my office, looking after my workmen all the morning; and after the office was done, did the same at night; and so home to supper and to bed.

11. Up; and all day, both forenoon and afternoon, at my*b* office, to see it finished by the Joyner and washed and everything in order; and endeed, now my closet is very convenient and pleasant for me. My uncle Wight came to me to my office this afternoon to speak with me about Mr. Maes's business[1] again, and from me went to my house to see my wife; and strange to think that my wife should by and by send for me after he was gone, to tell me that he should begin discourse of her want of children and his also, and how he thought it would be best for him and her to have one between them, and he would give her 500*l* either in money or jewell beforehand and make the child his heyre. He commended her body and discoursed that for all he knew the thing was lawful. She says she did give him a very warm answer, such as he did not excuse himself by*c* saying that he said this in jest but told her that since he saw what her mind

---

a repl. 'This' smudged   *b* repl. 'the'   *c* repl. symbol rendered illegible

---

1. See above, p. 43 & n. 2.

was, he would say no more to her of it, and desired her to make no words of it. It seemed he did say all this in a kind of counterfeit laugh; but by all words that passed, which I cannot now so well set down, it is plain to me that he was in good earnest, and that I fear all his kindness is but only his lust to her. What to think of it of a sudden I know not, but I think not to take notice yet of it to him till I have thought better of it. So, with my mind and head a little troubled, I received a letter from Mr. Coventry about a mast for the Dukes Yacht;[1] which, with other business, makes me resolve to go betimes to Woolwich tomorrow. So to supper and to bed.

12. Up by 4 a-clock and by water to Woolwich, where did some business and walked to Greenwich; good discourse with Deane best part of the way. There met by appointment Comissioner Pett and with him to Deptford, where also did some business; and so home to my office and at noon Mrs. Hunt and her cousin, child, and maid came and dined with me: my wife sick of those in bed. I was troubled at it; but however, could not help it, but attended them – till after dinner; and then to the office and there sat all the afternoon; and by a letter to me this afternoon from Mr. Coventry, I see the first appearance of a war with Holland.[2] So home and betimes to bed, because of rising tomorrow.

13. Up before 3 a-clock; and a little after upon[a] the water, it being very light as at noon and a bright sun rising; but by and by a rainbow appeared, the first that ever in a morning I saw, and then it fell a-raining a little but held up again; and I to Woolwich, where before all the men came to work, I with Mr. Deane spent two hours upon the new ship,[3] informing myself in the names

a repl. symbol rendered illegible

1. The *Anne*, at Greenwich; estimates for repairs had been submitted on 26 March: *CSPD 1663-4*, p. 87.
2. PRO, Adm. 106/8, f. 449; dated this day, urging on naval preparations. War was not declared until March 1665.
3. The *Royal Catherine*, launched on the following 26 October. Most of the men came to work at 5.30 a.m.: NWB, p. 40.

and natures of many parts of her, to my great content, and so back again without doing anything else; and after shifting myself, away to Westminster, looking after Mr. Maes's business and others. In the painted-chamber I heard a fine conference between the sum of the two Houses upon the bill for conventicles.[1] The Lords would be freed from having their houses searched by any but the Lord-Lieutenant of the county. And upon being found guilty, to be tried only by their peers; and thirdly, would have it added that whereas the Bill says that "that ⟨among other things⟩ shall be a conventicle wherein any such meeting is found doing anything contrary to the Liturgy of the Church of England," they would have it added "or practice."[2] The Commons to the Lords said that they knew not what might hereafter be found out which might be called the practice of the Church of England, for there are many things may be said to be the practice of the Church which were never established by any law, either common, Statute, or Cannon - as, singing of psalms – binding up prayers at the end of the Bible – and prayings extempore before and after sermon. And though these are things indifferent, yet things, for aught they at present know, may be started which may be said to be the practice of the Church which would not be fit to allow.

For the Lords' privileges, Mr. Waller[3] told them how tender their predecessors had been of the privileges of the Lords. But however, where the peace of the kingdom stands in competition with them, they apprehend those privileges must give place. He told them that he thought, if they should own all to be the privileges of the Lords which might be demanded, they should be

---

1. The bill 'to prevent and suppresse seditious conventicles', which received royal assent four days later (16 Car. II c. 4; the First Conventicle Act). Members of the public were admitted to conferences between the Houses, though not to the debates of the separate assemblies (cf. below, 5 May 1668). Two conferences were held this day on this bill: *LJ*, xi. 618. For the Painted Chamber, see *Comp.*: 'Westminster Palace'.

2. The bill in its final form incorporated these amendments. Search of peers' houses was to be authorised only by the sign-manual of the King, or by the action of a Lord-Lieutenant, or a Deputy-Lieutenant, or two J.P.s (one of whom was to be of the quorum). Trial for third offences was to be by their peers, and the phrase about the 'practice' of the Church was inserted.

3. Edmund Waller, the poet; M.P. for Hastings.

led like the man (who granted leave to his neighbour to pull off
his horse's tail, meaning that he could not do it at once) that hair
by hair had his horse's tail pulled off indeed.   So the Commons,
by granting one thing after another, might be so served by the
Lords.   Mr. Vaughan,[1] whom I could not to my grief perfectly
hear, did say: if that they should be obliged in this manner to
exempt the Lords from everything, it would in time come to
pass that whatever, be [it] never so great, that should be voted by
the Commons as a thing penall for a commoner, the contrary
should be thought a privilege to the Lords.

That also, in this business, the work of a Conventicle being but
the work of an hour, the cause of a search would be over before
a Lord-Lieutenant, who may be many miles off, can be sent
for.

And that all this dispute is but about 100*l*; for it is said in
the act that it shall be banishment or payment of 100*l*.

I thereupon heard the Duke of Lenox say that there might be
Lords who could not alway be ready to lose 100*l*, or some such
thing.

They broke up without coming to any end in it.

There was also in the Commons' house a great quarrel about
Mr. Prin,[2] and it was believed that he should have been sent to
the towre for adding something to a bill (after it was ordered to
be engrossed) of his own head – a bill for measures for wine and
other things of that sort and a bill of his own bringing in; but it
appeared he could not mean any hurt in it.   But however, the
King was fain to write in his behalf, and all was passed over.[3]

1. See above, p. 103 & n. 1.
2. William Prynne, M.P. for Bath.
3. It was a bill for the better levy-
ing of penalties on retailers of wine,
ale and beer; Prynne (who was
chairman of the committee to which
it had been referred) had altered it at
committee stage – not, as Pepys reports, after the order for ingrossment
was made. He meant only, as he said,
'to rectify some Matters mistaken in
it, and make the Bill agree with the
Sense of the House . . .'.   The matter
had been reported on the 11th, and

sent to a committee, whereupon it
was resolved on the 13th that he be
reprehended and pardoned. The
Speaker told him that the House was
'very sensible of this great Mistake, in
so antient and Knowing a Member,
to break so essential an Order of the
House, as to alter and interline a Bill
after Commitment': *CJ*, viii. 562,
563.   The bill's introduction dates
from 24 March; the Journals do not
reveal that it was Prynne who had
moved it; op. cit., pp. 536, 542.

But it is worth my remembrance that I saw old Ryly the Herald and his son; and spoke to his son, who told me in very bad words concerning Mr. Prin, that the King had given[a] him an office of keeping the Records, but that he never comes thither, nor had been there these six months – so that I perceive they expect to get his imployment from him.[1] Thus everybody is liable to be envied and supplanted.

At noon over to the Leg, where Sir G Ascue, Sir Rob. Parke-hurst and Sir W Pen dined. A good dinner and merry. Thence to White-hall, walking up and down a great while; but the Council not meeting soon enough, I went homeward, calling upon my Cosen Roger Pepys, with whom I talked; and heard so much from him of his desire that I would see my brother's debts paid and things still of that nature, tending to my parting with what I get with pain to serve others' expenses, that I was cruelly vexed. Thence to Sir R. Bernard and there heard something of Pigotts delay of paying our money, that that also vexed me mightily.[2] So home, and there met with a letter from my Cosen Scott which tells me that he is resolved to meddle no more

a repl. 'have'

---

1. William Ryley, sen. (d. 1667; now Lancaster Herald) had in 1660 been replaced as Clerk of the Records in the Tower by Prynne: since then he and his son William had served as Prynne's deputies. Prynne was given the office for life in 1665, and on his death in 1669 Sir Algernon May succeeded him. These criticisms may have had some basis of fact, for Prynne was both busy and unac-commodating, but substantially they are false. He did much to arrange, catalogue and make accessible the archives – mostly Chancery documents – in his charge, and in 1664 published an important collection – the fourth volume of his register of parliamentary writs. In 1661, accord-ing to his own claim, he performed prodigies in uncovering and sorting MSS – employing women and sol-diers in the work. Writing in Sep-tember 1661 to the Master of the Rolls, he revealed a distrust of his assistants. 'The work was so filthy and un-pleasant that Mr. Riley and others would not soil their hands or clothes, nor indanger their healths to assist me it it': HMC, *Verulam*, p. 58. For the state of the archives in general, see Wood, *L. & T.*, ii. 110; F. Peck, *Desiderata Curiosa* (1779), ii. 384; M. Noble, *Hist. College of Arms* (1805), pp. 289–92; R. B. Wernham in L. Fox (ed.), *Engl. hist. scholarship in 16th and 17th centuries*, pp. 11–30.

2. £209 was due this month: above, iv. 309 & n. 1.

with our business of Administering for my father,[1] which altogether makes me almost distracted, to think of the trouble that I
am like to meet with by other folks business, more then ever I
hope to have by my owne. So with great trouble of mind to
bed.

14. Up, full of pain, I believe by cold got yesterday. To the
office, where we sat; and after*a* office, home to dinner, being in
《 *Sicke.* 》 extraordinary pain.[2] After dinner, my pain increasing,
I was forced to go to bed; and by and by my pain ris
to be as great for an hour or two as ever I remember it was in
any fit of the stone, both in the lower part of my belly and in my
back also. No wind could I break. I took a glister, but it
brought away but a little and my heighth of pain fallowed it.
At last, after two hours lying thus in most extraordinary anguish,
crying and roaring, I know not whether*b* it was my great sweating that [made] me do it, but upon getting by chance among my
other tumblings, upon my knees in bed, my pain begin to grow
less and so continued less and less, till in an hour after I was in
very little pain, but could break no wind nor make any water;
and so continued and slept well all night.

15. *Lords day*. Rose, and as I had intended without reference
to this pain, took physic and it wrought well with me. My wife
lying from me tonight, the first time she did in the same house
ever since we were married I think (unless while my father was in
town that he lay with me); she took physic also today, and both
of our physics wrought well; so we passed our time today, our
physic having done working, with some pleasure talking; but I
was not well, for I could make no water yet but a drop or two
with great pain, nor break any wind.
In the evening came Mr. Vernatty to see me and discourse
about my Lord Peterborough's business.[3] And also my Uncle

a repl. 'were'   b repl. 'what'

---

1. See above, pp. 124–5 & n.
2. On this and the following days
Pepys seems to have suffered from the
same symptoms as those of 4–13

October 1663. He passed what were
probably two renal calculi on 7
March 1665.
3. See below, p. 153 & n. 1.

Wight and Norbury; but I took no notice nor showed any different countenance to my Uncle Wight or he to me, for all that he carried himself so basely to my wife the last week – but will take time to make my use of it. So being exceeding hot, to bed and slept well.

16. Forced to rise because of going to the Duke to St. James, where we did our usual business; and thence by invitation to Mr. Pierce's the surgeon, where I saw his wife, whom I had not seen in many months before. She holds her complexion still; but in everything else, even in this her new house and the best rooms in it and her closet, which her husband with some vain-glory took me to show me, she continues the veriest slattern that ever I knew in my life. By and by we to see an experiment of killing a dog by letting opium into his hind leg.[1] He and Dr. Clerke*a* did fail mightily in hitting the vein, and in effect did not do the business after many trials; but with the little they got in, the dog did presently fall asleep and so lay till we cut him up. And a little dog also, which they put it down his throate; he also staggered first, and then fell asleep and so continued; whether he recovered or no after I was gone, I know not – but it is a strange and sudden effect.

Thence walked to Westminster-hall, where the King was expected to come to prorogue the House; but it seems, afterward I hear, he did not come.

I promised to go again to Mr. Pierce's, but my pain grew so great, besides a bruise I got today in my right testicle, which now vexes me as much as the other, that I was mighty melancholy;[2] and so by coach home and there took another glister – but*b* find little good by it; but by sitting still, my pain of my bruise went away; and so after supper to bed – my wife and I having talked

a repl. 'Pie'-   *b* repl. 'and'

1. On 18 May a skin-grafting operation was carried out before the Royal Society, for which this may have been a preparatory exercise: Birch, i. 422, 428, 442. For a dissection of a dog in November 1664, see ib., p. 486. Gunther (iii. 130) states that anaesthesia by intravenous injections of opium had been induced in animals since c. 1656.

2. Cf. above, ii. 194, n. 4.

and concluded upon sending my father an offer of having Pall
come to us to be with us for her preferment, if by any means I
can get her a husband here; which though it be some trouble to
us, yet it will be better then to have her stay there till nobody will
have her, and then be flung upon my hands.

17. Slept well all night and lay long; then rose and wrote
my letter to my father about Pall, as we had resolved last night.
So to dinner and then to the office, finding myself better then I
was and making a little water, but not yet breaking any great stir
of wind; which I wonder at, for I cannot be well till I do do it.
After office, home and to supper and with good ease to bed.
And endeavoured to tie my hands that I might not lay them out
of bed, by which I believe I have got cold; but I could not
endure it.

18. Up and within all the morning, being willing to keep as
much as I could within doors. But receiving a very wakening
letter from Mr. Coventry about fitting of ships, which speaks
something like to be done,[1] I went forth to the office, there to
take order in things. And after dinner to White-hall to a Committee of Tanger, but did little. So home again and to Sir
W Pen – who, among other things of haste in this new order for
ships, is ordered to be gone presently to Portsmouth to look
after the work there. I stayed to discourse with him; and so
home to supper, where upon a fine couple of pigeons, a good
supper. And here I met a pretty Cabinet sent me by Mr. Shales,
which I gave my wife – the first of that sort of goods I ever had
yet – and very conveniently it comes for her closet. Stayed up
late finding out the private boxes,[2] but could not do some of
them; and so to bed, afeared that I have been too bold today in
venturing in the cold.
   This day I begin to drink Butter milke and whey – and I hope
to find great good by it.

---

1. PRO, Adm. 106/8, f. 463; 18
May; warning Pepys of the im-
minent arrival of an order from the
Duke, and urging speed because the
Dutch fleet was already at sea.

2. The   secret   drawers. John
Shales was navy victualler at
Portsmouth: an earlier present from
him is recorded above, p. 72.

19.   Up, it being very rayny weather, which makes it cooler then it was – by coach to Charing-cross with Sir W. Penn, who is going to Portsmouth this day; and left him going to St. James's to take leave of the Duke, and I to White-hall to a Committee of Tanger;   where God forgive how our report of my Lord Peterborough's account was read over and agreed to by the Lords without one of their understanding it.[1]   And had it been what it would, it had gone; and besides, not one thing touching the King's profit in it minded or hit upon.

Thence by coach home again, and all the morning at the office sat – and all the afternoon, till 9 at night, being fallen again to business; and I hope my health*a* will give me leave to fallow it.

So home to supper and to bed – finding myself pretty well. A pretty good stool, which I impute to my whey today – and break wind also.

20.   Up and to my office, whither by and by comes Mr. Cholmely;   and staying till the rest of the company came, he told me how Mr. Edwd. Mountagu is turned out of the Court – not return again.   His fault, I perceive, was his pride, and most of all his affecting to seem great with the Queene; and it seems endeed had more of her eare then everybody else, and would be with her talking alone two or three hours together.[2]   Insomuch that the Lords about the King, when he would be jesting with

a   repl. 'truth'

---

1. For these accounts, see above, p. 48, n. 1. On 11 June Pepys wrote to Vernatty that he was still at work on them: NMM, LBK/8, p. 109.

2. Mountagu (eldest son of the 2nd Lord Mountagu of Boughton) was Master of the Horse to the Queen Mother. His crime was to have tickled or squeezed the Queen's hand. Catherine had then asked the King what it meant, and the King is said to have minced no words in his reply. See Bodl., MS. Eng. Poet. d. 49, f. 168*v*.; A. Boyer, *Hist. Queen Anne* (1722), App. p. 46; MS. notes by Speaker Onslow (derived from 'a near relation of the Sandwich Family') in his copy (Goldsmiths' Lib., Univ. London) of Clarendon's *Life* (ii. 533). 'Ce nouveau Tantale,' wrote the French ambassador de Cominges to Louis XIV (19/29 May), 'n'a peu mesnages ses regards, et . . . il les a pousses si haut, qu'ils se sont allumés dans la source de la lumière': PRO, PRO 31/3/113, f. 182*v*.

them about their wifes, would tell the King that he must have a care of his wife too, for she hath now the gallant.   And they say the King himself did once ask Mountagu how his mistress (meaning the Queen) did.   He grew so proud and despised everybody, besides suffering nobody, he or*a* she, to get or do anything about the Queen, that they all laboured to do him a good turn.   They also say that he did give some affront to the Duke of Monmouth, which the King himself did speak to him of.   But strange it is that this man should, from the greatest negligence in the world, come to be the miracle of Attendance, so as to take all offices from everybody, either men or women, about the Queen – insomuch that he was observed as a miracle.   But that which is the worst, that which in a wise manner performed [would] turn to his greatest advantage, was by being so observed imployed to his greatest wrong, the world concluding that there must*b* be something more then ordinary to cause him to do thus.   So he is gone, nobody pitying, but laughing at him; and he pretends only that he is gone to his father, that is sick in the country.

By and by comes Povey, Creed and Vernatty; and so to their accounts, wherein more trouble and vexation with Povey.   That being done, I sent them going and myself fell to business – till dinner; so home to dinner, very pleasant.   In the afternoon to my office, where busy again; and by and by came a letter from my father, so full of trouble for discontents there between my mother and servants, and such troubles to my father from hence from Cave, that hath my brother's bastard, that I know not what in the world to do; but with great trouble, it growing night, spent some time walking, and putting care as much as I could out of my head, with my wife in the garden; and so home to supper and to bed.

21.   Up, called by Mr. Cholmly, and walked with him in the garden till others came to another Committee of Tanger – as we did meet as we used to do, to see more of Povy's folly; and so broke up and at the office sat all the morning, Mr. Coventry with us; and very hot we are getting out some ships.

At noon to the Change and there did some business; and thence home to dinner and so abroad with my wife by coach to the

a   repl. 'and'   *b*   MS. 'was must'

New Exchange and there laid out almost 40*s* upon her; and so called to see my Lady Sandwich, whom we found in her dining-room, which joyed us mightily; but she looks very thin, poor woman, being mightily broke.[1] She told us that Mr. Mountagu is to return to Court as she hears; which I wonder at and do hardly believe.

So home and to my office, where late; and so home to supper and to bed.

22. *Lords day.* Up and by water to White-hall to my Lord's lodgings; and with him walked to White-hall without any great discourse, nor do I find that he doth mind business at all. Here the Duke of Yorke called me to him to ask me whether I did intend to go with him to Chatham or no; I told him, if he commanded, but I did believe there would be business here for me; and so he told me, then it would be better to stay – which I suppose he will take better then if I had been forward to go.

Thence, after staying and seeing the throng of people to attend the King to chapel; but Lord, what a company of sad idle people they are – I walked to St. James with Collonell Remes; where stayed a good while and then walked to White-hall with Mr. Coventry, talking about business. So meeting Creed, took him with me home and to dinner, a good dinner; and thence by water to Woolwich, where mighty kindly received by Mrs. Falconer and her husband, who is now pretty well again – this being the first time I ever carried my wife thither. I walked to the Docke, where I met Mrs. Ackworth alone at home; and God forgive me, what thoughts I had; but I had not the courage to stay, but went to Mr. Pett's and walked up and down the yard with him and Deane, talking about the despatch of the ships now in haste; and by and by Creed and my wife and a friend of Mr. Falconers came with the boat and called me; and so by water to Deptford, where I landed; and after talking with others, walked to Halfway-house with Mr. Wayth, talking about the business of his supplying us with Canvas, and he told me in discourse several instances of Sir W. Batten's cheats.[2]

1. After her attack of measles.

2. The Board contracted with Robert Waith for the supply of 150 bolts of Ipswich canvas on 28 May: NWB, p. 41; cf. *CSPD 1664-5*, p. 134. Batten wanted to use a rival supplier, Potter: NWB, pp. 41, 48.

So to Halfway-house, whither my wife and them were gone before; and after drinking there, we walked and by water home, sending Creed and the other with the boat home. Then I wrote a letter to Mr. Coventry; and so a good supper of pease, the first I eat this year, and so to bed.

23. Up and to the office, where Sir J. Mennes, Sir W. Batten and myself met and did business, we being in a mighty hurry. The King is gone down with the Duke and a great crew this morning by break of day to Chatham.[1] Toward noon, I and my wife by water to Woolwich, leaving my wife at Mr. Falconers; and Mr. Hater and I with some officers of the yard on board to see several ships how ready*a* they are.[2] Then to Mr. Falconers to a good dinner, having myself carried them a vessel of Sturgeon and a Lampry pye. And then to the yard again; and among other things, did at Mr. Ackworths obtain a demonstracion of his being a knave; but I did not discover it till it be a little more seasonable.[3] So back to the Rope-yard and took my wife and Mr. Hater back, it raining mighty hard of a sudden; but we with the tilt kept ourselfs dry. So to Deptford; did something there; but Lord, to see how in both places the King's business, if ever it should come to a war, is likely to be done – there not being a man that looks or speaks like a man that will take pains or use any forecast to serve the King[4] – at which I am heartily troubled. So home, it raining terribly but we still dry. And at the office late, discoursing with Sir J. Mennes and W. Batten,

a MS. 'they ready'

---

1. The royal party stayed for two nights in a yacht while reviewing the naval preparations against the Dutch. A government newsletter (26 May) reported that the King satisfied himself that his battle-fleet could put to sea in eight days: Tanner 47, f. 153r.

2. See Pepys's notes, 'Minutes for W[oolwich] and Deptford. State of the Ships now in hand to see dispatched out' (23 May; partly in s.h.): PRO, SP 46/136, no. 133; *CSPD Add. 1660–85*, p. 102.

3. Cf. above, p. 130.

4. Writing this day to Coventry about his journey, Pepys reported 'every thing done after the old rate, without life or forecast'; the ships would not be ready to receive victuals for about a fortnight, and there would never be men enough without impressment: *Further Corr.*, pp. 25–6.

who, like a couple of sots, receive all I say but to little purpose. So late home to supper and to bed.

24. Up and to the office, where Sir J. Mennes and I sat all the morning; and after dinner, thither again and after dinner all the afternoon hard at the office till night; and so, tired, home to supper and to bed.

This day I heard that my Uncle Fenner is dead[1] – which makes me a little sad, to see with what speed a great many of my friends* are gone; and more, I fear for my father's sake, are going.

25. Took physic betimes and to sleep; then up, it working all the morning. At noon dined; and in the afternoon in my chamber, spending two or three hours to look over some unpleasant letters and things of trouble to answer my father in about Tom's business and others that vexed [me]. But I did go through it and by that means eased my mind very much. This afternoon also came Tom and Charles Pepys by my sending for; and received of me 40*l*, in part toward their 70*l* Legacy of my Uncles.[2]

Spent the evening talking with my wife, and so to bed.

26. Up to the office, where we sat, and I had some high words with Sir W. Batten about Canvas, wherein I opposed him and all his experience about seams in the middle and the profit of having many breadths and narrow; which I opposed to good purpose, to the rejecting of the whole business.[3]   At noon home to dinner; and thence took my wife by coach, and she to my Lady Sandwich to see her; I to Tom Trice to discourse about my father's giving over*a* his Administratorshipp to my brother.   And thence to Sir

a repl. 'our'

---

1. Thomas Fenner had married Katherine Kite, sister of Pepys's mother.
2. For the legacy from Robert Pepys, see above, iv. 42 & nn.
3. Cf. NWB, p. 22 (26 May): 'I stopped at a full Board, Collonell Reames being there, Sir W. Batten's project of bespeaking the W Country cloth to be of 15 inch wide – or 18, which the Board seemed inclined to have. And very high Sir W. Batten was with me how he should not understand a sail better than I.' Pepys (relying on the advice of sailmakers and on the Dutch example) argued that broad canvas, with few seams, was both cheaper and stronger. See notes in NWB, pp. 21+.

R. Bernard, and there received 19*l* in money and took up my
father's bond of 21*l* – that is, 40*l*, in part of Piggots 209*l* due to
us – which 40*l* he pays for 7 Roods of Meadow in Portholme.[1]
Thence to my wife and carried her to the Old Bayly; and there
we were led to the Questhouse by the church,[2] where all the
kindred were by themselfs at the burial of my uncle Fenner.
But Lord, what a pitiful rout of people there was of them – but
very good service and great company the whole was. And so
anon to church and a good sermon; and so home, having for
ease put my 19*l* into W. Joyces hand, where I left it. So to
supper and to bed – being in a little pain from some cold got
last night – lying without anything upon my feet.

27. Up, not without some pain by cold; which makes me
mighty melancholy, to think of the ill state of my health. To
the office, where busy till my brains ready to break with variety
of business, and vexed for all that to see the service like to suffer
by other people's neglect. Vexed also at a letter from my father,
with two troublesome ones inclosed from Cave and Noble – so
that I know not what to do therein.

At home to dinner at noon. But to comfort my heart,
Captain Taylor this day brought me 20*l* he promised me for my
assistance to him about his masts.[3]

After dinner to the office again, and thence with Mr. Wayth
to St. Catharin's to see some variety of Canvas's,[4] which endeed
was worth my seeing. But only, I was in some pain and so took
not the delight I should otherwise have done. So home to the
office and there busy till late at night; and so home to supper
and to bed.

This morning my Taylor brought me a very tall mayd to be
my cook-maid; she asked 5*l*: but my wife offered her but 3*l*-10*s* –
whether she will take it or no, I know not till tomorrow; but I
am afeared she will be over-high for us, she having last been a

1. See above, iv. 309 & n. 1.
2. St Sepulchre's, Holborn. The
.parish Quest House – so-called after
the 'quest' (inquest) juries which met
in it to enquire into matters of parish
or ward concern – served as an
assembly room for other purposes.

3. John Taylor, shipbuilder, of
Wapping, had recently sent in a bill
for masts: above, pp. 123–4, 136.
4. At Mr Lewen's, the sailmaker's,
where Pepys was shown Suffolk
cloth: NWB, p. 22. St Catherine's
was a precinct east of the Tower.

chamber-maid*ᵃ* and holds up her head, as my little girl Su observed.[1]

28. Up, pretty well as to pain and wind. And to the office, where we sat close and did much business. At noon I to the Change and thence to Mr. Cutler's, where I heard Sir W. Rider was; where I found them at dinner and dined with them – he having yesterday and today a fit of a pain like the gout, the first time he ever had it. A good dinner. Good discourse, Sir W. Rider especially much fearing the issue of a Dutch war – wherein I very highly commend him.[2] Thence home and at the office a while; and then home with Mr. Deane to a second lesson upon my Shipwrightry, wherein I go on with great pleasure. He being gone, I to the office late; and so home to supper and bed. But Lord, to see how my very going to the Change and being without my gowne presently brought me wind*ᵇ* and pain, till I came home and was well again; that I am come to such a pass that I shall not know what to do with myself. But I am apt to think that it is only my legs that I take cold in, from my having so long worn a gowne constantly.

29. *Sunday. Whitsunday. Kings Birth and Restauracion day.* Up; and having received a letter last night, desiring it from Mr. Coventry, I walked to St. James; and there he and I did long discourse together of the business of the office and the war with the Dutch and he seemed to argue mightily with the little reason that there is for all this.[3] For first, as to the wrong we pretend

a repl. 'cook-maid with'
b followed by folio (probably blank on both sides) cut out

1. This was probably the Jane (surname unknown), who was cook-maid from 27 June 1664 to 4 February 1665. The dispute was about her annual wage.
2. Rider was a merchant trading to W. Africa. According to Coventry, writing in 1665, he supported war against the Dutch: Longleat, Coventry MSS 102, ff. 4–5.
3. Cf. his later (and different)

arguments against the war set out in a long memorandum to Falmouth (c. March 1665; BM, Add. 32094, ff. 50+). 'This I confesse had bin more seasonably said before the King was engaged, and should have bin, if commanded': ib., f. 52v. Another copy in Longleat, Coventry MSS 102, ff. 3+. He claimed to have advised Clarendon and Arlington against war on 1 April 1665: HMC, *Rep.*, 5/315.

they have done us – that of the East Indys for their not delivering of Poleron, it is not yet known whether they have failed or no.[1] That of their hindering the *Leopard* cannot amount to above 3000*l*, if true.[2]   That of the Guiny Company, all they had done us did not amount to above 2 or 300*l* he told me, truly.[3]   And that now, from what Holmes without any commission hath done in taking an Island and two Forts, hath set us much in debt to them.[4]   And he believes that Holmes will have been so puffed up with this, that he by this time hath, being enforced with more strength then he had then, hath, I say, done a great deal more wrong to them.

He doth, as to the effect of the war, tell me clearly that it is not any skill of the Dutch that can hinder our trade if we will, we having so many advantages over them, of Windes, good ports, and men.   But it is our pride and the laziness of the merchant.

He seems to think that there may be some Negotiacion which may hinder a war this year; but that he speaks doubtfully, as unwilling, I perceive, to be thought to discourse any such thing.

The main thing he desired to speak with me about was to know whether I do understand my Lord Sandwiches intentions as to going to sea with this fleet; saying that the Duke, if he desires it, is most willing to it; but thinking that twelve ships is not a fleet fit for my Lord to be troubled to go out with, he is[a] not willing to offer it him till he hath some intimations of his mind to go or not.[5]

a   repl. 'will'

---

1. Pulo Run (in the Banda Sea), spice-island in the E. Indies, ceded by the Dutch in 1623, 1654 and 1662, was never in fact surrendered, and was retroceded to them in 1667. At the peace negotiations of 1667 the English asserted that this dispute was 'the true cause of the war': Feiling, p. 105.

2. In 1662–3 the Dutch had prevented an English E. Indiaman (escorted by the *Leopard*) from trading on the Malabar coast.   The loss was calculated at £53,560 in 1667: *Cal. court mins E. India Co. 1664–7* (ed. E. B. Sainsbury), p. 320.

3. For de Ruyter's attack on the Guinea coast, see above, p. 121, n. 2.

4. Holmes took the island of Goree and seven forts, all of which (except Cape Coast Castle, which became the English headquarters) were soon re-occupied by the Dutch. His orders had been to avoid hostilities.

5. Sandwich accepted the command, and there were 18 ships under him at first: Sandwich, p. 144. They cruised in the Downs and the Channel between July 1664 and February 1665.

He spoke this with very great respect as to my Lord, though methinks it is strange they should not understand one another better at this time then to need another's mediacion.

Thence walked over the park to White-hall, Mr. Povy with me, and was taken in a very great showre in the middle of the park, that we were very wet. So up into the House and with him to the King's closet, whither by^a and by the King came, my Lord Sandwich carrying the sword. A Bishop preached; but he speaking too low for me to hear behind the King's closet, I went forth and walked and discoursed with Collonell Reames, who seems a very willing man to be informed in his business of Canvas, which he is undertaking to strike in with us to serve the Navy.[1]

By and by my Lord Sandwich came forth and called me to him; and we fell into discourse a great while about his business, wherein he seems to be very open with me and to receive my opinion as he used to do; and I hope I shall become necessary to him again. He desired me to think of the fitness or not for him to offer himself to go to sea, and to give him my thoughts in a day or two.

Thence, after sermon, among the ladies on the Queenes side; where I saw Mrs. Stuart, very fine and pretty but far beneath my Lady Castlemaine.

Thence with Mr. Povy home to dinner, where extraordinary cheer. And after dinner, up and down to see his house.[2] And in a word, methinks for his perspective upon his wall in his garden[3] and the springs rising up – with the perspective in the little closet –[4] his room floored above with woods of several colours, like, but above the best Cabinet-work I ever saw – his grotto and vault, with his bottles of wine and a well therein to keep them cool – his furniture of all sorts – his bath at the top of his house[5] – good

a repl. 'after'

---

1. A contract was drawn up with Reymes on 2 June: *CSPD 1663–4*, p. 132.

2. One of the smaller houses on the w. side of Lincoln's Inn Fields, being assessed on 14 hearths as against the 36 of the largest, the Earl of Warwick's. Cf. Evelyn, iii. 375 & n. 2; 504. (R).

3. A *trompe l'oeil* by Robert Streeter: Evelyn, iii. 375 & n. 3. (OM).

4. See above, iv. 18 & n. 1 (and illust.); below, p. 212. (OM).

5. Bathrooms were great rarities.

pictures and his manner of eating and drinking, doth surpass all that ever I did see of one man in all my life.

Thence walked home and found my uncle Wight and Mr. Rawlinson, who supped with me. They being gone, I to bed, being in some pain from my being so much abroad today; which is a most strange thing, that in such warm weather the least ayre should get cold and winde in me. I confess it makes me mighty sad and out of all content in the world.

30. Lay long, the bells ringing, it being holiday;[1] and then up and all the day long in my study at home, studying of Ship=making with great content – till the evening; and then came Mr. How and sat and then supped with me. He is a little conceited, but will make a discreet man. He being gone, a little to my office and then home to bed – being in much pain from yesterday's being abroad; which is a consideration of mighty sorrow to me.

31. Up, and called upon Mr. Hollyard, with whom I advised and shall fall upon some course of doing something for my disease of the wind, which grows upon me every day more and more.[2] Thence to my Lord Sandwiches; and while he was dressing, I below discoursed with Captain Cocke and I think, if I do find it fit to keep a boy at all, I had as good be supplied from him with one as anybody.[3] By and by up to my Lord – and to discourse about his going to sea and the message I had from Mr. Coventry to him. He wonders, as he well may, that this course should be taken, and he every day with the Duke (who nevertheless seems most friendly to him), who hath not yet spoke one word to my Lord of his desire to have him go to sea. My Lord doth tell me clearly that were it not that he, as all other men that were of the parliaments side, are obnoxious to reproach, and so is forced to bear what otherwise he would not, he would never suffer everything ⟨to be⟩ done in the Navy and he never be consulted;[4]

1. In celebration of the King's birthday and restoration-day, which this year had fallen on a Sunday.

2. Cf. above, iv. 324 & n. 1.

3. See below, pp. 245, 258. Capt. Henry Cooke (Master of the Children of the Chapel Royal) often found employment for his choir-boys when their voices broke.

4. Sandwich was Lieutenant-Admiral to the Duke of York.

and it seems, in the naming of all these commanders for this fleet, he hath never been asked one Question. But we concluded it wholly inconsistent with his Honour not to go [with] this fleet, nor with the reputation which the world hath of his interest at Court; and so he did give me commission to tell Mr. Coventry that he is most willing to receive any commands from the Duke in this fleet, were it less then it is, and that perticularly in this service. With this message I parted; and by coach to the office, where I found Mr. Coventry and told him this. Methinks, I confess, he did not seem so pleased with it as I expected or at least could have wished; and asked me whether I had told my*a* Lord that the Duke doth not expect his going – which I told him I had. But now, whether he means really that the Duke, as he told me the other day, doth think the fleet too small for him to take, or that he would not have him go, I swear I cannot tell. But methinks other ways might have*b* been used to have put him by, without going in this manner about it; and so I hope it is out of kindness indeed.[1]

Dined at home; and so to the office, where a great while alone in my office, nobody near, with Bagwell's wife of Deptford; but the woman seems so modest that I durst not offer any court-ship to her, though I had it in my mind when I brought her in to me. But am resolved to do her husband a courtesy, for I think he is a man that deserves very well.

So abroad with my wife by coach to St. James, to one Lady Poultny's, where I found my Lord, I doubt at some vain pleasure or other. I did give him a short account of what I had done with Mr. Coventry, and so left him and to my wife again in the coach, and with her to the park; but the Queen being gone by the park to Kensington, we stayed not but straight home and to supper (the first time I have done so this summer); and so to my office doing business, and then to my monthly accounts; where to my great comfort I find myself better then I was still the last month, and now come to 930*l.*

a repl. 'him'   b repl. 'be'

---

1. James was not always friendly towards Sandwich: he had allowed him no credit, e.g., for the Algiers treaty of 1662: see above, iii. 122 & n. 1.

I was told today that upon Sunday night last, being the King's birthday – the King was at my Lady Castlemaine's lodgings (over the hither-gate at Lambert's lodgings)[1] dancing with fiddlers all night almost, and all the world coming by taking notice of it – which I am sorry to hear.

The[a] discourse of the town is only whether a war[b] with Holland or no. And we are preparing for it all we can, which is but little.

Myself subject more then ordinary to pain by winde, which makes me very sad – together with the trouble which at present lies upon me in my father's behalf, rising from the death of my brother – which are many and great. Would to God they were over.

a l.h. repl. s.h. 'My'   b MS. 'wars'

---

1. The Holbein gatehouse in Whitehall Palace, occupied by Maj.- Gen. Lambert during the Protector- ate. (R).

JUNE.

1. Up, having lain long, going to bed very late after the ending my accounts. Being up, Mr. Hollyard came to me; and to my great sorrow, after his great assuring me that I could not possibly have the stone again, he tells me that*a* he doth verily fear that I have it again and hath brought me something to dissolve it – which doth make me very much troubled and pray to God to ease me.

He gone, I down by water to Woolwich and Deptford to look after the despatch of the ships, all the way reading Mr. Spencer's book of Prodigys,[1] which is most ingeniously writ, both for matter and style.

Home at noon and my little girl got me my dinner; and I presently out by water and landed at Somerset-stairs and thence through Coventgarden, where I met with Mr. Southwell (Sir W. Pen's friend), who tells me the very sad newes of my Lord Tiviott's and 19 more commission-officers being killed at Tanger by the Moores, by an ambush of the enemy's upon them while they were surveying their lines; which is very sad, and he says afflicts the King much.[2]   Thence to W. Joyces, where by appointment I met my wife (but neither of them at home); and she and I to the King's house and saw *The Silent Woman*; but methought not so well done or so good [a] play as I formerly thought it to be, or else I am nowadays out of humour.[3]   Before

a repl. 'for cert'-

---

1. John Spencer, *A discourse concerning prodigies; wherein the vanity of presages by them is reprehended, and their true and proper ends asserted and vindicated* (octavo, 105 pp.; 1663); PL 920 (2nd ed., 1665).

2. The engagement had taken place on 3 May. For fuller accounts, see below, pp. 166-7, 179-80; Pepys's informant was Robert Southwell, jun., soon to be appointed a Clerk of the Privy Council (September 1664), Ambassador to Portugal (1665), etc.

3. This was the comedy by Ben Jonson (see above, i. 171 & n. 2). The cast listed by Downes (p. 4) includes Cartwright as Morose, Mohun as Truewit, Mrs Knepp as Epicoene and Kynaston as Dauphin. Kynaston had previously played Epicoene: above, ii. 7, n. 4. (A).

the play was done, it fell such a storm of Hayle that we in the middle of the pit were fain to rise,[1] and all the house in a disorder; and so my wife and I out and got into a little alehouse and stayed there an hour after the play was done before we could get a coach; which at last we did (and by chance took up Joyce Norton and Mrs. Bowles and set them at home); and so home ourselfs and I a little to my office and so home to supper and to bed.

2.[a] Up and to the office, where we sat all the morning; and then to the Change, where after some stay, by coach with Sir J. Mennes and Mr. Coventry to St. James and there dined with Mr. Coventry very finely; and so over the park to White-hall to a Committee of Tanger about providing provisions, money, and men for Tanger.[2] At it all the afternoon; but it is strange to see how poorly and brokenly things are done of the greatest consequence – and how soon the memory of this great man[3] is gone, or at least out of mind, by the thoughts of who goes next, which is not yet known. My Lord of Oxford, Muskerry, and several others are discoursed of. It seems my Lord Tiviotts design was to go out a mile and a half out of the town to cut down a wood in which the enemy did use to lie in ambush. He had sent several spyes; but all brought word that the way was clear, and so might be for anybody's discovery of an enemy before you are upon them. There they were all snapped, he and all his officers, and about 200 men as they say[4] – there being left now in the garrison but four Captains. This happened the 3d of May last, being not before the day twelvemonth of his entering into his government there; but at his going out in the morning, he said to some of his officers, "Gentlemen, let us look to ourselfs, for it was

a page headed l.h. 'June' repl. l.h. 'May'

---

1. To illuminate the auditorium of the Theatre Royal, there was a glazed cupola immediately above the pit, but it was not a good protection against bad weather. Pepys reports that it leaked again on 1 May 1668. (A).

2. Cf. PRO, CO 279/3, ff. 71–3.

3. The 1st Earl of Teviot, the Governor.

4. The correct figure would be nearer 400. This account may be compared with the official report of Sir Tobias Bridges to the King (printed Routh, pp. 67–8). A brief note of the action appeared in *The Intelligencer*, 6 June, p. 368.

this day three years that so many brave Englishmen were knocked on the head by the Moores, when Fines made his sally out."[1]

Here till almost night; and then home with Sir J. Mennes by coach, and so to my office a while and home to supper and bed – being now in constant pain in my back; but whether it be only wind or what it is, the Lord knows; but I fear the worst.

3. Up, still in a constant pain in my back, which much afflicts me with fear of the consequence of it. All the morning at the office; we sat at the office extraordinary, upon the business of our stores;[2] but Lord, what a pitiful account the Surveyor makes of it grieves my heart. This morning before I came out, I made a bargain with Captain Taylor for a ship for the Commissioners for Tanger,[3] wherein I hope to get 40 or 50*l.*

To the Change and thence home and dined; and then by coach to White-hall, sending my wife to Mr. Hunts. At the Committee for Tanger all the afternoon; where a sad consideration to see things of so great weight managed in so confused a manner as it is, so as I would not have the buying of an acre of land bought by – the Duke of Yorke and Mr. Coventry, for aught I see, being the only two that do anything like men. Prince Robert doth nothing but swear and laugh a little, with an oath or two, and that's all he doth.

Thence called my wife and home; and I late at my office and so home to supper and bed, pleased at my hopes of gains by today's work, but very sad to think of the state of my health.

4. Up and to St. James's by coach (after a good deal of talk before I went forth with J. Noble, who tells me that he will secure us against Cave – that though he knows and can prove it, yet nobody else can prove it to be Tom's child[4] – that the bond

1. See Routh, pp. 25–6. The sally, by a force under Maj. William Fiennes, had been made two years before.

2. Cf. Pepys's collection (in his own hand) of information on this subject in Rawl. A 174, ff. 19+: 'The Generall State of the Naval= Stores upon a Survey taken March 166¾ ...'. The Board seems to have been particularly concerned about the supply of masts in storage.

3. This was the *Eagle*, to be used for carrying victuals to Tangier: see below, p. 171 etc.; PRO, AO 1/310/1220.

4. Cf. above, pp. 113–14.

was made by one Hudson, a scrivener next to the Fountain tavern in the Old Bailey – that the children were born and christened and entered in the parish-book of St. Sepulchers[1] by the name of Anne and Elizabeth Taylor – and will give us security against Cave if we pay him the money); and there up to the Duke and was with him, giving him an account how matters go. And of the necessity there is of a power to Presse seamen, without which we cannot really raise men for this fleet of twelve sail. Besides that it will assert the King's power of pressing, which at present is somewhat doubted, and will make the Dutch believe that we are in earnest.[2] Thence by water to the office, where we sat till almost 2 a-clock. This morning Captain Ferrer came to the office to tell me that my Lord hath given him a promise of Young's place in the Wardrobe; and hearing that I pretend a promise to it,[3] he comes to ask my consent; which I denied him, and told him my Lord may do what he please with his promise to me, but my father's condition is not so as that I should let it go if my [Lord] will stand to his word. And so I sent him going, myself being troubled[a] a little at it.

After office I with Mr. Coventry by water to St. James, and dined with him and had excellent discourse from him. So to the Committee for Tanger all the afternoon, where still the same confused doings. And my Lord Fitzharding[4] now added to the Committee, which will signify much. It grieves me to see how brokenly things are ordered.

So by coach home and at my office late; and so to supper and to

a repl. 'a'

---

1. St Sepulchre's, Holborn; the record of the baptisms has not been traced.

2. On 7 June Secretary Bennet was ordered to prepare a warrant to the Admiral authorising a press, and it was issued on the 13th: *CSPD 1664–5*, p. 607; Duke of York, *Mem. (naval)*, p. 93. In September all members of the Navy Board were similarly empowered: PRO, C 66/3061/16–45. The power was 'somewhat doubted' not only be-

cause war had not yet been declared but also on general constitutional grounds. See *Cat.*, i. 120+; J. R. Hutchinson, *The Press-gang*; Ehrman, pp. 115+. For difficulties in applying it in the following autumn, see Tedder, pp. 106–7; and cf. below, vi. 43, 49; 30 June and 2 July 1666.

3. A promise had been made to Pepys's father: above, ii. 113 & n. 3.

4. A great favourite both of the King and of the Duke of York.

bed – my body, by plenty of breaking of wind, being just now pretty well again, having had a constant akeing in my back these five or six days.

Mr. Coventry, discoursing this noon about Sir W Batten (what a sad fellow he is), told me how the King told him the other day how Sir W. Batten, being in the ship with him and Prince Rupert when they expected to fight with Warwicke, did walk up and down sweating, with a napkin under his throat to dry up his sweat. And that Prince Rupert, being a most Jealous man, and perticularly of Batten, doth walk up and down, swearing bloodily to the King that Batten had a mind[a] to betray them today, and that the napkin was a signall; "But by God," says he, "if things go ill, the first thing I will do is to shoot him."[1]

He discoursed largely and bravely to me concerning the different sort of valours, the active and passive valour. For the latter, he brought as an instance Generall Blacke,[2] who in the defending of Taunton and Lime for the Parliament did through his stubborn sort of valour defend it the most *opiniastrement* that ever any man did anything – and yet never was the man that ever made any attaque by land or sea, but rather avoyded it on all, even fair occasions.[3] On the other side, Prince Rupert the boldest attaquer in the world for personal courage; and yet in the

a repl. 'my'

---

1. The incident was alleged to have occurred at the end of July 1648, when the parliamentarian and royalist fleets under Warwick and Rupert respectively met in the mouth of the Thames, but failed to come to action. Warwick appears to have avoided battle, and a storm later parted the ships. Batten was said to have missed a good opportunity of attacking an isolated squadron on its way in the dark from Portsmouth, alleging that they were only colliers. He was pronounced guiltless by Clarendon: *Hist.*, iv. 373. He had only just joined the fleet after escaping from London, and was distrusted by many royalists as a renegade parliamentarian who had once served under Warwick. E. Warburton, *Mem. Rupert* (1849), iii. 251–2; *Mar. Mirr.*, 12/241–2; John R. Powell, *Navy in Engl. Civil War*, pp. 172–5.

2. Robert Blake (d. 1657).

3. Blake had defended Lyme Regis with 500 men against Prince Maurice's 5000 until relieved in May 1644. Then he had taken Taunton, and held it against all odds for close on a year (July 1644–June 1645). Coventry's criticism is wide of the mark: Blake was capable of making attacks – as he did in taking Taunton, or, at sea, in his bold actions at Porto Farina in 1655 and Santa Cruz in 1657.

defending of Bristoll, no man did ever anything worse, he wanting the patience and seasoned head to consult and advise for defence and to bear with the evils of a Siege.[1] The like he says is said of my Lord Tiviott, who was the boldest adventurer of his person in the world, and from a mean man in few years was come to this greatness of command and repute only by the death of all his officers, he many times having the luck of being the only survivor of them all, by venturing upon services for the King of France that nobody else would.[2] And yet no man upon a defence – he being all fury and no judgment in a fight.

He tells me above all of the Duke of Yorke, that he is more himself, and more of judgment is at hand in him, in the middle of a desperate service then at other times – as appeared in the business of Dunkirke, wherein no man ever did braver things or was in hotter service in the close of that day, being surrounded with enemies; and then, contrary to the advice of all about him, his counsel carried himself and the rest through them safe – by advising that he might make[a] his passage with but a dozen with him; "For," says he, "the enemy cannot move after me so fast with a great body, and with a small one we shall be enough to deal with them."[3] And though he is a man naturally Martiall to the highest degree, yet a man that never in his life talks one word of himself or service of his own; but only that he saw such

a repl. 'do'

---

1. Rupert had surrendered Bristol in September 1645 after a short siege. He was blamed at the time, and deprived by the King of his command, but he was in fact without the means of defence.

2. He had served in the French army as a lieutenant-general in command of *Les Gardes Ecossaises*, c. 1644–59: W. Forbes-Leith, *The Scots men-at-arms . . . in France*, ii. 211–12.

3. This refers to the Duke's action in the Battle of the Dunes, near Dunkirk, June 1658, when (serving under the French) he forced his way from the right to the left wing of the Franco-Spanish lines. In his own account, he wrote that he took 20 men with him: 'The Smalness of my number prov'd my best security; for with those who still continued about me, I was strong enough to deal with any loose men, and yet was not so considerable as to provoke any bodys to disband after me' (*Mem. of James II, 1652–60*, ed. A. L. Sells, pp. 269–70). James does not mention any argument about the numbers of the party.

or such a thing, and lays it down for a maxime that a Hector can have no courage. He told me also, as a great instance of some men, that the Prince of Conde's[1] excellence is that there[a] not[b] ⟨being⟩ a more furious man in the world, danger in fight never disturbs him, more then just to make him Civill and to command in words of great obligation to his officers and men but without any the least disturbance in his judgment or spirit.

5. *Lords day.* About one in the morning I was knocked up by my mayds to come to my wife, who is very ill. I rose; and from some cold she got today or something else, she is taken with great gripings, a looseness and vomiting. I lay a while by her upon the bed – she being in great pain, poor wretch. But that being a little over, I to bed again and lay long; and then up and to my office all the morning, setting matters to rights in some accounts and papers; and then to dinner, whither Mr. Sheply,[2] lately come to town, came to me; and after dinner and some pleasant discourse, he went his way, being to go out of town again to Huntington tomorrow. So all the afternoon with my wife discoursing and talking; and in the evening to my office doing business and then home to supper and to bed.

6. Up, and found my wife very ill again, which troubles me – but I was forced to go forth. So by water with Mr. Gauden and others to see a ship hired by me for the Commissioners of Tanger and to give order therein.[3] So back to the office and by coach with Mr. Gauden to White-hall, and there to my Lord Sandwich; and here I met Mr. Townsend very opportunely and

a repl. 'though'   b repl. 'is'

---

1. Louis de Bourbon, 4th Prince de Condé (d. 1686); the great French soldier under whom the Duke of York had served.
2. Edward Shipley, Sandwich's steward at Hinchingbrooke.

3. See above, p. 167 & n. 3 Denis Gauden was the victualling contractor.

Captain Ferrer; and after some discourse we did accomodate the business of the Wardrobe place, that he shall have the reversion if he will take it out by giving a covenant that if Mr. Young dyes before my father, my father shall have the benefit of it [for] his life.[1]

So home; and thence by water to Deptford and there found our Trinity Brethren come from their election to church, where Dr. Britton made methought an indifferent sermon, touching the decency that we ought to observe in God's house, the church; but yet to see how ridiculously some men will carry themselfs, Sir W. Batten did at open table anon, in the name of the whole Society, desire him to print his sermon, as if the Doctor could think that they were fit judges of a good sermon.[2]

Thence by barge with Sir W. Batten to Trinity-house. It seems they have with much ado carried it for Sir G Carteret against Captain Harrison, poor man, who by succession ought to have been it; and most hands were for him, but only they were forced to fright the younger Brethren by requiring them to set their hands (which is an ill course); and then Sir G. Carteret carryed it.[3]

Here was at Dinner my Lord Sandwich, Mr. Coventry, my Lord Craven, and others. A great dinner and good company – Mr. Prin also, who would not drink any health; no, not the King's, but sat down with his hat on all the while; but nobody took notice of it to him at all.[4] But in discourse with the Doctor he did declare himself that he ever was, and hath expressed

1. Robert Ferrer succeeded to the place in October 1667 without Pepys pressing his father's claims.

2. It does not appear to have been printed.

3. Capt. Brian Harrison had been Deputy-Master in 1662–3. He was now made Deputy-Master again, and died shortly afterwards. The first vote was taken by show of hands; the second by signatures.

4. The drinking of healths (much commoner then than now) was disapproved of by Puritans, of whom only a minority were against drink-ing in itself. William Prynne was one of the most prominent Puritans in public life, and in 1628 had published *Healthe's Sicknesse, or A compendious and briefe discourse proving the drinking and pledging of healthes to be sinfull and utterly unlawfull unto Christians.* He was not in any case a republican. The practice of drinking toasts was said to have been introduced into England by soldiers serving in the Dutch Revolt in Elizabeth's reign: H. Peacham, *Compleat Gentleman* (1634, repr. 1906), p. 229.

himself in all his books, for mixt communion against the Presbyterian examinacion.[1]

Thence after dinner by water, my Lord Sandwich and all us Tanger men, where at the Committee, busy till night but with great confusion. And then by coach home, with this content however: that I find myself every day become more and more known, and shall one day hope to have benefit by it. I find my wife a little better. A little to my office; then home to supper and to bed.

7. Up and to the office (having by my going by water, without anything upon my legs yesterday, got some pain up me again), where all the morning. At noon a little to the Change and thence home to dinner, my wife being ill still in bed. Thence to the office, where busy all the afternoon till 9 at night; and so home to my wife – to supper and to bed.

8. All day before dinner with Creed, talking of many things; among others, of my Lord's going so often to Chelsy; and he, without my speaking much, doth tell me that his daughters do perceive all and do hate the place and the young woman there, Mrs. Betty Becke – for my Lord, who sent them thither only[a] for a disguise for his going thither, will come under pretence to see them, and pack them out of doors to the park and stay behind

a repl. 'he'

---

1. Prynne had quarrelled with the Presbyterians on this issue in 1645–6 and again in the 1650s. See esp. his *Vindication of foure serious questions* ... (1645). While he believed that excommunication was a necessary sanction, he held that it should be reserved for serious offences, and should involve exclusion from all the services of the church, not only from communion. The normal Presbyterian examination of communicants for their fitness to receive the sacrament implied, he thought, something dangerously near the Independent principle of reserving communion to those actually in a state of grace. Prynne was 'for mixt communion', i.e. for administering it to all members of the visible church, including sinners, if penitent. He stood for a single, broadly based, national church; his opponents for a collection of purified sects. See W. M. Lamont, *Marginal Prynne*, esp. p. 199.

with her.   But now the young ladies are gone to their mother to Kensington.[1]

To dinner.   And after dinner, till 10 at night in my study, writing of my old broken office-notes in shorthand all in one book,[2] till my eyes did ake, ready to drop out.   So home to supper and to bed.

9.   Up, and at my office all the morning.   At noon dined at home, Mr. Hunt and his kinswoman (wife in the country); after dinner I to the office, where we sat all the afternoon.   Then at night by coach to attend the Duke of Albemarle about the Tanger ship.[3]   Coming back, my wife spied me going home by coach from Mr. Hunts, with whom she hath gained much in discourse today concerning W. Howes discourse of me to him. That he was the man that got me to be Secretary to my Lord and all that I have thereby.   And that for all this I did never give him 6d in my life – which makes me wonder that this rogue dare talk after this manner, and I think all the world is grown false. But I hope I shall make good use of it.   So home to supper and to bed, my eyes[a] akeing mightily since last night.

10.   Up, and by water to White-hall and there to a Committee of Tanger.   And had occasion to see how my Lord Ashwith[4] deports himself; which is very fine endeed, and it joys my heart to see that there is anybody looks so near into the King's business as I perceive he doth in this business of my Lord Peterborough's accounts.

Thence into the parke and met and walked with Captain Sylas Taylor, my old acquaintance while I was of the Exchequer, and Dr. Whore – talking of music and perticularly of Mr. Berchen-

a l.h. repl. l.h. 'eey'-

---

1. At Dean Hodges's: below, p. 178. For Sandwich's affair with Betty Becke, see esp. above, iv. 389–90.

2. Unidentified; probably one of the memoranda books: q.v. above, iv. 241, n. 3.

3. Albemarle had written to Pepys on the 8th asking the whereabouts of one of the ships bound for Tangier: HMC, *Eliot Hodgkin*, p. 163.

4. *Recte* Ashley (later Shaftesbury).

shaw's way,[1] which Taylor magnifies mightily, and perhaps but what it deserves – but not so easily to be understood as he and others make of it. Thence home by water; and after dinner abroad to buy several things: as, a map and powder[a] and other small things; and so home to my office, and in the evening with Captain Taylor by water to our Tanger ship;[2] and so home well pleased, having received 26*l* profit today of my bargain for this ship – which comforts me mightily, though I confess my heart, what with my being out of order as to my health and the fear I have of the money my Lord oweth me and I stand endebted to him in, is much cast down of late.

In the evening home to supper and to bed.

11. Up and to the office, where we sat all the morning – where some discourse aris from Sir G. Carteret and Mr. Coventry which gives me occasion to think that something like a war is expected now indeed. Though upon the Change afterward, I hear too that an Embassador is landed from Holland, and one from their East India Company, to treat with ours[b] about the wrongs we pretend to.[3]

Mr. Creed dined with me; and thence after dinner by coach with my wife, only to take the ayre, it being very warm and pleasant, to Bowe and old Ford and thence to Hackny; there light and played at shuffle-board, eat cream and good cherries; and so with good refreshment home. There to my office, vexed with Captain Taylor about the delay of carrying down the ship hired by me for Tanger.[4] And late, about that and other things, at the office. So home to supper and to bed.

a repl. 'other'   *b* repl. 'us'

---

1. Some of Birchensha's rules for composing are recorded by Taylor: BM, Add. 4910, ff. 47r–49r. BM, Add. 3488 has Birchensha's 'Grand Scale' (c. 1665). (E).

2. The *Eagle*: above, p. 167.

3. Michiel van Gogh (ambassador from the States-General) and his retinue arrived at Gravesend on the 10th: *The Intelligencer*, 12 June, p. 378. For his embassy, see below, p. 181 & n. 3.

4. See below, pp. 276, 292; the *Eagle* was now to be sent down river.

12. *Lords day.* All the morning in my chamber, consulting my lesson of ship building. And at noon Mr. Creed by appointment came and dined with us and sat talking all the afternoon, till about church time my wife and I begin our great dispute about going to Griffins child's christening,[1] where I was to have been godfather; but[a] Sir J. Mennes refusing, he wanted an equal for me and my Lady Batten and so sought for others. Then the question was whether my wife should go; and she having dressed herself on purpose, was very angry and begin to talk openly of my keeping her within doors before Creed; which vexed me to the guts, but I had the discretion to keep myself without passion; and so resolved at last not to go, but to go down by water. Which we did, by H. Russell,[2] to the Halfway-house and there eat and drank; and upon a very small occasion had a difference again broke out, where without any the least cause she had the cunning to cry a great while and talk and blubber; which made me mighty angry in mind but said nothing to provoke her, because Creed was there. But walked home, being troubled in my mind also about the knavery and neglect of Captain Fudge and Taylor, who were to have had their ship for Tanger ready by Thursday last, and now the men by a mistake are come on board, and not any Maister or man or boy of the ship's company on board with them when we came by her side this afternoon. And also, I received a letter from Mr. Coventry[b] this day in complaint of it. We came home; and after supper Creed went home and I to bed. My wife made great means to be friends, coming to my bed's-side and doing all things to please me; and at last I could not hold out, but seemed* pleased and so parted; and I with much ado to sleep, but was easily wakened by extraordinary great rain; and my mind troubled the more, to think what the soldiers would do on board tonight in all this weather.

《13.》 So up at 5 a-clock, and with Captain Taylor on board her at Deptford and found all out of order, only the soldiers civil and Sir Arth. Bassett[3] a civil person. I rated at Captain

a repl. 'for'   *b* blot above name

1. Griffin (Griffith) was the office doorkeeper. The child (Thomas) was buried on the following 17 October.

2. Waterman to the Navy Office.
3. Captain of a company in the Governor's regiment, Tangier.

Taylor, whom contrary to my expectation I found a lying and a very stupid blundering fellow, good for nothing; and yet we talk of him in the Navy as if he had been a excellent officer,[1] but I find him a lying knave – and of no judgment or despatch at all.

After finding the condition of the ship, no master, not above four men, and many ships provisions, sails and other things wanting, I went back and called upon Fudge; whom I found, like a lying rogue, unready to*a* go on board; but I did so hare him that I made him get everything ready and left Taylor and H. Russell to quicken him; and so away and I by water on to White-hall, where I met his Royal Highness at a Tanger Committee about this very thing and did there satisfy him how things are; at which all was pacified without any trouble – and I hope may end well yet; but I confess I am at a vile trouble for fear the rogue should not do his work and I come to shame and loss of the money I did hope justly to have got by it.

Thence walked with Mr. Coventry to St. James's and there spent by his desire the whole morning reading of some old Navy books given him of old Sir John Cookes by the Arch-Bishop of Canterbury that now is;[2] wherein the order that was observed in the Navy then, above what it is now, is very observable, and fine things we did observe in our reading. Anon to dinner. After dinner, to discourse of the business of the Dutch war, wherein he tells me the Dutch do in every perticular, which are but few and small things that we can demand of them, whatever cry we unjustly make, do seem to offer at an accommodation – for they do own that it is not for their profit to have war with England; we did also talk of a History of the Navy of England,

a MS. 'to to'

1. John Taylor had been Master-Shipwright at the Chatham dockyard until his removal (by the Duchess of Albemarle's influence) in 1660: *CSPD 1664–5*, p. 68.

2. Coke had been Deputy-Treasurer of the Navy in 1591, a leading member of the commission of reform of 1618, and a Navy Commissioner, 1621–36. For the Caroline naval MSS in Coventry's possession, see Longleat, Coventry MSS 117. Others (which may be Coventry's) are listed in HMC, *Rep.*, 3/183*b*–184*a*. These latter include the tracts written by Sir William Monson (d. 1643), published by the Navy Records Society in 1902–14. How the MSS had come into Archbishop Sheldon's possession is not known; but Juxon, Sheldon's predecessor at Canterbury, had also been a Navy Commissioner.

how fit it were to be writ; and he did say that it hath been in his mind to propose to me the writing of the history of the late Dutch warr[1] – which I am glad to hear, it being a thing I much desire and sorts mightily with my genius* – and if done well, may recommend me much.   So he says he will get me an order for making of searches to all records &c. in order thereto, and I shall take great delight in doing of it.   Thence by water down to the Tower, and thither sent for Mr. Creed to my house, where he promised to be; and he and I down to the ship and find all things in pretty good order.   And I hope will end to my mind. Thence, having a gally, down to Greenwich and there saw the King's works, which are great a-doing there.[2]   And so to the Cherry-garden[3] and so carried some cherries home; and after supper to bed – my wife lying with me; which from my not being thoroughly well, nor she, we have not done above once these two or three weeks.

14.   Up and to the office, where we sat all the morning and had great conflict about the flags again – and am vexed, methought to see my Lord Berkely not satisfied with what I said. But however, I stop the King's being abused by the flag-makers for the present; I do not know how it may end, but I will do my best to preserve it.[4]

So home to dinner; and after dinner by coach to Kensington, in the way overtaking Mr. Laxton the Apothecary with his wife and daughters, very fine young lasses, in a coach.   And so both of us to my Lady Sandwich, who hath lain this fortnight here at Deane Hodges.[5]

1. Pepys collected materials but never wrote the history. Many of the MSS survive in the PL and Bodleian. The proposed history of the First Dutch War grew into an unfulfilled project for a general history of the navy: above, i, p. cvii. Similarly, Evelyn undertook to write the history of the Second Dutch War, but published only the preface, in 1674: Evelyn, esp. iii. 523, n. 1.

2. See above, p. 75 & n. 3.

3. A pleasure garden at Rotherhithe, the site being now marked by Cherry Garden pier and street. In Pepys's day Cherry Garden Stairs gave access to it. (R).

4. This was probably the dispute about the colours served in by Young and Whistler which Pepys alleged to be inferior to those of Mitchell: NWB, p. 44.

5. Dr Thomas Hodges, Dean of Hereford, Vicar of Kensington, Rector of St Peter's, Cornhill, and chaplain to the King.   He had two houses in Kensington.

Much company came hither today, my Lady Carteret &c.,
Sir Wm. Wheeler and his Lady, and above all Mr. Becke of
Chelsy and wife and daughter, my Lord's Mistress – one that
hath not one good feature in her face and yet is a fine lady, of a
fine Talle* and very well carriaged and mighty discreet. I took
all the occasion I could to discourse with the young ladies in her
company, to give occasion to her to talk; which now and then
she did and that mighty finely, and is I perceive a woman of such
an ayre, as I wonder the less at my Lord's favour to her, and I
dare warrant him she hath brains enough to entangle him. Two
or three hours we were in her company, going into Sir H. Finch's
garden[1] and seeing the fountayne and singing there with the
ladies; and a mighty fine cool place it is, with a great laver of
water in the middle, and the bravest place for music I ever heard.

After much mirth, discoursing to the ladies in defence of the
city against the country or court, and giving them occasion to
invite themselfs tomorrow to me to dinner to my venison
pasty, I got their mother's leave and so good-night – very well
pleased with my day's work; and above all, that I have seen my
Lord's Mistress.

So home to supper. A little at my office and to bed.

15. Up and by appointment with Captain Witham (the
Captain that brought the news of the disaster at Tanger where
my Lord Tiviott was slain) and Mr. Tooker to Beares Quay and
there saw, and more afterward at the several Granarys, several
parcels of Oates. And strange it is to hear how it will heat
itself if laid up green and not often turned. We came not to any
agreement, but did cheapen several parcels; and thence away,
promising to send again to them.

So to the Victualling office and thence home; and in our
garden I got Captain Witham to tell me the whole story of my
Lord Tiviotts misfortune,[2] for he was upon the guard with his
horse near the towne when at a distance he saw the enemy appear

1. Sir Heneage Finch (Solicitor-
General) had lived at Neyt Manor
(later known as Kensington Palace)
since 1663. He had made many
alterations both to the house and to
the grounds, which lay to the south
of it. It was bought by William III
in 1689, and little now remains of the
original building and gardens.
2. See above. p. 166–7.

upon a hill, a mile and half off, and made up to them and with much ado escaped himself; but what became of my Lord he neither knows nor thinks that anybody but the enemy can tell. Our loss was about 400.   But he tells me that the greater wonder is that my Lord Tiviott met no sooner with such a disaster; for every day he did commit himself to more probable danger then this, for now he had the assurance of all his Scouts that there was no enemy thereabouts; whereas he used every day to go out, with two or three with him to make his discoveries, in greater danger – and yet the man that could not endure to have anybody else to go a step out of order to endanger himself.   He concludes him to be the man of the hardest fate, to lose so much honour at one blow, that ever was.   His relation being done, he parted; and so I home to look after things for dinner.   And anon at noon comes Mr. Creed by chance, and by and by the three young ladies,[1] and very merry we were with our pasty, very well baked – and a good dish of roasted chickens – pease – lobsters – strawberries. And after dinner to cards; and about 5 a-clock by water down to Greenwich and up to the top of the hill and there played upon the ground at Cards; and so to the Cherry-garden and then by water, singing finely, to the Bridge and there landed; and so took boat again and to Somersett-house.   And by this time, the tide being against us, it was past 10 of the clock; and such a troublesome passage in regard of my Lady Paulina's fearfulness, that in all my life I never did see any poor wretch in that con- dition.   Being come hither, there waited for them their coach; but it being so late, I doubted what to do how to get them home. After half an hour's stay in the street, I sent my wife home by coach with Mr. Creed's boy – and myself and Creed in the coach home with them; but Lord, the fear that my Lady Paulina was in every step of the way; and endeed, at this time of the night it was no safe thing to go that road, so that I was even afeared myself, though I appeared otherwise.   We came safe, however, to their house, where all were abed.   We knocked them up, my Lady and all the family being in bed.   So put them into doors; and leaving them with the maids, bade them good-night and then into the town,[2] he and I, it being about 12 a-clock 《16.》 and past; and to several houses, Inns, but could get no lodging, all being in bed; at the last house, at last we

---

1. See above, p. 32, n. 2.   2. Kensington.

found some people drinking and roaring, and there got in; and after drinking, got an ill bed, where I lay in my drawers and stockings and waistcoat till 5 of the clock; and so up, and being well pleased with our frolic, walked to Knightsbridge and there eat a mess of cream; and so to St. James's and there walked a little; and so I to White-hall and took coach, and found my wife well got home last night and now in bed. So I to the office, where all the morning, and at noon to the Change; so home and to my office, where Mr. Ackworth came to me (though he knows himself and I know him to be a very knave); yet he came to me to discover the knavery of other people, like the most honest man in the world. However, good use I shall make of his discourse, for in this he is much in the right.[1] He being gone, I to the noon Change, Mr. Creed with me, after we had been by water to see a vessel we have hired to carry more soldiers to Tanger and also visited a rope-ground, wherein I learned several useful things. The talk upon the Change is that De Ruter is dead, with 50 men of his own ship, of the plague at Cales.[2] That the Hollands Embassador here doth endeavour to sweeten us with fair words and things likely to be peaceable.[3] Home, after I had spoke with my Cosen Rd. Pepys upon the Change

---

1. William Ackworth (Store-keeper, Woolwich) had been guilty of a 'plain cheat': above, p. 130 & n. 2. He now told Pepys of the mis-doings of the Clerk of the Cheque at Woolwich who was allegedly falsi-fying the petty-warrant and yard wages accounts: see Pepys's note in NWB, p. 54. Cf. Ackworth's letter to Coventry (7 June) complaining of ill management in the ropeyard: Rawl. A 174, ff. 38+.

2. A canard: de Ruyter did not die till 1676. But he was at this time seriously ill for about three weeks while cruising off 'Cales' (Cadiz): G. Brandt, *Michel de Ruiter* (trans., Amsterdam, 1698), p. 198.

3. The Dutch government at this point appears to have feared a war (see Downing's despatch, 20/30 May, in Lister, iii. 329–31), and had sent an embassy under van Gogh with proposals for a settlement. Downing had returned to London to take part in the discussions. For their failure, see below, p. 264 & n. 4. The optimism to which Pepys alludes was widely shared: see, e.g., PRO, SP 84/171, f. 14v (R. Duke to William-son, The Hague, 10/20 June); *CSPVen.* 1664–6, pp. 26–7 (de-spatch of Venetian ambassador in Paris, 22 June/1 July). Van Gogh had been received incognito by the King on the 13th (ten days or so before his public entry and audience), and was said to have argued that the grievances suffered by the English were to be blamed on the Dutch trading companies, not on the govern-ment: Tanner 47, ff. 167v, 176r, 179r–v.

about*a* supplying us with Bewpers from Norwich; which I should be glad of, if cheap.[1]   So home to supper and bed.

17.   Up, and to my office, where I despatched much business; and then down by water to Woolwich to make a discovery of a cheat providing for us in the working of some of our own-growned tows into new Cordage, to be sold to us for Riga cordage.[2]

Thence to Mr. Falconers, where I met Sir W. Batten and Lady and Captain Tinker, and there dined with them; and so to the dockyard and to Deptford by water and there very long, informing myself in the business of flags and Bewpers – and other things; and so home late, being weary and full of good informations today; but I perceive the corruptions of the Navy are of so many kinds that it is endless to look after them – especially while such a one as Sir W. Batten discourages every man that is honest. So home to my office; there very late and then to supper and to bed, mightily troubled in my mind to hear how Sir W. Batten and Sir J. Mennes do labour all they can to abuse or enable others to abuse the King.

18.   From morning till 11 at night (only, a little at dinner at home) at my office, very busy setting many businesses in order, to my great trouble but great content in the end.   So home to supper and to bed.

Strange to see how pert Sir W Pen is today, newly come from Portsmouth with his head full of great reports of his service and the state of the ships there.[3]   When that is over, he will be just

a repl. ? 'was'

---

1. Both Richard Pepys of London and his father William of Norwich were drapers. A contract for the supply of 26 Norwich bewpers by 'Mr. Pepys' (probably Richard) was concluded on 7 December 1664: *CSPD 1664–5*, p. 137.

2. Pepys had found on enquiry that if the cordage were already tarred, it was difficult to be certain where the hemp had come from: see his note on this case (13 June) in NWB, p. 33. For English 'tows' (hemp fibres), see above, iv. 259 & n. 4.

3. Penn reported that 'every ship there, upon his personal Survey off them, doth look other=gates . . . than the Surveyors book doth speak them to do': NWB, p. 10.

as another man again, or worse. But I wonder whence Mr. Coventry should take all this care for him, to send for him up only to look after his Irish business with my Lord Ormond,[1] and to get the Dukes leave for him to come with so much officiousness, when I am sure he knows him as well as I do,[a] as to his little service he doth.

19. *Lords day.* Up, and all the morning and afternoon (only at dinner at home) at my office, doing many businesses for want of time on the week-days. In the afternoon the greatest shower of rain of a sudden and the greatest and most continued Thunder that ever I heard I think in my life. In the evening home to my wife – and there talked seriously of several of our family concernments; and among others, of bringing Pall out of the country to us here, to try to put her off;* which I am very desirous, and my wife also, of. So to supper – prayers, which I have of late too much omitted. So to bed.

20. It[b] having been a very cold night last night, I had got some cold, and so in pain by wind; and a sure præcursor of pain, I find, is sudden letting off some farts; and when that stops, then my passages stop and my pain begins. Up, and did several businesses; and so with my wife by water[c] to White-hall – she to her father's, I to the Duke, where we did our usual business. And among other discourse of the Dutch, he was merrily saying how they print that Prince Robt., Duke of Albemarle, and my Lord Sandwich are to be Generalls; and soon after is to fallow them "*Vieux Pen*", and so the Duke called him in mirth Old Pen.[2]

a MS. 'to'   *b* repl. '20'   *c* repl. 'coach'

1. Ormond, the Lord Lieutenant, was now on a visit to England, and Penn probably wanted to discuss with him the question of his estates in co. Cork, which had several times been confirmed in his possession, most recently by an order of 7 April 1664, but which were still the subject of certain counterclaims. See above,

ii. 200 & n. 1; Penn, ii. 617–19. Penn also had a company of foot maintained on the Irish establish-ment; HMC, *Ormonde*, n.s., iii. 413.

2. Penn was just 43: '*vieux*' in the sense perhaps of 'old enemy'. He had fought against the Dutch in the war of 1652–4.

They have, it seems, lately wrote to the King to assure him that their setting-out ships were only to defend their fishing-trade and to stay near home, not to annoy the King's subjects; and to desire that he would do the like with his ships – which the King laughs at, but yet is troubled they should think him such a child, to suffer them to bring home their fish and East India Company's ships,*a* and then they will not care a fart for us.[1]

Thence to Westminster-hall, it being term-time. And meeting Pickering, he tells me how my Lady last week went to see Mrs. Becke the mother. And by and by the daughter came in. But that my Lady doth say herself (as he says) that, she knew not for what reason, for she never knew they had a daughter (which I do not believe), she was troubled and her heart did rise as soon as she appeared, and seems the most ugly woman that ever she saw. This, if true, were strange; but I believe it is not.

Thence to my Lord's lodgings and were merry with the young ladies; who make a great story of their appearing before their mother the morning after we carried them, the last week, home so late. And that their mother took it very well, at least without any anger. Here I heard how the rich widow, my Lady Gold, is married to one Neale, after he had received a box on the eare by her brother (who was there a sentinel in behalf of some Courtier) at the door; but made him*b* draw, and wounded him. She called Neale up to her and sent for a priest, married presently, and went to bed. The brother sent to the Court and had a Serjeant sent for Neale; but Neale sent for him up to be seen in bed, and she owned him for her husband.[2] And so all is past. It seems Sir H. Bennet did look after* her.

---

a repl. 'goods'   *b* repl. 'his'

---

1. The herring fleets had just gone out from most Dutch ports: PRO, SP 84/171, f. 24*r*. Six warships were reported to have been sent with them to the Scottish grounds (*CSPVen. 1664–6*, p. 28), but on 10/20 May the English ambassador had reported that the language of the States-General was still pacific: Lister, iii. 329–30. The English, knowing of the approach of a Dutch fleet of E. Indiamen, also sent a flotilla northwards, allegedly to protect English fishing: *CSPVen. 1664–6*, p. 34.

2. A licence for the marriage of Thomas Neale, groom-porter (bachelor, of 22) and Elizabeth Gould (widow, of 21) was issued on 13 June 1664. Cf. above, p. 1 & n. 2.

My Lady very pleasant. After dinner came in Sir Tho. Crew and Mr. Sidny, lately come from France; who is grown a little, and a pretty youth he is but not so improved as they did give him out to be, but like a child still.[1] But yet I can perceive he hath good parts and good inclinacions.[a]

Thence with Creed, who dined here, to Westminster to find out Mr. Hawly, and did; but he did not accept of my offer of his being Steward to my Lord at Sea.

Thence alone to several places about my law businesses, and with good success; at last, to Mr. Townsend at the Wardrobe and received kind words from him, to be true to me against Captain Ferrers his endeavours to get the place from my father, as my Lord hath promised him.

Here met Will How, and he went forth with me and by water back to White-hall to wait on my Lord, who is come back from Hinchingbrooke, where he hath been about four or five days. But I was never more vexed to see how an over-officious visitt is received, for he received me with as little concernment as in the mid of his discontent, and a fool I am to be of so servile a humour; and vexed with that consideration, I took coach home and could not get it off of my mind all night.

To supper and to bed – my wife finding fault with Besse for her calling upon Jane, that lived with us, and there heard Mrs. Harper and her talk ill of us and not told us of it – with which I was also vexed and told her soundly of it till she cried, poor wench, and I hope without dissimulation – and yet I cannot tell. However, I was glad to see in what manner she received it; and so to sleep.

21. Being weary yesterday with walking, I sleep long; and at last up and to the office, where all the morning. At home to dinner, Mr. Deane with me. After dinner, I to White-hall (setting down my wife by the way) to a Comittee of Tanger; where the Duke of Yorke, I perceive, doth attend the business

a l.h. repl. s.h. 'inc'-

1. Sidney Mountagu, Sandwich's second son, was now within a few weeks of his 14th birthday. He had been with tutors in Paris for the past three years.

very well, much better then any man there, or most of them.
And my [mind] eased of some trouble I lay under, for fear of
his thinking ill of me from the bad successe in the setting forth of
these men*ᵃ* to Tanger.

Thence with Mr. Creed and walked in the park. And so to the
New Exchange, meeting Mr. Moore, and he with us. I showed
him no friendly look, but he took no notice to me of the*ᵇ*
Wardrobe business[1] which vexes me. I perceive by him my
Lord's business of his family and estate goes very ill, and runs in
debt mightily. I would to God I were clear of it, both as to my
own money and the bond of 1000*l* which I stand debtor for*ᶜ*
him in to my Cosen Tho. Pepys.[2] Thence by coach home and to
my office a little; and so to supper and to bed.

22. Up, and I find Mr. Creed below, who stayed with me a
while; and then I to business all the morning. At noon to the
Change and Coffee-house, where great talk of the Dutch preparing of 60 sail of ships.[3] The plague grows mightily among
them, both at sea and land.[4]

From the Change to dinner to Trinity-house with Sir W
Rider and Cutler – where a very good dinner. Here Sir G
Ascue dined also, who I perceive desires to make himself known
among the seamen.[5] Thence home, there coming to me my
Lord Peterborough's sollicitor with a letter from him to desire
present despatch in his business of freight, and promises me 50*l* –
which is good news, and I hope to do his business readily for
him.[6] This much rejoiced me. All the afternoon at his business;

a repl. 'me'   *b* repl. 'it'   *c* repl. 'to'

---

1. Sandwich's accounts: cf. above,
p. 132.
2. See above, ii. 61, 62.
3. A government agent's report
gave the number as 40, of which
only 15 were said to be warships:
R. Duke to Secretary Williamson,
The Hague, 10/20 June: PRO,
SP 84/171, f. 14*r*.
4. Cf. Rugge, ii, f. 110*r*. For
the plague in Holland, see above, iv.
340 & n. 2.

5. He was a prominent naval commander under the Commonwealth,
now anxious for a commission: see
below, p. 288 & n. 2.
6. Peterborough's accounts as
Governor of Tangier (1661-2), still in
dispute, included a claim for freightage (of coal) which Peterborough had
paid for: PRO, CO 279/3, f. 211*v*.
The Tangier committee (including
Pepys) wrote to Povey, the Treasurer,
on the subject on 1 July: ib., f.146*r*.

and late at night comes the Sollicitor again, and I with him at 9 a-clock to Mr. Povy's and there acquainted him with the business. The money he won't pay without warrant – but that will be got done in a few days. So home by coach and to bed.

23. Up, and to the office, and there we sat all the morning. So to the Change and then home to dinner and to my office, where till 10 at night very busy; and so home to supper and to bed.

My Cosen Tho. Pepys was with me yesterday and I took occasion to speak to him about the bond I stand bound for my Lord Sandwich to him, in 1000*l*. I did very plainly, obliging him to secrecy, tell him how the matter stands, yet with all duty to my Lord, my resolution to be bound for whatever he desires me for him. Yet that I would be glad he had any other security. I perceive by Mr. Moore today that he hath been with my Lord; and my Lord, how he takes it I know not, but he is looking after other security and I am mighty glad of it.

W. How was with me this afternoon to desire some things to be got ready for my Lord against his going down to his ship;[1] which will be soon, for it seems the King and both the Queenes intend to visit him. The Lord knows how my Lord will get out of this charge, for Mr. Moore tells me today that he is 10000*l* in debt. And this will, with many other things*a* that daily will grow upon him (while he minds his pleasure as he doth), set him further backward. But it was pretty this afternoon to hear W How mince the matter and say that he doth believe that my Lord is in debt 2 or 3000*l* and then corrected himself and said, "No, not so; but I am afeared he is in debt 1000*l*."

I pray God get me well rid*b* of his Lordship as to his debt, and I care not.

24. Up, and out with Captain Witham in several places again to look for Oates for Tanger. And among other places, to the City Granarys, where it seems every company have their

a repl. 's'–   *b* repl. 'red'

---

1. The *London*: Sandwich, p. 144.

granary, and obliged to keep such a quantity of Corne alway there, or at a time of scarcity to issue so much at so much a bushell.[1]   And a fine thing it is to see their stores of all sorts for piles for the bridge and for pipes – a thing I never saw before.

Thence to the office and there busy all the morning.   At noon to my uncle Wights and there dined, my wife being there all the morning.   After[a] dinner to White-hall and there met with Mr Pierce[2] and he showed me the Queen's bed-chamber and her closet, where she had nothing but some pretty pious pictures and books of devotion.[3]   And her holy water at her head as she sleeps, with a clock by her bed-side wherein a lamp burns that tells her the time of the night at any time.[4]   Thence with him to the park and there met the Queen coming from chappell, with her Maids of honour all in Silver lace gowns again; which is new to me and that which I did not think would have been brought up again.

Thence he carried me to the King's closet; where such variety of pictures[5] and other things of value and rarity, that I was properly

a   repl. 'At'

---

1. Most of these granaries and storehouses were close to London Bridge.   This system of storage had been built up since c. 1520, the total provided by the companies being (in theory) 10,000 quarters of grain. The regulations were no longer observed: some of the companies employed private bakers to store grain for them; others evaded their obligations altogether.   W. H. and H. C. Overall (ed.), *Analytical index to Remembrancia of City of London*, pp. 372–91; N. S. B. Gras, *Evolution Engl. corn market*, pp. 82–8.

2. James Pearse, surgeon;   Groom of the Privy Chamber to the Queen.

3. Possibly the redecoration of the Queen's bedchamber (costing £3580 for the textiles alone) belongs to this period: *CSPD 1665–6*, p. 139.   A description of the closet in 1669 is in

Magalotti, pp. 177–8.   These rooms are not included in the MS. inventory (1667) of Charles II's pictures, but an indication of the pictures with which Catherine surrounded herself is to be found in the section devoted to the pictures in her custody in the following reign: *Cat. of coll. of pictures &c. belonging to King James* ... (1758), pp. 61–5.   These were almost entirely small pieces and of a religious nature. Charles had asked his sister Henrietta in December 1663 to buy 'images to put in prayer books' for the Queen, who could obtain none in England: C. H. Hartmann, *The King my brother*, p. 82.   (OM).

4. Examples of night-clocks of the period are in the Ilbert Collection in the BM.

5. See above, i. 258 & n. 1.

confounded and enjoyed no pleasure in the sight of them – which is the only time in my life that ever I was so at a loss for pleasure in the greatest plenty of objects to give it me.

Thence home, calling in many places and doing abundance of errands to my great content; and at night, weary, home, where Mr. Creed waited for me. And he and I walked in the garden, where he told me that he is now in a hurry fitting himself for sea. And that it remains that he deals as an ingenuous man with me in the business I wot of, which he will do before he goes.[1] But I perceive he will have me do many good turns for him first, both as to his bills coming to him in this office and also in his absence at the Committee of Tanger – which I promise, and as he acquits himself to me, I will willingly do. I would I knew the worst of it, what it is he intends; that so, I may either quit my hands of him or continue my kindness still to him.

25. We stayed late, and he lay with me all night – and ris very merry, talking; and excellent company he is, that is the truth of it, and a most cunning man. He being gone, I to the office, where we sat all the morning. At noon to dinner and then to my office, busy. And by and by home with Mr. Deane to a lesson upon raising a Bend of Timbers.[2]   And he being gone – I to the office; and there came Captain Taylor and he and I home; and I have done all very well with him as to the business of the last trouble,[3] so that come what will come, my name will be clear of any false doing with him. So to my office again late; and then to bed.

26. *Lords day.* Up, and Sir J Minnes set me down at my Lord Sandwiches, where I waited till his coming down. When he came too, could find little to say to me; but only a general question or two and so goodbye. Here his little daughter, my

---

1. See below, p. 213 & n. 2.
2. I.e. drawing the outline for the mould of a ship. Deane included a section on this subject ('To draw a bend of timber') in the book he wrote for Pepys in 1670: 'Sir Anthony Deane's Doctrine of Naval Architecture' (PL 2910, pp. 65–6).
3. Over the *Eagle*; see above, pp. 175, 176–7.

Lady Katharin, was brought, who is lately come from my father's at Brampton to have her cheeke[a] looked after, which is and hath long been sore. But my Lord will rather have it be as it is, with a scarr in her face, then endanger its being worse by tampering. He being gone, I went home, a little troubled to see he minds me no more; and with Creed with me, called at several churches – which, God knows, are[b] supplied with very young men, and the churches very empty.[1]

So home, and at our own church looked in and there heard one preach[c] which Sir Wm. Pen brought, which he desired us yesterday to hear, that had been his chaplain in Ireland – a very silly fellow. So home and to dinner; and after dinner a frolic took us we would go this afternoon to the Hope. So my wife dressed herself, and with good victuals and drink we took boat presently and, the tide with us, got down; but it was night and the tide spent by the time we got to Gravesend. So there we stopped but went not on shore; only Creede to get some cherries and send a letter to the Hope, where the fleet lies. And so it being rainy and thundering mightily and lightening, we returned. By and by the evening turned mighty clear and moonshine; we got with great pleasure home about 12 a-clock, which did much please us – he telling pretty stories in the boat. He lay with me all night.

27. Up; and he and I walked to Pauls churchyard and there saw Sir Harry Spillmans book,[2] and I bespoke it and others. And thence we took coach, and he to my Lord's and I to St. James, where we did our usual business; and thence I home and dined, and then by water to Woolwich and there spent the afternoon till night, under pretence of buying Captain Blackemans house and ground; and viewing the ground, took notice of Clothiers Cordage with which he, I believe, thinks to cheat the

a repl. ? 'k'-   b MS. 'a'   c MS. 'preacher'

1. For the expulsions which led to this situation, see above, iii. 186. Baxter's evidence is similar (M. Sylvester, *Reliq. Baxt.*, 1696, bk i, pt ii. 385), but Burnet (i. 342) remarked that 'the young clergy that came from the universities did good service'.

2. Spelman's *Glossarium Archaiologicum* (licensed almost a week later, on 2 July 1664: *Trans. Stat. Reg.*, ii. 345); PL 2472; see below, p. 198.

King.[1] That being done, I by water home, it being night first. And there I find our new mayd Jane[2] come, a cook-maid. So to bed.

28. Up; and this day put on a half-shirt first this summer, it being very hot; and yet so ill-tempered* I am grown, that I am afeared I shall ketch cold while all the world is ready to melt away.

To the office all the morning. At noon to dinner at home. Then to my office till the evening. Then out about several businesses; and then by appointment to the Change and thence with my uncle Wight to the Mum-house; and there drinking, he doth complain of his wife most cruelly, as the most troublesome woman in the world; and how she will have her will, saying she brought him a portion and God knows what[a] – by which, with many instances more, I perceive they do live a sad life together. Thence to the Miter, and there came Dr. Burnett to us and Mr. Maes. But the meeting was chiefly to bring the Doctor and me together, and there I begin to have his advice about my disease and then invited him to my house; and I am resolved to put myself into his hands. Here very late, but I drank nothing, nor will – though he doth advise me to take care of cold drinks. So home and to bed.

29. Up, and Mr. Sheply came to me, who is lately come to town. Among other things, I hear by him how the children[3] are sent for away from my father's, but he says without any great discontent. I am troubled there should be this occasion of difference, and yet I am glad they are gone, lest it should have come to worse.

a repl. 'not'

---

1. For the cordage, see below, p. 253 & n. 1. Pepys was again critical of Clothier in 1667: *CSPD 1667*, p. 158. Blackman's house appears to have been bought by the Ordnance Office, who then made over the gunyard to the use of the navy: ib., *1670*, p. 135.

2. Surname unknown; not to be confused with the other Janes whom the Pepyses employed – Jane Birch and Jane Gentleman. Jane III left the Pepyses on 4 February 1665.

3. Sandwich's daughters.

He tells me how my brave dog I did give him,[1] going out betimes one morning to Huntington, was set upon by five other dogs and worryed to pieces – of which I am a little and he the most sorry I ever saw man for such a thing.

Forth with him and walked a good way, talking; then parted and I to the Temple and to my Cosen Rog. Pepys; and thence by water to Westminster to see Deane Honiwood,[2] whom I had not visited a great while.   He is a good nature, but a very weak man; yet a Deane and a man in great esteem.   Thence walked to my Lord Sandwiches and there dined, my Lord there.   He was pleasant enough at table with me, but yet without any discourse of business or any regard to me when dinner was done; but fell to cards, and my Lady and I sat two hours alone talking of the condition of her family, being greatly*a* in debt and many children now coming up to provide for.   I did give her my sense very plain of it – which she took well and carried further then myself, to the bemoaning their condition and remembering how finely things were ordered about six years ago when I lived there and my Lord at Sea every year.

Thence home, doing several errands by the way.   So to my office and there till late at night – Mr. Comander coming to me for me to sign and seal the new draft of my Will; which I did do – I having altered something upon the death of my Brother Tom.[3]   So home to supper and to bed.

30.   Up, and to the office, where we sat all the morning.   At noon home to dinner, Mr. Wayth with me; and by and by comes in Mr. Falconer and his wife and dined with us – the first time she was ever here.   We had a pretty good dinner – very merry in discourse.   Sat after dinner an hour or two.   Then down by water to Deptford and Woolwich about getting of some business done, which I was bound to by my oath this month. And though in some things I have not come to the heighth of

a   MS. 'in greatly'

---

1. I.e. Pepys's father.   The dog was Towser, a mastiff.

2. Dr Michael Honywood, Dean of Lincoln.

3. Cf. above, p. 20, n. 2.

my vowe of doing all my businesses in paying all my petty debts
and receipt of all my petty monies due to me – yet I bless God
I am not conscious of any neglect in me that they are not done,
having not minded my*ª* pleasure at all. And so being resolved
to take no manner of pleasure*ᵇ* till it be done, I doubt not God
will forgive me for not forfeiting the 10*l* I promised.

Walked back from Woolwich to Greenwich all alone, save a
man that had a cudgell in his hand; and though he told me he
laboured in the King's yards and many other good arguments
that he is an honest man, yet God forgive me, I did doubt he
might knock me on the head behind with his club – but I got
safe home. Then to the making-up my month's accounts; and
find myself still a gainer and rose to 951*l*, for which God be
blessed. I end the month with my mind full of business and
some sorrow that I have not exactly performed all my vowes,
though my not doing is not my fault and shall be made good out
of my first leisure.

Great doubts yet whether the Duch war go on or no. The
fleet ready in the Hope, of twelve sail – the King and Queenes
go on board, they say, on Saturday next.

Young children of my Lord Sandwich gone with their maids
from my mother's; which troubles me, it being, I hear from
Mr. Sheply, with great discontent – saying that though they buy
good meate, yet can never have it before it stinks – which I am
ashamed of.

        a   repl. 'by'   *b*   repl. 'it'

JULY.

1. Up, and within all the morning – first bringing down my Tryangle* to my chamber below, having a new frame made proper for it to stand on.   By and by comes Dr. Burnett – who assures me that I have an Ulcer either in the Kidnys or Blather; for my water, which he saw yesterday, he is sure the Sediment is not slime gathered by heat, but is a direct pusse.   He did write me down some direction[a] what to do for it – but not with the satisfaction I expected.   I did give him a piece; with good hopes, however, that his advice will be of use to me – though it is strange Mr. Hollyard should never say one word of this ulcer in all his life to me.

He being gone, I to the Change and thence home to dinner; and so to my office, busy till the evening; and then by agreement came Mr. Hill and Andrew and one Cheswicke, a maister who plays very well upon the Spinette, and we sat singing Psalms till 9 at night, and so broke up with great pleasure; and very good company it is, and I hope I shall now and then have their company.   They being gone, I to my office till toward 12 a-clock, and then home and to bed.

Upon the Change this day I saw how uncertain the Temper of the people is – that from our discharging of about 200 that lay idle, having nothing to do upon some of our ships which were ordered to be fitted for service and their works are now done – the town doth talk that the King discharges all his men, 200 yesterday and 800 today, and that now he hath got 100000*l* in his hand, he values not a Dutch warr.[1]   But I undeceived a great many, telling them how it is.

---

a   opposite this entry a sheet is pasted in, containing a copy in Pepys's l.h. of Dr Burnet's prescription.   See below, App. p. 363.

---

1. Cf. the dismissals at Woolwich, 22 June: *CSPD Add. 1660–85*, p. 106. In fact, the King had on 13 June ordered 2000 seamen to be raised by impressment: ib., *1663–4*, p. 614.

2. Up and to the office, where all the morning. At noon to the Change; and there (which is strange) I could meet with nobody that I could invite home to my venison pasty, but only Mr. Alsop and Mr. Lanyon, whom I invited last night, and a friend they brought along with them. So home; and with our venison pasty we had other good meat*a* and good discourse. After dinner sat close to discourse about our business of the victualling of the garrison of Tanger – taking their prices of all provisions; and I do hope to order it so that they, and I also, may get something by it – which doth much please me, for I hope I may get nobly and honestly, with profit to the King.[1] They being gone, came Sir W Warren and he and I discoursed long about the business of masts;[2] and then in the evening to the office, where late writing letters, and then home to look over some Brampton papers, which I am under an oath to despatch before I spend one half-hour in any pleasure or go to bed before 12 a-clock; to which, by the grace of God I will be true. Then to bed.

When I came home, I found that tomorrow being*b* Sunday, I should gain nothing by doing it tonight, and tomorrow I can do it very well and better then tonight: I went to bed before my time, but with a resolution of doing the thing to better purpose tomorrow.

3. *Lords day.* Up and ready, and all the morning in my chamber looking over and settling some Brampton businesses. At noon to dinner, where the remains of yesterday's venison and a couple of brave green geese; which we are fain to eat alone, because they will not keep – which troubled us.

After dinner, I close to my business; and before the evening, did end it with great content and my mind eased by it. Then up and spent the evening walking with my wife, talking; and it thundering and lightening mightily all the evening – and this year have had the most thunder and lightening, they say, of any

a repl. 'and'   b blot above symbol

---

1. See below, p. 210.
2. Warren had offered to serve in small masts at prices agreed on in his former contract: Warren to Pepys, 22 June: Rawl. A 174, f. 3r.

in man's memory; and so it is it seems in France and everywhere else.[1] So to prayers and to bed.

4. Up, and many people with me about business; and then out to several places, and so at noon to my Lord Crews and there dined, and very much made on there by him. He offered me the selling of some land of his in Cambrigeshire, a purchase of about 1000*l* – and if I can compass it, I will. After dinner I walked homeward, still doing business by the way, and at home find my wife this day of her own accord to have lain out 25*s* upon a pair of pendances for her eares; which did vex me and brought both me and her to very high, and very foul words from her to me, such as trouble me to think she should have in her mouth, and reflecting upon our old differences,[2] which I hate to have remembered. I vowed to break them, or that she should go and get what she could for them again. I went with that resolution out of doors. The poor wretch afterward, in a little while, did send out to change them for her money again. I fallowed Besse her messenger at the Change and there did consult and sent her back; I would not have them changed, being satisfied that she yielded. So went home, and friends again as to that business; but the words I could not get out of my mind, and so went to bed at night discontented; and she came to bed to me, but all would not make me friends, but sleep and rise in the morning angry.

This day the King and the Queenes went to visit my Lord Sandwich and the fleet going forth, in the Hope.[3]

5. Up and to the office, where all the morning. At noon to the Change a little. Then with W Howe home and dined. So after dinner to my office and there busy till late at night – having had, among other things, much discourse with young Gregory[4] about the Chest business, wherein Sir W. Batten is so great a knave. And also with Alsop and Lanyon about the Tanger victualing, wherein I hope to get something for myself.

Late home to supper and to bed – being full of thoughts of a

---

1. See *Comp.*: 'Weather'.
2. This refers to their separation sometime before the diary opens: see above, ii. 153 & n. 3.

3. They returned on the same day: *The Newes*, 7 July, p. 440.
4. Edward Gregory, jun., purser of the *Sovereign*.

sudden resolution this day, taken upon the Change, of going down tomorrow to the Hope.

6. Up very betimes, and my wife also, and got us ready; and about 8 a-clock, having got some bottles of wine and beer and neat's tongues, we went to our barge at the Towre, where Mr. Pierce and his wife and a kinswoman and his sister, and Mrs. Clerke and her sister and cousin were to expect us. And so set out for the Hope, all the way down playing at Cards and other sports, spending our time pretty merry. Came to the Hope about one, and there showed them all the ship[s] and had a col-lacion of anchoves, Gammon &c.; and after an hour's stay or more imbarked again for home, and so to cards and other sports till we came to Greenwich; and there Mrs. Clerke and my wife and I on shore to an ale-house for them to do their business, and so to the barge again, having shown them the King's pleasure-boat.[1] And so home to the Bridge, bringing night home with us and it raining hard, but we got them on foot to the Beare and there put them into a boat; and I back to my wife in the barge and so to the Tower wharf and home – being very well pleased today with the company, especially Mrs. Pierce, who continues her com-plexion as well as ever[2] and hath at this day, I think, the best complexion that ever I saw on any woman, young or old, or child either, all days of my life. Also, Mrs. Clerkes kinswoman sings very prettily, but is very confident in it. Mrs. Clerke herself witty, but spoils all in being so conceited and making so great a flutter with a few fine clothes and some bad tawdry things worn with them.

But the charge of the barge lies heavy upon me, which troubles me; but it is but once, and I may make Pierce do me some courtesy as great.

Being come home, I weary to bed with sitting. The reason of Dr. Clerkes not being here was the King's being sick last night and let blood, and so he durst not come away today.[3]

1. The *Catherine*.
2. Cf. above, ii. 151 & n. 2.
3. The King had caught a chill ('*une petite indisposition*') through removing his wig and waistcoat during his visit to the fleet: de Cominges to de Lionne, 7/17 July;

PRO, PRO 31/3/113, f. 238r. 'Hav-ing received refreshment by rest and a gentle sweat', he quickly recovered (newsletter, 7 July; Tanner 47, ff. 185r, 186r). Pepys, had he known all this, would certainly not have shed his own waistcoat on the 7th.

7. Up; and this day begun, the first day this year, to put off my linen waistcoat.*   But it happening to be a cool day, I was afeared of taking cold – which troubles me and is the greatest pain I have in the world, to think of my bad temper of my health.

At the office all the morning.   Dined at home.   To my office to prepare some things against a Comitte of Tanger this afternoon.   So to White-hall and there found the Duke and 20 more reading their commission (of which I am, and was also sent to, to come) for the Royall Fishery, which is very large and a very serious Charter it is;[1] but the company generally so ill fitted for so serious a work[a] that I do much fear it will come to little.

That being done, and[b] not being able to do anything for lack of an oath for the Governor and Assistants to take, we rose.

Then our Committee for the Tanger=victualling met and did a little; and so up, and I and Mr. Coventry walked in the garden half an hour, talking of the business of our masts; and thence away and with Creed walked half an hour or more in the park; and thence to the New Exchange to drink some cream, but missed it; and so parted and I home, calling by the way for my new Bookes, viz., Sir H. Spillmans whole glossary[2] – Scapula's Lexicon[3] and Shakespeares plays[4] – which I have got money out of my stationers bills to pay for.   So home and to my office a while, and then home and to bed – finding myself pretty well for all my wastecoate being put off today.

The King is pretty well today, though let blood the night before yesterday.

a   repl. 'comp'-   b   repl. ? 'we'

---

1. See *Comp.*: 'Fishery'.   The charter was that of 8 April 1664.

2. See above, p. 190 & n. 2.

3. Joannes Scapula, *Lexicon Graeco-Latinum* (Amsterdam, 1652; PL 2668), one of the most commonly used dictionaries: Foster Watson, *Engl. grammar schools to 1660*, pp. 388, 512.

4. Probably one of the two issues of the Third Folio published in 1663 and 1664. Pepys retained a Fourth Folio (1685; PL 2635). It has been 'speculatively' suggested that the copy of the first issue of the Third Folio sold at Sotheby's in 1947 may be the copy which Pepys here refers to, since the initials 'S.P.' are stamped on the spine: Sotheby's, *Cat.*, 24–5 November 1947, no. 448. Mr H. M. Nixon thinks the guess unlikely.

8. Up, and called out by my Lord Peterburgh's gentleman to Mr. Povy's to discourse about getting of his money; wherein I am concerned, in hopes of the 50*l* my Lord hath promised me, but I dare not reckon myself sure of it, till I have it, in my mind,[1] for these Lords are hard to be trusted – though I well deserve it. I stayed at Povys for his coming in, and there looked over his stables and everything; but notwithstanding all the times I have been there, I do yet find many fine things to look on.

Thence to White-hall a little to hear how the King doth, he not having been well these three days. I find that he is pretty well again. So to Pauls churchyard about my books – and to the binders and directed the doing of my Chaucer, though they were not full neat enough for me, but pretty well it is – and thence to the clasp-makers to have it clasped and bossed.[2] So to the Change and home to dinner, and so to my office till 5 a-clock; and then came Mr. Hill and Andrews and we sung an hour or two. Then broke up and Mr. Alsop and his company came and consulted about our Tanger=victualling, and brought it to a good head. So they parted and I to supper and to bed.

9. Up, and at the office all the morning; in the afternoon by coach with Sir J. Mennes to White-hall and there to a Committee for Fishing; but the first thing was swearing to be true to the Company, and we were all sworn. But a great dispute we had (which methought is very Ominous to the Company); some, that we should swear to be true to the best of our power; and other, to the best of our understanding; and carried in the last (though in that we are the least able to serve the Company) because we would not be obliged to attend the business when we can, but when we list. This consideration did displease me, but it was voted and so went.[3]

We did nothing else, but broke up till a Committee of Guinny

---

1. The sentence would be clearer if 'in my mind' immediately followed 'reckon myself sure of it'. £600 was due to Peterborough from Tangier funds (Pepys to Vernatty, 11 June): NMM, LBK/8, p. 109.

2. Thomas Speght's edition of the *Workes* (1602) is still in the PL, bound in calf, and with clasps and bosses of brass: PL 2365.

3. No specific oath had been provided by the company's charter: see C. T. Carr (ed.), *Select charters of trading companies 1530–1707*, pp. 182+.

was sat and ended; and then met again for Tanger, and there I did my business about my Lord Peterburgh's order and my own for my expenses for the garrison lately. So home, by the way calling for my Chaucer and other books; and that is well done to my mind, which pleased me well. So to my office till late, writing letters; and so home to my wife to supper and bed – where we have ⟨not⟩[a] lain together because of the heat of the weather a good while, but now against her going into the country.

10. *Lords day.* Up, and by water towards noon to Somersetthouse; and walked to my Lord Sandwiches and there dined with my Lady and the children. And after some ordinary discourse with my Lady, after dinner took our leaves and [my] wife hers, in order to her going to the country tomorrow; but my Lord took not occasion to speak one word of my father or mother about the children at all[1] – which I wonder at, and begin I will not.[2]

Here my Lady showed us my Lady Castlemaynes picture, finely done – given my Lord,[3] and a most beautiful picture it is.

Thence with my Lady Jem and Mr. Sidny to St. Gyles church, and there heard a long poor sermon. Thence set them down and in their coach to Kate Joyces christening – where much company – good service of sweetmeats. And after an hour's stay left them and in my Lord's coach, his noble rich coach, home; and there my wife fell to putting things in order against her going tomorrow. And I to read and so to bed – where I not well, and so had no pleasure at all this night with my poor ⟪11.⟫ wife. But betimes up this morning; and getting ready, we by coach to Holborne, where at 9 a-clock they set out, and I and my man Will on horse by her to Barnett, a very

a repl. 'lain'

---

1. Sandwich's children had stayed at Brampton with Pepys's mother and father during the previous winter: above, p. 74 & n. 1.
2. Sc. Pepys would not mention them if Sandwich chose not to.
3. This remained at Hinching-

brooke until it was sold at Sotheby's on 4 December 1957 (no. 184): R. B. Beckett, *Lely*, pl. 90. It appears to have been a copy executed in Lely's studio and to be less good than the versions at Knole and Euston. (OM).

Barbara Villiers, Countess of Castlemaine, painted in the studio of Sir Peter Lely for the 1st Earl of Sandwich, and formerly at Hinchingbrooke

pleasant day, and there dined with her company, which was very good – a pretty gentlewoman with her that goes but to Huntington, and a neighbour to us in town.   Here we stayed two hours and then parted for altogether – and my poor wife I shall soon want,*a* I am sure.

Thence I and Will to see the Wells,[1] half a mile off; and there I drunk three glasses and went and walked, and came back and drunk two more.   The woman would have had me drunk three more; but I could not, my belly being full – but this wrought very well; and so we rode home round by Kingsland, Hackney, and Mile end,*b* till we were quite weary – and my water working at least seven or eight times upon the road, which pleased me well.   And so home, weary; and not being very well, I betimes to bed.

And there fell into a most mighty sweat in the night, about 11 a-clock; and there, knowing what money I have in the house[2] and hearing a noise, I begin to sweat worse and worse, till I melted almost to water.   I rung, and could not in half an hour make either of the wenches hear me; and this made me fear the more, lest they might be gag'd; and then I begin to think that there was some design in a stone being flung at the window over our stairs this evening, by which the thiefes meant to try what looking there would [be] after them and know our company.   These thoughts and fears I had, and do*c* hence apprehend the fears of all rich men that are covetous and have much money by them.   At last Jane rose and then I understand it was only the dog wants a lodging and so made a noyse.   So to bed, but hardly slept; at last did, and so till morning.

12.   And so rose, called up by my Lord Peterburghs gentleman about getting his Lords money today of Mr. Povy; wherein

a repl. 'what'   *b* repl. 'Mile end gree'-   *c* MS. 'to'

---

1. At Barnet Common, one mile south-west of Chipping (High) Barnet; discovered in 1652, and by this time well known, being near to London.   The well-house was later maintained by a trust established in 1677, but was demolished in 1840: VCH, *Herts.*, ii. 329; A. S. Foord, *Springs, streams and spas of London*, pp. 152–5.

2. About £1000: below, p. 281. For Pepys's banking methods, see below, p. 269, n. 1.

I took such order, that it was paid and I had my 50*l* brought me, which comforts my heart.

We sat at the office all the morning; then at home dined alone, sad for want of company and not being very well, and know not how to eat alone. After dinner, down with Sir G. Carteret, Sir J. Mennes and Sir W. Batten to view; and did like a place by Deptford-yard to lay masts in.[1] By and by comes Mr. Coventry; and after a little stay, he and I down to Blackewall, he having a mind to see that yard; which we did, and fine storehouses there are and good dockes, but of no great profit to him that oweth* them for aught we see.[2]

So home by water with him – having good discourse by the way; and so I to the office a while, and late home to supper and to bed.

13. Up and to my office. At noon (after having at an ale-house hard by discoursed with one Mr. Tyler, a neighbour, and one Captain Sanders about the discovery of some pursers that have sold their provisions), I to my Lord Sandwich, thinking to have dined there; but they not dining at home, I with Captain Ferrers to Mr. Barwell the King's Squire Sadler, where about this time twelvemonth[3] I dined before at a good venison pasty. The like we had now, and very good company, Mr. Tresham and others.

Thence to White-hall to the Fishery, and there did little. So by water home, and there met Lanyon &c. about Tanger matters; and so late to my office and thence home and to bed.

Mr. Moore was with me late, to desire me to come to my Lord Sandwich tomorrow morning; which I shall, but wonder what my business is.

14. My mind being doubtful what the business should be, I rose little after 4 a-clock, and abroad; walked to my Lord's and nobody up, but the porter ris out of bed to me. So I back again to Fleet-street and there bought a little book of law; and thence, hearing a psalm sung, I went into St. Dunstans and there

1. See below, p. 231 & n. 1.
2. The yard was owned by Henry Johnson, who built most of the E. Indiamen of this period: see Henry

Green and R. Wigram, *Chronicles of Blackwall Yard.*
3. On 20 August 1662.

heard prayers read, which it seems is done there every morning at 6 a-clock, a thing I never did do at a chapel, but the College chapel, in all my life.

Thence to my Lord's again; and my Lord being up, was sent for up, and he and I alone: he did begin with a most solemn profession of the same confidence in and love for me that he ever had, and then told me what a misfortune was fallen upon me and him: in me, by a displeasure which my Lord Chancellor did show to him last night against me in the highest and most passionate manner that ever any man did speak, even to the not hearing of anything to be said to him. But he told me that he did say all that could be said for a man as to my faithfullness and duty to his Lordshipp, and did me the greatest right imaginable. And what should the business be but that I should be forward to have the trees in Clarendon-park marked and cut down; which he it seems hath bought of my Lord Albemarle – when God knows I am the most innocent man in the world in it, and did nothing of myself nor knew of his concernment therein, but barely obeyed my Lord Treasurer's warrant for the doing thereof.[1] And said that I did most ungentlemanlike with him, and had justified the rogues in cutting down a tree of his; and that I had sent the veriest fanatique[2] that is in England to mark them, on*a* purpose to nose him – all which, I did assure my Lord, was most utterly false, and nothing like it true – and told my Lord the whole passage. My Lord doth seem most nearly* affected with him; partly I believe for me, and partly for himself. So he advised me to wait presently upon my Lord and clear myself in the most perfect manner I could, with all submission and assurance that I am his creature both in this and all other things, and that I do own that all I have is derived through my Lord Sandwich from his Lordshipp. So, full of horror, I

a repl. 'and'

---

1. The mark was that of the navy's broad arrow. The Lord Treasurer was responsible for royal forests. For the interests of Clarendon and Albemarle in the estate, see above, pp. 60–1 & n. The Crown had in fact reserved felled timber for its own use. The Chancellor's objection was that the navy purveyors were marking standing timber. Deane and his colleague Mayors had sent in their report from the Three Lions, Salisbury, on 4 July. Lister, iii. 342; *CSPD 1663–4,* pp. 502, 633; *CTB,* i. 194; *CSPClar.,* v. 365, 378, 386.

2. Anthony Deane.

went and found him busy in trials of law in his great room;[1]
and it being sitting-day, durst not stay, but went to my Lord and
told him so – whereupon he directed me to take him after
dinner; and so away I home, leaving my Lord mightily concerned for me.

I to the office and there sat busy all the morning.   At noon to
the Change, and from the Change over with Alsopp and the
others to the Popes-head tavern and there stayed a quarter of an
hour; and concluded upon this, that in case I get them no more
then 3s-1½d per week a man, I should have of them but 150l per
annum, but to have it without any adventure* or charge.[2]   But if
I got them 3s-2d, then they would give me 300l in the like manner.
So I directed them to draw up their tender in a line or two
against the afternoon, and to meet me at White-hall.   So I left
them and to my Lord Chancellors; and there coming out after
dinner, I accosted him, telling him that I was the unhappy Pepys
that hath fallen into his high displeasure, and came to desire
him to give me leave to make myself better understood to his
Lordshipp – assuring him of my duty and service.   He answered
me very pleasingly: that he was confident upon the score of my
Lord Sandwiches character of me – but that he had reason to think
what he did, and desired me to call upon him some evening:
I named tonight, and he accepted of it.   So with my heart light,
I to White-hall, and there, after understanding by a stratagem
and yet appearing wholly desirous not to understand Mr.[a]
Gaudens price when he desired to show it me – I went down and
ordered matters in our tender so well, that at the meeting by and
by I was ready, with Mr. Gaudens and his,[3] both directed in a
letter to me, to give the board their two tenders; but there being
none but the Generall Monke and Mr. Coventry and Povy and I,
I did not think fit to expose them to view now, but put it off till
Saturday – and so with good content rose.

a   repl. 'his'

---

1. Clarendon then lived at Worcester House in the Strand.   He trans-
acted much public business in his
private house;   sessions both of
Chancery and of the Privy Council
were held there during his bouts of
illness.

2. This concerned the contract for
victualling: see below, p. 210 & n. 3.

3. I.e. Alsop's (or Lanyon's).

Thence I to the Half-Moone against the Change to acquaint Lanyon and his friends of our proceeding; and thence to my Lord Chancellors and there heard several Tryalls, wherein I perceive my Lord is a most able and ready man. After all done, he himself called, "Come, Mr. Pepys, you and I will take a turn in the garden." So he was led downstairs, having the goute, and there walked with me I think above an hour, talking most friendly yet cunningly. I told him clearly how things were. How ignorant I was of his Lordships concernment in it. How I did not do nor say one word singly; but what was done was the act of the whole Board. He told me by name that he was more angry with Sir G. Carteret then with me, and also with the whole body of the Board. But thinking who it was of the Board that knew him least, he did place his fear upon me. But he finds that he is indebted to none of his friends there. I think I did thoroughly appease him, till he thanked me for my desire and pains to satisfy him. And upon my desiring to be directed who I should of his servants advise with about this business, he told me nobody, but would be glad to hear from me himself. He told me he would not direct me in anything, that it might not be said that the Lord Chancellor did labour to abuse the King or (as I offered) direct the suspending the Report of the Purveyors; but I see what he means, and will make it my work to do him service in it. But Lord, to see how he is incensed against poor Deane, as a fanatic, rogue, and I know not what – and what he did was done in spite to his Lordshipp among all his friends and tenants. He did plainly say that he would not direct me in anything, for he would not put himself into the power of any man to say that he did so and so; but plainly told me as if he would be glad I did something.

Lord, to see how we poor wretches dare not do the King good service for fear of the greatness of these men.

He named Sir G. Carteret and Sir J. Mennes and the rest; and that he was as angry with them all as me.

But it was pleasant to think that while he was talking to me, comes into the garden Sir G. Carteret, and my Lord avoided speaking with him, and made him and many others stay expecting him, while I walked up and down above an hour I think – and would have me walk with my hat on.

And yet after all this, there hath been so little ground for all this

his jealousy of me, that I am sometimes afeared that he doth this only in policy, to bring me to his side by scaring me; or else, which is worse, to try how faithful I would be to the King. But I rather think the former of the two.

I parted with great assurance how I acknowledged all I had to come from his Lordship; which he did not seem to refuse – but with great kindness and respect parted. So I by coach home, calling at my Lord's, but he not within.

At my office late; and so home to eat something, being almost starved for want of eating my dinner today; and so to bed – my head being full of great and many businesses of import to me.

15. Up, and to my Lord Sandwiches; where he sent for me up and I did give my Lord an account of what had passed with my Lord Chancellor yesterday; with which he was well pleased – and advised me by all means to study in the best manner I could to serve him in this business. After this discourse ended, he begun to tell me that he had now pitched upon his day of going to sea, upon Monday next; and that he would now give me an account how matters are with him. He told me that his work now in the world is only to keep up his interest at Court, having little hopes to get more considerably; he saying that he hath now about 8000*l* per annum. It is true, he says, he oweth about 10000*l*. But he hath been at great charges in getting things to this pass in his estate – besides his building and goods*a* that he hath bought. He says he hath now evened his reckonings at the Wardrobe till Michaelmas last,*b* and hopes to finish it to Lady-day before he goes. He says, now there is due too, 7000*l* to him there, if he knew how to get it paid, besides 2000*l* that Mr. Mountagu doth owe him.[1] As to his interest, he says*c* that he hath had all the injury done him that ever man could have by another bosom-friend that knows all his secrets,

---

a MS. 'good goods'   *b* repl. 'next'   *c* 'he says' repeated twice

---

1. Edward Mountagu of Boughton, Sandwich's cousin, had been in charge of his affairs during his absence on the Mediterranean voyage, 1661–2. Sandwich's finances are summarised in Harris, i. 255+. £8000 was a very large income (the average for the nobility according to Gregory King's 1688 figures was £3200), but Sandwich was extravagant. For the Wardrobe debts, see above, iii. 287 & n. 2.

by Mr. Mountagu.[1] But he says that the worst of it all is past and he gone out and hated, his very person, by*a* the King,[2] and he believes the more upon the score of his carriage to him; and that the Duke of Yorke did say a little while since, in his closet, that he did hate him because of his ungrateful carriage to my Lord of Sandwich. He says he is as great with the Chancellor, or greater, then ever in his life. That with the King he is the like; and told me an instance, that whereas he formerly was of the private council to the King before he was last sick, and that by that sickness an interruption was made in his attendance upon him, the King did not constantly call him, as he used to do, to his private council, only in businesses of the sea and the like; but of late, the King did send a message to him by Sir Hary Bennet, to excuse the King to my Lord that he had not of late sent for him as he used to do to his private council, for it was not out of any distaste, but to avoid giving offence to some others, whom he did not name but my Lord supposes it might be Prince Rupert, or it may be only that the King would rather pass it by an excuse then be thought unkind. But that now he did desire ⟨him⟩ to attend him constantly; which he hath of late done, and the King never more kind to him in his life then now. The Duke of Yorke, as much as is possible; and in the business of late, when I was to speak to my Lord about his going to sea, he says that he finds the Duke did it with the greatest ingenuity* and love in the world;[3] "and whereas," says my Lord, "here is a wise man hard by that thinks himself so and would be thought so, and it may be is in a degree so (naming by and by my Lord Crew), would have had me conditioned with him that Prince Rupert nor anybody should come over my *b* head, and I know not what" – the Duke himself hath caused in his commission that he be made Admirall of this and what other ships or fleets shall hereafter be put out after these – which is very noble.[4] He tells

a repl. 'to'   *b* MS. 'his'

1. See above, iv. 46–7.
2. See above, p. 153 & n. 2.
3. Sandwich had in May suspected that there was some political prejudice at work against him.
4. For the commission, see Carte 75, f. 136. When this squadron was reinforced at the end of October Sandwich was made joint-commander with Rupert. On 11 November the Duke himself took command. Sandwich, p. 157; Tedder, pp. 109, 110.

me, in these cases and that of Mr. Mountagus and all others, he finds that bearing of them patiently is his best way, without noise or trouble; and things wear out of themselfs and come fair again. "But," says he, "take it from me never to trust too much to any man in the world, for you put yourself into his power; and the best-seeming friend and real friend as to the present may have or take occasion to fall out with you; and then out comes all."

Then he told me for Sir Harry Bennet: though they were alway kind, yet now it is become to an acquaintance and familiarity above ordinary; that for these month[s] he hath done no business but with my Lord's advice in his chamber; and promises all faithful love to him, and service upon all occasions. My Lord says that he hath the advantage of being able by his experience to help and advise him; and he believes that that chiefly doth invite Sir Harry to this manner of treating him.

"Now," says my Lord, "the only and the greatest Embarras that I have in the world is how to behave myself to Sir H. Bennet and my Lord Chancellor, in case that there doth lie anything under the Embers about my Lord Bristoll,[1] which nobody can tell. For then," says he, "I must appear for one or other, and I will lose all I have in the world rather then desert my Lord Chancellor; so that," says he, "I know not for my life what to do in that case" – for Sir H. Bennett's love is come to that heighth, and his confidence, that he hath given my Lord a Character and will oblige my Lord to correspond with him.

"This," says he,[a] "is the whole condition of my estate and interest; which I tell you because I know not whether I shall see you again or no." Then as to the voyage, he thinks it will be of charge to him, and no profit; but that he must not now look after nor think to encrease, but study to make good what he hath, that what is due to him from the Wardrobe or elsewhere may be paid; which otherwise would fail, and all a man hath be but small content to him.

So we seemed to take leave one of another; my Lord of me,

a repl. 'is'

---

1. Now in disgrace after his attempted impeachment of Clarendon in July 1663. Bennet had supported him.

Frances Stewart, later Duchess of Richmond, by Sir Peter Lely

(*Reproduced by gracious permission of Her Majesty the Queen*)

desiring me that I would write to him and give him information upon all occasions in matters that concern him – which, put together with what he preambled with yesterday, makes me think that my Lord doth truly esteem me still, and desires to preserve my service to him – which I do bless God for.

In the middle of our discourse my Lady Crew came in to bring my Lord Word that he hath another son,[1] my Lady being brought to bed just now. I did not think her time had been so nigh; but she is well brought to bed, for which God be praised – and send my Lord to study the laying up of something the more.

Thence with Creed to St. James; and missing Mr. Coventry, to White-hall, where staying for him in one of the galleries, there comes out of the Chayre roome Mrs. Steward in a most lovely form, with her hair all about her eares, having her picture taking there.[2] There was the King and twenty more I think, standing by all the while, and a lovely creature she in this dress seemed to be.

Thence to the Change by coach, and so home to dinner – and then to my office. In the evening Mr. Hill, Andrews and I to my chamber to sing, which we did very pleasantly; and then to my office again, where very late; and so home with my mind, I bless God, in good state of ease and body of health; only, my head at this Juncture very full of business how to get something – among others, what this rogue Creed will do before he goes to sea – for I would fain be rid of him and see what he means to do – for I will then declare myself his firm friend or enemy.

---

1. James, his sixth son; so-named perhaps in compliment to the Duke of York.

2. Frances Stewart was much painted at this period. The sitting here referred to could have been to Huysmans (see below, p. 254), or to Lely for the portrait in the set of portraits (now at Hampton Court) painted c. 1662–5 for the Duchess of York and seen by Pepys on 21 August 1668. The latter seems, on grounds of style, to have been painted a little earlier than 1664, but certainly shows her with her hair about her ears: R. B. Beckett, *Lely*, pl. 100. The Chair Room appears to have been an important but very small royal chamber, judging from the pictures and works of art it contained temp. Charles I. These are catalogued after the pictures in the Long Gallery towards the Orchard, which it probably adjoined: O. Millar (ed.), *Abraham van der Doort's Catalogue* (Walp. Soc., vol. 37), pp. 62+. (OM).

16. Up in the morning, my head mightily confounded with the great deal of business I have upon me today. But to the office and there despatched Mr. Creed's business pretty well, about his bill.[1] But then there comes W. Howe for my Lord's Bill of Imprest for 500*l* to carry with him this voyage. And so I was at a loss how to carry myself in it, Creed being there;[2] but there being no help, I delivered it to them both and let them contend; which I perceive they did both endeavour to have it, but W. Howe took it and the other had the discretion to suffer it. But I think I cleared myself to Creed, that it passed not from*a* any practice of mine. At noon rose and did some necessary business at the Change. Thence to Trinity-house to a dinner which Sir G. Carteret makes there as Maister this year. Thence to White-hall to the Tanger Comittee; and there above my expectation got the business of our contract for the Victualling carried for my people – *viz.*, Alsop, Lanyon and Yeabsly.

And by their promise I do thereby get 300*l* per annum to myself – which doth overjoy me; and the matter is left to me to draw up.[3] Mr. Lewes was in the gallery, and is mightily amused at it; and I believe Mr. Gauden will make some stir about it, for he wrote to Mr. Coventry today about it, to argue why he should for the King's convenience have it; but Mr. Coventry most justly did argue freely for them that served cheapest.

Thence walked a while with Mr. Coventry in the gallery and first find that he is mighty cold in his present opinion of Mr. Peter Pett, for his flagging and doing things so lazily there.[4] And he did also surprize me with a question why Deane did not bring in their report of the Timber of Clarindon. What he means thereby, I know not; but at present put him off. Nor do I know how to steer myself – but must think of it and advise with my Lord Sandwich.

a repl. with

---

1. See above, p. 46, n. 1; below, p. 213 & n. 2.

2. Pepys had successfully plotted with Howe for the latter to displace Creed as Sandwich's Secretary and Deputy-Treasurer of the fleet now setting out.

3. See below, pp. 226, 229, 263; and PRO, CO 279/3, f. 245*r* for details. Pepys later refers to this contract as his 'Plymouth business'.

4. At Chatham, where he was Navy Commissioner.

Thence with Creed by coach to my Lord Sandwiches, and there I got Mr. Moore to give me my Lord's hand for my receipt of 109*l* more of my money of Sir*a* G. Carteret, so that then his*b* debt to me will be under 500*l* I think.[1] This doth ease my mind also.

Thence carried him and W Howe into London and set them down at Sir G. Carteret to receive some money; and I home and there busy very late; and so home to supper and to bed with my mind in pretty good ease – my business being in a pretty good condition everywhere.

17. *Lords day.* All the morning at my office doing business there, it raining hard. So dined at home alone. After dinner walked to my Lord's – and there found him and much other guest[s] at table at dinner, and it seems they have christened his young son today, called him James; I got a piece of cake. I got my Lord to sign and seal my business about*b* my selling of Brampton land;[2] which though not so full as I would, yet is as full as I can at present. Walked home again, and there fell to read; and by and by comes my Uncle Wight, Dr. Burnett and another gentleman, and talked and drank – and the Doctor showed me the manner of eating Turpentine;[3] which pleases me well, for it is with great ease. So they being gone, I to supper and to bed.

18. Up, and walked to my Lord's and there took my leave of him, he seeming very friendly to me, in as serious a manner as ever in his life – and I believe he is very confident of me. He sets out

a repl. 'Mr.'   *b* repl. 'the'   *c* repl. 'at'

1. See above, ii. 61, n. 5
2. PL, Freshfield MSS, no. 15 (in Pepys's hand, with signatures and seals of parties and witnesses); endorsed 'Confirmacion of the Sale of some Lands late Capt. Pepys's for the paymt of Debts, Legacys and other Charges'. It authorised the sale of land to William Prior and others and of 'a further parcell of land in Brampton and Offord'. The executors were required under the agreement made with the heir-at-law (Thomas Pepys of London) to obtain the consent of Lord Sandwich and of Thomas Pepys of Hatcham before selling land from the estate in order to meet the charges on it (annuities of £55 p.a. and a debt of £821): above, iv. 42 & n. 2. Pepys of Hatcham added his signature later: below, vi. 100.
3. Pills for the stone: see above, pp. 1–2 & n.

this morning for Deale. Thence to St. James to the Duke and there did our usual business. He discourses very freely of a war with Holland, to begin about winter; so that I believe we shall come to it. Before we went up to the Duke, Sir G. Carteret and I did talk together in the parke about my Lord Chancellors business of the timber, he telling me freely that my Lord Chancellor was never so angry with him in all his life as he was for this business, in great passion – and that when he saw me there, he knew what it was about. And plots now with me how we may serve my Lord – which I am mightily glad of and I hope together we may do it.

Thence to Westminster to my barbers, to have my perriwig he lately made me cleansed of its nits; which vexed me cruelly, that he should put such a thing into my hands. Here meeting his maid Jane, that hath lived with them so long, I talked with her; and sending her of an errand to Dr. Clerkes, did meet her and took her into a little alehouse in Brewers-yard and there did sport with her, without any knowledge of her though – and a very pretty innocent girl she is. Thence to my Lord Chancellors; but he being busy, I went away to the Change and so home to dinner. By and by comes Creed, and I out with him to Fleet-street, and he to Mr. Povy's. I to my Lord Chancellor's; and missing him again, walked to Poveys and there saw his new perspective in his closet.[1] Povy, to my great surprize and wonder, did here attacque me in his own and Mr. Bland's behalf, that I should do for them both with the new contractors for the victualling of the garrison[2] – which I am ashamed that he should ask of me; nor did I believe that he was a man that did seek benefit in such poor things. Besides that he professed that he did not believe that I would have any hand myself in the contract, and yet here declares that he himself would have profit by it; and himself did move me that Sir W Rider might joyne, and Ford with Gauden. I told him I had no interest in them; but[a] I fear they must do something to him – for he told me that

a blot (? with fingermark) in upper margin

---

1. See above, p. 161 & n. 4.   2. At Tangier.
(OM).

those of the Molle[1] do promise to consider him.   Thence home, and Creed with me; and there he took occasion to own his obligations to me, and did lay[a] down twenty pieces in gold upon my shelf in my closet; which I did not refuse, but wish and expected should have been more; but however, this is better then nothing, and now I am out of expectation and shall from hence-forward know how to deal with him.[2]

After discourse of settling his matters here, we went out by coach; and he light at the Temple and there took final leave of me, in order to his fallowing my Lord tomorrow.   I to my Lord Chancellor and discoursed his business with him.   I perceive, and he says plainly, that he will not have any man to have it in his power to say that my Lord Chancellor did contrive the wronging the King of his timber, but yet I perceive he would be glad to have service done him therein; and told me Sir G. Carteret hath told him that he and I would look after his business, to see it done in the best manner for him.   Of this I was glad, and so away.   Thence home, and late with my Tanger men about drawing up their agreement with us,[3] wherein I find much trouble; and after doing as much as we could tonight, broke up and I to bed.

19.   Up and to the office, where we sat all the morning.   At noon dined alone at home.   After dinner, Sir W. Batten and I down by water to Woolwich; where coming to the Rope-yard, we are told that Mr. Falconer, who hath been ill of a relapse these two days, is just now dead.   We went up to his widow, who is sick in bed also; the poor woman in great sorrow, and entreats our friendship, which we shall I think in everything do for her; I am sure I will.   Thence to the Docke, and there in Sheldons garden eat some fruit.   So to Depford a little and thence home, it raining mightily; and being cold, I doubted my health after it.   At[b] the office till 9 a-clock about Sir W Warrens

a repl. 'give'   *b* repl. 'home'

---

1. The contractors for the Tangier mole.
2. This payment was made in return for Pepys's services in the passing of Creed's accounts for his previous voyage: see above, iv. 198, 391 & nn.
3. See above, p. 210 & n. 3.

contract for masts.   And then at home with Lanyon and Yeabsly till 12 and past, about their contract for Tanger; wherein they and*a* I differed, for I would have it drawn to the King's advantage as much as might be – which they did not like, but parted good friends; however, when they were gone, I wished that I had forborne any disagreement till*b* I had had their promise to me in writing.

They being gone, I to bed.

20.   Up, and a while to my office.   And then home with Mr. Deane, till dinner discoursing upon the business of my Lord Chancellors timber in Clarindon-park and how to make a report therein without offending him; which at last I drew up, and hope it will please him.[1]   But I would to God neither I nor he ever had had anything to have done with it.

Dined together with a good pig.   And then out by coach to White-hall to the Comittee for Fishing; but nothing done, it being a great day today there, upon drawing at the Lottery of Sir Arth. Slingsby.[2]   I got in and stood by the two Queens and the Duchesse of York, and just behind my Lady Castlemayne, whom I do heartily adore; and good sport it was to see how most that did give their ten pounds did go away with a pair of gloves only for their lot, and one gentlewoman, one Mrs. Fish, with the only blanke.   And one I stayed to see drew a suit of

a   l.h. repl. s.h. 'do'   b   repl. 'and'

---

1. See above, pp. 203–4 & nn. The report has not been traced.

2. This took place at 2 p.m. in the Banqueting Hall, by the King's permission.   The goods consisted of a coach, plate, jewels and a variety of furnishings (tapestry, gilt-leather hangings, chairs, cabinets and marble tables): *The Newes*, 23 June, p. 405; ib., 14 July, p. 456; *The Intelligencer*, 18 July, p. 464.   Evelyn's view (19 July) was the same as Pepys's: 'the sale was thought to be contriv'd very unhandsomely by the master of it, who was in truth a meer shark'.

Lotteries, as well as being commonly used for raising public funds in all countries of W. Europe, were also granted as favours to private individuals, though in England they were supposed to number no more than eight a year at this time: *CSPD 1664–5*, p. 141.   Sir Arthur Slingsby, Bt (of Patrixbourne, near Canterbury) was a younger brother of Sir Robert, late Comptroller of the Navy, and was presumably now granted a lottery in return for his services to the King in exile.

hangings valued at 430*l*; and they say are well worth the money, or near it. One other suit there is better then that – but very many lots of three and four score pounds. I observed the King and Queens did get but as poor lots as any else. But the wisest man I met with was Mr. Cholmly, who insured as many as would from drawing of the one blanke for 12*d* – in which case there was the whole number of persons to one, which I think was 3 or 400. And so he insured about 200 for*a* 200 shillings, so that he could not have lost if one of them had drawn it – for there was enough to pay the 10*l*; but it happened another drew it, and so he got all the money he took. I left the lottery and went to a play, only a piece of it; which was at the Dukes house, *Worse and Worse* – just the same manner of play, and writ I believe by the same man, as *The Adventures of Five Hours* – very pleasant it was. And I begin to admire Harris more then ever.[1]

Thence to Westminster to see Creed, and he and I took a walk in the park. He is ill, and not able yet to set out after my Lord, but will do tomorrow. So home and late at my office; and so home to bed.

This evening being moonshine, I played a little late upon my flagelette in the garden.

But being at Westminster-hall, I met with great news: that Mrs. Lane is married to one Martin, one that serves Captain Marsh. She is gone abroad with him today, very fine. I must have a bout with her very shortly, to see how she finds marriage.

21. Up, and to the office, where we sat all the morning; among other things, making a contract with Sir W. Warren for almost 1000 Gottenburg masts, the biggest that ever was made in the Navy and wholly of my composing, and a good one

a repl. 'shilling'

---

1. Henry Harris, a leading actor in the Duke of York's Company, could play comic and romantic parts equally well. *Worse and worse* was an adaptation (now lost) by the 2nd Earl of Bristol, of a Spanish comedy, probably Caldéron's *Peor está que estaba*: see Downes, p. 26. *The adventures of five hours* was not by Bristol, but by Samuel Tuke: see above, iv 8 & n. 2. (A).

I hope it is for the King.[1]   Dined at Sir W. Batten, where I have
not eat these many months.   Sir G. Carteret, Mr Coventry,
Sir J. Mennes and myself there only, and my Lady.   A good
venison pasty, and very merry and pleasant I made myself with
my Lady, and she as much to me.   This morning to the office
comes Nich. Osborne, Mr. Gauden's clerk, to desire of me what
piece of plate I would choose to have, a 100*l* or thereabouts,
bestowed upon me in – he having order to lay out so much, and
out of his freedom with me doth of himself come to make this
question: I a great while urged my unwillingness to take any,
not knowing how I could serve Mr. Gauden; but left it wholly
to himself.   So at noon I find brought home in fine leather cases
a pair of the noblest Flaggons that ever I saw all days of my life.
Whether I shall keep them or no, I cannot tell; for it is to oblige
me to him in that business of the Tanger victualing, wherein I
doubt I shall not; but glad I am to see that I shall be sure to get
something on one side or other, have it which will.   So with a
merry heart, I looked upon them and locked them up.

After dinner to my Lord Chancellors; a good account of his
business, and he is very well pleased therewith – and carries himself with great discretion to me, without seeming over-glad or
beholding to me; and yet I know that he doth think himself
very well served by me.

Thence to Westminster and to Mrs. Lane's lodging to give her
joy.   And there suffered me to deal with her as I used to do;
and by and by her husband comes, a sorry simple fellow, and
his letter to her, which she proudly showed me, a simple, silly,
nonsensical thing.   A man of no discourse, and I fear married

---

1. By this contract (signed 28
July) 977 masts were to be delivered
to Deptford by 24 September: *CSPD
1664–5*, p. 125.   The agreement was
much criticised: immediately by
Batten, and in 1669–70 by the Brooke
House Committee, who suspected
that Warren was unduly favoured.
See B. Pool, *Navy Board contracts
1660–1832*, p. 28. Pepys remained
of the opinion that it was best to rely
on a single experienced contractor
for the supply of masts: see esp. his

letters to Commissioner Pett (16
June 1665) in *Shorthand Letters*, pp.
44–5.   For further references to the
contract, see below, 2 July, 29 November 1668 and nn.   Papers on the dispute about it are in PL 2554; PL
2874, pp. 400+, 515+, 559+;
NWB, pp. 161–2; HMC, *Lindsey
1660–1702*, pp. 116–50; Longleat,
Coventry MSS 96, ff. 52r, 54–67,
118r, 294r, ib., 97, ff. 114–15, 242–6;
CTB, v. 1299–1300.

her to make a prize of; which he is mistaken in. And a sad wife I believe she will prove to him, for she urged me to appoint a time, as soon as he is gone out of town, to give her a meeting next week.

So by water with a couple of Cosens of Mrs. Lane's; and set them down at Queenehive and I through bridge home. And there late at business and so home to supper and to bed.

22. Up and to my office, where busy all the morning. At noon to the Change, and so home to dinner and then down by water to Deptford; where coming too soon, I spent an hour in looking round the yard and putting Mr. Shish to measure a piece or two of timber; which he did most cruelly wrong and to the King's loss, 12 or 13s in a piece of 28 f[oot] in contents.[1]   Thence[a] to the Clerke of the Cheques, from whose house Mr. Falconer was buried today – Sir J. Mennes and I the only principall-officers that were there.

We walked to church with him; and then I left them without staying the sermon, and straight home by water and there find, as I expected, Mr. Hill and Andrews and one slovenly and ugly fellow, Seignor Pedro, who sings Italian songs to the Theorbo most neatly; and they spent the whole evening in singing the best piece of musique, counted of all hands in the world, made by Seignor Charissimi[2] the famous master in Rome.   Fine it was indeed, and too fine for me to judge of.

They have spoke to Pedro to meet us every week, and I fear it will grow a trouble to me if we once come to bid guests to meet us, especially idle masters – which doth a little displease me to consider.

They gone, comes Mr. Lanyon, who tells me Mr. Alsop is now

a repl. 'And I observe'

---

1. Jonas Shish was Assistant Master-Shipwright at Deptford yard. According to Pepys's note on this trial (NWB, p. 59), Pepys reckoned the timber as measuring 27 ft and Shish at 37 ft – which would imply an overcharge of 20s. In a letter to Commissioner Pett of July, Pepys had reported that Shish was allowing the blockmakers to measure blocks wrongly: *Further Corr.*, pp. 26–7.

2. Giacomo Carissimi (d. 1674); most famous for his vocal compositions, in particular for his quasi-operatic chamber cantatas and oratorios. (E).

become dangerously ill and fears his recovery, which shakes my expectation of 300*l* per annum by that business. And therefore bless God for what*a* Mr. Gauden hath sent me; which from some discourse today with Mr. Osborne, swearing that he knows not anything of this business of the victualling but the contrary, that it is not that that moves Mr. Gauden to send it me, for he hath had order for it any time these two months. Whether this be true or no, I know not; but I shall hence with the more confidence keep it.

To supper and to the office a little and to walk in the garden, the moon shining bright and fine warm fair weather. And so home to bed.

23. Up, and all the morning at the office. At noon to the Change, where I took occasion to break the business of my Lord Chancellors*b* timber to Mr. Coventry in the best manner I could. He professed to me that till Sir G. Carteret did speak of it at the table after our officers were gone to survey it, he did not know that my Lord Chancellor had anything to do with it. But now he says that he had been told by the Duke that Sir G. Carteret had spoke to him about it, and that he had told the Duke that were he in my Lord Chancellor's case, if he were his father, he would rather fling away the gains of 2 or 3000*l* then have it said that that timber, which should have been the King's if it had continued the Duke of Albemarles, was concealed*c* by us in favour of my Lord Chancellor. "For," says he, "he is a great man, and all such as he, and he himself perticularly, have a great many enemies that would be glad of such a advantage against him."

When I told him*d* it was strange that Sir J. Mennes and Sir G. Carteret, that knew my Lord Chancellor's concernment therein, should not at first inform us – he answered me: that for Sir J. Mennes, he is looked upon to be an old good companion, but by nobody at the other end of the towne[1] as any man of business; and that my Lord Chancellor, he dares say, never did tell him of it. Only, Sir G. Carteret, he doth believe, must needs know

a repl. 'our'   *b* MS. 'Treasurers'   *c* MS. 'not concealed'
          d MS. 'it'

---

1. At Whitehall.

it, for he and Sir J Shaw[1] are the greatest confidants he hath in the world.

So for himself, he said, he would not mince the matter; but was resolved to do what was fit, and stand upon his own legs therein. And that he would speak to the Duke, that he and Sir G. Carteret might be appointed to attend my Lord Chancellor in it.

All this disturbs me mightily; I know not what to say to it, nor how to carry myself therein; for a compliance will discommend me to Mr. Coventry and a discompliance to my Lord Chancellor. But I think to let it alone, or at least meddle in it as little more as I can.

From thence walked toward Westminster; and being in an idle and wanton humour, walked through Fleet-alley, and there stood a most pretty wench at one of the doors. So I took a turn or two; but what by sense of honour and conscience, I would not go in. But much against my will, took coach and away to Westminster-hall, and there light of Mrs. Lane and plotted with her to go over the water; so met at Whites stairs in Channel-row, and over to the old house at Lambeth-marsh and there eat and drank and had my pleasure of her twice – she being the strangest woman in talk, of love to her husband sometimes, and sometimes again she doth not care for him – and yet willing enough to allow me a liberty of doing what I would with her. So spending 5 or 6*s* upon her, I could do what I would; and after an hour's stay and more, back again and set her ashore there again, and I forward to Fleetstreete and called at Fleet-alley, not knowing how to command myself; and went in and there saw what formerly I have been acquainted with, the wickedness of those houses and the forcing a man to present expense. The woman, endeed, is a most lovely woman; but I had no courage to meddle with her, for fear of her not being wholesome, and so counterfeited[a] that I had not money enough. It was pretty to see how cunning that Jade was; would not suffer me to have to do in any manner with her after she saw I had no money;

a   MS. 'counterfeiting'

---

1. Sir John Shaw, merchant and customs farmer. Among his many offices he held a surveyorship of the royal forests.

but told me then I would not come again, but she now was sure I would come again – though I hope in God I shall not, for though she be one of the prettiest women I ever saw, yet I fear her abusing me.

So desiring God to forgive me for this vanity, I went home, taking some books home from my bookseller and taking his lad home with me, to whom I paid 10*l* for books I have laid up money for and laid out within these three weeks – and shall do no more a great while I hope.

So to my office, writing letters; and then home and to bed, weary of the pleasure I have had today and ashamed to think of it.

24. *Lords day.* Up, in some pain*a* all day from yesterday's passages, having taken cold I suppose. So stayed within all day, reading of two or three good plays. At night to my office a little, and so home after supper to bed.

25. Up, and with Sir J. Mennes and Sir W. Batten by coach to St. James; but there the Duke being gone out, we to my Lord Berkely's chamber, Mr. Coventry being there. And among other things, there met with a printed copy of the King's Comission for the repair of Pauls;[1] which is very large, and large power for collecting money and recovering of all people that had bought or sold formerly anything belonging to the church.

And here I find my Lord Mayor of the City set in order before the Archbishop or any nobleman, though all the greatest officers of state are there.

But yet I do not hear by my Lord Berkely, who is one of them, that anything is like to come of it.

Thence back again homeward, and Sir W. Batten and I to the Coffee-house. But no news; only, the plague is very hot still and increases among the Dutch.[2]

Home to dinner, and after dinner walked forth; and do what I could, I could not keep myself from going through Fleet-lane,

a repl. 'time'

---

1. *His majesties commission concerning the reparation of the cathedral church of St. Paul* (1663). For the repairs, see above, iv. 261 & n. 1.

2. See above, iv. 340, n. 2. The weekly death-roll in Amsterdam was now c. 700: *CSPClar.*, v. 410.

but had the sense of safety and honour not to go in, and the rather, being a holiday,[1] I feared I might meet with some people that might know me.

Thence to Charing-cross and there called at Unthankes[2] to see what I owed, but found nothing; and here being a couple of pretty ladies, lodgers, in the kitchen, I stayed a little there. Thence to my Barber Gervas's, who this day buries his child which he had lately; which it seems was born without a passage behind, so that it never voided anything in the week or fortnight that it hath been born.

Thence to Mr. Reeves, it coming just now in my head to buy a Microscope – but he was not within. So I walked all round that end of the town, among the loathsome people and houses;[3] but God be thanked, had no desire to visit any of them. So home, where I met Mr. Lanyon, who tells me Mr. Alsop is past hopes – which will mightily disappoint me in my hopes there, and yet it may be not. I shall think whether it will be safe for me to venture myself or no – and come in as an adventurer.[4]

He gone, Mr. Cole (my old Jack Cole)[5] comes*a* to see and speak with me; and his errand, in short, to tell me that he is giving over his trade. He can do no good in it, and will turn what he hath into money and go to sea – his father being dead and leaving him little, if anything. This I was sorry to hear, he being a man of good parts, but I fear debauched.

I promised him all the friendship I can do him; which will end in little, though I truly mean it. And so I made him stay with me till 11 at night, talking of old*b* school stories, and very pleasing ones; and truly, I find that we did spend our time and thoughts then otherwise then I think boys do now, and I think as well as my thoughts at the best are now. He supped with me, and so away and I to bed.

And strange to see how we are all divided that were bred so

a repl. 'comes)'   *b* repl. 'odd'

---

1. St James's Day. Cf. below, p. 222, n. 2.

2. His wife's tailor.

3. Reeves's shop was in Long Acre, which (with Fleet Alley near by) was a well-known prostitutes' quarter.

4. In the business of victualling Tangier.

5. A schoolfellow at St Paul's.

long at school together, and what various fortunes we have run, some good, some bad.

26. All the morning at the office. At noon to Anth. Joyces to our gossips dinner;[1] I had sent a dozen and a half of bottles of wine thither and paid my double share besides, which is 18s. Very merry we were, and when the women were merry and ris from table, I above with them, ne'er a man but I; I begin discourse of my not getting of children and prayed[a] them to give me their opinions and advice; and they freely and merrily did give me these ten among them. 1. Do not hug my wife too hard nor too much. 2. Eat no late suppers. 3. Drink Juyce of sage. 4. Tent and toast. 5. Wear cool Holland-drawers. 6. Keep stomach warm and back cool. 7. Upon my query whether it was best to do at night or morn, they answered me neither one nor other, but when we have most mind to it. 8. Wife not to go too straight-laced. 9. Myself to drink Mum and sugar. 10. Mrs. Ward did give* me to change my plat. The 3rd, 4th, 6th, 7th, and 10th they all did seriously declare and lay much stress upon them, as rules fit to be observed indeed, and especially the last: to lie with our heads where our heels do, or at least to make the bed high at feet and low at head.

Very merry all, as much as I could be in such sorry company.

Great discourse of the fray yesterday in Moore-fields, how the Butchers at first did beat the Weavers (between[b] whom there hath been ever an old competition for mastery), but at last the weavers rallied and beat them.[2] At first the butchers knock down all for weavers that had green or blue aprons, till they were fain to pull them off and put them in their breeches. At last, the butchers were fain to pull off their sleeves, that they might not be known, and were soundly beaten out of the field, and some deeply wounded and bruised – till at last the weavers went out

a repl. 'they'   *b* MS. 'being'

---

1. Held to celebrate the birth of the Joyces' child: see above, p. 200.
2. This fight between the rival apprentices arose from the fact that 25 July was Election Day for the

Weavers' Company. The day was also celebrated by a service, with bells, at Cripplegate Church, and a dinner. Cf. GL, MS. 4648/1, n.p.

tryumphing, calling, "A hundred pound for a Butcher!" Toward [evening] I to Mr. Reeves to see a Microscope, he having been with me today morning, and there chose one which I will have.

Thence back and took up young Mrs. Harman, a pretty-bred and pretty-humored woman, whom I could love well, though not handsome, yet for her person and carriage and black eye. By the way met her husband going for her, and set them both down at home; and so home to my office a while, and so to supper and bed.

27. Up; and after some discourse with Mr. Duke, who is to be Secretary to the Fishery and is now Secretary to the Committee for Trade, who I find a very ingenious man, I went to Mr. Povys and there heard a little of his empty*a* discourse; and fain he would have Mr. Gauden been the victualler for Tanger, which none but a fool would say to me, when he knows he hath made it his request to me to get him something of these men that now do it. Thence to*b* St. James's; but Mr. Coventry being ill and in bed, I did not stay, but to White-hall a little, walked up and down, and so home to fit papers against the afternoon. And after dinner to the Change a little and then to White-hall, where anon the Duke of Yorke came and a Committee we had of Tanger; where I read over my rough draft of the contract for Tanger Victualling and acquainted them with the death of Mr. Alsopp, which Mr. Lanyon had told me this morning – which is a sad consideration, to see how uncertain a thing our lives are and how little to be presumed of in our greatest undertakings.

The words of the contract approved of, and I home; and there came Mr. Lanyon to me and brought my neighbour Mr. Andrews to me, whom he proposes for his partener in the room of Mr. Alsopp; and I like well enough of it.

We read over the contract together and discoursed it well over, and so parted; and I am glad to see it once over in this condition again, for Mr. Lanyon and I had some discourse today about my share in it; and I hope, if it goes on, to have my first hopes of 300*l* per annum.

They gone, I to supper and to bed.

This afternoon came my great store of Coles in, being ten Chaldron, so that I may see how long they will last me.

a repl. 'em'-   *b* 'to' repeated

28. At the office all the morning. Dined, after Change, at home, and then abroad and seeing *The Bondman* upon the posts, I consulted my oaths and find I may go safely this time without breaking it;[1] I went thither, notwithstanding my great desire to have gone to Fleete ally, God forgive me, again. There I saw it acted; it is true, for want of practice they had many of them forgot their parts a little, but Baterton and my poor Ianthe out-do all the world.[2] There is nothing more taking in the world with me then that play.[3]

Thence to Westminster to my barbers; and strange to think how when I found that Jervas himself did intend to bring home my periwig, and not Jane his maid, I did desire not to have it at all, for I had a mind to have her bring it home. I also went to Mr. Blagraves, about speaking to him for his kinswoman to come live with my wife; but they are not come to town, and so I home by coach and to my office, and then to supper and to bed.

My present posture is this. My wife in the country and my maid Besse[a] with her, and all quiet there. I am endeavouring to find a Woman for her to my mind; and above all, one[b] that understands musique, especially singing. I am the willinger to keep one because I am in good hopes to get 2 or 300*l* per annum extraordinary by the business of the victualing of Tanger – and yet Mr. Alsop, my chief hopes, is dead since my looking after it, and now Mr. Lanyon I fear is falling sick too.

I am pretty well in health; only, subject to wind upon any cold, and then immediate and great pains.

a repl. 'Jane'　　　*b* MS. 'whom'

---

1. Pepys had sworn not to go to plays more often than once a month (above, p. 33), and had seen one as recently as 20 July, but as he saw only 'a piece of it', he evidently thought that he was entitled to see another. On this occasion he saw a performance of Philip Massinger's tragicomedy (q.v. above, ii. 49 & n. 2) at the LIF. (A).

2. In this play, Thomas Betterton played Pisander, who is disguised as the bondman, Marullo. 'Ianthe' (his wife) probably played Cleora. The faulty memorising of parts by Restoration actors was sometimes due to poor discipline, but their large repertoire of plays and frequent changes of programme must also be taken into account. During his career Thomas Betterton had to master over 120 major roles. (A).

3. Between 1 March 1661 and this date, Pepys saw *The Bondman*, in whole or in part, seven times. (A).

All our discourse is of a Dutch war; and I find it is likely to come to it, for they are very high and desire not to compliment us at all as far as I hear, but to send a good fleet to Guinny to oppose us there. My Lord Sandwich newly gone to sea, and I, I think, fallen into his very good opinion again; at least, he did before his going, and by his letter since, show me all manner of respect and confidence.

I am over-Joyed in hopes that upon this month's account I shall find myself worth 1000*l*, besides the rich present of two silver and gilt flagons which Mr. Gauden did give me the other day.

I do now live very prettily at home, being most seriously, quietly, and neatly served by my two maids, Jane and the girl Su – with both of whom I am mightily well pleased.

My greatest trouble is the settling of Brampton estate, that I may know what to expect and how to be able to leave it when I die,*a* so as to be just to my promise to my Uncle Tho. and his son.[1] The next thing is this cursed trouble my Brother Tom is likely to put us to by his death, forcing us to law with his Creditors, among others Dr. Tom Pepys, and that with some shame, as trouble.[2] And the last, how to know in what manner, as to saving or spending, my father lives, lest they should run me in debt as one of my uncles executors, and I never the wiser nor better for it. But in all this I hope shortly to be at leisure to consider and inform myself well.

29. At the office*b* all the morning, despatching of business. At noon to the Change after dinner, and thence to Tom Trice about Dr. Pepys's business; and thence, it raining, turned into Fleete-ally and there was with Cocke an hour or so. The jade,

a MS. 'day'   *b* repl. 'home'

---

1. By the final clause of the agreement made with Thomas Pepys and his son Tom in February 1663, Pepys had agreed to strict limits on his right to sell any of the estate: above, iv. 42 & n. 2. And in the event of the failure of male heirs of the executor's family, the estate was to pass to the family of Thomas Pepys, as heir-at-law: below, 26 May 1667.
2. On 10 July John Pepys had written to his son Samuel: 'the fowle mouthed doctor is resolved to be trouble som' (Rawl. A 182, f. 329*r*). See the correspondence in *Family Letters*, pp. 8–13.

whether she [thought] I would not give her money or not*a* enough, she would not offer to invite to do anything, but the contrary, saying she had them; which I was glad of, for I had no mind to meddle with her. But had my end, to see what a cunning jade she was, to see her impudent tricks and ways of getting money, and raising the reckoning by still calling for things, that it came to 6 or 7s presently. So away home – glad I escaped without any inconvenience; and there came Mr. Hill, Andrews and Seignor Pedro, and great store of Musique we had, but I begin to be weary of having a master with us, for it spoils methinks the ingenuity of our practice.

After they were gone comes Mr. Bland to me and sat till 11 at night with me, talking of the garrison of Tanger and serving them with pieces-of-eight.[1] A mind he hath to be imployed there, but dares not desire any courtesy of me; and yet would fain engage me to be for him, for I perceive they do all find that I am the busy man to see the King have right done him, by enquiring out other Bidders. Being quite tired with him, I got him gone, and so to bed.

30. All the morning at the office. At noon to the Change, where great talk of a rich present brought by an East India ship from some of the princes of India, worth to the King 70000*l* in two precious stones.[2] After dinner to the office and there all the afternoon – making an end of several things against the end of the Month, that I may clear all my reckonings tomorrow. Also, this afternoon with great content I finished the contract for Victualing of Tangier with Mr. Lanyon and the rest, and to my comfort got him and Andrews to sign to the giving me 300*l* per annum – by which, at least, I hope to be a 100*l* or 2 the better.

a MS. 'no'

---

1. He wrote to Pepys on the subject on the 30th: PRO, CO 279/3, ff. 224–5.

2. There were three (not two) stones, which the King showed to the French ambassador, wrapped in a red satin bag. De Cominges thought them of no great value: J. J. Jusserand, *French Ambassador*, pp. 228–9. They were a present from an Armenian styling himself Governor of Maliapur, who asked in return to be given a ship: *Cal. court mins E. India Company*, *1664–7* (ed. E. B. Sainsbury), pp. 59–60.

Wrote many letters by the post, to ease my mind of business and to clear my paper of Minutes,[1] as I did lately oblige myself to clear every thing against the end of the month. So at night, with my mind quiet and contented, to bed. This day I sent a side of venison and six bottles of wine to Kate Joyce.[2]

31. *Lords day.* Up and to church, where I have not been these many weeks. So home; and thither, inviting him yesterday, comes Mr. Hill, at which I was a little troubled; but made up all very well, carrying him with me to Sir J. Mennes, where I was invited and all our families to a venison pasty. Here, good cheer and good discourse. After dinner, Mr. Hill and I to my house*a* and there to Musique all the afternoon. He being gone in the evening, I to my accounts; and to my great joy and with great thanks to Almighty God, I do find myself most clearly worth 1014*l* – the first time that ever I was worth 1000*l* before – which is the heighth of all that ever I have for a long time pretended to. But by the blessing of God upon my care, I hope to lay up something more in a little time, if this business of the victualing of Tangier goes on as I hope it will.

So with praise to God for this state of fortune that I am brought to as to wealth – and my condition being as I have at large set it down two days ago in this book – I home to supper and to bed, desiring*b* God to give me the grace to make good use of what I have and continue my care and diligence to gain more.

a repl. 'office'   *b* MS. 'discerning'

---

1. At this time Pepys kept monthly 'memorandums' of things to be done: cf. below, p. 284. He had a life-long habit of drawing up 'papers of minutes' of this sort. Several survive from a later period: e.g. *Priv.*

Corr., i. 165; *Tangier Papers*, pp. 251 252.
2. She was just out of childbed: above, p. 200.

AUGUST.

1. Up, my mind very light from my last night's accounts. And so up and with Sir J. Mennes, Sir W. Batten, and Sir W. Penn to St. James; where among other things, having prepared with some industry every man a part this morning and no sooner (for fear they should either consider of it or discourse of it one to another), Mr. Coventry did move the Duke and obtain it that one*a* of the Clerke's of the Clerk of the Acts shall have an addition of 30*l* a year, as Mr. Turner hath – which I am glad of, that I may give T. Hater 20*l* and keep 10*l* toward a boy's keeping.[1]

Thence Mr. Coventry and I to the Atturny's chamber at the Temple; but not being there, we parted and I home and there with great joy told T. Hater what I had done, with which the poor wretch was very glad – though his modesty would not suffer him to say much.

So to the Coffee-house, and there all the house full of the victory Generall Souche (who is a Frenchman, a soldier-of-fortune, commanding part of the German army) hath had against the Turke – killing 4000 men and taking most extraordinary spoil.[2] Thence, taking up Harman and his wife, carried them to Anth. Joyces – where we had my venison in a pasty, well done; but Lord, to see how much they made of it, as if they had never eat any before. And very merry we were, but Will most troublesomely so. And I find he and his wife have a most wretched

a repl. 'the very eldest'

---

1. Thomas Turner (as chief clerk) had been given an extra allowance in 1660: above, i. 228 & n. 2. A Council order in Pepys's favour for an additional £30 p.a. was issued on 3 August (BM, Add. 9314, f. 6*r*), and in consequence Tom Edwards began work for him on 27 August.

2. Louis Ratuit, Comte de Souches, had just won the battle of Lewenz, in Hungary, on 9/19 July. The news had appeared in *The Intelligencer* published this day (pp. 494–6), but the number of killed was there given as 'above 6000'. Cf. *A true and perfect relation of the battail and victory lately obtained near Lewentz against twenty five thousand Turks, Tartars and Moldavians* (1664). For the war, see above, iv. 316, n. 1.

life one with another. But we took no notice, but were very merry as I could be in such company. But Mrs. Harman is a very pretty humoured wretch, whom I could love with all my heart, being so good and innocent company. Thence to Westminster to Mr. Blagraves; and there, after singing a thing or two over, I spoke to him about a woman for my wife and he offered me his kinswoman; which I was glad of, but she is not at present well. But however, I hope to have her. Thence to my Lord Chancellors; and thence with Mr. Coventry, who appointed to meet me there, and with him to the Atturny Generall and there with Sir Ph. Warwicke consulted of a new commission to be had through the Broad Seale, to enable us to make this contract for Tanger=Victualing.[1] So home, and there talked long with Will about the young woman of his family which he spoke of for to live with my wife;[2] but though she hath very many good qualitys, yet being a neighbour's child, and young and not very staid, I dare not venture of having her, because of her being able to spread any report of our family upon any discontent among the hearts of our neighbours.

So that my dependence is upon Mr. Blagrave. And so home to supper and to bed.

Last night at 12 a-clock I was waked with knocking at Sir W Pen's door; and what was it but people's running up and down to bring him word that his Brother (Captain Pen),[3] who hath been a good while it seems sick, is dead.

2. At the office all the morning. At noon dined, and then to the Change and there walked two hours or more with Sir W Warren – who after much discourse in general of Sir W. Batten's dealings, he fell to talk how everybody must live by their places; and that he was willing, if I desired it, that I should go shares with him in anything that he deals in. He told me again and again too, that he confesses himself my debtor 100*l*, for my service and friendship to him in his present great contract

1. Issued on 17 August, the patent gave the Commissioners power to receive money both for this contract and for the construction of the mole: PRO, CO 279/3, ff. 240+.
2. Mary Mercer, daughter of the family with whom Will Hewer now lodged. She served Mrs Pepys for two years from September 1664.
3. George Penn, twenty years older than Sir William and once a merchant in Sanlúcar, Spain.

of masts,[1] and that between this and Christmas he shall be in stock and will pay it me.   This I like well, but do not desire to become a merchant and there[fore] will put it off, but desired time to think of it.

Thence to the King's play-house and there saw *Bartholomew fayre*, which doth still please me and is, as it is acted, the best comedy in the world I believe.[2]   I chanced to sit by Tom Killigrew – who tells me that he is setting up a Nursery;[3] that is, is going to build a house in Moore fields wherein he will have common plays acted.   But four operas it **shall have in the** year, to act[a] six weeks at a time – where we shall have the best Scenes and Machines, the best Musique, and everything as Magnificent as is in Christendome;   and to that end hath sent for voices and painters and other persons from Italy.

Thence homeward;   called upon my Lord Marlborough, and so home and to my office;   and then to Sir W Pen and with him and[b] our fellow-officers and servants of the house, and none else, to church to lay his brother in the ground – wherein nothing handsome at all, but that he lays him under the communion table in the chancel – about 9 at night.[4]   So home and to bed.

3.   Up betimes and set some Joyners on work to new lay my floor in our Wardrobe, which I intend to make a room for Musique.[5]   Thence abroad to Westminster;   among other things, to Mr. Blagrave's and there have his consent for his kinswoman to come to be with my wife for her woman;   at which I am well pleased – and hope she may do well.

a   repl. 'act'   b   repl. 'to'

---

1. See above, pp. 215–16 & n.

2. This was the comedy by Ben Jonson, now at the TR, Drury Lane. Pepys had revised his opinion since his notice at 8 June 1661.   (A).

3. Thomas Killigrew was manager of the King's Company and of the Theatre Royal where they played. A 'nursery' was a minor theatre for the training of young actors.   On 30 March 1664 Killigrew and Davenant received royal licence to institute a theatre of this kind.   Killigrew was

probably referring to this project, but he was unable to set up his nursery at Moorfields: below, 12 February 1667.   (A).

4. The register of St Olave's records the burial under 3 August: *Harl. Soc. Reg.*, 46/198.   It was a sign of social standing to be buried in the chancel and at night.

5. Until his departure in November 1663 Will Hewer had occupied this room: above, iv. 320, 382.

Thence to White-hall to meet with Sir G. Carteret about hiring some ground to make our mast-dock at Deptford;[1] but being Council morning, failed. But met with Mr. Coventry and he and I discoursed of the likeliness of a Duch warr, which I think is very likely now, for the Duch do prepare a fleet to oppose us at Guinny.[2] And he doth think we shall, though neither of us hath a mind to it,[a] fall into it of a sudden. And yet the plague doth increase among them and is got into their fleet, and Updam's own ship[3] – which makes it strange they should be so high.

Thence to the Change, and thence home to dinner and down by water to Woolwich to the rope-yard; and there visited Mrs. Falconer, who tells me odd stories how Sir W. Penn was rewarded by her husband with a gold watch (but seems not certain of what Sir W. Batten told me, of his daughter having a life* given her in 80*l* per annum) for his helping him to his place, and yet cost him 150*l*[4] to Mr. Coventry besides. He did much advise, it seems, Mr[s]. Falconer not to marry again, expressing that he would have him make his daughter his heire, or words to that purpose – and [it is] that that makes him, she thinks, so cold in giving her any satisfaction. And that W. Boddam hath publicly said, since he came down thither to be clerk of the Ropeyard, that it hath this week cost him 100*l* and would be glad that it would cost him but half as much more for the place. And that he was better before then now; and that if he had been to have bought it, he would not have given so much for it. Now, I am sure Mr. Coventry hath again and again said that he would take nothing, but would give all his part in it freely to him, that so the widow

a repl. 'us'

---

1. This was in working order in 1666 and was used for reserves: *Shorthand Letters*, p. 81; R. G. Albion, *Forests and seapower*, pp. 209–10. Cf. also W. Camden, *Britannia* (1772 ed.), i. 255.

2. See below, pp. 272–3 & n.

3. Cf. Downing to Clarendon, 19/29 July: 'Just now one of Obdam's footmen is come to town with news

that six out of Obdam's ships and eight [others] . . . are carryed to the Pest-house, having the plague upon them' (Lister, iii. 333).

4. At 21 May 1667 below the sum is given as £200. Unlike the watch and the annuity, it is not mentioned in Pepys's note (31 August) in NWB, p. 61. See below, pp. 248–9 & n.

might have something. What the meaning of this is I know not, but that Sir W. Penn doth get something by it.

Thence to the Docke yard and there saw the new ship[1] in great forwardness. So home and to supper; and then to the office, where late, Mr. Bland and I talking about Tanger business. And so home to bed.

4. Up betimes and to the office, fitting myself against a great dispute about the East India Company,[2] which spent afterward with us all the morning. At noon dined with Sir W Pen, a piece of beef only, and I counterfeited a friendship and mirth which I cannot have with him. Yet out with him by his coach, and he did carry me to a play and pay for me at the King's house, which is *The Rivall Ladys*, a very innocent and most pretty witty play[3] – I was much pleased with it; and it being given me, I look upon it as no breach to my oath.[4]

Here we hear that Clun, one of their best actors, was the last night, going out of towne (after he had acted *The Alchymist*, wherein was one of his best parts that he acts) to his country-house, was set upon and murdered; one of the rogues taken, an Irish fellow.[5] It seems, most cruelly butchered and bound – the house will have a great miss of him. Thence visited my Lady Sandwich – who tells me my Lord Fitzharding is to be made a Marquis.[6]

1. The *Royal Catherine*, launched on 26 October.

2. ? about the convoying of the E. Indiaman which was just about to sail: *CSPD 1663-4*, p. 671.

3. A tragicomedy by Dryden, based upon a Spanish plot, first acted and published in 1664. (A).

4. His companion having paid for their admission, Pepys did not think that he was breaking his oath (above, p. 33) to visit theatres only once a month. (A).

5. Walter Clun had been murdered while on his way to his country house in Kentish Town. According to a contemporary poem on his death (reprinted in *A little ark*, ed. G. Thorn-Drury, pp. 30-1), Clun was killed, not on 3 August, but on Tuesday the 2nd.

The part he had played was that of Subtle, a leading character in Jonson's comedy, *The Alchemist*. (A).

6. He was already an Irish viscount. He was never made a marquess, but in March 1665 became Earl of Falmouth and Baron Botetort of Langport in the English peerage. Charles probably delayed the grant until parliament had been prorogued, in order to avoid pressure from a host of other aspirants to the peerage. See C. H. Hartmann, *The King's friend*, pp. 174-8. The date of Fitzharding's earldom given in GEC (17 March 1664) is wrong. On 15 December 1664 Pepys reports a rumour that he intended to succeed Albemarle as General.

Thence home to my office late; and so to supper and to bed.

5. Up very betimes and set my plasterer to work about whiting and colouring my Musique roome; which having with great pleasure seen done, about 10 a-clock I dressed myself, and so mounted upon a very pretty Mare, sent me by Sir W Warren according to his promise yesterday – and so through the City, not a little proud, God knows, to be seen upon so pretty a beast; and to my Cosen W. Joyces, who presently mounted*a* too, and he and I out of town toward Highgate, in the way, at Kentish towne, showing me the place and manner of Cluns being killed and laid in a ditch; and yet was not killed*b* by any wounds, having only one in his arm, but bled to death through his strugling. He told me also the manner of it – of his going home so late, drinking with his whore – and manner of having it found out.

Thence forward to Barnett and there drank, and so by night to Stevenige, it raining a little but not much; and there to my great trouble find that my wife was not come, nor any Stamford coach gone down this week, so that she cannot come. So, vexed and weary and not thoroughly out of pain neither in my old parts – I after supper to bed. And after a little sleep, W Joyce comes in his shirt into my chamber, with a note and a messenger from my wife that she was come by Yorke coach to Bigglesworth, and would be with us tomorrow morning. So, I mightily pleased at her discreet action in this*c* business, I with peace to sleep again till next morning. So up; and here lay Deane Honiwood[1] last night: I met and talked with him this morning, and a simple priest he is,*d* though a good well-meaning man. W Joyce and I to a game at Bowles on the green there – till 8 a-clock; and then comes my wife in the coach, and a coach full of women, only one man riding by, gone down last night to meet a sister of his coming to town. So, very joyful, drank there, not lighting; and we mounted and away with them to Welling, and there light and dined very well, and merry and glad

《6.》

a repl. two symbols rendered illegible   b preceded by blot
    c MS. 'his'   d repl. 'this'

---

1. Michael Honywood, Dean of Lincoln.

to see my poor wife.   Here very merry as being weary I could
be; and after dinner out again and to London.   In our way, all
the way the mightiest merry, at a couple of young gentl[e]men
come down to meet the same gentlewoman, that ever I was in my
life, and so W. Joyce too – to see how one of them was horsed
upon a hard-trotting Sorrell horse, and both of them soundly
weary and galled.   But it is not to be set down how merry we
were all the way.

   We light in Holdborne;*a* and so by another coach my wife and
maid home, *b* and I by horseback; and so at home found all things
well and most mighty neat and clean.   So after welcoming my
wife, a little to the office; and so home to supper and then, weary
and not very well, to bed.

   7.   *Lords day.*   Lay long, caressing my wife and talking – she
telling me sad stories of the ill, improvident, disquiet, and sluttish
manner that my father and mother and Pall live in the country;
which troubles me mightily and I must seek to remedy it.   So
up and ready – and my wife also; and then down and I showed
my wife, to her great admiration and joy, Mr. Gaudens present
of plate, the two Flaggons; which endeed are so noble that I
hardly can think that they are yet mine.   So blessing God for it,
we down to dinner, mighty pleasant; and so up after dinner for
a while and I then to White-hall; walked thither – having at
home met with a letter of Captain Cooke's, with which he had
sent a boy for me to see, whom he did intend to recommend to
me.   I therefore went, and there met and spoke with him.
He gives me great hopes of the boy, which pleases me; and at
Chappell I there met Mr. Blagrave, who gives a report of the
boy; and he showed me him and I spoke to him, and the boy
seems a good willing boy to come to me, and I hope will do well.
I am to speak to Mr. Townsend to hasten his clothes for him,[1]

a l.h. written over l.h. 'Hob'-   *b* repl. 'him'

1. Tom Edwards, of the Chapel
Royal, now entered Pepys's service.
It was customary for the children of
the Chapel Royal to receive a suit of
clothes from the Great Wardrobe
when, their voices breaking, they left
the service of the King. The Lord
Chamberlain issued a warrant for
Tom's livery on 12 August: PRO,
LC 5/61, p. 167.

and then he is to come. So I walked homeward and met with Mr. Spong;[1] and he with me as far as the Old Exchange, talking of many ingenuous things, Musique, and at last of Glasses, and I find him still the same ingenuous man that ever he was; and doth, among other fine things, tell me that by his Microscope of his own making he doth discover that the wings of a Moth is made just as the feathers of the wing of a bird, and that most plainly and certainly. While we were talking, came by several poor creatures, carried by by Constables for being at a conventicle.[2] They go like lambs, without any resistance. I would to God they would*a* either conform, or be more wise and not be ketched. Thence parted with him, mightily pleased with his company, and away homeward, calling at Dan Rawlinson and supped there with my Uncle Wight; and then home and eat again for form sake with her, and then to prayers and to bed.

8. Up, and abroad with Sir W. Batten by coach to St. James; where by the way he did tell me how Sir J Minnes would many times arrogate to himself the doing of that that all the Board have equal share in; and more, that to himself which he hath had nothing to do in*b* – and perticularly the late paper given in by him to the Duke, the translation of a Duch print concerning the quarrel between us and them; which he did give as his own when it was Sir Rich Fords wholly.[3] Also, he told me how Sir W. Penn (it falling in our discourse touching Mrs. Falconer) was at first very great for Mr. Coventry to bring him in guests*, and that at high rates, for places;*c* and very open was he to me therein.

After business done with the Duke, I*d* to the Coffee-house and so home to dinner; and after dinner, to hang up my fine pictures

---

a repl. 'will'   *b* repl. 'it'   *c* repl. 'his'   *d* MS. 'I home'

---

1. John Spong, maker of optical instruments.

2. Seventy Quakers were committed to Newgate this day, mostly from meetings held at Wheeler St and at Mile End Green: J. Besse, *Coll. of sufferings of . . . Quakers* (1753), i. 394.

3. Neither the original nor the translation has been identified. There were many such broadsheets and pamphlets. Ford was one of the leaders of the merchant interest now pressing for war against the Dutch.

in my dining-room, which makes it very pretty. And so my wife and I abroad to the Kings play-house, she giving me her time of the last month, she having not seen any then; so my vow is not broke at all, it costing me no more money then it would have done upon her had she gone both her times that were due to her.[1] Here we saw *Flora's Figarys:*[2] I never saw [it] before, and by the most ingenuous performance of the young jade Flora,[3] it seemed as pretty a pleasant play as ever I saw in my life.

So home to supper and then to my office late – Mr. Andrews and I to talk about our victualing commission; and then he being gone, I to set down my four days past journalls and expenses; and so home to bed.[a]

9. Up and to my office, and there we sat all the morning. At noon home, and there by appointment Mr. Blagrave came and dined[b] with me, and brought a friend of his of the Chappell with him. Very merry at dinner; and then up to my chamber and there we sung a psalm or two of Lawes's.[4] Then he[c] and I a little talk by ourselfs of his kinswoman that is to come to live with my wife; who is to come about ten days hence – and I hope will do well. They gone, I to my office and there, my head being a little troubled with the little wine I drank, though mixed with beer, but it may be a little more then I used to do and yet I cannot say so, I went home and spent the afternoon with my wife, talking. And then in the evening a little to my office; and so home to supper and to bed.

This day came the news that the Emperour hath beat the Turke. Killed the Grand Vizier and several great Bassa's – with an army of 80000 men killed and routed. With some considerable loss of his own side, having lost three Generalls, and the French Forces

---

a repl. 'my'   b repl. 'dined'   c repl. 'drunk'

---

1. Pepys's vow not to visit theatres more than once a month had already been severely strained on 28 July and 4 August. (A).

2. *Flora's Vagaries*, a comedy by Richard Rhodes, first acted in 1663 and published in 1670. (A).

3. A role later played by Nell Gwyn; below, 5 October 1667. (A).

4. See above, p. 128 & n. 2. (E).

all cut off almost[1] – which is thought as good a service to the Emperour as beating the Turke almost – for had they conquered, they would have been as troublesome to him.[2]

10. Up; and being ready, abroad to do several small businesses; among others, to find out one to engrave my tables upon my new sliding-Rule with silver plates, it being so small that Browne that made it cannot get one to do*a* it. So I found out Cocker, the famous writing-master,[3] and got him to do it; and I sat an hour by him to see him design it all, and strange it is to see him with his natural eyes to cut so small at his first designing it, and read it all over without any missing, when for my life I could not with my best skill read one word or letter of it – but it is use; but he says that the best light, for his life, to do a very small*b* thing by (contrary to Chaucer's words to the sun: that he should lend his light to them that small seals grave),[4] it should be by an artificiall light of a candle, set to advantage as he could do it.[5] I find the fellow, by his discourse, very ingenuous; and among other things, a great admirer and well read in all our English poets and undertakes to judge of them all, and that not

a repl. 'to'   *b* preceding part of entry crowded into bottom of page

---

1. This was Montecuculi's victory at St Gothard, in Hungary, on 22 July/ 1 August, the decisive battle of the campaign, which led to the conclusion of a peace between the Emperor and the Sultan in the same month. The news as Pepys gives it is exactly and almost verbally the same as the report from Brussels (5/15 August) published in *The Newes*, 11 August, pp. 518–19. The Grand Vizier (Ahmed Kiuprilli) was not killed, but Turkish losses included the Pasha of Buda and the son of the Khan of Krim Tartary. *The Intelligencer*, 22 August, pp. 540–1; W. Coxe, *Hist. house Austria*, ii. 370–1.

2. The Emperor had suspected his French allies (whose losses are here exaggerated) of caballing with the Hungarians and of holding secret correspondence with the Turks.

3. Edward Cocker (d. 1675), author of several works on penmanship and arithmetic, whose name (in the phrase 'according to Cocker') became synonymous with exactitude.

4. A reminiscence of *Troilus and Criseyde*, bk iii, ll. 1461–3: 'What profrestow thi light here for to selle?/Go selle it hem that smale selys grave;/We wol the nought, us nedeth no day have' (ed. R. K. Root). For Pepys's knowledge of Chaucer, see above, iv. 184 & n. 1.

5. See below, pp. 291–2.

impertinently. Well pleased with his company and better with
his beginning upon my Rule, I left him and home; whither Mr.
Deane by agreement came to me and dined with me, and by
chance Gunner Batters's wife.

After dinner, Deane and I great discourse again about my Lord
Chancellors timber[1] – out of which I wish I may get well.

Thence I to Cockers again and sat by him, with good discourse
again for an hour or two; and then left him and by agreement
with Captain Sylas Taylor (my old acquaintance at the Exchequer) to the post-office[2] to hear some Instrument Musique of
Mr. Berchenshaws before my Lord Brunkard and Sir Rob.
Murrey. I must confess, whether it be that I hear it but seldom,
or that really voices is better, but so it is, that I found no pleasure
at all in it, and methought two voyces were worth twenty of it.

So home to my office a while, and then to supper and to bed.

11. Up; and through pain, to my great grief forced to wear
my gowne to keep my legs warm. At the office all the morning;
and there a high dispute against Sir W. Batten and Sir W. Penn
about the breadth of Canvas again,[3] they being for the making of
it narrower, I and Mr. Coventry and Sir J. Mennes for the
keeping it broader. So home to dinner; and by and by comes
Mr. Creed, lately come from the Downes, and dined with me.
I show him a good countenance, but love him not for his base
ingratitude to me.[4] However, abroad, carried my wife to buy
things at the New Exchange, and so to my Lady Sandwiches
and there merry, talking with her a great while, and so home;
whither[a] comes Cocker with my Rule, which he hath ingraved
to admiration for goodness and smallness of work: it cost me
14s the doing – and mightily pleased I am with it. By and by, he
gone, comes Mr. Moore and stayed talking with me a great while

a repl. same symbol badly formed

1. See above, pp. 203–4 & n.
2. Presumably to the 'faire ban-
quetting house covered with lead' in
the garden behind the Post Office
which then stood opposite the Stocks
and at the Junction of Threadneedle
St and Cornhill. After the Fire
Princes St was made across the area:
BM, Add. 5098, ff. 228–34. (R).
3. Cf. above, p. 157 & n. 3.
4. Cf. above, p. 213.

about my Lord's businesses, which I fear will be in a bad condition for his family, if my Lord should miscarry at sea. He gone, I late to my office; and cannot forbear admiring and consulting my new Rule. And so home to supper and to bed.

This day for a wager before the King, my Lords of Castle-haven and Aran (a son of my Lord of Ormonds), they two*a* alone did run down and kill a stout Bucke in St. James's parke.

12. Up, and all the morning busy at the office with Sir W Warren about a great contract for New England Masts;[1] wherein I was very hard with him, even to the making him angry. But I thought it fit to do it, as well as just for me on the King's behalf. At noon to the Change a little; and so to dinner and then out by coach, setting my wife and maid down, going to Stevens the Silver-smith's to change some old silver lace[2] and to go buy new silk lace for a petticoat.

I to White-hall and did much business at a Tanger committee – where among other things, speaking about propriety of the houses there and how we ought to let the portugeses have right done them, as many of them as continue or did sell the houses while they were in possession – and something further in their favour[3] – the Duke (in an anger I never observed in him before) did cry, says he, "All the world rides us, and I think we shall never ride anybody."

Thence home; and though late, yet Pedro being there he sang a song and parted; I did give him 5s, but find it burdensome and so will break up the meeting. At night is brought home our poor Fancy,[4] which to my great grief continues lame still, so that I wish she had not been brought ever home again, for it troubles me to see her.

a MS. 'do'

---

1. Signed on 16 August: *CSPD 1664–5*, p. 132.

2. The silver thread would be burnt out from the old cloth and sold to the silversmith.

3. The question of compensation to the former owners of houses was not settled until 1684: *Tangier Papers*, p. 63; Routh, p. 56. It had been provided for by the marriage treaty of 1661 by which the territory had come into British possession.

4. Pepys's dog: her death is recorded at 16 September 1668.

13. Up; and before I went to the office comes my Taylor
with a coat I have made to wear within doors, purposely to come
no lower then my knees; for by my wearing a gown within
doors comes all my tenderness about my legs.   There comes also
Mr. Reeve with a Microscope and Scotoscope;[1] for the first I did
give him 5*l*. 10*s*, a great price; but a most curious bauble it is, and
he says as good, nay, the best he knows in England, and he makes
the best in the world.   The other he gives me, and is of value;
and a curious curiosity it is to [see]*a* objects in a dark room
with.   Mightily pleased with this, I to the office, where all the
morning.   There, offered by Sir W. Penn his coach to go to
Epsum and carry my wife, I stepped out and bade my wife make
her ready; but being not very well, and other things advising
me to the contrary, I did forbear going; and so Mr. Creed dining
with me, I got him to give my wife and me a play this afternoon, lending him*b* money to do it – which is a fallacy that
I have found now once to avoid my vowe with, but never to be
more practised I swear.   And to the new play at the Dukes
house, of *Henery the 5th* – a most noble play, writ by my Lord
Orery;[2] wherein Baterton, Harris, and Ianthes parts are most
incomparably wrote and done,[3] and the whole play the most full
of heighth and raptures of wit and sense that ever I heard; having
but one incongruity or what did not please me in it – that is, that
King Harry promises to plead for Tudor to their*c* mistress,
Princesse Katherine of France, more then when it comes to it
he seems to do; and Tudor refused by her with some kind of

a   MS. 'look' (struck through but not replaced)
b   repl. 'me'   *c*   repl. 'his'

———————

1. A portable *camera obscura*.
2. A rhymed heroic drama, published in 1668. This is the first record
of a performance. Roger Boyle, Earl
of Orrery, is said to have begun to
write plays when Charles II urged him
to justify his claims for the dramatic
virtues of rime. (A).
3. According to Downes (pp. 27–
8), King Henry (Harris) wore the

Duke of York's coronation suit in
this production; Owen Tudor (Betterton), King Charles's; the Duke of
Burgundy (Smith), the Earl of
Oxford's. He adds that the play
was 'Excellently Perform'd and acted
10 days successively'. 'Ianthe' (Mrs
Betterton) played Princess Katharine,
for whose hand King Henry and
Owen Tudor are rivals. (A).

indignity, not with the*a* difficulty and honour that it ought to have been done in to him.[1]

Thence home and to my office; wrote by the post, and then to read a little in Dr. Powre's booke of discovery by the Microscope,[2] to enable me a little how to use and what to expect from my glasse.

So to supper and to bed.

14. *Lords day.* After long lying discoursing with my wife, I up; and comes Mr. Holliard to see me, who concurs with me that my pain is nothing but cold in my legs breeding wind, and got only by my using to wear a gowne. And that I am not at all troubled with any ulcer,[3] but my thickness of water comes*b* from my over-heat in my back. He gone, comes Mr. Herbert, Mr. Honiwoods man, and dined with me – a very honest, plain, well-meaning man I think him to be; and by his discourse and manner of life, the true Embleme of an old ordinary serving-man.

After dinner, up to my chamber and made an end of Dr. Powre's book of the Microscope, very fine and to my content; and then my wife and I with great pleasure, but with great difficulty before we could come to find the manner of seeing anything by my Microscope – at last did, with good content, though not so much as I expect when I come to understand it better. By and by comes W. Joyce in his silk suit and cloak lined with velvett. Stayed talking with me, and I very merry at it. He supped with me; but a cunning, crafty fellow he is, and dangerous to displease, for his tongue spares nobody.

After supper I up to read a little, and then to bed.

15. Up, and with Sir J. Mennes by coach to St. James and

a MS. 'a'   *b* repl. 'coming'

---

1. See Act V, ll. 307–406. (A).
2. Henry Power, *Experimental philosophy . . . containing new experiments microscopical, mercurial, magnetical . . .* (1664); one of the earliest books on microscopy. Pepys's copy (PL 1422) has one marginal note (at p. 44) and an index

(of 'the several minute Bodies micrographically illustrated') in the hand of one of Pepys's amanuenses. These were inserted much later than the diary period.
3. Dr Burnet had attributed the pain to an ulcer: above, p. 194.

there did our business with the Duke; who tells us more and more signs of a Dutch warr and how we must presently set out a fleet for Guinny – for the Dutch are doing so, and there I believe the war will begin.[1]   Thence home with him again, in our way he talking of his cures abroad while he was with the King as a Doctor; and above all men, the pox.   And among others, Sir J. Denham he told me he had cured after it was come to an ulcer all over his face to[a] a miracle.[2]

To the Coffee-house I, and so to the Change a little and then home to dinner with Creed, whom I met at the Coffee-house. And after dinner, by coach set him down at the Temple, and I and wife to Mr. Blagraves.   They being none of them at home, I to the Hall, leaving her there; and thence to the Trumpett, whither came Mrs. Lane and there begins a sad story how her husband, as I feared, proves not worth a farding, and that she is with child and undone if I do not get him a place.   I had my pleasure here of her; and she, like an impudent jade, depends upon my kindness to her husband; but I will have no more to do with her, let her brew as she hath baked – seeing she would not take my counsel about Hawly.   After drinking we parted; and I to Blagrave and there discoursed with Mrs. Blagrave about her kinswoman, who it seems is sickly even to Frantiqueness some-times; and among other things, chiefly from love and melancholy upon the death of her servant.*   Insomuch, that she telling us all most simply and innocently, I fear she will not be able to come to us with any pleasure; which I am sorry for, for I think she would have pleased us very well.   In comes he, and so to sing a[b] song, and his niece with us, but she sings very meanly.   So through the hall and thence by coach home, calling by the way at Charing-cross and there saw the great Dutchman that is come over, under whose arm I went with my hat on and could not reach higher then his eyebrowes with the tip of my fingers, reaching as

a   repl. 'it'   *b*   smudge above symbol

---

1. See below, p. 258 & n. 1, and cf. the Duke's strong words to the Dutch ambassador: below, p. 264 & n. 4.

2. Mennes had had no medical training, but was an amateur of chemistry and anatomy.

high as I could.¹   He is a comely and well-made man, and his
wife a very little but pretty comely Dutch woman.   It is true
he wears pretty high-heeled shoes, but not very high, and doth
generally wear a Turbant, which makes him show yet taller then
really he is,² though he is very tall as I have said before.   Home
to my office, and then to supper, and then to my office again late,
and so home to bed – my wife and I troubled that we do not
speed better in this business ⟨of her woman⟩.

16.   Wakened about 2 a-clock this morning with the noise of
Thunder, which lasted for an hour; with such continued Lighten-
ings, not flashes but flames, that all the sky and ayre was light;
and that for a great while, not a minute's space between new
flames all the time; such a thing as I never did see, nor could
have believed had ever been in nature.   And being put into a
great sweat with it, could not sleep till all was over – and that
accompanied with such a storm of rain as I never heard in my life.
I expected to find my house in the morning overflowed with the
rain breaking in, and that much hurt must needs have been done
in the City with this lightening; but I find not one drop of rain in
my house, nor any news of hurt done.   But it seems it hath been
here and all up and down the counties hereabouts, the like tempest
– Sir W. Batten saying much of the greatness thereof at Epsum.³
Up, and all the morning at the office.   At noon busy at the
Change about one business or other; and thence home to dinner
and so to my office all the afternoon, very busy; and so to supper
anon and then to my office again a while, collecting observations

1. Cf. *Verney Mem.*, ii. 236 [1664]:
'There is a Giant come out of Holond
and he is 9 fut hy & 2 inches. I
believe my poor Nike would stand
between his legs . . .'.   James Yonge,
a naval surgeon, saw him in 1666 and
put his height at just under 9 ft:
Journal (ed. Poynter), p. 105.   Yonge
calls him 'the Boor van Litterkirk'
(Lekkerkerk) and reports his death
in 1666.   He was possibly the same
giant whom John Ray saw in Bruges
in 1663: *Observations Topographical
. . .* (1673), p. 6.

2. These (together with the use of
long sweeping clothes) were common
tricks of the trade: cf. Wood, *L. &
T.*, ii. 226.

3. Dr D. J. Schove writes: 'The
thunderstorms were recorded as far
away as Norfolk, and the associated
squall was noted also in the Downs:
Samuel Clarke, "Observations of the
weather . . . 1657–86" (Norf. and
Norwich Rec. Off., MS. 9374, 8A1);
Sandwich, p. 149.'

out of Dr.[a] Powres booke of Microscopes, and so home to bed. Very stormy weather tonight for Winde.

This day we had news that my Lady Pen is landed and coming hither, so that I hope the family will be in better order and more neat then it hath been.

17. Up; and going to Sir W. Batten to speak to him about business, he did give me three bottles of his Epsum water, which I drunk and it wrought well with me and did give me many good stools, and I found myself mightily cooled with them and refreshed.

Thence I to Mr. Honiwood and my father's old house, but he was gone out; and there I stayed talking with his man Herbert, who tells me how Langford[1] and his wife are very foul-mouthed people and will speak very ill of my father, calling him old rogue in reference to the hard pennorths he sold him of his goods,[b] when the rogue need not have bought any of them – so that I am resolved he shall get no more money by me. But it vexes me to think that my father should be said to go away in debt himself; but that I will cause to be remedied, whatever comes of it.

Thence to my Lord Crews and there with him a good while; before dinner talked of the Duch war and find that he doth much doubt that we shall fall into it without the money or consent of Parliament that is expected, or the reason for it that is fit to have for every war.

Dined with him; and after dinner talked with Sir Tho. Crew, who told me how Mr. Edwd. Mountagu is for ever blown up, and now quite out with his father again; to whom he pretended that his[c] going down was not that he was cast out of the court, but that he had leave to be absent a month – but now he finds the truth.[2]

Thence to my Lady Sandwich, where by agreement my wife

a repl. 'my'   *b* repl. 'g'-   *c* MS. 'is'

---

1. The tailor who had succeeded to Tom Pepys's house and business.

2. Edward Mountagu was the son of the 2nd Lord Mountagu of Bough-

ton. For his recent disgrace, see above, p. 153 & n. 2; for his earlier quarrel with his father, see above, iii. 289 & n.

dined; and after talking with her, I carried my wife to Mrs. Pierces and left her there, and so to Captain Cookes but he was not at home; but I there spoke with my boy Tom Edwards and directed him to go to Mr. Townsend (with whom I was in the morning) to have measure taken of his clothes to be made him there out of the Wardrobe – which will be so done, and then I think he will come to me.

Thence to White-hall; and after long staying, there was no committee of the Fishery as was expected. Here I walked long with Mr. Pierce, who tells me the King doth still sup^a every night with my Lady Castlemayne, who he believes hath lately slunk a great belly away, for from very big she is come to be down again.

Thence to Mrs. Pierces, and with her and my wife to see Mrs. Clarke; where with him and her very merry, discoursing of the late play of *Henery the 5th* – which they conclude the best that ever was made; but confess with me that Tudor's being dismissed in the manner he is is a great blemish to the play.[1] I am mightily pleased with the Doctor, for he is the only man I know that I would learn to pronounce by, which he doth the best that ever I heard any man.

Thence home and to the office late; and so to supper and to bed.

My Lady Pen came hither first tonight to Sir W. Pen's lodgings.

18. Lay too long in bed, till 8 a-clock; then up, and Mr. Reeve came and brought an Anchor and a very fair lodestone. He would have had me bought it, and a good stone it is; but when he saw that I would not buy it, he said he [would] leave it for me to sell for him. By and by he comes to tell me that he had present occasion for 6*l* to make up a sum, and that he would pay me in a day or two; but I had the unusual wit to deny him, and so by and by we parted – and I to the office, where busy all the morning sitting.

Dined alone at home, my wife going today to dine with Mrs.

a repl. same symbol badly formed

---

1. See above, p. 241 & n. 1. (A).

Pierce; and thence with her and Mrs. Clerke to see a new play, *The Court Secret*.[1]

I busy all the afternoon; toward evening to Westminster and there in the hall a while; and then to my barbers, willing to have any opportunity to speak to Jane, but wanted it. So to Mrs. Pierces, who was come home and she and Mrs. Clerke busy at cards; so my wife being gone home, I home, calling by the way at the Wardrobe and met Mr. Townsend, Mr. Moore and others at the Taverne thereby;[2] and thither I to them and spoke with Mr. Townsend[a] about my boy's clothes, which he says shall be soon done – and then I hope I shall be settled, when I have one in the house that is Musicall.

So home and to supper, and then a little to my office, and then home to bed. My wife says the play she saw is the worst that ever she saw in her life.

19. Up and to the office, where Mr. Coventry and Sir W. Penn and I sat all the morning, hiring of ships to go to Guinny, where we believe the war with Holland will first break out.[3] At noon dined at home; and after dinner my wife and I to Sir W. Penn's to see his Lady the first time – who is a well-looked, fat, short, old Dutchwoman,[4] but one that hath been heretofore pretty handsome; and is now very discreet and I believe hath more wit then her husband. Here we stayed talking a good while. And very well pleased I was with the old woman at first visit. So away home, and I to my office; my wife to go see my aunt Wight, newly come to town.

a MS. 'Townsends'

---

1. A tragicomedy by James Shirley, written in 1642 and published in 1653. This is the first record of a performance. According to Langbaine (p. 475), it was acted at the TR, Drury Lane. (A).

2. Probably the Horn: cf. above, iv. 102.

3. A squadron of 12 ships was made ready by early October and put under the command of Rupert. It was meant to follow the Dutch squadron which was preparing to sail to Guinea. Rupert's ships were weatherbound at Portsmouth on 15 October, and never got farther. Tedder, pp. 105–6.

4. *Née* Margriet Jaspers (d. 1682). She had lived at Kinsale since at least 1661 (HMC, *Ormonde*, n.s., iii. 37), and was now about 42.

Creed came to me, and he and I out; among ⟨other⟩ things,*a* to*b* look out a man to make a case for to keep my Stone that I was cut of in.[1]   And he to buy Daniels *History*;[2] which*c* he did, but I missed of my end.

So parted upon Ludgate-hill and I home and to the office, where busy till supper; and home to supper to a good dish of fritters, which I bespoke and were done much to my mind; then to the office a while again, and so home to bed.

The news of the Emperour's victory over the Turkes is by some doubted, but by most confessed to be very small (though great) of what was talked; which was 80000*d*[3] men to be killed and taken of the Turkes side.

20.   Up and to the office a while, but this day, the Parliament meeting only to be Adjourned to November (which was done accordingly),[4] we did not meet; and so I forth to bespeak a case to be made to keep my Stone in, which will cost me 25*s*.   Thence I walked to Cheapeside, there to see the effect of a fire there this morning since 4 a-clock – which I find in the house of Mr. Bois that married Dr Fuller's niece;[5] who are both out of town, leaving only a maid and man in town.   It begin in their house and hath burned much and many houses backward, though none forward – and that in the great uniforme pile of buildings in the

a followed by 'thing' (struck through)   *b* MS. 'he'   *c* repl. 'in'
d followed by superior '*l*' (struck through)

---

1. The bladder-stone removed in 1658. Evelyn relates that on 10 June 1669 Pepys carried the stone ('as big as a tenis-ball') to Evelyn's brother, who was suffering from the same complaint, to 'encourage his resolution to go thro the operation'.
2. Probably the 4th edition (1650) of Samuel Daniel's *The collection of the historie of England*; first published in 1612 and 1618, and one of the most popular histories of the time. Pepys kept the 5th edition of 1685 (PL 2230).
3. Probably a slip for '8000'.

Estimates in the London newspapers put the figure at 6000–8000: e.g. *The Newes*, 18 August, pp. 533–4. (80,000 was the total number of the Turkish army according to Pepys's report at 9 August.) The Turks in fact lost *c.* 16,000 men: J. W. Zinkeisen, *Geschichte des osman. Reiches* (Gotha, 1840–63), iv. 931.
4. It was prorogued (not adjourned) until 24 November: *LJ*, xi. 623.
5. For the marriage, see above, iii. 163. William Fuller, a friend of Pepys, was Bishop of Limerick.

middle of Cheapside. I am very sorry for them for the Doctors sake. Thence to the Change and so home to dinner. And thence to Sir W. Batten's; whither Sir Rd Ford comes, the Sheriffe, who hath been at this fire all the while; and he tells me upon my question, that he and the Mayor were there, as it is their duties to be, not only to keep the peace, but they have power of commanding the pulling down of any house or houses to defend the whole City.

By and by comes in the Common Cryer of the City[1] to speak with him; and when he was gone – says he – "You may see by this man the constitution of the Magistracy of this City; that this fellow's place, I dare give him (if he will be true to me) 1000*l* for his profits every year, and expect to get 500*l* more to myself thereby. When," says he, "I in myself am forced to spend many times as much."

By and by comes Mr. Coventry; and so we met at the office to hire ships for Guinny, and that done, broke up. I to Sir W. Batten's, there to discourse with Mrs. Falconer, who hath been with Sir W. Penn this evening, after Mr. Coventry had promised her half what W. Bodham had given him for his place.[2] But Sir W. Penn, though he knows that, and that Mr Bodham hath said that his place hath cost him 100*l* and would 100*l* more, yet is he so high against the poor woman that he will not hear to give her a farding – but it seems doth listen after a lease, wherein he expects Mr. Falconer hath put in his daughter's life.[3] And he is afeared that that is not done; and did tell Mrs. Falconer that he would see it and know what is done therein in spite of her; when,[a] poor wretch, she neither doth nor can hinder him the

a repl. same symbol badly formed

---

1. Richard Alexander.
2. John Falconer, Clerk of the Ropeyard at Woolwich, had died on 19 July, and on that same day his widow had written to Pepys, who had befriended her in the past, asking for some compensation from her husband's successor in view of his great expenses: *CSPD 1663–4*, p. 646.

3. An annuity of £80 promised to Penn's daughter, Margaret: above, p. 231 & n. 4; below, p. 253. Falconer's will, proved on 22 August, contained nothing to this effect. Penn's aim had apparently been to secure for his daughter an annuity which Falconer had arranged for his first wife: NWB, p. 61.

knowing it. Mr. Coventry knows of this business of the Lease, and I believe doth think of it as well as I. But the poor woman is gone home without any hopes but only Mr. Coventry's own nobleness.

So I to my office and wrote*a* many letters; and so to supper and to bed.

21. *Lords day*. Waked about 4 a-clock with my wife's having a looseness – and people's coming in the yard to the pump to draw water several times, so that fear of this day's fire made me fearful; and called Besse and sent her down to see, and it was Griffins maid for water to wash her house. So to sleep again and then lay talking till 9 a-clock. So up and drunk three bottles of Epsum-water, which wrought well with me. I all the morning, and most of the afternoon after dinner, putting papers to rights in my chamber, and the like in the evening till night at my office, and renewing and writing fair over my vowes. So home to supper – prayers and to bed.

Mr. Coventry told us yesterday the Duke was gone, ill of a fit of an ague, to bed. So we sent this evening to see how he doth.

22. Up and abroad, doing very many errands to my great content which lay as burdens upon my mind and memory. Home to dinner, and so to White-hall, setting down my wife at her father's, and I to the Tanger Committee, where several businesses I did to my mind, and with hopes thereby to get something. So to Westminster-hall; where, by appointment 《*Dr. Pepys*》 I had made, I met with Dr. Tom Pepys but avoided all discourse of difference with him, though much against my Will; and he, like a doting coxcomb as*b* he is, said he could not but demand his money, and that he would have his right, and that let all anger be forgot, and such sorry stuff, nothing to my mind.[1] But only I obtained this satisfaction, that

a MS. 'rome'   *b* repl. 'forbore'

---

1. Dr Thomas Pepys (physician) had lent £30 to his cousin, Tom Pepys the tailor, to set him up in business, of which £8 was still out- standing: above, p. 85, n. 1; cf. Rawl. A 182, ff. 340–1 (an angry letter, undated, from the doctor to John Pepys, sen.).

he told me that about Sturbridge last[1] was twelve-month or two year, he was at Brampton, and there my father did tell him that what he had done for my brother in giving him his goods and setting him up[a] as he had done was upon condition that he should give my brother John 20*l* per annum; which he charged upon my father, he tells me in answer, as a great deal of hard measure that he should expect that with him that had a brother so able as I am to do that for him.   This is all that he says he can say as to my father's acknowledging that he had given Tom his goods.[2]   He says his Brother Roger will take his oath that my father hath given him thanks for his counsel for his giving of Tom his goods – and setting him up in that manner that he hath done; but the former part of this he did not speak fully so bad, nor as certain what he could say.

So we walked together to my Cosen Joyces, where my wife stayed for me; and then I home and her by coach.   And so to my office; then to supper and to bed.

23.   Lay long, talking with my wife and angry a while about her desiring to have a French maid all of a sudden; which I took to arise from yesterday's being with her mother.   But that went over, and friends again; and so she be well qualitied, I care not much[b] whether she be French or no, so a protestant.   Thence to the office; and at noon to the Change, where very busy getting ships for Guiny and for Tanger.   So home to dinner; and then abroad all the afternoon, doing several errands to comply with my oath of ending many businesses before Bartholomew day, which is two days hence.[3]   Among others, I went into New Bridewell in my way to Mr. Cole and there I saw the new model;[4] and is very handsome, several at work.   And among others, one pretty whore brought in last night, which works very

---

a   repl. symbol rendered illegible   *b*   repl. 'this'

---

1. Sturbridge Fair (still the largest of English fairs – it was Bunyan's Vanity Fair) was held for just over a fortnight every September, near Cambridge.

2. John Pepys, sen., claimed that he had given the tailoring business over to Tom and so could not be held responsible for his debts: cf. below, 21 March 1666.

3. A slip: Bartholomew's Day was the 24th.

4. The new-model workroom. New Bridewell was a house of correction.

lazily. I did give them 6*d* to drink, and so away – to Grayes Inn, but missed Mr. Cole and so homeward; called at Harman's and there bespoke some chairs for a room. And so home and busy late; and then to supper and to bed. The Dutch East India fleet are now come home safe, which we are sorry for.[1] Our fleets on both sides[2] are hastening out to Guinny.

24. Up by 6 a-clock and to my office with Tom Hater, despatching business in haste. At 9 a-clock to White-hall about Mr. Maces's business at the Council, which stands in an ill condition still.[3] Thence to Grayes Inne but missed of Mr. Cole the lawyer and so walked home, calling among the Joyners in Woodstreete to buy a table; and bade in many places but did not buy till I came home to see the place where it is to stand, to judge how big it must be. So after Change, home and a good dinner; and then to White-hall to a Committee of the Fishery, where my Lord Craven and Mr. Gray mightily against Mr. Creeds being joined in the*a* warrant for Secretary with Mr. Duke.[4] However, I did get it put off till the Duke of Yorke was there – and so broke up, doing nothing. So walked home; first to the Wardrobe and there saw one suit of clothes made for my boy and linen*b* set out – and I think to have him the latter end of this week. And so home, Mr. Creed walking the greatest part of the way with me, advising what to do in his case, about his being Secretary to us in conjunction with Duke – which I did give him the best I could; and so home and to my office, where very much business; and then home to supper and to bed.

25. Up and to the office – after I had spoke to my tailor, Langford (who came to me about some work), desiring to know

a repl. 'Mr.'   *b* repl. same symbol badly formed

---

1. Tromp had escorted it *via* the Shetlands, and it reached port on 15–17 August. According to the official English newspaper, it was 'not so rich as was expected': *The Newes*, 25 August, p. 551.

2. I.e. both Dutch and English.

3. The dispute about the Portu-guese sugar duties: see above, p. 43 & n. 2. This meeting is not recorded in the Council Register and must have been of a committee.

4. Nothing came of this proposal: below, p. 262. John Creed was already secretary to the Tangier committee.

whether he knew of any debts that my father did owe of his own in the City; he tells me no, not any; I did on purpose try him, because of what words he and his wife have said of him (as Herbert told me the other day); and further did desire him, that if he knew of any or could hear of any, that he should bid them come to me and I would pay them – for I would not, that because he doth not pay my brother's debts, that therefore he should be thought to deny the payment of his own.

All the morning at the office busy. At noon to the Change; among other things, busy to get a little by the hire of a ship for Tanger. So home to dinner; and after dinner comes Mr. Cooke to see me; it is true he was kind to me at Sea, in carrying messages to and fro to my wife from sea, but I did do him kindnesses too, and therefore I matter not much to compliment or make any regard of his thinking me to slight him, as I do for his folly about my brother Tom's mistress.[1]

After dinner and some talk with him, I to my office, there busy, 《 *Jacke Noble* 》 – till by and by Jacke Noble came to me to tell me that he had Cave in prison, and that he would give me and my father good security that neither we nor any of our family should be troubled with the child – for he could prove that he was fully satisfied for him; and that if the worst came to the worst, the parish must keep it. That Cave did bring the child to his house, but they got it carried back again and that thereupon he put*a* him in prison. When he saw that I would not pay him the money, nor made anything of being secured against the child, he then said that then he must go to law; not himself, but come in as a witness for Cave against us. I could have told him that he could bear witness that Cave is satisfied, or else there is no money due to himself. But I let alone any such discourse, only getting as much out of him as I could. I perceive he is a rogue, and hath enquired into everything and consulted with Dr Pepys. And that he thinks, as Dr. Pepys told him, that my

a repl. 'got'

---

1. Cooke had served with Pepys in the *Naseby* in the spring of 1660, and Pepys had once lent him 30s.: above, ii. 109. He had busied himself as a marriage broker for Tom and had offered far too great a portion: above, iii. 232.

father, if he could, would not pay a farding of the debts. And yet I made him confess that in all his lifetime he never knew my father to be asked for money twice, nay, not once, all the time he lived with him. And that for his own debts, he believed he would do so still; but he meant only for these of Tom.

He said now, that Randall and his wife and the Midwife could prove from my brother's own mouth that the child was his, and that Tom had told them the circumstances of time, upon November the 5 at night, that he got it on her.

I offered him if he would secure my father against being forced to pay the money again, I would pay him; which at first he would do, give his own security; and when*a* I asked more then his own, he told me yes, he would, and those able* men, Subsidy men. But when we came by and by to discourse of it again, he would not then do it but said he would take his course and Joyne with Cave and release him; and so we parted.

However, this vexed me, so as I could not be quiet but took Coach to go speak with Mr. Cole; but met him not within, so back, buying a table by the way, and at my office late; and then home to supper and to bed, my mind disordered about this roguish business: in everything else, I thank God, well*b* at ease.

26. Up by 5 a-clock, which I have not been many a day, and down by water to Deptford; and there took in Mr. Pumpfield the rope-maker and down with him to Woolwich to view Clothiers cordage; which I found bad, and stopped the receipt of it.[1] Thence to the rope-yard and there, among other things, discoursed with Mrs. Falconer, who tells me that she hath found the writing, and Sir W Pen's daughter is not put into the lease for her life as he expected;[2] and I am glad of it. Thence to the Docke-yard and there saw the new ship[3] in very great forwardness; and so by water to Deptford a little and so home; and shifting myself, to the Change and there did business; and thence

a repl. 'though'   *b* repl. badly-formed symbol

---

1. Cf. above, p. 191 & n. 1. According to Pepys's notes in NWB, p. 61 (26 August), it was 'well enough made, but of most cruel course stuff.'
2. See above, p. 248 & n. 3.
3. The *Royal Catherine*.

down by water to White-hall, by the way, at Three Cranes,
putting into an alehouse and eat a bit*a* of bread and cheese. There
I could not get into the park; and so was fain to stay in*b* the
gallery over the gate[1] to look to the passage into the park (into
which the King hath forbid of late anybody's coming) to watch
his coming that had appointed me to come;[2] which he did
by and by with his lady. And we went to Guardeners-lane and
there, instead*c* of meeting with one that was handsome and could
play well (as they told me), she is the ugliest beast, and plays so
basely as I never heard anybody, so that I should loathe her being
in my house. However, she took us by and by and showed us
endeed some pictures at one Hiseman's,[3] a picture-drawer, a
Dutchman, which is said to exceed Lilly; and endeed there is,
both of the Queenes and maids of honour (perticularly Mrs.
Stewards, in a buff doublet like a soldier), as good pictures I think
as ever I saw. The Queene is drawn in one like a shepherdess –
in the other like St. Katharin, most like and most admirably.*d*[4]
I was mightily pleased with this sight endeed. And so back
again to their lodgings, where I left them. But before I went,
this man that carried me, whose name I know not but they call
him Sir John, a pitiful fellow, whose face I have long known

a MS. 'bid'　　　*b* repl. 'to'　　　*c* repl. 's'-
d preceding part of entry crowded into bottom of page

---

1. The Holbein gate. (R).

2. Pepys was at this time enquiring
after a lady's maid for his wife, but
he has made no previous mention of
the arrangement to meet this person.

3. Jacob Huysmans, a Fleming.

4. Huysmans' portrait of Frances
Stewart (later Duchess of Richmond)
in male attire was probably painted
for Charles II and is still in the royal
collection; it may have been the
portrait for which she was sitting at
Whitehall on 15 July 1664: see
above, p. 209; O. Millar, *Tudor,
Stuart and early Georgian pictures in
coll. H.M. Queen* (1963), no. 291.
The portrait of the Queen as a shepherdess was recorded in the MS. inventory of Charles II's pictures
in the Queen's Gallery at Hampton
Court, and is now at Windsor Castle:
ib., no. 289. The portrait of her as
St Catherine was recorded in the same
inventory, in store at Whitehall
(measurements given as 75 × 41 ins.),
but does not appear in later royal
inventories. A version of the design
is now in St James's Palace (ib., no.
290); another is in a private collection in Portugal. Either of these
could be the portrait missing from
the royal collection. Copies of the
design are at Gorhambury, Castle
Bromwich, Ugbrooke and Drum-
lanrig. It was engraved by Richard
Tompson (d. 1693). (OM).

but upon what score I know not – but he could have the confidence to ask me to lay down money for him to renew the lease
of his house; which I did give eare to there, because I was there
receiving a civility from him, but shall not part with my money.

There I left them and I by water home, where at my office
busy late; then home to supper and so to bed.

This day my wife tells me Mr. Pen, Sir Wms son, is come
back from France and came to visit her – a most modish person,
grown, she says, a fine gentleman.[1]

27. Up and to the office, where all the morning. At noon
to the Change and there almost made my bargain about a ship[2]
for Tanger, which will bring me in a little profit with Captain
Taylor. Off the Change with Mr Cutler and Sir W Rider to
Cutlers house; and there had a very good dinner, and two or
three pretty young ladies of their relations there. Thence to my
Case=maker for my Stone=case; and had it to my mind, and cost
me 24*s* – which is a great deal of money, but it is well done and
pleases me. So doing some other small errands, I home and there
find my boy Tom Edwards come – sent me by Captain Cooke,
having [been] bred in the King's chapel these four years. I purpose to make a clerk of him; and if he deserves well, to do well
by him.[3] Spent much of the afternoon to set his chamber in
order; and then to the office, leaving him at home. And late at
night, after all business was done, I called*a* Will and told him
my reason of taking a boy, and that it is of necessity, not out of
any unkindness to him, nor should be to his injury. And then

a repl. 'took'

---

1. William Penn (later the Quaker
leader) had been abroad since July
1662, first in Paris and Saumur, then
in Turin, whence he had been recalled
by his father on the approach of war
with Holland. Cf. P. Gibson to
Penn, March 1712: 'I remember your
honour very well, when you newly
came out of France, and wore panta-
loon breeches . . .' (qu. Penn, ii. 616).
For portraits of Penn at this age, see

DNB; N. & Q., 17 October 1868,
p. 382.

2. ? the *Union*; see below, p. 340.

3. Tom seems never to have disappointed these hopes. In 1668 he
was married off to Jane Birch, the
Pepyses' favourite maid, and later
became an Admiralty clerk. His son
Samuel (a godson of Pepys) became
a naval officer and received a ring at
Pepys's funeral.

talked about his landlord's daughter to come to my wife, and I think it will be.[1] So home and find my boy a very schoole-boy that talks inocently and impertinently;* but at present it is a sport to us, and in a little*a* time he will leave it. So sent him to bed, he saying that he used to go to bed at 8 a-clock. And then all of us to bed, myself pretty well pleased with my choice*b* of a boy. All the news this day is that the Dutch are with 22 sail of ships of warr crewsing up and down about Ostend; at which we are alarmed.[2] My Lord Sandwich is come back into the Downes with only eight sail, which is or may be a prey to the Dutch, if they knew our weakness and inability to set out any more speedily.[3]

28. *Lords day.* Up, and with my boy alone to church – the first time I have had anybody to attend me to church a great while. Home to dinner and there met Creed; who dined, and we merry together, as his learning is such and judgment that I cannot but be pleased with it. After dinner I took him to church into our gallery with me, but slept the best part of the sermon, which was a most silly one. So he and I to walk to the Change a while, talking from one pleasant discourse to another; and so home, and thither came my Uncle Wight and aunt and supped with us, mighty merry. And Creed lay with us all night. So to bed – very merry to think how Mr. Holliard (who came in this evening to see me) makes* nothing but proving as a most clear thing that Rome is antichrist.

29. Up betimes, intending to do business at my office, by 5 a-clock. But going out, met at my door Mr. Hughes, come to speak with me about office business; and told me that as he

a repl. same symbol badly formed   *b* repl. 'boy'

---

1. This was Mary, 17-year-old daughter of William Mercer of St Olave's parish, 'a decayed merchant' (below, p. 265) in whose house Will Hewer was now living; an attractive girl, dismissed by Mrs Pepys on 3 September 1666.

2. Tromp and Opdam's fleets had joined: Downing to Clarendon, 23 August/2 September (Lister, iii. 338+). They sailed north and convoyed home the E. India fleet.

3. Sandwich did not send any of his fleet to spy out the Dutch movements until 11 September: Sandwich, pp. 149, 151, 153.

St Olave's, Hart Street, 1736. Engraving by W. H. Toms.

(*Guildhall Library*)

came this morning from Deptford, he left the King's yard a-fire. So I presently took a boat and down; and there found, by God's providence, the fire out; but if there had been any wind, it must have burned all our stores – which is a most dreadful consideration.

But leaving all things well, I home and out abroad, doing many errands. Mr. Creed also out, and my Wife to her mother's. Creed and I met at my Lady Sandwiches and there dined; but my Lady is become as handsome, I think, as ever she was.[1] And so good and discreet a woman I know not in the world.

After dinner I to Westminster to Jervas's a while; and so doing many errands by the way, and necessary ones, I home. And thither came the woman, with her mother, which our Will recommends to my wife. I like her well, and I think will please us. My wife and they agreed, and she is to come the next week – at which I am very well contented, for then I hope we shall be settled; but I must remember that never since I was housekeeper I ever lived so quietly, without any noise or one angry word almost, as I have done since my present maids, Besse, Jane and Susan, came and were together. Now I have taken a boy and am taking a woman, I pray God we may not be worse; but I will observe it. After being at my office a while – home to supper and to bed.[a]

30. Up and to the office, where sat long; and at noon to dinner at home. After dinner comes Mr. Pen to visit me, and stayed an hour talking with me. I perceive something of learning he hath got, but a great deal, if not too much, of the vanity of the French garbe and affected manner of speech and gait – I fear all real profit he hath made of his travel will signify little. So he gone, I to my office and there very busy till late at night; and so home to supper and to bed.

31. Up by 5 a-clock and to my office, where T. Hater and Will met me; and so we despatch a great deal of my business as to the ordering my papers and books, which were behind-hand.

a 'be worse . . . bed' crowded into bottom of page

---

1. After her recent attack of measles.

All the morning very busy at my office. At noon home to dinner and there my wife hath got me some pretty good oysters, which is very soon, and the soonest I think I ever eat any. After dinner I up to hear my boy play upon a lute which I have this day borrowed of Mr. Hunt; and endeed, the boy would with little practice play very well upon the Lute – which pleases me well. So by coach to the Tanger Committee, and there have another small business, by which I may get a little small matter of money. Stayed but little there; and so home and to my office very late, casting up my month's accounts; and blessed be God, find myself worth 1020*l* – which is still the most I ever was worth.

So home and to bed.

Prince Robt. I hear this day – is to go to command this fleet going to Guinny against the Dutch.[1] I doubt few will be pleased with his going, being accounted an unhappy* man. My mind at good rest; only, my father's troubles with Dr Pepys and my brother Tom's Creditors in general do trouble me.

I have got a new boy that understands Musique well, as coming to me from the King's Chappell, and I hope will prove a good boy. And my wife and I are upon having a woman, which for her content I am contented to venture upon the charge of again; and she is one that our Will finds out for us, and understands a little Musique and I think will please us well; only, her friends* live too near us.

Pretty well in health since I left off wearing of a gowne within doors all day and then go out with my legs into the cold, which brought me daily pain.

---

1. Sandwich had written from the Channel on 20 August urging haste: *CSPD 1663-4*, p. 671. Rupert took the command, but his ships were joined to Sandwich's on 15 October and never left the Channel.

SEPTEMBER.

1. A sad rainy night. Up and to the office, where busy all the morning. At noon to the Change and thence brought Mr. Pierce the surgeon and Creed and dined very merry and handsomely; but my wife not being well of those, she not with us. And we cut up the great cake Morecocke lately sent us – which is very good.[1] They gone, I to my office and there very busy till late at night; and so home to supper and to bed.

2. Up very betimes and walked (my boy with me) to Mr. Coles;[2] and after long waiting below, he being under the barber's hands, I spoke with him and he did give me much hopes of getting my debt that my brother owed me, and also that things would go well with my father. But going to his atturnys that he directed me to, they tell me both that though I could bring my father to a confession of a judgment, yet he knowing that there are specialties out against him, he is bound to plead his knowledge of them to me before he pays me, or else he must do it in his own wrong. I took a great deal of pains this morning in the thorough understanding hereof, and hope[a] that I know the truth of our case, though it be but bad – yet better then to run spending money and all to no purpose. However, I will enquire a little more.

Walked home, doing very many errands by the way, to my great content. And at the Change met and spoke with several persons about serving us with pieces-of-eight at Tanger. So[b] home to dinner above stairs, my wife not being well of those in bed – I dined by her bed-side. But I got her to rise, and abroad

a repl. 'therefore'   b repl. 'if'

---

1. John Moorcock, timber merchant, sent in a tender for the supply of elm on this very day: *CSPD 1664–5*, p. 131.

2. Barrister, of Gray's Inn.

259

with me by coach to Bartholomew Fayre,[1] and our boy with us, and there showed them and myself the dancing on the ropes and several other the best shows. But pretty it is, to see how our boy carries himself, so innocently clownish as would make one laugh. Here till late and dark. Then up and down to buy combes for my wife to give her maids; and then by coach home and there at the office set down my day's work; and then home to bed.

3. I have had a bad night's rest tonight, not sleeping well, as my wife observed, and once or twice she did wake me; and I thought myself to be mightily bit with fleas, and in the morning she chid her maids for not looking the fleas a-days. But when I rise, I find that it is only the change of the weather from hot to cold, which (as I was two winters ago) doth stop my pores, and so my blood tingles and iches all day all over my body and so continued to do, all the day long just as I was then; and if it continues to be so cold, I fear I must come to the same pass. But sweating cured me then, and I hope and am told will this also.

《*Health.*》

《*health.*》

At the office; sat all the morning. Dined at home; and after dinner to White-hall to the Fishing Committee, but not above four of us met, which could do nothing; and a sad thing it is to see so great a work so ill fallowed – for at this pace it*a* can come to nothing but disgrace to us all. Broke up and did nothing.

So I walked to Westminster, and there at my barber's had good luck to find Jane alone; and there I talked with her and got the poor wretch to promise to meet me in the abbey on tomorrow come sennit, telling me that her maister and mistress have a mind to get her a husband, and so will not let her go abroad without them*b* – but only in sermon time a-Sundays she doth go out. I would I could get a good husband for her, for she is one I alway thought a good-natured as well as a well-looked girl.

a MS. 'I'   *b* repl. 'her'

---

1. See above, ii. 166, n. 2.

Thence home, doing some errands by the way; and so to my office, whither Mr. Holliard came to me to discourse about the privileges of the Surgeon's hall as to our signing of bills, wherein I did give him a little, and but a little, satisfaction; for we won't lose our power of recommending them once approved of by the hall.[1]

He gone, I late to send by the post &c.; and so to supper and to bed – my itching and tickling continuing still, the weather continuing cold. And Mr. Holliard tells me that sweating will cure me at any time.

4. *Lords day.* Lay long in bed; then up and took physique, Mr. Hollyard['s]. But it being cold weather and myself negligent of myself, I fear I took cold and stopped the working of it. But I feel myself pretty well.

All the morning looking over my old wardrobe and laying by things for my brother John and my father, by which I shall leave myself very bare in clothes, but yet as much as I need and the rest would but spoil in the keeping.

Dined, my wife and I, very well. All the afternoon my wife and I above, and then the boy and I to singing of psalms, and then came in Mr. Hill and he sung with us a while; and he being gone, the boy and I again to the singing of Mr. Porter's mottets,[2] and it is a great joy to me that I am come to this condition, to maintain a person in the house able to give me such pleasure as this boy doth by his thorough understand of music, as he sing[s] anything at first sight.

Mr. Hill came to tell me that he had got a gentlewoman for

1. Thomas Hollier (Pepys's surgeon) was now one of the Wardens of the Company of Barber Surgeons, who claimed the right under their charter of nominating ships' surgeons and of supplying them with surgical goods. In a letter of 18 October, Hollier (and others of the Company's officers) agreed under protest to admit the recommendations of the Board or the requests of commanders 'in filling up the bills for surgeons': *CSPD* *1664–5*, p. 36; see also ib., p. 87. (Apothecaries had often made out the bills and recommended the surgeons.) For the decline of the Company's privileges from the 1650s onwards, see J. J. Keevil, *Medicine and the navy, 1200–1900*, ii. 32–3; cf. Duke of York, *Mem. (naval)*, p. 80.

2. Walter Porter, *Mottets of two voyces for treble or tenor and bass* (1657); not in the PL. (E).

my wife, one Mrs. Ferrabosco, that sings most admirably.[1] I seemed glad of it; but I hear she is too gallant for me and am not sorry that I misse her.

Then I to the office, setting some papers right; and so home to supper and to bed – after prayers.

5. Up and to St. James and there did our business with the Duke – where all our discourse of war, in the highest measure. Prince Robt. was with us – who is fitting himself to go to sea in the *Heneretta*. And afterward in White-hall, I met him and Mr. Gray and he spoke to me; and in other discourse, says he, "God damn me, I can answer but for one ship, and in that I will do my part; for it is not in that as in [an] army, where a man can command everything."

By and by to a committee for the Fishery, the Duke of Yorke there – where after Duke[2] was made Secretary, we fell to name a committee; whereof I was willing to be one because I would have my hand in that business, to understand it and be known in doing something in it. And so after cutting out work for that committee, we ris; and I to my wife to Unthankes, and with her from shop to shop, laying out near 10*l* this morning in clothes for her. And so I to the Change, where a while, and so home and to dinner, and thither came W. Bowyer and dined with us; but strange to see how he could not endure onyons in sauce to lamb, but was overcome with the sight of it and so was forced to make his dinner of an egg or two.[a] He tells us how Mrs. Lane is undone by her marrying so bad, and desires to speak with me; which I know is wholly to get me to do something for her to get her husband a place which he is in no wise fit for.

After dinner I down to Woolwich with a galley, and then to

a 'of it . . . two' crowded into corner of lower margin

---

1. Ferrabosco is the name of a large and influential Italian family of musicians, at least five members of which became celebrated in England, and so identification is difficult. See J. Pulver (*Biog. dictionary of old Engl. music*), pp. 184–8, who thinks the reference here is to a daughter-in-law of the third Alfonso Ferrabosco, a royal instrumentalist until the Commonwealth period, during which he died. At 30 May 1667 Pepys mentions the Duchess of Newcastle's woman: 'the Ferrabosco . . . they say sings well'. (E).

2. George Duke.

Deptford and so home – all the way reading Sir J Suck[l]ings *Aglaura*,[1] which methinks is but a mean play – nothing of design in it.

Coming home, it is strange to see how I was troubled to find my wife but in a necessary compliment, expecting Mr. Pen to see her; who had been there and was by her people denied – which he having been three times, she thought not fit he should be any more. But yet even this did raise my jealousy presently* and much vex me. However, he did not come, which pleased me; and I to supper and to the office till 9 a-clock or thereabouts, and so home to bed.

my Aunt James had been here today with Kate Joyce twice to see us – the second time my wife was at home; and they it seems are going down to Brampton, which I am sorry for for the charge that my father will be put to. But it must be borne with – and my mother hath a mind to see them. But I do condemn myself mightily[a] for my pride and contempt of my aunt and kindred that are not so high as myself, that I have not seen her all this while, nor invited her all this while.

6. Up and to the office, where we sat all the morning. At noon home to dinner. Then to my office and there waited, thinking to have had Baggwell's wife come to me about business, that I might have talked with her; but she came not. So I to White-hall by coach with Mr. Andrews; and there I got his contract for the victualling of Tanger signed and sealed by us there. So that all that business is well over, and I hope to have made a good business of it – and to receive 100*l* by it the next week – for which God be praised.[2] Thence to W. Joyces and Anthonys to invite them to dinner to meet my aunt James at my house, and the rather because they are all to go down to my father's the next week, and so I would be a little kind to them before they go.

So home, having called upon Doll, our pretty Change woman,

a repl. 'very'

---

1. Originally a tragedy, this play had been awkwardly transformed into a tragicomedy; see above, iii.

204, n. 5. PL 905 (1658 ed.). (A).
2. Cf. above, p. 210.

for a pair of gloves trimmed with yellow ribbon*a* (to [match the] petticoat she bought yesterday), which costs me 20*s*. But she is so pretty, that, God forgive me, I could not think it too much; which is a strange slavery that I stand in to beauty, that I value nothing near it.

So going home and my coach stopping in Newgate-market over against a poulterer's shop, I took occasion to buy a rabbit; but it proved a deadly old one when I came to eat it – as I did do after an hour's being at my office; and after supper, again there till past 11 at night. And so home and to bed.

This day, Mr. Coventry did tell us how the Duke did receive ⟪*Duch.*⟫ the Dutch Embassador the other day – by telling him that whereas they think us in Jest, he believes that the Prince (Rupert), which goes in this fleet to guinny, will soon tell them that we are in earnest; and that he himself will do the like here in the head of fleet here at home. And that for the Meschants,[1] which he[2] told the Duke there were in England which did hope to do themselfs good by the King's being at war, says he,[3] "the English have ever united all this private differences to attend Forraigne," and that Cromwell, notwithstanding the Meschants in his time (which were the Cavaliers), he did never find them interrupt him in his foreign businesses. And that he did not doubt but to live to see the Dutch as fearful of provoking the English under the government of a King, as he remembers them to have been under that of a Coquin.[4] I writ all this story to my Lord Sandwich tonight into the Downes, it being very good and true, word for word from Mr. Coventry today.

a repl. 'ribbed'

---

1. I.e. the puritan fanatics. Some of them were said this summer to be promising the Dutch to raise a fifth column of 20,000 in England should war break out: see despatch (10/20 June) from The Hague in PRO, SP 84/171, f. 14*r*.

2. The Dutch ambassador.

3. The Duke of York.

4. The English government was using strong language to the Dutch ambassadors who were about to leave. Pepys's summary is confirmed by the report in *CSPVen. 1664–6*, p. 44 (newsletter, undated). The King had used similar language: 'They had only to send their fleet to Guinea and they would find one ready to receive them, and perhaps another on the road to stop them': (ib., loc. cit.). Rupert's fleet in fact got no farther than Portsmouth, and the Dutch ships were recalled to harbour before the end of the year. James took command of the Channel fleet for a few weeks in November–December.

7. Lay long today, pleasantly discoursing with my wife about the dinner we are to have for the Joyces a day or two hence. Then up and with Mr. Margetts to Limehouse to see his ground and ropeyard there; which is very fine, and I believe we shall imploy it for the Navy – for the King's grounds are not sufficient to supply our dispense if a warr comes.[1] Thence back to the Change – where great talk of the forwardness of the Dutch; which puts us all to a stand, and perticularly myself for my Lord Sandwich, to think him to lie where he is for a Sacrifice if they should begin with us.

So home and Creed with me, and to dinner; and after dinner, I out to my office, taking in Bagwells wife, who I knew waited for me; but company came to me so soon, that I could have no discourse with her as I intended, of pleasure. So anon abroad with Creed; walked to Bartholomew fayre, this being the last day, and there saw the best dancing on the ropes that I think I ever saw in my life – and so all say. And so by coach home – where I find my wife hath had her head dressed by her woman Mercer, which is to come to her tomorrow; but my wife being to go to a christening tomorrow, she came to do her head up tonight.

So a while to my office, and then to supper and to bed.

8. Up and to the office, where busy all the morning. At noon dined at home – and I by water down to Woolwich by a gally, and back again in the evening. All haste made in setting out this Guinny fleet, but yet not such as will ever do the King's business if we come to a warr.[2] My [wife] this afternoon, being very well dressed by her new woman, Mary Mercer (a decayed merchant's daughter that our Will helps us to), did go to the christening of Mrs. Mill's the parson's wife's child, where she never was before.[3] After I was come home, Mr. Povey came to me and took me out to supper to Mr. Bland's, who is making now all haste to be gone for Tanger. Here pretty merry, and

1. George Margetts was given a contract for cordage on 29 November 1664 (*CSPD 1664–5*, p. 133), but his ropeyard does not appear to have been taken over.

2. Probably because the fleet was too small and included too many converted merchantmen: *CSPD 1664–5*, pp. 3, 4.

3. The child was a daughter (Elizabeth), and the godparents included Sir W. Batten: *Harl. Soc. Reg.*, 46/72.

good discourse; fain to admire the knowledge and experience of Mrs. Bland, who I think as good a merchant as her husband.[1] I went home and there find Mercer, whose person I like well and I think will do well, at least I hope so. So to my office a little and then to bed.

9. Up, and to put things in order against dinner, I out and bought some things; among others, a dozen of Silver Salts. Home and to the office, where some of us met a little; and then home and at noon comes my company – *viz.*, Anth. and Will Joyce and their wifes – my aunt James newly come out of Wales, and my Cosen Sarah Gyles – her husband[2] did not come, and by her I did understand afterward that it was because he was not yet able to pay me the 40s she had borrowed a year ago of me. I was as merry as I could, giving them a good dinner; but W. Joyce did so talk, that he made everybody else Dumb, but only laugh at him. I forgot, there was Mr. Harman and his wife. My aunt a very good harmelesse woman. All their talk is of her and my two she-Cosen Joyces and Will's little boy Will (who was also here today) [going] down to Brampton to my father's next week – which will be trouble and charge to them; but however, my father and mother desire to see them, and so let them. They eyed mightily my great Cupboard of plate, I this day putting my two Flaggons upon my table; and endeed, it is a fine sight and better then ever I did hope to see of my own. Mercer dined with us at table, this being her first dinner in my house.

After dinner left them and to White-hall, where a small Tanger committee; and so back again home and there my wife and Mercer and Tom and I sat till 11 at night, singing and fiddling; and a great joy it is to see me maister of so much pleasure in my house, that it is, and will be still I hope, a constant pleasure to me to be at home. The girle plays pretty well upon the Harpsicon, but only ordinary tunes; but hath a good hand. Sings a little, but hath a good voyce and eare. My boy, a brave boy, sings finely and is the most pleasant boy at present, while his ignorant boy's tricks last, that ever I saw. So to supper, and with great pleasure to bed.

1. For women as merchants, see above, iii. 300 & n. 2.

2. Sarah Gyles's husband Thomas.

10. Up and to my*ᵃ* office, where we sat all the morning. And I much troubled to think what the end of our great sluggishness will be, for we do nothing in this office like people able to carry on a warr. We must be put out, or other people put in.

Dined at home. And then my wife and I and Mercer to the Dukes house and there saw *The Rivalls*,[1] which is no excellent play, but good action in it – especially, Gosnell comes and sings and dances finely; but for all that, fell out of the Key, so that the Musique could not play to her afterward; and so did Harris also, go*ᵇ* out of the tune to agree with her.[2]

Thence home, and late writing letters; and this night I received by Will 105*l* – the first fruits of my endeavours in the late Contract for victualling of Tanger – for which God be praised. For I can with a safe conscience say that I have therein saved the King 5000*l* per annum, and yet got myself a hope of 300*l* per annum without the least wrong to the King.

So to supper and to bed.

11. *Lords day.* Up, and to church in the best manner I have gone a good while; that is to say, with my wife and her woman Mercer along with us and Thom my boy waiting on us.

A dull sermon. Home; dined. Left my wife to go to church alone; and I walked in haste, being late, to the Abby at Westminster according to promise to meet Jane Welsh; and there wearily walked, expecting her till 6 a-clock from 3. But no Jane came, which vexed me. Only, part of it I spent with Mr. Blagrave walking in the Abbey, he telling me the whole government and discipline of White-hall chapel and the caution now used against admitting any debauched persons – which I was glad to hear, though he tells me there are persons bad enough. Thence, going home, went by Gervas's; and there stood Jane

a repl. 'the'
b 'and dances . . . go' crowded into bottom of page

1. Davenant's insipid adaptation of *The two noble kinsmen*, a comedy by John Fletcher and another Elizabethan playwright (possibly Shakespeare). Davenant's version was published in 1668. The cast listed by Downes (pp. 23–4) includes Betterton as Philander and Smith as Polynices. (A).

2. Winifred Gosnell was formerly Mrs Pepys's maid; she probably played Celania, a role later taken by Mrs Davis. Harris played Theocles. (A).

at the door, and so I took her in and drank with her, her maister and mistress being out of door. She told me how she could not come to*a* me this afternoon, but promised another time. So I walked home, contented with my speaking with her, and walked to my uncle Wights, where they were all at supper; and among others, fair Mrs. Margtt Wight, who endeed is very pretty. So after supper home to prayers and to bed. This afternoon, it seems, Sir J Minnes fell sick at church; and going down the gallery stairs, fell down dead; but came to himself again and is pretty well.

12. Up, and to my Cosen Anth. Joyce's and there took leave of my aunt James and both Cosens their wifes, who are this day going down to my father's by coach. I did give my aunt xxs to carry as a token to my mother, and xs to Pall.

Thence by coach to St. James and there did our business as usual with the Duke. And saw him with great pleasure play with his little girle[1] – like an ordinary private father of a child.

Thence walked to Jervas's, where I took Jane in the shop alone and there heard of her her maister and mistress were going out; so I went away and came again half an hour after. In the mean-time went to the Abby and there went in to see the tombs with great pleasure. Back again to Jane, and there upstairs and drank with her; and stayed two hours with her, kissing her – but nothing more. Anon took boat and by water to the neat-houses over against Fox-hall[2] to have seen Greatorex dive,[3] which Gervas

a repl. 'at the time she'

---

1. Princess Mary, born 30 April 1662; afterwards Queen Mary II.
2. The Neat Houses, Chelsea, opposite Vauxhall. See above, ii. 158, n. 2.
3. Several experiments under the auspices of the Royal Society were made with diving-bells. In July 1661 the society's amanuensis stayed under water for 28 minutes in a bell let down in the river at Deptford: Birch, i. 35; Evelyn, 19 July. James Maule and Robert Hooke are mentioned at about this time as inventors

of apparatus, but not Greatorex: *CSPD 1660–1*, pp. 320, 490; Birch, i. 399–400, 422, 425, 431, 433. Prof. Eva G. R. Taylor (*Math. Practitioners*, pp. 105, 229) states that Greatorex, acting on the advice of Jonas Moore, made experiments of this sort on behalf of the Royal Society in order to demonstrate the usefulness of diving-bells in the construction of the mole at Tangier. Both diving-bells and diving-suits had been known in England since the late 16th century: Oppenheim, p. 345.

and his wife were gone to see; and there I found them (and did it the rather for a pretence for my having been so long at their house); but being disappointed of some necessaries to do it, I stayed not, but back to Jane; but she could not go out with me, and so I to Mr. Creed's lodgings and with him walked up and down in the New Exchange, talking mightily of the convenience and necessity of a man's wearing good clothes. And so after eating a mess of Creame, I took leave of him, he walking with me as far as Fleet Conduict; he offering me, upon my request, to put out some money for me into Backwells hand at 6 per cent interest, which he seldom gives – which I will consider of, being doubtful of trusting any of these great dealers because of their mortality; but then the convenience of having one's money at an hour's call is very great.[1]

Thence to uncle Wights and there supped with my wife, having given them a brave barrel of oysters of Povys giving me. So home and to bed.

13. Up and to the office, where we sat busy all morning. Dined at home; and after dinner to Fishmongers hall, where we met the first time upon the Fishery committee – and many good things discoursed of concerning[a] making of Farthings, which was proposed as a way of raising money for this business; and then that of Lotterys, but with great confusion.[2] But I hope we shall fall into greater order.

---

a   repl. 'but'

---

1. Pepys now had c. £1000 in his house: below, p. 281. Nothing came of this proposal, but in 1666 he deposited £2000 at Vyner's: below, 1 February 1666. He continued, however, to keep large sums in cash in his study. Even substantial merchants did the same: R. North, *Life of . . . Sir Dudley North* (1744), p. 148. Certainly bankers were often broken – Pepys at 6 July 1665 reports a run on Backwell caused by his going abroad. The 6% here mentioned was the maximum statutory rate of interest fixed by an act of 1660. In 1666 Vyner allowed Pepys 7% for money recoverable at will.

2. Three methods of raising funds for the Royal Fishery were now proposed – voluntary collections; the grant of monopolies for coining farthings; and the grant of licences authorising public lotteries. The coinage scheme was never tried. For the use of lotteries for raising public money, see Sir W. Petty, *Econ. Writings* (ed. Hull), pp. 64–5. They had been used in 1639 for the benefit of the Fishery Association of 1632. Cf. also above, p. 214.

So home again and to my office; where after doing business, home and to a little Musique – after supper; and so to bed.

14. Up; and wanting some things that should be laid ready for my dressing myself, I was angry; and one thing after another made my wife give Besse warning to be gone – which the idle [jade], whether out of fear or ill-nature or simplicity I know not, but she took it and asked leave to go forth to look a place, and did – which vexed me to the heart, she being as good a natured wench as ever we shall have, but only forgetful.

At the office all the morning; and at noon to the Change and there went off with Sir W. Warren and took occasion to desire him to lend me 100*l* – which he said he would let me have with all his heart presently, as he had promised me a little while ago to give me, for my pains in his two great contracts of masts, 100*l*;[1] and that this should be it – to which end I did move it to him; and by this means I hope*a* to be possessed of the 100*l* presently, within two or three days.

So home to dinner; and then to the office and down to Blackwall by water to view a place found out for laying of masts; and I think it will be most proper.*b*   So home and there find Mr. Pen come to visit my wife and stayed with them till sent for to Mr. Blands, whither by appointment I was to go to supper.   And against my will left them together; but God knows without any ⟨reason of⟩ fear in my conscience of any evil between them – but such is my natural folly.   Being thither come, they would needs have my wife; and so Mr. Bland and his wife (the first time she was ever at my house or my wife at hers) very civilly went forth and brought her and W Pen; and there Mr. Povy and we supped nobly and very merry – it being to take leave of Mr. Bland, who is upon going soon to Tanger.   So late home to prayers and to bed.

15. At the office all the morning.   Then to the Change and so home to dinner, where Luellin dined with us; and after dinner

----

a   MS. 'have'   *b*   symbol smudged

----

1. For these contracts, see above,   promise, see above, pp. 229–30.
p. 216, n. 1; p. 239, n. 1; for the

many people came in and kept me all the afternoon; among other, the Maister and Wardens of Chyrurgeons' hall, who stayed arguing their cause[1] with me. I did give them the best answer I could; and after their being two hours with me, parted; and I to my office to do business, which is much on my hands, and so late home to supper and to bed.

16. Up betimes and to my office, where all the morning very busy putting papers to rights. And among other things, Mr. Gauden coming to me, I had a good opportunity to speak to him about his present,[2] which hitherto hath been a burden to me, that I could not do it, because I was doubtful that he meant it as a temptation to me to stand by him in the business of Tangier victualling. But he clears me it was not, and that he values me and my proceedings therein very highly – being but what became me; and that what he did was for my old kindnesses to him in despatching of his business – which I was glad to hear; and with my heart in good rest and great joy, parted and to my business again. At noon to the Change, where by appointment I met Sir*a* W Warren; and afterward to the Sun tavern, where he brought to me, being all alone, a 100*l* in a bag; which I offered him to give him my receipt for, but he told me no, it was my owne, which he had a little while since promised me and was glad that (as I had told him two days since) it would now do me courtesy. And so most kindly he did give it me, and I as joyfully, even out of myself, carried it home in a coach – he himself expressly taking care that nobody might see this business done, though I was willing enough to have carried a servant with me to have received it; but he advised me to do it myself. So home with it and to dinner. After dinner, I forth with my boy to buy several things, Stooles and Andirons and candlesticks, &c., household stuff. And walked to the Mathematical instrument-maker in Moore-fields[3] and bought a large pair of compasses.

a repl. 'Mr.'

---

1. See above, p. 261 & n. 1.
2. The two silver flagons: see above, p. 216.
3. Probably Walter Hayes (fl.
1651–92), at the sign of the Cross Daggers, next door to the Pope's Head Tavern.

And there met Mr. Pargiter,[1] and he would needs have me to drink a cup of Horse-redish ale, which he and a friend of his, troubled with the stone, have been drinking of – which we did, and then walked into the fields as far almost as Sir G. Whitmores,[2] 《*Russia.*》 all the way talking of Russia – which he says is a sad place;[3] and though Mosco is a very great city, yet it is, from the distance between house and house, and few people compared with this – and poor sorry houses, the Emperor himself living in a wooden house[4] – his exercise only flying a hawke at pigeons and carrying pigeons ten or twelve mile off and then laying wagers which pigeon shall come soonest home to her house. All the winter within doors, some few playing at Chesse but most drinking their time away. Women live very slavishly there. And it seems, in the Emperor's Court no room hath above two or three windows, and those the greatest not a yard wide or high – for warmth in winter time. And that the general cure for all diseases there is their sweating-houses – or people that are poor, they get into their ovens, being heated, and there lie. Little learning among things of any sort – not a man that speaks Latin, unless the Secretary of State by chance.

Mr. Pargiter and I walked to the Change together and there parted; and so I to buy more things and then home; and after a little at my office – home to supper and to bed. ⟨This day old Hardwicke[5] came and redeemed a watch he had left with me in pawn for 40*s* seven years ago; and I let him have it.⟩[a]

Great talk that the Dutch will certainly be out this week and

a   addition crowded in between paragraphs

---

1. Francis Pargiter, merchant, of the Muscovy Company.

2. Baumes House, Hoxton; the house of Sir George Whitmore (Lord Mayor 1631–2; d. 1654), which Pepys had known as Whitmore's house in his boyhood rambles across these fields. Engraving in D. Lysons, *Environs* (1792–1811), ii, opp. p. 488.

3. To the western traveller Russia was a land of poverty, superstition, tyranny and no inns. Cf. similar accounts in Samuel Collins, *Present state of Russia* (1671); M.S. Anderson, *Britain's discovery of Russia, 1553–1815*, ch. ii.

4. The Kremlin was built of stone and brick, but some of the winter lodgings attached to it were of wood, which was held to make the living quarters warm and dry: Collins, op. cit., p. 57.

5. ? Ralph Hardwicke, Council messenger.

will sail*ᵃ* directly to Guiny, being conveyed out of the Channel with 42 sail of ships.[1]

17. Up and to the office, where Mr. Coventry very angry to see things go so coldly as they do; and I must needs say it makes me fearful every day of having some change of the office; and the truth is, I am of late a little guilty of being remiss myself, of what I used to be. But I hope I shall come to my old pass again— my family being now settled again.

Dined at home; and to the office, where late busy in setting all my businesses in order, and I did a very great and a very contenting afternoon's work.

This day my aunt Wight sent my wife a new scarfe, with a compliment for the many favours she had received of her; which is the several things we have sent her. I am glad enough of it, for I see my Uncle is so given up to the Wights that I hope for little more of them.[2] So home to supper and to bed.

18. *Lords day*. Up and to church, all of us. At noon comes Anth. and W. Joyces (their wifes being in the country with my father) and dined with me, very merry as I can be in such company.*ᵇ* After dinner walked to Westminster (tiring them by the way, and so left them, Anthony in Cheapside and the other in the Strand) and there spent all the afternoon in the Cloyster, as I had agreed with Jane Welsh; but she came not, which vexed me, staying till 5 a-clock; and then walked homeward and by coach to the Old Exchange, and thence to my aunt Wights and

a MS. 'say' *b* repl. 'clo'-

---

1. In fact, it was not this fleet but the Dutch Mediterranean squadron under de Ruyter which was to sail (on secret instructions) to Guinea. The fleet in the Texel, which England was so anxiously watching, was mostly recalled into harbour in November. Downing, English ambassador at The Hague, was quite deceived as to which fleet would move: below, pp. 328, 333; Lister, iii. 343–5; HMC, *Heathcote*, p. 167; *CSPD 1664–5*, p. 11 (a report, similar to Pepys's, dated this day); J. Beresford, *Godfather of Downing St*, pp. 172–4.

2. Uncle William Wight was rich and childless, and Pepys had for some time been suspended between hope and despair in observing the variable relations between him and his family.

invited her and my uncle to supper. And so home; and by and by they came and we eat a rare barrel of oysters Mr. Povey sent me this morning, and very merry at supper; and so to prayers and to bed.

Last night it seems my aunt Wight did send my wife a new scarfe, laced, as a token for her many givings to her. It is true, now and then we give them small toys, as oranges, &c. – but my aime is to get myself something more from my uncles favour then this.

19. Up, my wife and I having a little anger*a* about her woman already, she thinking that I take too much*b* care of her at table to mind her (my wife) of cutting* for her – but it soon over! and so up and with Sir W. Batten and W. Penn to St. James and there did our business with the Duke; and thence homeward straight, calling at the Coffee-house and there had very good discourse with Sir   Blunt[1] and Dr. Whistler[2] about Ægypt and other things. So home to dinner, my wife having put on today her winter new suit of Moyre, which is handsome. And so after dinner I did give her 15*l* to lay out in linen and necessaries for the house and to buy a suit for Pall; and I myself to White-hall to a Tanger committee, where Collonell Reames hath brought us so full and methodicall an account of all matters there, that I never have nor hope to see the like of any public business while I live again.[3] The committee up, I to West-

_a_ l.h. repl. s.h. rendered illegible   _b_ MS. 'make'

---

1. Presumably Sir Henry Blount (d. 1682), the traveller whose account of Egypt and the Middle East (*Voyage to the Levant*) had been published in 1636.

2. Daniel Whistler, F.R.S.; physician and virtuoso.

3. On 11 September Bullen Reymes had returned from Tangier, where he had been sent in June. His lengthy report (now untraced) on both Tangier and Sallee, and on the needs of the garrison, had been presented to the Privy Council on the 18th, and received with great com-

mendation. Reymes wrote in his diary: 'The King was so well pleased with my booke, which he held in his hand and perused all the time, as ... all of them confessed, they never had so good an account in all their life. And I overheard the King say to himselfe, as he was turning over the booke, "Indeed, indeed, it was very well done and playne"' (qu. H. A. Kaufman, *Concientious Cavalier*, p. 196). A subcommittee was appointed to send men and money immediately: PRO, CO 279/3, ff. 230+.

minster to Jervas's and spoke with Jane, who I find cold and not so desirous of a meeting as before; and it is no matter, I shall be the freer from the inconveniences that might fallow thereon – besides offending God Almighty and neglecting my business. So by coach home and to my office, where late; and so to supper and to bed.

I met with Dr. Pierce today; who speaking of Dr. Fraizer's

《*Dr. Fraizer*》 being so earnest to have such a one (one Collins) go Chyrurgeon to the Princes person, and will have him go in his terms and with so much money put into his[1] hands,[a] he tells me (when I was wondering that Fraizer should order things with the Prince in that confident manner) that Fraizer is so great with my Lady Castlemayne and Steward and all the ladies at Court, in helping to slip their calfes when there is occasion, and with the great men in curing of their claps, that he can do what he please with the King in spite of any man, and upon the same score with the Prince – they all having more or less occasion to make use of him.

Sir G Carteret tells me this afternoon that the Dutch are not

《*Dutch*》 yet ready to set out; and by that means do lose a good wind, which would carry them out and keep us in. And moreover, he says that they begin to bogle in the business, and he thinks may offer terms of peace for all this; and seems to argue that it will be well for the King too[2] – and I pray God send it.

Collonell Reames did, among other things, this day tell me how

《*Lord Tiviott.*》 it is clear that if my Lord Tiviott had lived, he would have quite undone Tanger, or designed himself to be master of it. He did put the King upon most great, chargeable, and unnecessary works there. And took that course industriously, to deter all other merchants but himself to deal

---

a   MS. 'times'

---

1. Fraizer's. Alexander Fraizer was physician-in-ordinary to the King and the most trusted of his medical advisers. Jerome Collins had written to Pepys on the 17th, informing him that he (Collins) had been appointed surgeon to Rupert by the King's 'positive orders', and would require special medicines: *CSPD 1663-4*, p. 11.

2. On the following day Pepys repeated most of this news in a letter to Sandwich: *Further Corr.*, p. 27.

there and to make both King and all others pay what he pleased for all was brought thither.

20. Up and to the office, where we sat all the morning. At noon to the Change and there met by appointment with Captain Poyntz, who hath some place, or title to a place, belonging to gameing;[1] and so I discoursed with him about the business of our improving of the Lotterys to the King's benefit, and that of the Fishery; and had some light from him in that business – and shall, he says, have more in writing from him. So home to dinner and then abroad to the Fishing committee at Fishmongers hall, and there sat and did some business considerably; and so up and home, and there late at my office, doing much business; and I find with great delight that I am come to my good temper of business again – God continue me in it. So home to supper, it being washing day, and to bed.

21. Up, and by coach to Mr. Povy's and there got him to sign the payment of Captain Taylors bills for the remainder of freight for the *Eagle*, wherein I shall be gainer about 30*l*.[2] Thence with him to Westminster by coach, to Houseman's the great picture-drawer and saw again very fine pictures, and have his promise, for Mr. Povy's sake, to take pains in what picture I shall set him about; and I think to have my wife's.[3] But it is a strange thing to observe, and fit for me to remember, that I am at no time so unwilling to part with money as when I am concerned in the getting of it most (as, I thank God, of late I have got more in this*a* month, *viz.* near 250*l*) then ever I did in half a year before in my life, I think.

Thence I to White-hall with him; and so walked to the Old Exchange and back to Povy's to dinner, where great and good company; among others, Sir John Skeffington, whom I knew at

a repl. 'his'

---

1. John Poyntz was Clerk Comptroller of the office of the Master of the Revels, which licensed lotteries and entertainment of all sorts.

2. See below, p. 292 & n. 2.

3. Huysmans was probably at this time at the height of his popularity: see above, p. 254 & n. 4. I know of no painting of Mrs Pepys by him. (OM).

Magdalen College, a fellow-commoner, my fellow-pupil, but one with whom I had no great acquaintance, he being then (God knows) much above me.[1]   Here I was afresh delighted with Mr. Povys house and pictures of perspective; being strange things, to think how they do delude one's eye, that methinks it would make a man doubtful of swearing that ever he saw anything.[2]

Thence with him to St. James's, and so to White-hall to a Tanger committee – and hope I have light of another opportunity of getting a little money, if Sir W Warren will use me kindly for deals to Tanger.   And with that hopes went joyfully home and there received Captain Taylors money, received by Will today; out of which (as I said above) I shall get above 30*l.*   So with great comfort to bed after supper.

By discourse this day, I have great hopes from Mr. Coventry that the Dutch and we shall not fall out.

22.   Up, and at the office all the morning.   To the Change at noon; and among other things, discoursed with Sir Wm. Warren what I might do to get a little money by carrying of Deales to Tanger, and told him the opportunity I have there of doing it. And he did give me some advice, though not so good as he would have done at any other time of the year, but such as I hope to make good use of and get a little money by.

So to Sir G Carteret's to dinner, he and I and Captain Cocke all alone – and good discourse.   And thence to a committee of Tanger at White-hall; and so home, where I find my wife not well – and she tells me she thinks she is with child; but I neither believe nor desire it.   But God's will be done.

So to my office late, and home to supper and to bed, having got a strange cold in my head by flinging off my hat at dinner[3] and sitting with the wind in my neck.

1. Skeffington was made a fellow-commoner in his third year at Magdalene in 1651, the year in which Pepys entered college – Samuel Morland being tutor to them both: Magd. Coll., Reg. Bk no. 2, p. 11*b*. Skeffington was the son and heir of Sir Richard Skeffington, Kt, of Coventry, and succeeded to a cousin's baronetcy in 1652. He was now

M.P. for Co. Antrim, and became Viscount Massereene in 1665.
2. Pepys's delight in the effect of illusion created in Povey's pictures is a clear expression of one very marked aspect of contemporary taste. Cf. above, iv. 18, n. 1.   (OM).
3. Men normally wore hats at meals.

23. My cold and pain in my head increasing and the palate of my mouth falling, I was in great pain all night. My wife also was not well, so that a maid was fain to sit up by her all night.

Lay long in the morning. At last, up; and among others, comes Mr. Fuller, that was the wit of Cambridge and *Prævaricator* in my time,[a] came and stayed all the morning with me, discoursing – and his business to get a man discharged, which I did do for him.[1]

Dined with little heart at noon. In the afternoon, against my will to the office, where Sir G Carteret and we met about an order of the Council for the hiring him a house, giving him 1000*l* fine and 70*l* per annum for it.[2] Here Sir J. Mennes took occasion, in the most childish and most unbeseeming manner, to reproach us all; but most himself, that he was not valued as Controller among us, nor did anything but only set his hand to paper (which is but too[b] true); and everybody had a palace, and he no house to lie in, and wished he had but as much to build him a house with as we have laid out in Carved work. It was to no end to oppose, but all bore it, and after laughed at him for it.[3]

So home and late reading *The Siege of Rhodes*[4] to my wife, and then to bed – my head being in great pain and my palate still down.

a MS. 'mind'   b repl. 'true'

---

1. Thomas Fuller, Fellow of Christ's, 1649–61, was now Rector of Navenby, Lincs. As *praevaricator*, he was a licensed jester at the disputation in philosophy, making learned but nonsensical play with the question under dispute. A sample of his wit (verses on *An anima hominis sit tabula rasa*) is in W. T. Costello, *Scholastic curriculum at early 17th-cent. Cambridge*, pp. 27–9. He was now interceding to protect a waterman from the pressgang: below, p. 292.

2. The order had been issued on 21 September: BM, Add. 36782, f. 21r. The house (for the use of the Navy Treasury) was in Broad St and

replaced the old building in Leadenhall St. (R).

3. In 1661 Mennes had succeeded John Davis (an office clerk) in one of the official houses in the Navy Office building: above, ii. 114. His complaint was perhaps that it did not belong *ex officio* to the Comptroller and was not grand enough.

4. Davenant's opera; see above, ii. 130 & n. 2. Pepys had a copy of the 1663 edition, in which the two parts were published together for the first time: below, vi. 320; 5 August 1666. Both parts are also printed in the 1673 edition of Davenant's *Works*: PL 2347. (A).

24. Up and to the office, where all the morning busy. Then home to dinner; and so after dinner comes one Phillips, who is concerned in the Lottery,[1] and from whom I collected much concerning that business. I carried him in my way to White-hall and set him down at Somersett-house. Among other things, he told me that Monsieur du Puis, that is so great a man at the Duke of Yorkes, and this man's great opponent, is a knave and by quality but a tailor.[2]

To the Tanger Comittee; and there I opposed Collonell Legg's estimate of supplies of provisions to be sent to Tanger, till all were ashamed of it and he fain, after all his good husbandry and seeming ignorance and joy, to have the King's money saved – yet afterward he discovered all his design to be to keep the furnishing of these things to the officers of the Ordnance.[3] But Mr. Coventry seconded me, and between us we shall save the King some money in the year. In one business of deals, in 520*l*, I offer to save 172*l* and yet propose getting money to myself by it.

So home and to my office; and business being done, home to supper and so to bed, my head and throat being still out of order mightily.

This night Prior of Brampton came and paid me 40*l*. And I find this poor painful man is the only thriving and purchasing man in the town almost.[4] We were told today of a Duch ship of 3 or 400 Tons, where all the men were dead of the plague and the ship cast ashore at Gottenburgh.[5]

1. Phillips was probably Robert Phillips, Groom of the King's Bedchamber. For the lottery, see above, p. 214 & n. 2.

2. Lawrence Dupuy was Yeoman of the Robes to the Duke of York. Courtiers obtained a stranglehold on lotteries, though the licences were intended at the Restoration to be granted for the benefit of loyal and indigent officers. Dupuy had with others been licensed in December 1663 to set up a lottery for the benefit of the Fishery: *CSPD 1663–4*, p. 397. There is a complaint of his dishonesty ib., p. 454 (? January 1664).

3. William Legge was Lieutenant of the Ordnance. Cf. Pepys's note (24 September) in NWB, p. 63: 'It is worth considering how Collonell Legg, being lately brought into the Tanger Comittee by Sir H. Bennet, hath given great attendance, which I alway construed to arise from his care of the King's business.'

4. William Prior had bought a house and some land from the estate of Robert Pepys: above, iii. 287 & n. 1.

5. I have not traced this story elsewhere; possibly a canard. For the plague in Holland, see above, iv. 340, n. 2.

25.*ª* *Lords day.* Up; and my throat being yet very sore and my head out of order – we went not to church; but I spent all the morning reading of *The Madd Lovers*[1] – a very good play. And at noon comes Harman and his wife, whom I sent for to meet the Joyces, but they came not; it seems Will hath got a fall off his horse and broke his face.

However, we were as merry as I could in their company, and we had a good Chine of beef. But I have no taste nor stomach through my cold, and therefore little pleased with my dinner.

It raining, they sat talking with us all the afternoon. So anon they went away and then I to read another play, *The Custome of the Country*,[2] which is a very poor one methinks. Then to supper, prayers, and bed.

26. Up; pretty well again, but my mouth very scabby, my cold being going away – so that I was forced to wear a great black patch: but that would not do much good. But it happens we did not go to the Duke today. And so I stayed at home, busy all the morning; and at noon, after dinner, to the Change and thence home to my office again, where busy, well imployed till 10 at night; and so home to supper and to bed – my mind a little troubled that I have not of late kept up myself so briske in business, but minded my ease*ᵇ* a little too much and my family, upon the coming of Mercer and Tom – so that I have not kept company, nor appeared very active with Mr. Coventry; but now I resolve to settle to it again. Not that I have idled all my time; but as to my ease, something; so I have looked a little too much after Tanger and the Fishery – and that in the sight of Mr. Coventry. But I have good reason to love myself for serving Tanger, for it is one of the best flowers in my garden.

27. Lay long sleeping, it raining and blowing very hard.

    a MS. '24'   *b* repl. 'business' followed by illegible symbol

---

1. A tragicomedy by Fletcher: see above, ii. 34 & n. 3. (A).

2. A comedy by Fletcher and Massinger, written between 1619 and 1622, and published in 1647. Pepys had a copy of it (and of *The mad lover*) in his 1679 Folio of the plays of Beaumont and Fletcher: PL 2623. (A).

Then up and to the office, my mouth still being scabby, and a patch on it. At the office all the morning. At noon dined at home; and so after dinner (Lewellin dining with me and in my way talking about Deering)[1] to the Fishing committee and had there very many fine things argued – and I hope some good will come of it. So home, where my wife having (after all her merry discourse of being with child) her months upon her, is gone to bed. I to my office very late, doing business. Then home to supper and to bed. Tonight Mr. T. Trice and Piggot came to see me, and desire my going down to Brampton Court; where for Piggots sake, for whom it is necessary I should go, I would be glad to go, and will, contrary to my purpose, endeavour it.[2] But having now almost 1000*l*, if not above, in my house, I know not what to do with it;[3] and that will trouble my mind, to leave in the house and I not at home.

28. Up, and by water with Mr. Tooker down (to Woolwich first, to do several businesses of the King's); then on board Captain Fisher's ship, which we hire to carry goods to Tanger – all the way, going and coming, I reading and discoursing over some papers of his, which he, poor man, having some experience, but greater conceit of it then is fit, did at the King's first coming over make proposals of, ordering in a new manner the whole revenue of the kingdom.[4] But God knows, a most weak thing; however, one paper of his I keep, wherein he doth state the main branches of the public Revenue – fit to consider and remember. So home, very cold and fearful of having got some pain; but thanks be to God, I was well after it. So to dinner; and after dinner by coach to White-hall, thinking to have met at a Comittee of Tanger; but nobody being there but my Lord Rutherford, he would needs carry me and another scotch lord to a play; and so we saw, coming late, part of *The Generall*, my Lord Orery's

1. Sir Edward Dering, timber merchant, whom Llewellyn served as clerk.
2. See below, p. 298.
3. Cf. above, p. 269, n. 1.
4. John Tooker of Putney (now employed by the Navy Board as a river shipping agent) had been an excise official during the Protectorate: *CSPD 1656-7*, p. 134. These papers have not been traced.

⟨Broghill⟩ second play;[1] but Lord, to see how no more, either in words, sense or design, it is to his *Harry the 5th* is not imaginable, and so poorly acted, though in finer clothes, is strange. And here I must confess breach of a vow in appearance,[2] but I not desiring it but against my will, and my oath being to go neither at my own charge nor another's, as I had done by becoming liable to give them another, as I am to Sir W. Penn and Mr. Creed. But here I neither know which of them paid for me; nor, if I did, am I obliged ever to return the like, or did it by desire or with any willingness. So that with a safe conscience, I do think my oath is not broke, and judge God Almighty will not think it otherwise.

Thence to W. Joyces and there find my aunt and Cosen Mary[3] come home from my father's with great pleasure and content. And thence to Kate's[4] and found her also mighty pleased with her journey and their good usage of them. And so home, troubled in my conscience at my being at a play. But at home I find Mercer playing on her Vyall, which is a pretty instrument; and so I to the Vyall and singing till late, and so to bed – my mind at a great loss how to go down to Brampton this week to satisfy Piggot. But what with the fears of my house – my money – my wife and my office, I know not how in the world to think of it – Tom Hater being out of town and I having near 1000*l* in my house.

29. *Michaelmas day.* Up, and to the office, where all the morning. Dined at home and Creed with me. After dinner I to Sir G Carteret, and with him to his new house he is taking in Broadstreete; and there surveyed all the rooms and bounds in order to the drawing up a lease thereof. And that done, Mr Cutler (his landlord) took me up and down and showed me all his ground and houses, which is extraordinary great, he having

1. Written in 1661; one of the earliest of the heroic dramas of the Restoration period, first acted in 1662 in Dublin under the title *Altemera*; now at the TR, Drury Lane. First published in 1853 (J. O. Halliwell-Phillips, ed., *A brief description of . . . MSS . . . in Plymouth* etc.; best edition by William S. Clark (*Dramatic works Orrery*, 1937, vol. i). (A).

2. I.e. not to go to theatres more often than once a month: above, p. 33. He had been to the LIF on 10 September. (A).

3. I.e. Aunt James and Mary, wife of William Joyce.

4. Wife of Anthony Joyce.

bought all the Augustin-fryers; and many many a 1000*l* he hath and will bury there. So home to my business, clearing my papers and preparing my accounts against tomorrow for a monthly and a great Auditt. So to supper and to bed.

Fresh newes came of our beating the Dutch at Guiny quite out of all their castles almost,[1] which will make them quite mad here at home, sure. And Sir G. Carteret did tell me that the King doth joy mightily at it; but asked him, laughing, "But," says he, "how shall I do to answer this to the Embassador when he comes?"

Nay, they say that we have beat them out of the New Netherlands too[2] – so that we have been doing them mischiefe a great while in several parts of the world, without public knowledge or reason.

Their Fleete for Guinny is now, they say, ready and abroad, and will be going this week.*a*[3]

Coming home tonight, I did go to examine my wife's house-accounts; and finding things that seemed somewhat doubtful, I was angry, though she did make it pretty plain; but confessed that when she doth misse a sum, she doth add something to other things to make it. And upon my being very angry, she doth protest she will here lay up something for*b* herself to buy her a neckelace with – which madded me and doth still trouble me, for I fear she will forget by degrees the way of living cheap and under a sense of want.

a   smudge below symbol   *b*   repl. 'to'

---

1. These were the exploits of Capt. Robert Holmes on the voyage which did so much to provoke the Second Dutch War. For an account, see R. Ollard, *Man of war*, pp. 85+. Setting out with a small squadron in September 1663, he had struck a series of quick blows against the Dutch trading stations in W. Africa, taking, between January and mid-May, all the Dutch ports in that region (loosely called the 'Guinea coast') except Elmina, seat of the Dutch government. As a gesture of appeasement (nothing more), Holmes was lodged in the Tower for two months on his return: see below, vi. 6 & n. 2. Pepys later acquired a copy of his log of the voyage: PL 2698.

2. On 30 July the Dutch surrendered New Amsterdam (i.e. Long Island and Manhattan, an enclave of Dutch-occupied territory surrounded by English colonies) to a force of three ships and 300 men under Richard Nicholls. See C. H. Wilson in *EHR*, 72/469+.

3. See above, p. 273, n. 1.

30. Up, and all day, both morning and afternoon, at my accounts, it being a great month both for profit and layings-out – the last being 89*l* – for kitchen, and clothes for myself and wife, and a few extraordinaries for the house. And my profits, besides salary, 239*l*. So that I have this week, notwithstanding great layings-out (and preparations for laying-out, which I make as paid this month), my balance doth come to 1203*l* – for which the Lord's name be praised.

Dined at home at noon, staying long looking for Kate Joyce and my aunt James and Mary; but they came not. So my wife abroad to see them, and took Mary Joyce to a play – then in the evening came and sat working by me at the office. And late home to supper and to bed, with my heart in good rest for this day's work – though troubled to think that by[a] last month's negligence, besides the making me neglect business and spend money and lessen myself, both as to business and the world and myself, I am fain to preserve my vowe by paying 20*s* dry money into the poor's box, because I had not fulfilled all my Memorandums[1] and paid all my petty debts and received all my petty Credits of the last month. But I trust in God I shall do so no more.

a   MS. 'my'

---

1. It was Pepys's habit to make   cf. above, p. 227, n. 1.
monthly lists of things he had to do:

OCTOBER.

1. Up and at the office both forenoon and afternoon, very busy, and with great pleasure in being so. This morning, Mrs. Lane (now Martin) like a foolish woman came to the Hors=shoo hard by, and sent for me while I was at the office to come to speak with her, by a note sealed up – I know, to get me to do something for her husband; but I sent her an answer that I would see her at Westminster. And so I did not go, and she went away, poor soul.

At night home to supper, weary and my eyes sore with writing and reading – and to bed.

We go now on with great Vigour in preparing against the Dutch, who they say will now fall upon us without doubt, upon this high news come of our beating them so wholly in Guiny.

2. *Lords day.* My wife not being well to go to church, I walked with my boy through the City, putting in at several churches; among others, at Bishops-gate, and there saw the picture usually put before the King's book, put up in the church; but very ill painted, though it were a pretty piece to set up in a church.[1] I entended to have seen the Quakers, who they say do meet every Lord's day at the Mouth at Bishops-gate;[2] but I could see none stirring, nor was it fit to ask for the place. So I walked over Moore-fields, and thence to Clerkenwell church and

---

1. The picture (in St Botolph's; now no longer there) was copied from the engraving by William Marshall, printed as frontispiece to the *Eikon Basilike* (1648), which showed Charles I spurning his earthly crown and accepting a crown of thorns in exchange. Description in E. Hatton, *New view of London* (1708); i. 168-9.
2. This is probably a confusion between the Mouth tavern, Without Bishopsgate, and the Bull and Mouth,

Aldersgate St: George Fox, *Short Journal* (ed. Penney), p. 296. At the latter was held the most important Quaker meeting in the city. The room there had been used by Friends since 1654; destroyed by the Fire, it was later rebuilt and served as a meeting-place until 1740: W. Beck and T. F. Ball, *London Friends' meetings*, ch. ix. The Quakers were the boldest of all nonconformists in defying the laws against conventicles.

there (as I wished) sat next pew to the fair Butler,[1] who endeed is a most perfect beauty still. And one I do very much admire myself for my choice of her for a beauty – she having the best lower part of her face that ever I saw all days of my life. After church I walked to my Lady Sandwiches through my Lord Southamptons new buildings in the fields behind Grays Inn;[2] and endeed they are a very great and a noble work. So I dined with my Lady; and the same innocent discourse that we used to have. Only, after dinner, being alone, she asked me my opinion about Creed, whether he would have a wife or no and what he was worth, and proposed Mrs. Wright[3] for him; which she says she heard he was once enquiring after. She desired I would take a good time and manner of proposing it; and I said I would, though I believed he would love nothing but money, and much was not to be expected there she said.

So away back to Clerken-well church, thinking to have got sight of *la belle* Boteler again, but failed; and so after church walked all over the fields home; and there my wife was angry with me for not coming home and for gadding abroad to look after beauties, she told me plainly; so I made all peace, and to supper. This evening came Mrs. Lane (now Martin) with her husband to desire my help about a place for him; it seems poor Mr. Daniel is dead, of the Victualling-Office – a place too good for this puppy to fallow him in – but I did give him the best words I could; and so after drinking a glass of wine, sent them going, but with great kindness. So to supper, prayers, and to bed.

3.[a] Up. With Sir J. Mennes by coach to St. James's, and there all the news now of very hot preparations for the Dutch; and being with the Duke, he told us he was resolved to make a

a repl. '2'

---

1. The sister of a friend: see above, ii. 125.

2. The development by Lord Treasurer Southampton of what is now Bloomsbury Sq. His mansion, afterwards known as Bedford House, occupied the whole n. side of the square, having 50 hearths: Mdx R.O., Hearth Tax, 1664, 2, mb. 8. (R).

3. Nan Wright, Lady Sandwich's niece. It was another niece of hers, Betty Pickering, whom Creed married in 1668.

Tripp himself, and that Sir W Pen should go in the same ship with him[1] – which honour, God forgive me, I could grudge him for his knavery and dissimulation, though I do not envy much the having the same place myself. Talk also of great haste in the getting out another fleet and building some ships;[2] and now it is likely we have put one another, by eachother's dalliance, past a retreate.

Thence, with our heads full of business, we broke up, and I to my barbers and there only saw Jane and stroked her under the chin; and away to the Exchange and there long about several businesses, hoping to get money by them. And thence home to dinner and there found Hawly. But meeting Bagwell's wife at the office before I went home, I took her into the office and there kissed her only. She rebuked me for doing it; saying, that did I do so much to many[a] bodies else, it would be a stain to me. But I do not see but she takes it well enough; though in the main, I believe she is very honest. So after some kind discourse, we parted, and I home to dinner; and after dinner down to Deptford, where I found Mr. Coventry; and there we made an experiment of Hollands and our Cordage and ours out-did it a great deal, as my book of observations tells perticularly.[3] Here we were late. And so home together by water; and I to my office, where late putting things in order. Mr. Bland came this

a repl. 'any'

---

1. In a letter of 4 October to Sandwich, Pepys, remarking (as he does here) that 'the business now grows very hot between the Dutch and us', told of the preparation to set forth a fleet of 17 sail under the Duke in the *Royal James*, with Penn as her commander: *Further Corr.*, pp. 27–8. This was James's first taste of command at sea. He put himself at the head of Sandwich's and Rupert's squadrons in the Solent on 11 November, and stayed at sea, daring the Dutch to come out of harbour, until the end of November: *CSPD 1664–5*, p. 96. Penn shifted his flag to the *Charles* when the Duke went aboard her on the 18th: ib., pp. 75, 76, 81.

2. The Admiralty Committee of the Privy Council now drew up a programme of shipbuilding: for the Admiral's comments (13 November), see *CSPD 1664–5*, p. 67. Meantime reports of the fitting out of ships poured in from the dockyards (7 October; ib., p. 27) and 37 were made ready or nearly ready to sail a month later: ib., p. 57.

3. NWB, p. 34 (3 October). Coventry was not too pleased, since he had been instrumental in buying Dutch cordage.

night to me to take his leave of me, he going to Tanger; wherein I wish him good successe.[1]

So home to supper and to bed – my mind troubled at the businesses I have to do, that I cannot mind them as I ought to do and get money – and more that I have neglected, by[a] frequenting and seeming more busy publicly then I [ought to] have done of late in this hurry of business. But there is time left to recover it, and I trust in God I shall.

4. Up, and to the office, where we sat all the morning. And this morning Sir W Pen went to Chatham to look after the ships now going out thence – and perticularly that wherein the Duke and himself goes. He took Sir G Ascue with him, whom I believe he hath brought into play.[2] At noon to the Change; and thence home, where I find my aunt James and the two she-Joyces. They dined and were merry with us. Thence after dinner to a play, to see *The Generall*;[3] which is so dull and so ill acted, that I think it is the worst I ever saw or heard in all my days. I happened to sit next to Sir Ch. Sidly;[4] who I find a very witty man, and did at every line take notice of the dullness of the poet and badness of the action, and that most pertinently; which I was mightily taken with – and among others, where by Altemira's command Clarimont the Generall is commanded to rescue his Rivall whom she loved, Lucidor, he after a great deal of demurre breaks out – " Well – Ile save my Rivall and make her confess. That I deserve, while he doth but possesse."[5] "Why, what! Pox!" says Sir Ch. Sydly, "would he have him have more, or what is there more to be had of a woman then the possessing her?"

a MS. 'my'

---

1. John Bland went as a merchant; he served as the first mayor in 1668–9, and later became Comptroller of His Majesty's Revenues there.

2. Ascue, now made captain of the *Henry*, had held no commission since 1660. On 13 May he had dined with Penn and Pepys; and again on 22 June, at Trinity House – 'to make himself known among the seamen':

above, p. 186.

3. See above, p. 282 & n. 1. The episode subsequently mentioned typifies the extravagances of this kind of play. (A).

4. Sedley, dramatist and man of fashion.

5. 'I'le save my Rivall and make *her* confesse/'Tis I deserve what hee does but possesse': III, ii. 143–4. (A).

Thence, setting all them at home, I home with my wife and Mercer, vexed at my losing my time and above 20*s* in money and neglecting my business to see so bad a play. Tomorrow, they told us, should be acted, or the day after, a new play called *The Parsons Dreame*, acted all by women.[1]

So to my office and there did business; and so home to supper and to bed.

5. Up betimes and to my office. And thence by coach to New Bridewell to meet with Mr. Poyntz to discourse with him (being master of the workhouse there) about making of Bewpers for us – but he was not within. However, his clerk did lead me up and down through all the houses. And there I did with great pleasure see the many pretty works and the little children imployed, everyone to do something; which was a very fine sight and worthy incouragement.[2] I cast away a Crowne among them, and so to the Change – and among the Linnen wholesale-Drapers to enquire about Callicos, to see what can be done with them for the supplying our want of Bewpers for flags. And I think I shall do something therein to good purpose for the King.[3]

1. Thomas Killigrew's exceptionally bawdy comedy, *The parson's wedding*, was written in 1640 and published in 1664: see below, p. 294. This is the first reference to a post-Restoration performance. The exploitation of actresses in highly suggestive roles was common at the time. According to Langbaine (p. 313), the prologue to this revival was 'spoken by Mrs Marshal in Man's Cloaths'. (A).

2. Povey later recommended Pepys to get sailcloth and bewpers for Tangier from the same workhouse: Povey to Pepys, 19 May 1665 (PRO, CO 279/4, f. 90r). The linen part of the business failed sometime after 1667 (Poyntz's memorandum in Longleat, Coventry MSS 101, ff. 94–9), but the sailmaking continued: *CSPD Add. 1660–85*, p. 266. Pepys became a governor of Bridewell in

1675: E. G. O'Donoghue, *Bridewell Hosp.*, p. 162. The employment of child labour was not considered cruel until the late 18th century.

3. Pepys now bought calico on his own account (below, p. 351) instead of inviting tenders. He then had it made up into flags, and sold them to the Navy Board in defiance of the rule which forbade officials to engage in trade with the navy. See B. Pool, *Navy Board contracts, 1660–1832*, p. 39. For Pepys's defence of his conduct, see below, 21 September 1666 & n., and *Priv. Corr.*, pp. 253+ (an answer to criticism from the Brooke House Committee, 1669). Calico was used for flags in Spain, but never successfully in England, being too heavy to fly, apart from not wearing well: cf. NWB, p. 66; *CSPD 1664–5*, p. 273.

So to the Coffee-house and there fell in discourse with the Secretary of the Virtuosi of Gresham College,[1] and had very fine discourse with him. He tells me of a new-invented Instrument to be tried before the College anon, and I intend to see it. So to Trinity-house, and there I dined among the old dull fellows. And so home – and to my office a while; and then comes Mr. Cocker to see me and I discoursed with him about his writing and ability of sight, and how I shall do to get some glass or other to help my eyes by Candle light; and he tells me he will bring me the helps he hath within a day or two, and show me what he doth.

Thence to the Musique-meeting at the post office, where I was once before.[2] And thither anon come all the Gresham College and a great deal of noble company. And the new instrument was brought, called the Arched Viall – where, being tuned with Lutestrings and played on with Kees like an Organ – a piece of Parchment is alway kept moving; and the strings, which by the keys are pressed down upon it, are grated, in imitation of a bow, by the parchment; and so it is intended to resemble several vyalls played on with one bow – but so basely and harshly, that it[a] will never do.[3] But after three hours' stay, it could not be Fixt in tune; and so they were fain to go to some other Musique of instruments, which I am grown quite out of love with;[4] and so I, after some good discourse with Mr. Spong, Hill, Grant, Dr Whisler, and others by turns, I home to my office and there late; and so home – where I understand my wife hath spoke to Jane[5] and ended matters of difference between her and her, and she stays with us; which I am glad of, for her fault is nothing but sleepiness and forgetfulness; otherwise, a good-natured, quiet, well-meaning, honest servant, and one[b] that will do as she is bid, so one called upon her and will see her do it.

a MS. 'I'   b repl. 'so'

1. Henry Oldenburg, first secretary of the Royal Society.
2. See above, p. 238.
3. It was a harpsichord-like instrument in appearance: Evelyn, 5 October 1664. See *Comp.*: 'Music'. (E).

4. Cf. above, p. 238.
5. A mistake for Bess, who is referred to at 14 September and 10 November as good-natured but forgetful.

This morning by 3 a-clock, the Prince and King, and Duke with him, went down the River; and the Prince under sail the next tide after, and so is gone from the Hope. God give him better success then he used to have.[1]

This day Mr. Bland went away hence towards his Voyage to Tanger.

This day also, I had a letter from an unknown hand, that tells me that Jacke[a] Angier,[2] he believes, is dead at Lisbon, for he left him there ill.

6.[b] Up, and to the office, where busy all the morning; among other things, about this of the flags and my bringing in of Callicos to oppose Young and Whisler. At noon by promise, Mr. Pierce and his wife and Madam Clerke and her niece came and dined with me, to a rare Chine of beefe – and spent the afternoon very pleasantly all the afternoon. And then to my office in the evening, they being gone, and late at business; and then home to supper and to bed – my mind coming to itself in fallowing of my business.

7. Lay pretty while, with some discontent, abed, even to the having bad words with my wife, and blows too, about the ill serving-up of our victuals yesterday; but all ended in love. And so I rose and to my office, busy all the morning. At noon dined at home, and then to my office again; and then abroad to look after Callicos for Flaggs, and hope to get a small matter by my pains therein and yet save the King a great deal of money. And so home to my office; and there came Mr. Cocker and brought me a Globe of glasse and a frame of oyled paper (as I desired),[3] to

a repl. 'Tom'
b repeated before second sentence which begins new page

---

1. Rupert had had indifferent success as a naval commander, 1648–52. He now led a small squadron intended for W. Africa, but got no farther than Spithead, where the fleet was enlarged and reformed under the Duke of York. It then cruised in the Channel for a few weeks. Cf. *CSPD 1664–5*, p. 27; above, p. 287 & n. 1.

2. The relative from Cambridge who had asked Pepys for a job about a year before: above, iv. 363.

3. Cf. above, p. 237.

show me the manner of his gaining light to grave by and to lessen the glaringnesse of it at pleasure, by an oyled paper. This I bought of him, giving him a Crowne for it; and so, well satisfied, he went away and I to my business again; and so home to supper, prayers, and to bed.

8. All the morning at the office, and after dinner, abroad; and among other things, contracted with one Mr. Bridges[1] at the White beare on Cornhill, for 100 pieces of Callico to make flags; and as I know I shall save the King money, so I hope to get a little for my pains and venture of my money myself.

Late in the evening doing business; and then comes Captain Taylor, and he and I, till 12 a-clock at night, arguing about the freight of his ship *Eagle*, hired formerly by[a] me to Tanger; and at last we made an end, and I hope to get a little money, some small matter, by it.[2]

So home to bed – being weary and cold, but contented that I have made an end of that business.

9. *Lords day.* Lay pretty long; but however, up time enough with my wife to go to church. Then home to dinner; and Mr. Fuller (my Cambridge acquaintance) coming to me about what he was with me lately,[3] to release a waterman, he told me he was to preach at Barking church; and so I to hear him, and he preached well and neatly. Thence, it being time enough, to our own church; and there stood privately[b] at the great doore to gaze upon a pretty lady and from church dogged her home, whither she went to a house near Tower-hill; and I think her to be one of the prettiest women I ever saw. So home and at my office a while, busy; then to my Uncle Wights, whither it seems my wife went after sermon, and there supped; but my aunt and uncle in a very ill humour one with another, but I made shift with much ado to keep them from scolding;

a symbol smudged   *b* l.h. repl. s.h.

---

1. Richard Bridges, linen draper; he does not appear to have supplied the navy before.

2. Cf. above, p. 175.

3. See above, p. 278 & n. 1.

and so after supper, home – and to bed without prayers, it being cold and tomorrow washing-day.

10. Up; and it being rainy, in Sir W. Penn's Coach to St. James and there did our usual business with the Duke. And more and more preparations every day appear against the Dutch. And (which I must confess doth a little move my envy) Sir W. Penn doth grow every day more and more regarded by the Duke, because of his service heretofore in the Dutch warr – which I am confident is by some strong obligations he hath laid upon Mr. Coventry, for Mr. Coventry must needs know that he is a man of very mean parts, but only a bred seaman.

Going home in Coach with Sir W. Batten, he told me how Sir J. Mennes, by the means of Sir R. Ford, was the last night brought to his house and did discover* the reason of his so long discontent with him; and now they are friends again – which I am sorry for. But he told it me so plainly, that I see there is no thorough understanding between them, nor love; and so I hope there will be no great combinacion in anything, nor do I see Sir J. Mennes very fond, as he used to be. But Sir W. Batten doth rail still against Mr. Turner and his wife[1] (telling me he is a false fellow, and his wife a false woman and hath rotten teeth and false, set in with wire); and as I know they are so, so I am glad he finds it so.

To the Coffee-house; and thence to the Change and there with Sir W Warren to the Coffee-house behind the Change and sat alone with him till 4 a-clock, talking of his businesses first and then of business in general; and discourse how I might get money and how to carry myself to advantage, to contract no envy and yet make the world see my pains – which was with great content to me, and a good friend and help I am like to find him – for which God be thanked.

So home to dinner at 4 a-clock, and then to the office and there late; and so home to supper and to bed – having sat up till past 12 at night to look over the account of the Collections for the Fishery; and to [see] the loose and base manner that monies so

1. Thomas Turner was clerk to   of £100 under Mennes's will.
Mennes; his wife received a legacy

collected are disposed of in, would make a man never part with a penny in that manner. And above all, the inconvenience of having a great man, though never so seeming-pious, as my Lord Pembroke is; he is too great to be called to an account, and is abused by his servants and yet obliged to defend them for his own sake.[1] This day by the blessing of God, my wife and I have been married nine years[2] – but my head being full of business, I did not think of it, to keep it in any extraordinary manner. But bless God for our long lives and loves and health together, which the same God long continue, I wish from my very heart.

11. Up, and to the office, where we sat all the morning. My wife this morning went, being invited, to my Lady Sandwich, and I alone at home at dinner, till by and by Luellin comes and dines with me. He tells me what a bawdy loose play this *parsons wedding*[3] is, that is acted by nothing but women at the Kings house – and I am glad of it. Thence to the Fishery in Thames-street – and there several good discourses about the letting of the Lotterys; and among others, one Sir Tho. Clifford, whom yet I know not, doth speak very well and neatly.[4]

Thence to my Cosen Will Joyces to get him to go to Brampton with me this week; but I think he will not, and I am not a whit sorry for it, for his company would be both chargeable and troublesome.

So home and to my office. And then to supper and then to my office again till late; and so home with my head and heart full of business, and so to bed.[a]

My wife tells me the sad news of my Lady Castlemaynes being

a   blot in MS.

---

1. Philip Herbert, 5th Earl of Pembroke, was in charge of the voluntary collections for the Royal Fishery under both the Council of 1661 and the Corporation of 1664. In the event Pepys and George Duke, the Corporation's secretary, spared neither him nor his agent Thomas King in the report they presented on 25 October. King was M.P. for Harwich, and the moving spirit in the Fishery business. Pembroke was reputedly a Quaker.
2. For the date of the wedding, see above, ii. 194, n. 3, and *Comp.*
3. See above, p. 289 & n. 1. (A).
4. For the lotteries, see above, p. 269, n. 2; below, p. 300, n. 1. Clifford (d. 1673) became Secretary of State (1672), and Lord Treasurer (1672–3).

now become so decayed that one would not know her; at least, far from a beauty, which I am sorry for.

This day, with great joy, Captain Titus told us the perticulars of the Frenche's expedition against Gigery, upon the Barbary Coast in the Straights, with 6000 chosen men. They have taken the Fort of Gigery, wherein was five men and three guns – which makes the whole story of the King of Frances policy and power to be laughed at.[1]

12. This morning, all the morning at my office, ordering things against my Journy tomorrow. At noon to the ⟨Coffee-house⟩,[a] where very good discourse.

For news, all say De Ruyter is gone to Guiny before us. Sir J Lawson is come to Portsmouth. And our fleet is hastening all speed; I mean, this new fleet.[2] Prince Rupert with his is got into the Downes.

At home dined with me W. Joyce and a friend of his. W Joyce will go with me to Brampton. After dinner, I out to Mr. Bridges the linen-draper and evened with [him] for 100 pieces of Callico, and did give him 208*l.* 18*s.* 00*d* – which I now trust the King for – but hope both to save the King money and to get a little by it to boot.

Thence by water up and down all the timber-yards to look out some Dram timber;[3] but can find none for our turn at the price

a   repl. 'Change'

---

1. The French had attacked Jijelli (in Algeria) on 13/23 July, led by the Duc de Beaufort, Grand Admiral of France, at the head of 8000 men (including one English battalion) shipped from Toulon in a fleet of 63 sail. The enemy had withdrawn from the fort, but in October they returned, and on the 29th drove the French out again. Louis XIV was attempting to create a French counterpoise to Tangier. See E. Mercier, *Hist. de l'Afrique septentrionale,* iii. 261–5.

2. Lawson had sailed into Portsmouth from the Mediterranean on the 11th, and had brought with him news of de Ruyter's taking abroad great supplies of victuals in Spain. The Dutch squadron had in fact left Cadiz harbour for the Guinea Coast on 27 September: G. Brandt, *Michel de Ruiter* (trans., Amsterdam, 1698), p. 221; *The Newes,* 13 October, p. 664. 'This new fleet' was the Duke of York's: see above, p. 291.

3. A variety of Baltic timber: see above, iii. 118 & n. 3.

I would have, and so I home.   And there at my office late, doing business against my Journy, to clear my hands of everything for two days.

So home and to supper and bed.

13.   After being at the office all the morning, I home and dined; and taking leave of my wife, with my mind not a little troubled how she would look after herself or house in my absence, especially too, leaving a considerable sum of money in the office, I by coach to the Red Lyon in Aldersgate Streete and there by agreement met W Joyce and Tom Trice, and mounted – I upon a very fine mare that Sir W Warren helps me to.   And so very merrily rode till it was very dark, I leading the way through the dark to Welling; and there, not being very weary, to supper and to bed – but very bad accomodation at the Swan.[1]

In this day's Journy I met with Mr. White, Cromwells Chaplin that was, and had a great deal of discourse with him.   Among others, he tells me that Richard is and hath long been in France, and is now going into Italy – he owns publicly that he doth correspond and return him all his money.   That Richard hath been in some straits at the beginning, but relieved by his friends. That he goes by another name, but doth not disguise himself nor deny himself to any man that challenges him.[2]   He tells me for certain, that offers had been made to[a] the old man of marriage between the King and his daughter, to have obliged him; but

a   repl. 'him' and an illegible symbol

---

1. Possibly the inn since renamed the Wellington.

2. Richard Cromwell was now living in Paris and elsewhere in France under assumed names. A servant of his wife, examined in March 1666, deposed that he had no income except £600 p.a. 'in right of his wife' and was 'not 6*d.* the better for being the son of the pretended

Protector': *CSPD 1665–6*, p. 299. According to this servant, Jeremiah White (Oliver's chaplain) still had possession of Richard's mother's estate in 1666, and 'will not come into account for the same'. Richard's friends were now urging him to go to Italy or Spain, as war with Holland and France seemed to be inevitable.

he would not.[1] He thinks (with me) that it never was in his power to bring in the King with the consent of any of his officers about him. And that he scorned to bring him in as Monke did, to secure himself and deliver everybody else. When I told him of what I found writ in a French book of one Monsieur Sorbiere, that gives an account of his observations here in England – among other things, he says that it is reported that Cromwell did in his life-time transpose many of the bodies of the kings of England from one grave to another, and that by that means it is not known certainly whether the head that is now set up upon a post be that of Cromwell or of one of the kings[2] – Mr. White tells me that he believes he never had so poor a low thought in him to trouble himself about.[a] He says the hand of God is much to be seen; that all his children are in good condition enough as to estate, and that their relations that betrayed their family are all now either hanged or very miserable.

a followed by 'it' (struck through)

---

1. The story was that certain Presbyterian leaders had projected a marriage alliance between Charles II and Frances, youngest daughter of Oliver Cromwell ('the old man'), towards the end of 1654. It is told in the life of Roger Boyle, Earl of Orrery, by his chaplain, Thomas Morrice, in Morrice, *A collection of state letters* . . . (1742), pp. 21–2. According to Morrice, Cromwell rejected the suggestion out of hand, on the ground that Charles would never forgive him for the death of his father.

2. The book is Samuel-Joseph Sorbière's *Relation d'un voyage en Angleterre* . . . (Paris, 1664; not in the PL). The story (which struck Sorbière as 'un bruit ridicule') is at pp. 165–6 in the Cologne edition of 1667. Cf. above, i. 309; ii. 31. There seems no doubt that this was in fact Cromwell's head: see K. Pearson

and G. M. Morant, *Portraiture of O. Cromwell*, esp. pp. 107+. For a contrary view, see F. J. Varley, *Cromwell's latter end*. The head remained for display at Westminster Hall for about 25 years, when it was blown down in a storm. In 1710 it was said to be in London in a collection of curios: Von Uffenbach, *London in 1710* (trans. and ed. Quarrell and Mare), p. 82. In 1812 a head (allegedly the same one) found its way (*via* a pawnbroker's shop) into the possession of a Suffolk family – the Wilkinsons of Woodbridge – whence it passed in 1960 to Cromwell's college, Sidney Sussex, Cambridge, where it was given decent burial in the ante-chapel. *Journal R. Arch. Inst.*, 68/237+; *N. & Q.*, corr. in vols for 1864 and 1926; *The Times*, 31 December 1874; ib., 15 April 1957; *Sid. Suss. Annual*, 1960, p. 26.

14. Up by break of day and got to Brampton by 3 a-clock – where my father and mother overjoyed to see me – my mother ready to weep every time she looked upon me. After dinner my father and I to the Court and there did all our business to my mind, as I have set down in a paper perticularly expressing our proceedings at this Court.[1] So home, where W. Joyce full of talk and pleased with his journey. And after supper, I to bed and left my father, mother and him laughing.

15. My father and I up and walked alone to Hinchingbrooke; and among the other late chargeable works that my Lord hath done there, we saw his water-works and the *Ora*,[2] which is very fine – and so is the house all over. But I am sorry to think of the money at this time spent therein. Back to my father's (Mr. Sheply being out of town) and there breakfasted, after making an end with Barton about his businesses.[3] And then my mother called me into the garden and there, but all to no purpose, desiring me to be friends with John; but I told her I cannot, nor endeed easily shall; which afflicted the poor woman, but I cannot help it.[4] Then taking leave, W Joyce and I set out, calling T. Trice at Bugden; and thence got by night to Stevenage and there mighty merry, though I in bed more weary then the other two days, which I think proceeded from our galloping so much – my other weariness being almost all over. But I find that a coney-skin in my breeches preserves me perfectly from galling – and that eating after I come to my Inne, without drinking, doth keep me from being stomach-sick; which drink doth presently* make me.

We lay all in several beds in the same room; and W Joyce full of his impertinent tricks and talk, which then made us merry, as any other fool would have done. So to sleep.

16. *Lords day.* It raining, we set out; and about 9 a-clock got to Hatfield in church-time, and I light and saw my simple

---

1. Pigott's debt was now settled: see above, iv. 309 & n. 1. The paper does not appear to have survived: cf. below, 13 June 1667 & n.

2. For the works, see above, i.

314, n. 1. The *ora* were presumably the spouts.

3. See above, ii. 204 & n. 2.

4. For this quarrel, see above, p. 91.

Lord Salsbury sit there in his gallery.[1] Stayed not in the church; but thence mounted again, and to Barnett by the end of sermon and there dined at the Red Lyon.[2] Very weary again, but all my weariness yesterday night and today in my thighs only, the rest of my weariness in my shoulders and arms being quite gone. Thence home, parting company at my Cosen Anth. Joyces by 4 a-clock. Weary, but very well, to bed at home, where I find all well. Anon my wife came to bed; but for my ease rose again and lay with her woman.

17. Rose very well and not weary, and with Sir W. Batten to St. James's. There did our business. I saw Sir J Lawson since his return from sea first this morning, and hear that my Lord Sandwich is come from Portsmouth to town. Thence I to him; and finding him at my Lord Crews, I went with him home to his house, and much kind discourse. Thence my Lord to Court and I with Creed to the Change. And thence with Sir W Warren to a cook's shop and dined, discoursing and advising him about his great contract he is to make tomorrow. And do every day receive great satisfaction in his company, and a prospect of just advantage by his friendship. Thence to my office doing some business; but it being very cold, I, for fear of getting cold, went early home to bed – my wife not being come home from my Lady Jemimah, with whom she hath been at a play and at Court today.

18. Up and to the office; where among other things, we made a very great contract with Sir W Warren for 3000 load of Timber.[3] At noon dined at home. In the afternoon to the Fishery, where very confused and very ridiculous my Lord Cravens proceedings, especially his finding fault with Sir J

1. The church was the parish church of St Etheldreda. By 'simple' Pepys may mean senile: the Earl was now over 73 and his wits had never been of the brightest – 'a man of no words,' wrote Clarendon, 'except in hunting and hawking, in which he only knew how to behave himself': *Hist.* ii. 543.

2. Now nos 74–6, High St. (Inf. from Mr W. McB. Marcham.) (R).

3. Some of the terms the Board insisted on in this contract (the provision, e.g., of 46 pieces fit for beams for the broadest parts of 2nd-rates) are detailed in NMM, LBK/8, p. 113. A load was 50 cu. ft.

Collidon and Collonell Griffin's report in the accounts of the
Lottery=men.[1]   Thence I with Mr. Gray[2] in his coach to White-
hall; but the King and Duke being abroad, we returned to
Somersett-house.   In discourse, I find him a very worthy and
studious gentleman in the business of Trade; and among other
things, he observed well to me how it is not the greatest wits but
the steady man that is a good merchant: he instanced[a] in Ford and
Cocke, the last of whom he values above all men as his oracle,
as Mr. Coventry doth Mr. Jolliffe.   He says that it is concluded
among merchants, that where a Trade hath once been and doth
decay, it never recovers again; and therefore, that the manufacture of Cloath of England will never come to esteem again.[3]
That among other faults, Sir Rd. Ford cannot keep a secret;
and that it is so much the part of a merchant to be guilty of that
fault, that the Duke of Yorke is resolved to commit no more
secrets to the merchants of the Royall Company.[4]   That Sir
Ellis Layton is, for a speech of forty* words, the wittiest man that
ever he knew in his life; but longer, he is nothing; his judgment
being nothing at all, but his wit most absolute.[5]   At Somersett-
house he carried me in and there I saw the Queenes new rooms,[6]
which are most stately and nobly furnished; and there I saw her,
and the Duke of Yorke and Duchesse were there.   The Duke
spied me, and came to me and talked with me a very great
while about our contract this day with Sir W Warren; and
among other things, did with some contempt ask whether we
did except* Pollards – which Sir W. Batten did yesterday (in

a   MS. 'instant'

1. For this lottery, see above, p.
269 & n. 2.
2. Thomas Grey, member of the
Fishery Corporation.
3. Wool had lost a little ground
(though not as much as is here suggested) to the new-fashioned fabrics
made from linen and cottons.
4. The Royal African Company,
of whom the Duke was a member,
would now be especially concerned
with the struggle with the Dutch for
W. Africa.
5. Leighton was secretary to the
Royal African Company; an over-
successful Scot, widely admired for
his wit and widely distrusted as a
social climber. Named Elisha by
puritan parents, he preferred to be
known as Ellis. He rose in the
service of the Dukes of York and of
Buckingham, and was a Roman
Catholic convert. For his wit, see
below, vi. 334, 27 March 1667;
HMC, *Rep.*, 7/402.
6. The Queen Mother's: for the
new building, see above, p. 63 &
n. 1.

spite, as the Duke, I believe by my Lord Barkely, doth well enough know) did among other things, in writing propose.

Thence home by coach, it raining hard, and to my office, where late; then home to supper and to bed.

This night the Duch Embassador desired and had an Audience of the King. What the issue of it was I know not – both sides I believe desire peace but neither will begin, and so I believe a warr will fallow. The Prince is with his fleet at Portsmouth – and the Duch are making all preparations for warr.

19. Up, and to my office all the morning. At noon dined at home. Then abroad by coach to buy for the office *Herne upon the Statute of Charitable uses*,[1] in order to the doing something better in the Chest then we have done, for I am ashamed to see Sir W. Batten possess himself so long of so much money as he hath done. Coming home, weighed my two silver Flaggons at Stevens's; they weigh 212 oz. 27 dwt. – which is about 50*l* – at 5*s*. per oz.; and then they judge the fashion to be worth above 5*s*. per ounce more. Nay, some say x*s*. an ounce the fashion – but I do not believe; but yet am sorry to see that the fashion is worth so much and the silver come to no more.

So home and to my office, where very busy late. My wife at Mercer's mother's and I believe W. Hewer with them; which I do not like, that he should ask me leave to go about business and then to go and spend his time in sport and leave me here busy. To supper and to bed – my wife coming in by and by, which though I know there was no hurt in it, I do not like.

20. Up and to the office, where all the morning. At noon my uncle Tho. came; dined with me and received some money of me. Then I to my office, where I took in with me Bagwells wife; and there I caressed her, and find her every day more and more coming, with good words and promise of getting her

---

1. John Herne, *The law of charitable uses, wherein the statute of 43. Eliz. chap. 4. is set forth and explained; with directions how to sue out and prosecute commissions grounded upon that statute* ... (first published 1660; 2nd ed. 1663); not in the PL. The statute of 1601 'empowered the Lord Chancellor to issue commissions to bishops and others to enquire by jury into the value and application of revenues of charitable foundations': Sir W. S. Holdsworth, *Hist. Engl. law*, iv. 398.

husband a place, which I will do. So we parted, and I to my Lord Sandwich at his lodgings; and after a little stay, away with Mr. Cholmely to Fleet-street, in the way he telling me that Tanger is like to be in a bad condition with this same Fitzgerald,[1] he being a man of no honour nor presence, nor little honesty, and endeavours to raise the Irish and suppress the English interest there, and offends everybody – and doth nothing that I hear of well – which I am sorry for.

Thence home, by the way taking two silver Tumblers home which I have bought; and so home and there late, busy at my office; and then home to supper and to bed.

21. Up, and by coach to Mr. Coles and there conferred with him about some law business; and so to Sir W Turners and there bought me cloth, coloured for a suit and cloak, to line with plush[a] the cloak – which will cost me money, but I find that I must go handsomely, whatever it costs me; and the charge will be made up in the fruits it brings.

Thence to the Coffee-house and Change, and so home to dinner; and then to the office all the afternoon, whither comes W How to see me, being come[b] from, and going presently back to sea with my Lord. Among other things, he tells me Mr. Creed is much out of favour with my Lord, from his freedom of talk and bold carriage and other things, with which my Lord is not pleased; but most I doubt, his not lending my Lord money and Mr. Moores reporting what his answer was, I doubt in the worst manner.[2] But however, a very unworthy rogue he is; and therefore let him go for one good-for-nothing, though wise to the heighth above most men I converse with.

In the evening (W. How being gone) comes Mr. Martin to trouble me again to get him a Lieutenant's place, for which he is as fit as a fool can be – but I put him off like an asse as he is; and so setting my papers and books in order, I home to supper and to bed.

a   repl. 'plash'   b   repl. 'coming'

---

1. Col. John Fitzgerald, Deputy-Governor, had returned in July to take charge after the death of the Governor (Teviot) in May. He was in command of the Irish regiment.

The forecast proved correct: see, e.g., below, p. 344 & n. 3.

2. Creed was now reputedly worth £10,000: below, p. 338.

22. Up, and to the office, where we sat all the morning. At noon comes my uncle Tho and his daughter Mary, about getting me to pay them the 30*l* due now, but payable in law to her husband.[1] I did give them the best answer I could and so parted, they not desiring to stay to dinner. After dinner I down to Deptford and there did business; and so back to my office, where very late busy; and so home to supper and bed.

23. *Lords day.* Up and to church. At noon comes unexpected Mr. Fuller the Minister,[2] and dines with me – and also I had invited Mr. Cooper, with one I judge came from sea. And he and I spent the whole afternoon together, he teaching me some things in understanding of plats.[3] At night to the office doing business, and then home to supper; then a psalm, to prayers, and to bed.

24. Up, and in Sir J. Minnes's coach (alone with Mrs. Turner as far as Pater Noster-row, where I set her down) to St. James and there did our business; and I had the good luck to speak what pleased the Duke about our great contract in hand with Sir W Warren against Sir W. Batten, wherein the Duke is very earnest for our contracting.

Thence home to the office till noon; and then dined and to the Change, and off with Sir W Warren for a while, consulting about managing his contract.[4] Thence to a committee at Whitehall of Tanger, where I had the good luck to speak something to very good purpose about the Molle at Tanger; which was well received, even by Sir J Lawson and Mr. Cholmly, the undertakers against whose interest I spoke – that I believe I shall be valued for it.[5] Thence into the galleries to talk with my Lord

---

1. This was a legacy from the estate of Robert Pepys of Brampton: see above, ii. 134, n. 2. Mary's husband was Samuel de Santhune.

2. See above, p. 278, n. 1.

3. Cooper, once master of the *Reserve*, had in 1662 taught Pepys his multiplication tables and the rudiments of naval architecture.

4. Cf. above, p. 299 & n. 3. Perhaps as a result of these consultations Warren wrote this day to the Board protesting against the Board's terms and making suggestions for the revision of his contract: Rawl. A 174, f. 63r.

5. But see below, p. 343.

Sandwich; among ⟨other⟩ things, about the Princes writing up to tell us of the danger he and his fleet lies [in] at Portsmouth of receiving affronts from the Dutch[1] – which my Lord said he would never have done had he lien there with one ship alone; nor is there any great reason for it, because of the sands. However, the fleet will be ordered to go and lay themselfs up at the Cowes – much beneath the prowesse of the Prince I think, and the honour of the nation, at the first to be found to secure themselfs. My Lord is well pleased to think that if the Duke and the Prince goes, all the blame of any miscarriage will not light on him. And that if anything goes well,[a] he hopes he shall have the share of the glory – for the Prince is by no means well esteemed of by anybody.

Thence home; and though not very well, yet up late about the Fishery business, wherein I hope to give an account how I find the Collections to have been managed – which I did finish to my great content. And so home to supper and to bed.

This day the great Oneale died; I believe, to the content of all the protestant pretenders in Ireland.[2]

25. Up and to the office, where we sat all the morning and finished Sir W. Warren's great contract for timber; with great content to me, because just in the terms I wrote last night to Sir W. Warren, and against the terms proposed by Sir W. Batten.

At noon home to dinner and there find Creed and Hawly. After dinner comes in Mrs. Ingram,[3] the first time, to make a visit to my wife. After a little stay I left them, and to the committee of the Fishery, and there did make my report of the

a repl. ? 'bad'-

---

1. Rupert's letter has not been traced.
2. Daniel O'Neill, Postmaster-General, was after Ormond the most influential Irishman of his time. The Irish land settlement provoked many disputes between Cromwellian settlers ('protestant pretenders') and dis-

possessed royalists. For O'Neill's part, see *Rawdon Papers* (ed. E. Berwick, 1819), p. 151; *CSP Ireland 1662–5*, p. 534. He was himself a convert to Protestantism.

3. Probably Anne, wife of Rowland Ingram, of St Olave's parish; a friend of the Warrens.

late public Collections for the Fishery,¹ much to the satisfaction of the Comittee, and I think much to my reputation, for good notice was taken of it and much it was commended.

So home (in my way taking care of a piece of plate for Mr. Chr. Pett, against the lanching of his new great ship tomorrow at Woolwich, which I singly did move to His Royall Highness yesterday, and did obtain it for him, to the value of 20 peeces).² And he, under his hand, doth acknowledge to me that he did never receive so great a kindness from any man in the world as from me herein. So to my office and then to supper; and then to my office again, where busy late, being very full nowadays of business, to my great content I thank God; and so home to bed – my house being full of a design to go tomorrow, my wife and all her servants, to see the new ship lanched.

26. Up – my people rising mighty betimes to fit themselfs to go by water; and my boy, he could not sleep, but wakes about 4 a-clock and in bed lay playing on his lute till daylight, and it seems did the like last night till 12 a-clock.

About 8 a-clock, my wife, she and her woman and Besse and Jane and W. Hewers and the boy, to the water-side and there took boat. And by and by, I out of doors to look after the Flagon, to get it ready to carry to Woolwich.

That being not ready, I stepped aside and found out Nellson, he that Whistler buys his Bewpers of, and did there buy five pieces at their price. And am in hopes thereby to bring them down, or buy ourselfs all we spend of Nellson at the first hand.³

1. A copy (in a clerk's hand) is in PRO, SP 29/103, no. 130; 25 October; signed by Pepys. Summaries in *CSPD 1664–5*, p. 44; J. R. Elder, *Royal fishery companies*, pp. 103–4. Pepys reported the receipt of £1076 from 32 counties and made suggestions for improving the methods of collection.

2. This was a gilt flagon (66 oz.) bought at Backwell's: Backwell Ledger M, f. 412*v* (MS. in possession of Williams and Glyn's Bank). Plate was customarily given to the royal navy's shipbuilders, the value being determined by the rate of the ship. At this period it took the form of a flagon from which the shipwright drank the healths of the monarch and the Admiral at the ship's launch: *Further Corr.*, pp. 118, 186.

3. Cf. NWB, p. 66: 'This day it came in my head and I did go to Nellson's house ... [He] was not at home; the servant showed me some ... He had only five pieces in the house; I bought and paid for them at 7s 6d.'

This jobb was greatly to my content. And by and by, the Flaggon being finished at the Burnishers, I home; and there fitted myself and took a hackney-coach I hired[a] (it being a very cold and fowle day) to Woolwich, all the way reading in a good book touching the Fishery;[1] and that being done, in the book upon the statutes of Charitable uses,[2] mightily to my satisfaction.

At Woolwich, I there up to the King and Duke and they liked the plate well. Here I stayed above with them while the ship was[b] lanched; which was done with great success, and the King did very much like the ship, saying she had the best bow that ever he saw.[3]

But Lord, the sorry talk and discourse among the great courtiers round about him, without any reverence in the world, but with so much disorder.

By and by the Queen comes and her maids of honour; one whereof, Mrs. Boynton, and the Duchesse of Buckeingham, had been very sick coming by water in the barge (the water being very rough); but what silly sport they made with them, in very common terms methought,[4] was very poor, and below what people think these great people say and do.

The launching being done, the King and company went down to take barge; and I sent for Mr. Pett and put the Flaggon into the Dukes hand, and he, in the presence of the King, did give it, Mr. Pett taking it upon his knee. This, Mr. Pett is wholly beholding to me for, and he doth know and I believe will acknowledge it.

Thence I to Mr. Ackworths and there eat and drank with

a MS. 'heard'   *b* repl. 'l'-

---

1. Possibly *Ichthyothera; or The royal trade of fishing* . . . (1662, 30 pp.; not in the PL); but several such books were published.

2. See above, p. 301, n. 1.

3. The ship was the *Royal Catherine*; a 2nd-rate, built by Christopher Pett. The King in a letter to Rupert of 27 October called her 'the finest ship that has yet been built' (Sir G. Bromley, *Coll. of original royal letters*, 1787, p. 284); and de Cominges, the French ambassador, in a despatch to Louis XIV of the same day has similar praise: 'le plus beau et le plus royal que j'aye jamais veu' (PRO, PRO 31/3/113, f. 384r). The launch is described in *The Newes*, 27 October, p. 696. For the King's knowledge of shipbuilding, see above, iv. 123, n. 1.

4. de Cominges wrote that the King himself on this occasion showed pleasure in seeing others seasick.

London Bridge, from downstream.   Engraving by John Norden, 1624.

Commissioner Pett and his wife. And thence to Sheldens, where Sir W. Batten and his Lady were. By and by I took coach, after I had enquired for my wife or her boat but found none. Going out of the gate, an ordinary woman prayed me to give her room to London; which I did, but spoke not to her all the way, but read as long as I could see my book again.

Dark when we came to London, and a stop of coaches in Southworke; I stayed above half an hour and then light; and finding Sir W. Batten's coach, heard they were gone into the Beare at the Bridge-foot, and thither I to them. Presently, the stop is removed; and then going out to find my coach, I could not find it, for it was gone with the rest. So I fain to go through the dark and dirt over the bridge, and my leg fell in a hole broke on the bridge; but the constable standing there to keep people from it, I was ketched up, otherwise I had broke my leg – for which mercy the Lord be praised. So at Fanchurch I find my coach staying for me, and so home – where the little girl[1] hath looked to the house well, but no wife come home; which made me begin to fear her, the water being very rough, and cold and dark. But by and by, she and her company come in all well, at which I was glad, though angry.

Thence I to Sir W. Batten's and there sat late with him, Sir R Ford, and Sir John Robinson – the last of whom continues still the same fool he was, crying up what power he has in the City, in knowing their temper and being able to do what he will with them. It seems the City did last night very freely lend the King 100000*l*, without any security but the King's word, which was very noble.[2] But this loggerhead and Sir R. Ford would make us believe that they did it. Now Sir R Ford is a cunning man and makes a fool of the other, and the other believes whatever the other tells him. But Lord, to think that such a man should be Lieutenant of the Towre and so great a man as he is, is a strange thing to me.

---

1. Susan.

2. The city had lent £100,000 in June; now a second loan of the same amount was advanced, the Common Council expressing their gratitude to the King for his help in preventing the construction of a bridge between Westminster and Lambeth, 'which as is conceived would have been of dangerous consequence to the state of this city': Sharpe, ii. 407; *CSPD 1664–5*, p. 43. (Westminster Bridge was not built until 1750.)

With them late, and then home and with my wife to bed – after supper.

27.　Up, and to the office, where all the morning busy.　At noon Sir G. Carteret, Sir J. Mennes, Sir W. Batten, Sir W. Penn and myself were treated at the Dolphin by Mr. Foly the Ironmonger,[a][1] where a good plain dinner; but I expected Musique, the missing of which spoiled my dinner.　Only, very good merry discourse at dinner.

Thence with Sir G. Carteret by coach to White-hall to a committee of Tanger:　and thence back to London, and light in Cheapeside and I to Nellsons;　and there met with a rub[b] at first, but took him out to drink and there discoursed, to my great content, so far with him that I think I shall agree with him for Bewpers, to serve the Navy with.[2]　So with great content home and to my office, where late.　And having got a great cold in my head yesterday, home to supper and to bed.

28.　Slept ill all night, having got a very great cold the other day at Woolwich in head, which makes me full of snot.　Up in the morning, and my tailor brings me home my fine new coloured cloth suit, my cloak lined with plush, as good a suit as ever I wore in my life and mighty neat, to my great content.

To my office, and there all the morning.　At noon to Nellsons and there bought 20 pieces more of Bewpers, and hope to go on with him to a contract.　Thence to the Change a little; and thence home with Luellin to dinner, where Mr. Deane met me by appointment; and after dinner he and I up to my chamber and there hard at discourse, and advising him what to do in his

a repl. 'sm'-　　　*b* blot above symbol

---

1. Robert Foley, ironmonger to the navy.

2. Cf. NWB, p. 66.　Nelson had at first refused to let Pepys have 20 pieces of cloth, protesting he had 'not enough to serve his constant custo- mers. . . . I would not be put off . . ., but took him to the alehouse back again, and there he and I talked calmely and came almost to a conclusion.'

business at Harwich;[1] and then to discourse of our old business of Ships, and taking new rules of him to my great pleasure; and he being gone, I to my office a little and then to see Sir W. Batten, who is sick of a greater cold then I; and thither comes to me Mr. Holliard, and into the chamber to me; and poor man (beyond all I ever saw of him), was a little drunk, and there sat talking and finding acquaintance with Sir W. Batten and my Lady by relations on both sides, that there we stayed very long. At last broke up and he home, much overcome with drink – but well enough to get well home. So I home to supper and to bed.

29. Up; and it being my Lord Mayor's show, my boy and three maids went out; but it being a very foul rainy day from morning to night, I was sorry my wife let them go out. All the morning at the office. At dinner at home. In the afternoon to the office again; and about 4 a-clock by appointment to the Kings-head tavern upon Fishstreete-hill, whither Mr. Wolfe (and Parham by his means) met me to discourse about the Fishery;[2] and great light I had by Parham, who is a little conceited but a very knowing man in his way, and in the general fishing-trade of England.

Here I stayed three hours and eat a barrel of very fine oysters of Wolfes giving me; and so it raining hard – home and to my office, and then home to bed.

All the talk is that de Ruter is come over-land home with six or eight of his Captaines, to command here at home, and their ships[a] kept abroad in the Straights[3] – which sounds as if they had a mind to do something with us.

30. *Lords day.* Up; and this morning put on my new fine coloured cloth suit, with my cloak lined with plush – which is a

a repl. 'fl'-

---

1. Anthony Deane had been appointed Master-Shipwright there on 10 October, by Pepys's influence, and was now discussing with the Board the state of the stores and a proposed increase in the wages of his servants: below, 19 May 1666; Duke of York, *Mem. (naval)*, p. 111; NMM, LBK/8, p. 113.

2. Both William Wolfe and Richard Parham were members of the Fishmongers' Company.

3. A canard: de Ruyter and his fleet were on their way to Guinea.

dear and noble suit, costing me about 17*l.* To church and then home to dinner; and after dinner, to a little musique with my boy, and so to church with my wife; and so home and with her all the evening, reading and at musique with my boy, with great pleasure; and so to supper, prayers, and to bed.

31. Very busy all the morning; at noon Creed to me and dined with me; and then he and I to White-hall, there to a committee of Tanger – where it is worth remembering, when Mr. Coventry proposed the retrenching some of the charge of the horse, the first word asked by the Duke of Albemarle was, "Let us see who commands them" (there being three troops): one of them he calls to mind was by Sir Toby Bridges. "Oh", says he, "there is a very good man; if you must reform ⟨two of⟩ them, be sure let him command the troop that is left."[1]

Thence home; and there came presently to me Mr. Young and Whistler, who find that I have quite overcome them in their business of flags; and now they come to entreat my favour, but I will be even with them.[2]

So late to my office and there till past one in the morning, making up my month's accounts; and find that my expense this month in clothes hath kept me from laying-up anything; but I am no worse, but a little better then I was; which is 1205*l* – a great sum, the Lord be praised for it.

So home to bed – with my mind full of content therein, and vexed for my being so angry in bad words to my wife tonight, she not giving me a good account[a] of her layings-out to my mind tonight.

This day I hear young Mr. Stanly, a brave young [gentleman]

a repl. same symbol badly formed

---

1. Bridges had served with distinction under Albemarle in Scotland in the 1650s, and recently, as commander of the cavalry at Tangier, he had been put in temporary charge of the garrison after the death in action of Teviot, the Governor, in May 1664. He received a knighthood and a medal for his services. Routh, pp. 72, 310, 332; Sir C. Firth and G. Davies, *Reg. hist. Cromwell's army*, pp. 298, 305, 306.

2. Cf. NWB, p. 67: 'This night ... Young and Whistler did come to me in a most humble manner ... I told them what I had done and what I could do. How all was now in my power ... so leaving them to make a lower demand, but yet giving them good words, I sent them away.'

that went out with young Jermin with Prince Rupert, is already dead of the small-pox at Portsmouth.[1]

All preparations against the Dutch; and the Duke of Yorke fitting himself with all speed to go to the fleet which is hastening for him – being now resolved to go in the *Charles*.

---

1. Edward Stanley of the *Henrietta* was the fourth son of the 7th Earl of Derby. News of his death had been sent to the Navy Board on the 30th; his four servants now left the ship: *CSPD 1664–5*, p. 48.

Henry Jermyn was Master of the Horse to the Duke of York, and nephew of the 1st Earl of St Albans. Both had attended Rupert's farewell supper given before the voyage on 12 September: ib., p. 7.

NOVEMBER.

1. Up and to the office, where busy all the morning. At noon (my wife being invited to my Lady Sandwiches) all alone dined at home upon a good goose with Mr. Wayth[1] – discoursing of business. Thence I to the committee of the Fishery and there we sat, with several good discourses and some bad and simple ones and with great disorder, and yet by the men of business of the town. But my report in the business of the collections[2] is mightily commended and will get me some reputation; and endeed is the only thing looks like[a] a thing well done since we sat.

Thence with Mr. Parham to the tavern, but I drank no wine; only, he did give me another barrel of oysters. And he brought one Major Greene, an able fishmonger, and good discourse to my information. So home and late at business at my office. Then to supper and to bed.

2. Up betimes, and down with Mr. Castle to Redriffe, and there walked to Deptford to view a parcel of brave Knees of his, which endeed are very good. And so back again – home – I seeming very friendly to him, though I know him to be a rogue and one that hates me with his heart.[3] Home and to dinner, and so to my office all the afternoon, where in some pain in my backe, which troubled me; but I think it comes only with stooping and from no other matter.

At night to Nellsons and up and down about[b] business, and so home to my office; then home to supper and to bed.

3. Up, and to the office – where strange to see how Sir W.

a repl. 'but'   *b* repl. 'above'

---

1. Robert Waith, paymaster to the Navy Treasurer.
2. See above, pp. 304–5 & n.
3. Castle was Batten's son-in-law. Pepys has a note in NWB, p. 71 (10 November) of his over-charging for this knee-timber. For the dispute which followed, see below, p. 347 & n. 1.

Penn is flocked to by people of all sorts against his going to sea.[1]
At the office did much business; among other, an end of that
that hath troubled me long, the business of Bewpers and
Flaggs.[2] At noon to the Change; and thence by appointment
was met with Bagwells wife, and she fallowed me into Moore-
fields and there into a drinking-house – and all alone eat and
drank together. I did there caress her; but though I did make
some offer, did not receive any compliance from her in what was
bad, but very modestly she denied me; which I was glad to see
and shall value her the better for it – and I hope never tempt her
to any evil more. Thence back to the town and we parted;
and I home and there at the office late – where Sir W. Penn came
to take his leave of me, being tomorrow (which is very sudden
to us) to go on board to lie on board;[a] but I think will come
ashore again before the ship, the *Charles*, can go away. So home
to supper and to bed.

This night Sir W. Batten did, among other things, tell me
strange news which troubles me: that my Lord Sandwich will
be sent Governor to Tanger[3] – which in some respects indeed
I should be glad of, for the good of the place and the safety of
his person; but I think his honour will suffer, and it may be his
interest fail by his distance.

4. Waked very betimes and lay long awake, my mind being
so full of business. Then up and to St. James, where I find Mr.
Coventry full of business, packing up for his going to sea with
the Duke. Walked with him, talking, to White-hall; where to
the Duke's lodgings, who is gone thither to lodge lately.[4] I
appeared to the Duke; and thence Mr. Coventry and I an hour
in the long gallery, talking about the management of our office.
He tells me the weight of despatch will lie most upon me. And
told me freely his mind touching Sir W. Batten and Sir J. Mennes
– the latter of whom, he most aptly said, was like a lapwing;

a   preceded by 'board' (struck through)

---

1. He was in command of the
Duke of York's flagship.
2. See above, p. 289 & n. 2.
3. A canard.

4. He lived at Whitehall in the
winter and at St James's in the
summer.

that all he did was to keep*a* a flutter, to keep others from the nest that they would find. He told me an odd story of the former, about the Light-houses: how just before, he had certified to the Duke against the use of them, and what a burden they are to trade – and presently after, at his being at Harwich, comes to desire that he might have the setting one up there – and gets the usefulness of it certified also by the Trinity-house.[1]

After long discoursing and considering all our stores and other things – as, how the King hath resolved upon Captain Taylor and Collonell Middleton, the first to be commissioner for Harwich and the latter for Portsmouth[2] – I away to the Change and there did very much business. So home to dinner, and Mr. Duke, our Secretary for the Fishery, dined with me. After dinner, to discourse of our business – much to my content. And then he away and I by water among the smiths on the other side; and to the ale-house with one and was near buying four or five anchors, and learned something worth my knowing of them. And so home and to my office, where late, with my head very full of business; and so away home to supper and to bed.

5. Up, and to the office, where all the morning. At noon to the Change and thence home to dinner; and so with my wife to the Duke's house to a play, *Macbeth*; a pretty good play, but admirably acted.[3] Thence home, the coach being forced to go round by London-wall home because of the Bonefires – the day being mightily observed in the City.[4]

a repl. 'give'

---

1. See below, vi. 3 & n. 4.
2. Both John Taylor and Thomas Middleton began work this month, although (as was not unusual) their patents of appointment were not issued until some months later. All the royal yards (except Woolwich and Deptford, which were reasonably close to the Navy Office) were now staffed with resident commissioners. The post at Harwich lapsed after the war in 1668.
3. Probably the first of Davenant's

spectacular adaptations, at the LIF, of Shakespeare's tragedy. He added such devices as a sinking cave and flying machines for the witches. His final version was published in 1674. The cast listed by Genest (i. 139–140) includes Betterton as Macbeth, Harris as Macduff, Smith as Banquo and Mrs Betterton as Lady Macbeth. (A).
4. See *Comp.*: 'Gunpowder Treason Day'.

To my office late at business; and then home to supper and to bed.

6. *Lords day.* Up, and with my wife to church. Dined at home. And I all*ᵃ* the afternoon close at my office, drawing up some proposals to present to the committee for the Fishery tomorrow – having a great good intention to be serviceable in that business if I can. At night to supper with my uncle Wight, where very merry; and so home – to prayers and to bed.

7. Up, and with Sir W. Batten to White-hall, where mighty thrusting about the Duke, now upon his going. We were with him long; he advised us to fallow our business close and to be directed in his absence by the committee of the Councell for the Navy.[1]

By and by a meeting of the Fishery, where the Duke was; but in such haste, and things looked so superficially over, that I had not a fit opportunity to propose my paper that I wrote yesterday; but I had showed it to Mr. Gray and Wren[2] before, who did like it most highly as they said, and I think they would not dissemble in that manner in a business of this nature. But I see the greatest businesses are done so superficially, that I wonder anything succeeds at all among us that is public.

a repl. 'am'

---

1. The Admiralty Committee, a standing committee of the Privy Council for naval affairs (originally appointed on 9 November 1660), was now given full powers to act in the Duke's absence on his behalf, and was expanded to include three new members, making a total of 15. By an order of 9 November, it was to meet at least three times a week, beginning on 11 November, and its business had precedence of private affairs. Members of the Navy Board attended only when summoned. Below, vi. 58; Secretary Nicholas's notes of meetings, in BM, Egerton 2543, ff. 145+; *EHR*, 27/271. Cf. Clarendon, *Life*, ii. 326. The committee is variously referred to in subsequent entries as 'Lords of the Admiralty', 'Lords Commissioners', 'Committee of the Lords', and 'the Lords'.

2. Thomas Grey and Matthew Wren, both members of the Fishery Corporation.

Thence, somewhat vexed to see myself frustrated in the good I hoped to have done and a little reputation to have gained, and thence to my barber's; but Jane not being in the way, I to my Lady Sandwich and there met my wife and dined. But I find that I dine as well myself; that is, as neatly and my meat as good and well-dressed as my good Lady doth in the absence of my Lord.

Thence by water, I to my barber's again; and did meet in the street my Jane, but could not talk with her but only a word or two; and so by coach called my wife and home, where at my office late; and then it being washing-day, to supper and to bed.

8. Up, and to the office – where by and by Mr. Coventry came; and after doing a little business, took his leave of us, being to go to sea with the Duke tomorrow.

At noon I and Sir J. Mennes and Lord Berkely (who with Sir J. Duncum and Mr. Chichly are made Maisters of the Ordnance)[1] to the Office of the Ordnance to discourse about Wadding for guns. Thence to dinner, all of us, to the Lieutenant of the Towers – where a good dinner, but disturbed in the middle of it by the King's coming into the Tower; and so we broke up, and to him and went up and down the store-houses and magazines; which are, with the addition of the new great Store house, a noble sight.[2]

He gone, I to my office, where Bagwell's wife stayed for me; and together with her a good while, to meet again shortly. So all the afternoon at my office – till late; and then to bed – joyed in my love and ability to fallow my business.

This day Mr. Lever sent my wife a pair of silver candlesticks, very pretty ones – the first man that ever presented me to whom I have not only done little service, but apparently did him the

1. On 31 October Lord Berkeley of Stratton, Sir John Duncombe and Thomas Chicheley had been appointed to execute the office of Master of the Ordnance, made vacant by the death of Sir William Compton: *CSPD 1664–5*, p. 49.

2. A commission had been appointed by the Ordnance Office in March 1664 to review the state of the wharf and of certain buildings: *CSPD 1663–4*, p. 520.

greatest disservice in his business of accounts, as Purser generall, of any man at the board.[1]

9. Called up, as I had appointed, by H. Russell,[2] between 2 and 3 a-clock; and I and my boy Tom by water with a galley down to the Hope, it being a fine starry night. Got thither by 8 a-clock and there, as expected, found the *Charles*, her mainmast setting. Comissioner Pett aboard. I up and down to see the ship I was so well acquainted with[3] – and a great work it is, the setting so great a mast. Thence the Comissioner and I on board Sir G Ascue in the *Henery* – who lacks men mightily, which makes me think that there is more believed to be in a man that hath heretofore been imployed then truly there is; for one would never have thought, a month ago, that he could have wanted 1000 men at his heels.[4] Nor do I think he hath much of a seaman in him; for he told me, says he, "Heretofore we use to find our ships clean and ready, everything to our hands in the Downes; now I come and must look to see things done like a slave, things that I never minded nor cannot look after;" and by his discourse I find that he hath not minded anything in her at all.

Thence, not staying, the wind blowing hard, I made use of the *Jemmy* Yacht and returned to the Tower in her – my boy being a very droll boy and good company. Home and eat something, and then shifted myself and to White-hall; and there, the King being in his Cabinet council (I desiring to speak with Sir G Carteret), I was called in and demanded by the King himself many Questions, to which I did give him full answers. There was at this council my Lord Chancellor, Archbishop of Canterbury, Lord Treasurer, the two Secretarys, and Sir G Carteret.

Not a little contented at this chance of being made known to

---

1. William Lever had been Purser-General to Sandwich's fleet in the Mediterranean, 1661–2. He had delayed presenting his accounts until June 1664, and Pepys then queried them, out of a distrust of Mennes (who passed them), and from information received from two of his purser friends (Lewis and Pierce). See Pepys's notes (28 June 1664) in

NWB, pp. 55–6. Lever was employed again as Purser-General in 1665. The usual assumption was that pursers were rogues: cf. below, vi. 306 & n. 1.

2. Waterman to the Navy Office.

3. In 1660 Pepys had sailed on her with Mountagu (Sandwich) to bring back the King from exile.

4. Cf. above, p. 186, n. 5.

these persons, and called often by my name by the King – I to Mr. Pierce's to take leave of him, but he not within but saw her; and made very little stay but straight home to my office, where I did business, and then to supper and to bed.

The Duke of Yorke is this day gone away to Portsmouth.

10. Up; and not finding my things ready, I was so angry with Besse as to bid my wife for good and all to bid her provide herself a place – for though she be very good-natured, she hath no care nor memory of her business at all.

So to the office, where vexed at the malice of Sir W. Batten and folly of Sir J. Mennes against Sir W. Warren. But I prevented, and shall do, though to my own disquiet and trouble.

At noon dined with Sir W. Batten and the Auditors of the Exchequer at the Dolphin, by Mr. Wayth's desire; and after dinner fell to business relating to Sir G Carterets account. And so home to the office, where Sir W. Batten begins too fast to show his knavish tricks, in giving what price he pleases for commodities.[1]

So abroad, intending to have spoke with my Lord Chancellor about the old business of his wood at Clarindon;[2] but could not, and so home again and late at my office. And then home to supper and bed.

My little Guirle Susan is fallen sick of the meazles we fear, or at best of a Scarlett feavour.

11. Up, and with Sir J. Mennes and Sir W. Batten to the council chamber at White-hall, to the committee of the Lords for the Navy[3] – where we were made to wait an[a] hour or two before called in. In that time, looking upon some books of Heraldry of Sir Edw. Walkers making,[4] which are very fine, there I observed the Duke of Monmouth's armes are neatly done, and

---

a repl. 'a'

---

1. Particularly for his son-in-law Castle's knee-timber: NWB, p. 71.
2. See above, p. 204, etc.
3. See above, p. 315, n. 1.
4. There is a MS. now in the College of Arms entitled 'Sir Edward Walker's Nobility Temp. Car. II', which includes both the arms subsequently mentioned: Sir A. Wagner, *Records Coll. of Arms*, p. 33. Walker was Garter King of Arms.

his title, "The most noble and high-born prince, James Scott, Duke of Monmouth, &c.;" nor could Sir J. Mennes or anybody there tell whence he should take the name of Scott.[1]   And then I found my Lord Sandwich his title under his armes is "The most noble and mighty Lord, Edward, Earl of Sandwich, &c."

Sir Edw. Walker afterward coming in, in discourse did say that there was none of the families of princes in Christendom that do derive themselfs so high as Julius Cæsar, nor*a* so far by a thousand years, that can directly prove their rise.   Only, some in Germany do derive themselfs from the patrician*b* familys of Rome, but that uncertainly.   And among other things, did much enveigh against the writing of Romances; that five hundred years hence, being wrote of matters in general true, as the Romance of *Cleopatra*,[2] the world will not know which is the true and which the false.

Here was a gentleman attending here that told us he saw the other day, and did bring the draft of it to Sir Fr. Prigeon,[3] of a monster born of an hostlers wife at Salsbury; two women-children perfectly made, joyned at the lower part of their*c* bellies, and every part perfect as two bodies, and only one payre of legs, coming forth on one side from the middle where they were joined.   It was alive 24 hours, and cried and did as all hopeful children do; but being showed too much to people, was killed.

By and by we were called in, where a great many lords – Annesly in the chair.   But Lord, to see what work they will make us, and what trouble we shall have to inform men in a business they are to begin to know when the greatest of our hurry is, is a thing to be lamented – and I fear the consequence will be bad to us.[4]

a repl. 'so'   *b* repl. 'pr'-   *c* repl. 'the'

---

1. He had assumed it on being knighted (14 February 1663) in anticipation of his marriage on the following 20 April to Anne Scott, Countess of Buccleuch.

2. The long romance by La Calprenè de (d. 1663), published in 1647–58, of which English translations had appeared in 1652–8 and 1663; not in the PL.

3. Prujean, a fashionable physician.

4. The discussion was mainly about victualling: BM, Egerton 2543, f. 145r–v.   The committee now required the Board to report in person or in writing three times a week: Pepys to Coventry, 12 November (*Further Corr.*, pp. 28–9).

Thence I by coach to the Change; and thence home to dinner, my head akeing mightily with much business.

Our little girl better then she was yesterday.

After dinner out again by coach to my Lord Chancellors, but could not speak with him. Then up and down to seek Sir Ph. Warwick, Sir G Carteret, and my Lord Berkely, but failed in all; and so home and there late at business.

Among other things, Mr. Turner making his complaint to me how my clerks do all the work and get all the profit,[1] and he hath no comfort nor cannot subsist, I did make him apprehend how he is beholding to me more then to anybody, for my suffering him to act as Pourveyour of petty provisions.[2] And told him so largely my little value of anybody's favour, that I believe he will make no complaints again a good while.

So home to supper and to bed – after prayers and having my boy and Mercer give me some, each of them some, music.

12. Up, being frighted that Mr. Coventry was come to town and now at the office. So I run down, without eating or drinking or washing, to the office; and it proved my Lord Berkely.

There all the morning. At noon to the Change and so home to dinner, Mr. Wayth with me; and then to the office, where mighty busy till very late; but I bless God I go through with it very well, and hope I shall.

13. *Lords day.* The morning to church, where mighty sport to hear our Clerke*a* sing out of tune, though his master sits by him that begins and keeps the tune aloud for the parish.[3]

Dined at home very well. And spent all the afternoon with my wife within doors – and getting a speech out of *Hamlett*, "To bee or not to bee," without book.[4]

a repl. 'Chap'-

---

1. An old complaint of his: above, iii. 27.

2. See above, ii. 54 & n. 1.

3. St Olave's had been without an organ since 1644: cf. below, 4 April 1667 & n.

4. Pepys greatly admired Better-

ton's interpretation of Hamlet, and refers to the soliloquy at 15 August 1665. Morelli, his domestic musician, set it as a recitative song c. 1680. PL 2591, ff. 37r–40r; see Emslie in *Shakespeare Quart.*, 6/159+. (E).

In the evening, to sing psalms; and in came Mr. Hill to see me, and then he and I and the boy finely to sing; and so anon broke up after much pleasure. He gone, I to supper and so to prayers and to bed.

14. Up, and with Sir W. Batten to White-hall to the Lords of the Admiralty[1] and there did our business betimes. Thence to Sir Ph. Warwicke about Navy business – and my Lord Ashly; and afterward to my Lord Chancellor, who is very well pleased with me and my carrying of his business. And so to the Change, where mighty busy; and so home to dinner, where Mr. Creed and Moore; and after dinner I to my Lord Treasurers, to Sir Ph. Warwicke there, and then to White-hall to the Duke of Albimarle about Tanger; and then homeward to the Coffee-house to hear news: and it seems the Dutch, as I afterward find by Mr.[a] Coventrys letters, have stopped a ship of masts of Sir W Warrens, coming for us in a Swedes ship; which they will not release upon Sir G Downings claiming her – which appears as the first act of hostility – and is looked upon as so by Mr. Coventry.[2]

The *Elias*, coming from New England (Captain Hill commander), is sunk; only the Captain and a few men saved. She foundered in the sea.[3]

So home, where infinite busy till 12 at night; and so home to supper and to bed.

a repl. 'Sir G Downings letters'

---

1. See above, p. 315, n. 1 (not Lords of the Admiralty in the modern sense).

2. Coventry wrote: 'matters begin to grow to an heigth'. See his two letters to Pepys and to the Board, 12 November, Portsmouth: Rawl. A 174, ff. 491+, 497+ (the first endorsed by Pepys: 'Sir Wm. Warrens mast ship stopt . . . the first act lookeing like Hostility'). The ship (the *St Jacob*) was released in late December, only after Downing, the English envoy, had twice obtained

orders to that effect: *CSPClar.*, v. 440, 453 etc.

3. Cf. Lanyon to Pepys, Plymouth, 11 November: Rawl. A 174, f. 145r. She was a frigate serving in Holmes's squadron which had taken New York. There were 21 survivors out of a ship's company of 107: NWB, p. 74; *CSPD 1664-5*, pp. 60, 70, 80; ib., *Add. 1660-85*, pp. 113-14, 119. Pepys has a note on the 'sorry . . . inquiry' made into her loss in NWB, p. 85.

15. That I might not be too fine for the business I intend this day, I did leave off my fine new[a] cloth suit lined with plush and put on my poor black suit; and after office done (where much business but little done), I to the Change; and thence Bagwell's wife with much ado fallowed me through Moor-fields to a blind alehouse, and there I did caress her and eat and drank, and many hard looks and sithes the poor wretch did give me, and I think verily was troubled at what I did; but at last, after many pro-testings, by degrees I did arrive at what I would, with great pleasure. Then in the evening, it raining, walked to the town to where she knew where she was; and then I took coach and to White-hall to a Committee of Tanger, where, and everywhere else I thank God, I find myself growing in repute; and so home and late, very late, at business, nobody minding it but myself; and so home to bed – weary and full of thoughts. Businesses grow high between the Dutch and us on every side.

16. My wife not being well, waked in the night; and strange to see how dead sleep our people[b] sleeps, that she was fain to ring an hour before anybody would wake. At last one rose and helped my wife; and so to sleep again.

Up, and to my business; and then to White-hall, there to attend the Lords Commissioners; and so directly home and dined with Sir W. Batten and my Lady, and after dinner had much discourse tending to profit with Sir W. Batten, how to get ourselfs into the prize-office,[1] or some other fair way of obliging the King to consider us in our extraordinary pains.

Then to the office, and there all the afternoon very busy, and so till past 12 at night; and so home to bed.

This day my wife went to the burial of a little boy of W. Joyces.

17. Up, and to my office and there all the morning mighty busy, and taking upon me to tell the Comtroller how ill his matters were done. And I think, endeed, if I continue thus, all

a repl. 'I'–   *b* repl. symbol rendered illegible

---

1. See below, p. 327 & n. 2.

the business of the office will come upon me, whether I will or no.

At noon to the Change and then home with Creed to dinner; and thence I to the office, where close at it all the afternoon till 12 at night; and then home to supper and to bed.

This day I received from Mr. Foly,[1] but for me to pay for if I like it, an Iron chest, having now received back some money I have laid out for the King; and I hope to have a good sum of money by me thereby in a few days – I think above 800*l*. But when I came home at night, I could not find the way to open it – but which is a strange thing, my little girl Susan could carry it alone from one table clear from the ground and set upon another, when neither [I] nor*a* anyone in my house but Jane the cook-maid could do it.

18. Up, and to the office and thence to the committee of the Fishery at White-hall; where so poor simple doings about the business of the Lottery, that I was ashamed to see it – that a thing so low and base should have anything to do with so noble an undertaking.

But I had the advantage this day to hear Mr. Williamson discourse, who came to be a contractor with others for the Lotterys; and endeed, I find he is a very Logicall man and a good speaker.[2]

But it was so pleasant to see my Lord Craven the chaireman, before many persons of worth and grave – use this comparison, in saying that certainly those that would contract for all the lotteries would not suffer us to set up the Virginia Lottery for plate before them. "For," says he, "if I occupy a wench first, you may occupy her again your heart out; you can never have her maiden-head after I have once had it," – which he did [say] more loosely, and yet as if he had fetched a most grave and worthy instance. They made mirth, but I and others were ashamed of it.

Thence to the Change, and thence home to dinner, and

a MS. 'nor nor'

---

1. Ironmonger to the navy.
2. With four others, Joseph Williamson (secretary to Arlington) was in June 1665 appointed to manage the Fishery Corporation's monopoly of lotteries: *CSPD 1664–5*, p. 438.

thence to the office a good while; and thence to the council-chamber at White-hall to speak with Sir G. Carteret.   And here by accident heard a great and famous cause between Sir G. Lane and one Mr. Phill. Whore – an Irish business, about Sir G Lane's endeavouring to reverse a decree of the late Comissioners of Ireland in a Rebells case for his land, which the King had given as forfeited to Sir G. Lane – for whom the Sollicitor did argue most angell-like.[1]   And one of the Comissioners, Baron   ,[2] did argue for the other and for himself and his bretheren who had decreed it.   But the Sollicitor doth so pay the Comissioners, how four all along did act for the papists and three only for the protestants, by which they were over-voted.   But at last, one word (which was omitted in the Sollicitors repeating of an Act of Parliament in the case) being insisted on by the other part, the Sollicitor was put to a great stop; and I could discern he could not tell what to say, but was quite out.   Thence home, well pleased with this accident; and so home to my office, where late, and then to supper and to bed.

This day I had a letter from Mr. Coventry that tells me that my Lord Brunkard is to be one of our Commissioners, of which I am very glad, if any more must be.[3]

1. See PRO, PC 2/57, f. 154r. The notes of counsel's arguments before the English Privy Council given as undated and illegible in *CSP Ireland 1662–4*, pp. 505–6, may refer to this day's proceedings. The commissioners were those appointed under the act of settlement to adjudge disputes about land in Ireland, and they were almost always accused of prejudice. It was once said that three of them were for the King, three for the Anglo-Irish and one for himself: ib., p. 231. The litigants here were Sir George Lane, Ormond's secretary, and Philip Hore of Kilshachan.   Details in *CSP Ireland 1662–4*, pp. 30–1 etc.; *CSPClar.*, v. 319 etc.   The Solicitor [-General] was Sir Heneage Finch.

2. Supply 'Rainsford'.   Sir Richard

Rainsford was Baron of the Exchequer and President of the Court of Claims in Ireland, 1663.

3. Coventry to Pepys, 17 November: Rawl. A 174, ff, 482–3. In a letter of 12 November Coventry had written that Sir W. Rider was 'in nomination' for the post: ib., ff. 491–2. But, as both Coventry and Pepys recognised, there were objections to the appointment of merchants to the Board: ib., f. 483r. Brouncker's warrant was issued on 12 November and his patent on 7 December. His appointment was perhaps welcome to Pepys because of his ability as a ship-designer and mathematician.   He was President of the Royal Society, 1662–77.

19. All the morning at the office. And without dinner, down by galley up and down the river to visit the yards and ships now ordered forth, with great delight; and so home to supper and then to office late to write letters; then home to bed.*a*

20. *Lords day.* Up, and with my wife to church – where Pegg Pen very fine in her new coloured silk suit, laced with silver lace. Dined at home, and Mr. Sheply, lately come to town, with me – a great deal of ordinary discourse with him. Among other things, praying him to speak to Stankes to look after our business.¹ With him, and in private with Mr. Bodham, talking of our ropeyard stores at Woolwich, which are mighty low – even to admiration. They gone, in the evening comes Mr. Andrews and sings with us. And he gone, I to Sir W. Batten's, where Sir J. Minnes and he and I to talk about our letter to my Lord Treasurer;² where his folly and simple confidence so great, in a report so ridiculous that he hath drawn up to present to my Lord, nothing of it being true, that I was ashamed and did roundly, and in many words for an hour together, talk boldly to him – which pleased Sir W. Batten and my Lady; but I was in the right, and was the willinger to do so before them, that they might see that I am somebody, and shall serve him so in his way another time.

So home, vexed at this night's passage, for I had been very hot with him: so to supper, prayers, and to bed, out of order with this night's vexation.

21. Up; and with them to the Lords at White-hall, where they do single me out to speak to and to hear – much to my content. And received their commands perticularly in several businesses. Thence by their order to the Atturny Generall's

a entry crowded into bottom of page

----

1. Will Stankes looked after John Pepys's land at Brampton. Edward Shipley was Sandwich's steward at Hinchingbrooke.

2. See below, p. 330 & n. 2.

about a new warrant for Captain Taylor, which I shall carry for him to be Comissioner, in spite of Sir W. Batten; and yet endeed, it is not I, but the ability of the man, that makes the Duke and Mr. Coventry stand by their choice.[1]

I to the Change and there stayed long, doing business. And this day for certain, news is come that Teddiman hath brought in 18 or 20 Duchmen, merchants, their Burdeaux fleet, and two men of war to Portsmouth. And I had letters this afternoon that three are brought into the Downes and Dover[2] – so that the war is begun: God give a good end to it.

After dinner at home all the afternoon, busy; and at night with Sir W. Batten and Sir J. Mennes[a] looking over[b] the business of stating the accounts of the Navy charge to my Lord Treasurer, where Sir[c] J. Mennes's paper served us in no stead almost, but was all false; and after I had done it with great pains, he being by, I am confident he understands not one word in it. At it till 10 at night almost.

Thence by coach to Sir Ph. Warwickes by his desire, to have conferred with him; but he being in bed, I to White-hall to the

---

a blot in lower margin   *b* symbol blotted   *c* repl. 'his'

---

1. The Admiralty Committee had on the 11th stayed John Taylor's appointment in face of Batten's objection that he was a 'fanatic'. Pepys had written to Coventry urging Taylor's claims, and Coventry (despite his scruples against appointing a merchant) had said, in a letter to Secretary Bennet (14 November): 'Certain it is that his abilities are great and his dispatch hath heretofore been eminent. . . . As to his being a fanatic, I have nothing to say for or against it, but I believe you will have need of all hands to the work now cut out': *CSPD 1664–5*, p. 68. See *Further Corr.*, pp. 28–30; *Shorthand Letters*, pp. 3–4, 7, 18. For Coventry's letters to Pepys, see Rawl. A 174, ff. 468+, 489*v* 490*r*.

2. John Strode to Navy Board, Dover Castle, 20 November: *CSPD 1664–5*, p. 82. Teddiman had left Portsmouth on the 15th. Most of these ships had been driven into English harbours by the bad weather; no letters of marque had been issued yet. The French ambassador was soon busy claiming the captured wine: below, p. 354. Another Dutch fleet from Bordeaux got through in December–January. Cf. *The Newes*, 24 November, p. 756, 15 December, p. 806; *The Intelligencer*, 28 November, p. 764, 12 December, p. 798; *CSPD 1664–5*, pp. 66, 95; *CSPVen. 1664–6*, pp. 72, 121; HMC, *Heathcote*, p. 171; HMC, *Finch*, p. 95.

Secretary's and there wrote to Mr. Coventry;[1] and so home by coach again. A fine clear moonshine night, but very cold.

Home to my office a while, it being past 12 at night; and so to supper and to bed.

22. At the office all the morning. Sir G. Carteret, upon a motion of Sir W. Batten's, did promise, if we would write a letter to him, to show it to the King on our behalf, touching our desire of being Commissioners of the Prize office. I wrote a letter to my mind;[2] and after eating a bit at home (Mr. Sheply dining and taking his leave[a] of me), abroad and to Sir G Carteret with the letter; and thence to my Lord Treasurer's, where with Sir Ph. Warwicke[3] long studying all we could to make the last year swell as high as we could. And it is much to see how he doth study for the King to do it, to get all the money from the Parliament, all he can – and I shall be serviceable to him therein, to help him to heads upon which to enlarge the report of the expense.[4] He did observe to me how obedient this Parliament was for a while; and the last sitting, how they begun to differ

a repl. 'life'

---

1. NMM, LBK/8, pp. 125–7 (dated 22 November); printed in *Shorthand Letters*, pp. 5–8; concerning stores and the appointment of commissioners at Portsmouth and Harwich.

2. Copy (mostly in Hayter's hand, with the opening sentence in Pepys's) in PRO, SP 46/136, no. 224 (summary in *CSPD Add. 1660–85*, p. 116); copy (in Hewer's hand) in NMM, LBK/8, pp. 127–8 (printed in *Further Corr.*, p. 31); dated this day and signed by Mennes, Batten and Pepys. They asked Carteret to bring to the King's attention their claims to places on the commission – 'being doubtfull least by our Silence we might loose the favour wee humbly hope for'. They gave excellent reasons – among them the precedent of the last Dutch war – but to no avail. The politicians landed all the jobs: on 24 December the members of the Navy Committee of the Privy Council were appointed Commissioners (with Secretary Bennet as their Comptroller and Ashley as their Treasurer), and the sub-commissioners at the ports were, with few exceptions, all M.P.s. See below, p. 342 & n. 6; *CSPD 1664–5*, pp. 43, 60, 122; HMC, *Heathcote*, p. 175.

3. Secretary to Southampton (the Lord Treasurer), and the mainstay of the Treasury at this time.

4. Parliament was about to reassemble on the 24th, and the government was to ask for a new grant of money in view of the approach of war.

and to carp at the King's officers; and what they will do now, he says, is to make agreement for the money, for there is no guess to be made of it. He told me he was prepared to convince the parliament that the Subsidys are a most ridiculous tax (the four last not rising to 40000*l*) and unæquall.[1] He talks of a tax of assessement of 70000*l* for five years, the people to be secured that it shall continue no longer then there is really a warr – and the charges thereof to be paid.*a*[2]

He told me that one year of the late Dutch war cost 1623000*l*.*b*[3] Thence to my Lord Chancellors, and there stayed long with Sir W. Batten and Sir J. Mennes to speak with my Lord about our Prize-Office business; but being sick and full of visitants, we could not speak with him, and so away home.

Where Sir Rd. Ford did meet us, with letters from Holland this day that it is likely the Duch fleet will not come out this year; they have not victuals to keep them out, and it is likely they will be frozen before they can get back.[4]

---

a two blots in lower margin   *b* figure blotted

---

1. The four subsidies of 1663 brought in rather more than Warwick here maintains: c. £80,000 from Easter 1663 to Easter 1664, according to W. A. Shaw (*CTB*, vol. i, p. xxxi), and c. £63,250 from Easter to Michaelmas 1664, according to C. D. Chandaman ('The English Public Revenue, 1660–1688', unpub. thesis, Univ. London, 1954, p. 407). But subsidies, being based on long-outdated assessments, were unproductive and inequitable, and this was the last time that they were levied.

2. The 'assessment', introduced in 1643 and the principal direct tax during the Interregnum, was a tax mainly on land. The total to be levied was stipulated by the act, and the taxpayer was more stringently rated than in the subsidy. In December the Commons granted an assessment of c. £2½m. levied in 36 months (16–17 Car. II c. 1). When the assessment had been last levied, in December 1661, a promise had been inserted in the act that it would not be levied again. The war now forced its adoption, and assessments came to replace subsidies.

3. The opening year (1652–3) of the First Dutch War was the most expensive. The totals given in BM, Add. 11602, and Rawl. A 195 a, f. 241r are rather lower than Warwick's estimate: £1,402,081 and £1,410,312 respectively.

4. See the similar report in Coventry to Bennet, 30 November: *CSPD 1664–5*, p. 96. Another view was that the Dutch were anxious for peace: *CSPVen. 1664–6*, pp. 56, 58, 61.

Captain Cocke is made Steward for sick and wounded seamen.[1]

So home to supper, where troubled to hear my poor boy Tom hath a fit of the stone, or some other pain like it. I must consult Mr. Holliard for him.

So at one in the morning, home to bed.

23. Up, and to my office, where close all the morning about my Lord Treasurer's account, and at noon home to dinner. And then to the office all the afternoon, very busy till very late at night; and then to supper and to bed.

This evening Mr. Hollyard came to me and told me that he hath searched my boy, and he finds he hath a stone in his bladder – which grieves me to the heart, he being a good-natured and well-disposed boy – and more, that it should be my misfortune to have him come to my house.

Sir G Carteret was here this afternoon; and strange to see how we plot to make the charge of this war to appear greater then it is, because of getting money.

24. Up and to the office, where all the morning busy answering of people. About noon out with Comissioner Pett, and he and I to a Coffee-house to drink Jocolatte, very good; and so by coach to Westminster,[a] being the first day of the Parliaments meeting. After the House had received the King's speech and what more he had to say, delivered in writing[2] (the Chancellor being sick), it rose; and I with Sir Ph. Warwicke home and conferred our matters about the charge of the Navy, and am more to give him in the excessive charge of this year's

a repl. 'White-hall'

---

1. I.e. Treasurer to the Commission for the Sick and Wounded Mariners and Prisoners of War, which was now (28 October) appointed for the duration of the war. The commissioners, who received their instructions on 23 November, were Sir William Doyley, Sir Thomas Clifford, Col. Bullen Reymes and John Evelyn. For their work, see J. J. Sutherland Shaw in *Mar. Mirr.*, 25/306+. Evelyn gives the date of Cocke's election to the office as the 15th; the Privy Council Register has an order appointing him Receiver on the 11th: PRO, PC 2/57, f. 150.

2. *LJ*, xi. 624-6. The speech was followed by an account of relations with the Dutch.

expense. I dined with him, and Mr. Povy with us[a] and Sir Edmd. Pooly, a fine gentleman, and Mr. Chichly;[1] and fine discourse we had and fine talk – being proud to see myself accepted in such company and thought better then I am. After dinner Sir Phillip and I to talk again; and then away home to the office, where sat late, beginning our sittings now in the afternoon because of the parliament; and they being rose, I to my office, where late, till almost one a-clock; and then home to bed.

25. Up, and at my office all the morning to prepare an account of the charge we have been put to extraordinary by the Dutch already; and I have brought it to appear 85270*ol*; but God knows, this is only a scare to the Parliament, to make them give the more money.[2]

Thence to the Parliament-house and there did give it to Sir Ph. Warwicke, the House being hot upon giving the King a supply of money. And I by coach to the Change and took up Mr. Jenings along with me (my old acquaintance), he telling me the mean manner that Sir Samuel Morland lives near him, in a house he hath bought and laid out money upon; in all, to the value of 1200*l* – but is believed to be a beggar. And so I ever thought he would be.[3]

From the Change, with Mr. Deering and Luellin to the White-horse[a] tavern in Lombard-street – and there dined with them, he giving me a dish of meat, to discourse in order to my serving Deering;[4] which I am already obliged to do, and shall do it –

a repl. 'me'   b repl. 'White-wh'-

---

1. Pooley was M.P. for Bury St Edmund's and a clerk extraordinary to the Privy Council. Thomas Chicheley was M.P. for Cambridge-shire and had just been appointed an Ordnance Commissioner.

2. £800,000 was the figure used in the King's speech at the opening of the session: *LJ*, xi. 624. Coventry, writing to Secretary Bennet (24 November), criticised even that as excessive: *CSPD 1664-5*, pp. 88-9.

3. Morland (now a baronet and a courtier) had been Pepys's tutor at Magdalene. For his money affairs, see above, iv. 275 & n. 1. This house was probably in Bloomsbury: Eva G. R. Taylor, *Math. Practitioners*, p. 230.

4. Edward Dering was a timber merchant, Llewellyn his clerk.

and would be glad he were a man trusty, that I might venture something along with him.

Thence home; and by and by, in the evening, took my wife out by coach, leaving her at Unthankes, while I to White-hall and to Westminster-hall, where I have not been to talk a great while; and there hear that Mrs. Lane and her husband live a sad life together, and he is gone to be a pay-master to a company to Portsmouth to serve at sea. She big with child. Thence I home, calling my wife – and at Sir W. Batten's hear that the House hath given the King 2500000*l* to be paid for this war, only for the Navy, in three years time; which is a joyful thing to all the King's party I see – but was much opposed by Mr. Vaughan and others, that it should be so much.[1] So home and to supper and to bed.

26. Up and to the office, where busy all the morning. Home a while to dinner; and then to the office, where very late, busy till quite weary, but contented well with my despatch of business; and so home to supper and to bed.

27.*a* ⟨*Lords day.*⟩ To church in the morning. Then dined at home, and to my office and there all the afternoon setting right my business of Flaggs; and after all my pains, find reason not to be sorry, because I think it will bring me considerable profit.[2]

a repl. '25'

---

1. Voted by 172 to 102 (*CJ*, viii. 568), this was much the largest grant ever made to any Stuart government, though sufficient, Pepys thought, for only 2½ years of war: Pepys to Sandwich, 3 December, *Shorthand Letters*, p. 20. Collection was to be spread over three years. Vaughan had moved to reduce the total to £500,000. The proposal to make it 'only for the Navy' (i.e. to appropriate the proceeds to a naval war) was not pursued now, but was incorporated in the Additional Aid of 1665:

below, vi. 292 & n. 3. For the passage of the present bill, see ib., p. 33 & n. 4. Several writers, relying on Clarendon's misleading account (*Life*, ii. 309-10), have exaggerated the willingness of the Commons to pass this vote. A detailed account of the debate on this day is in BM, Add. 32094, ff. 24-7 (Sir T. Clifford to W. Coventry, 25 November).

2. See above, p. 291. For the payments made to him from December 1664 onwards, see PRO, Adm. 20/5, p. 245; ib., 20/6, pp. 31, 166.

In the evening came Mr. Andrews and Hill, and we sung with my boy Ravenscrofts four-part psalms,[1] most admirable music. Then (Andrews not staying) we to supper; and after supper fell into the rarest discourse with Mr. Hill about Rome and Italy,[2] the most pleasant that I ever had in my life. At it very late, and then to bed.

28.[a]　Up, and with Sir J. Mennes and W. Batten to White-hall, but no committee of Lords (which is like to do the King's business well).[b]　So to Westminster, and there to Gervas and was a little while with Jane; and so to London by coach and to the Coffee-house – where[c] certain news of our peace made by Captain Allen with Argier,[3] which is good news. And that the Duch have sent part of their fleet round by Scotland and resolve to pay off the rest half-pay, promising the rest in the Spring; hereby keeping their men.[4] But how true this, I know not. Home to dinner. Then came Dr. Clerke to speak with me about sick and wounded men, wherein he is like to be concerned.[5] And after him, Mr. Cutler;[6] and much talk with him, and with him to White-hall to have waited on the Lords by order; but no meeting neither tonight, which will spoil all.

I think I shall get something by my discourse with Cutler. So home; and after being at my office an hour with Mr. Povey talking about his business of Tanger, getting him some money allowed him for freight of ships, wherein I hope to get some-

a repl. '26'　　*b* bracket follows 'business' in MS.
　　　　　c repl. 'where' (blotted)

---

1. Thomas Ravencroft, *The whole book of psalmes* (1621); PL 612. The 'Norwich tune' transcribed from this collection is in P. M. Young, *Samuel Pepys music book*, p. 17 (reproduced in D. G. Weiss, *Samuel Pepys, curioso*, p. 39). (E).

2. Thomas Hill was a merchant. Pepys never visited Italy.

3. Signed 30 October; a repetition (with one additional clause) of Lawson's treaty of 1662 which the Algerines had repudiated; printed in *Somers Tracts* (ed. Scott), vii. 554+.

4. Cf. the similar news about the laying-up of the Dutch fleet in Downing's despatch to Bennet, The Hague, 29 November/8 December: PRO, SP 84/173, ff. 51r–52v. See below, p. 338. The unfounded rumour about their sending ships north of Scotland persisted for several weeks: below, p. 354 & n. 3.

5. He later inspected some of the wounded in Evelyn's district: Evelyn, 17 March 1665.

6. William Cutler, merchant.

thing too. He gone, I home, hungry and almost sick for want of eating; and so to supper and to bed.

29. Up, and with Sir W. Batten to the committee of Lords at the council-chamber – where Sir G. Carteret told us what he hath said to the King, and how the King inclines to our request of making us Comissioners of the Prize-office. But meeting him anon in the gallery, he tells me that my Lord Barkely is angry we should not acquaint him with it; so I found out my Lord and pacified him; but I know not whether he was so in earnest or no, for he looked very frowardly. Thence to the parliament-house, and with Sir W. Batten home and dined with him, my wife being gone to my Lady Sandwiches; and then to the office, where we sat all the afternoon; and I at my office till past 12 at night and so home to bed.

This day I hear that the King should say that the Dutch do begin to comply with him – Sir John Robinson told Sir W. Batten that he heard the King say so. I pray God it may be so.

30. Up, and with Sir W. Batten and Sir J. Mennes to the committee of the Lords and there did our business; but Lord, what a sorry despatch those great persons give to business. Thence to the Change and there hear the certainty and circumstances of the Duch having called in their fleet and paid their men half-pay, the other to be paid them upon their being ready upon beat-of-drum to come to serve them again – and in the meantime to have half-pay. This is said.

Thence home to dinner, and so to my office all the afternoon. In the evening my wife and Sir W Warren*a* with me to Whitehall, sending her with the coach to see her father and mother. He and I up to Sir G Carteret and first I alone, and then both, had discourse with him about things of the Navy; and so I and he calling my wife at Unthankes, home again and long together, talking how to order things in a new contract for Norway goods,[1] as well to the King's as to his advantage.

a blot in MS.

---

1. Concluded on 3 December (for Gothenburg masts): *CSPD 1664–5*, p. 137.

He gone, I to my monthly accounts; and bless God, I find I have encreased my last balance, though but little – but I hope ere long to get more.   In the meantime, praise God for what I have, which is 1209*l.*   So, with my heart glad to see my accounts fall so right in this time of mixing of monies and confusion, I home to bed.

DECEMBER.

1. Up betimes and to White-hall to a committee of Tanger. And so straight home and hard to my business at my office till noon; then to dinner, and so to my office and by and by we sat all the afternoon; then to my office again till past*a* one in the morning, and so home to supper and to bed.

2. Lay long in bed. Then up and to the office, where busy all the morning. At home dined. After dinner, with my wife and Mercer to the Dukes house and there saw *The Rivalls*, which I had seen before. But the play not good, nor anything but the good actings of Baterton and his wife and Harris.[1]

Thence homeward, and the coach broke with us in Lincoln's-Inn Fields; and so walked to Fleet-street and there took coach and home and to my office – whither by and by comes Captain Cocke and then Sir W Batten; and we all to Sir J Minnes and I did give them a barrel of oysters I had given me, and so there sat and talked; where good discourse of the late troubles, they knowing things, all of them very well – and Cocke from the King's own mouth, being then intrusted himself much, doth know perticularly that the Kings credulity to Cromwells promises private to him – against the advice of his friends and the certain discovery of the practices and discourses of Cromwell in council (by Major Huntington) – did take away his life, and nothing else.[2]

Then to some loose atheisticall discourse of Cockes, when he

a repl. 'all v'-

---

1. Cf. above, p. 267 & n. 1. Betterton played Philander; Mrs Betterton, Heraclia; Harris, Theocles. (A).

2. Cf. Clarendon, *Hist.*, iv. 260-1; Ludlow, i. 196, n. 1. Maj. Robert Huntingdon, who commanded Cromwell's own troop, had acted as intermediary between Cromwell and Charles I in 1647-8, but had resigned his commission in August 1648. Several pamphlets were published on his defection to Charles, but neither there nor elsewhere has any mention been found of Cocke's association at this time with the King.

was almost drunk; and then about 11 a-clock broke up, and I to my office to fit up an account for Povey, wherein I hope to get something. At it till almost 2 a-clock; then home to supper and to bed.

3. Up,[a] and at the office all the morning; and at noon to Mr. Cutlers and there dined with Sir W Rider and him; and thence Sir W. Rider and I by coach to White-hall to a committee of the Fishery – there only to hear Sir Edwd. Ford's proposal about Farthing's;[1] wherein, O God, to see almost everybody interested for him, only my Lord Annesly,[2] who is a grave, serious man. My Lord Barkely was there, but is the most hot, fiery man in discourse, without any cause, that ever I saw – even to breach of civility to my Lord Anglesy in his discourse opposing to my Lord's. At last, though without much satisfaction to me, it was voted that it should be requested of the King, and that Sir Edw. Fords proposal is the best yet made. Thence by coach home – the Duke of Yorke being expected tonight with great joy from Portsmouth, after his having been abroad at sea three or four days with the fleet; and the Dutch are all drawn into their harbours[3] – but it seems like a victory. And a matter of some reputation to us it is, and blemish to them; but in no degree like what it is esteemed at – the weather requiring them to do so.[4] Home, and at my office late; and then to supper and to bed.

a preceded by 'Up' (struck through) in margin

---

1. See above, iv. 366 & n. 1. This meeting is reported in HMC, *Rep.*, 6/331.

2. Arthur Annesley, 1st Earl of Anglesey. His gravity, combined with his love of speechifying, made him in fact a formidable bore: see Clarendon's opinion (and the King's) in Lister, iii. 494. Burnet (i. 174) refers to his 'faculty of speaking indefatigably upon every subject'.

3. See Coventry to the Navy Board, from the Channel fleet (30 November and 2 December): *CSPD 1664-5*, pp. 96, 100-1.

4. Cf. Pepys to Sandwich, 3 December: 'I do congratulate your lordship with your return to Portsmouth so much like a victory, your enemy fleeing, but could be glad to apprehend more reason than I yet do of the inference the World generally draws from it . . .' (NMM, LBK/8, p. 138; printed in *Shorthand Letters*, p. 20).

4. *Lords day.* Lay long in bed; and then up and to my office, there to despatch a business in order to the getting something out of the Tanger business,*a* wherein I have an opportunity to get myself paid upon the score of freight;[1] I hope a good sum.

At noon home to dinner, and then in the afternoon to church. So home; and by and by comes*b* Mr. Hill and Andrews and sung together long and with great content. Then to supper and broke up – pretty discourse, very pleasant and ingenious; and so to my office a little, and then home (after prayer) to bed.

This day (I hear) the Duke of Yorke is come to town – though expected last night, as I observed; but by what hindrance stopped I can [not] tell.

5. Up, and to White-hall with ‘ Sir J Minnes; and there among an infinite crowd of great persons did kiss the Dukes hand but had no time to discourse. Thence up and down the gallery, and got my Lord of Albemarles hand to my bill for Povey. But afterward was asked some scurvy questions by Povey about my demands, which troubled [me], but will do no great hurt I think. Thence, vexed, home; and there by appointment comes my Cosen Roger Pepys and Mrs. Turner and dined with me, and very merry we were. They stayed all the afternoon till night; and then after I had discoursed an hour with Sir W Warren, plainly declaring my resolution to desart him if he goes on to Joyne with Castle, who, and his family, I for great provocations I love not – which he takes with some trouble, but will concur in everything with me he says.[2] Now I am loath, I confess, to lose him, he having been the best friend I have had ever in this office. So he being gone, we all, it being night, in Madam Turner's coach to her house, there to see, as she tells us, how fat Mrs. The is grown. And so I find her, but not as I expected. But mightily pleased I am to hear the mother commend her daughter Betty, that she is like to be a great beauty,

a repl. symbol rendered illegible   *b* followed by blot

1. Probably the freight of the *William*: below, p. 340 & n. 2.
2. Warren joined with Castle (Batten's son-in-law) in a contract

concluded later this month for 1500 loads of timber: Rawl. A 174, ff. 58+.

and she sets much by her.   Thence I to White-hall and there saw
Mr. Coventry come to town – and with all my heart am glad to
see him.   But could have no talk with him, he being but just
come.

Thence back and took up my wife, and home;[1] where a while
and then home to supper and bed.

6.   Up, and in Sir W. Batten's coach to White-hall; but the
Duke being gone forth, I to Westminster-hall and there spent
much time till towards noon, to and fro with people.   So by
and by Mrs. Lane comes and plucks me by the cloak to speak to
me, and I was fain to go to her shop; and pretending to buy
some bands, made her go home and I by and by fallowed her
and there did what I would with her; and so after many discourses and her intreating me to do something for her husband,
which I promised to do, and buying a little band of her, which I
intend to keep too – I took leave, there coming a couple of foot-
boys to her with[a] a coach to fetch her abroad, I know not to
whom.   She is great with child, and she says I must be godfather, but I do not entend it.   Thence by coach to the Old
Exchange and there hear that the Dutch are fitting their ships out
again;[2] which puts us to new discourses and to alter our thoughts
of the Duch as to their want of courage or force.   Thence by
appointment to the White-horse taverne in[b] Lumbard Streete and
there dined with my Lord Rutherford, Povey, Mr. Gauden,
Creed and others – and very merry; and after dinner, among
other things, Povey and I withdrew and I plainly told him that I
was concerned in profit, but very justly, in this business of the
Bill that I have been these two or three days about; and he
consents to it, and it shall be paid.

He tells me how he believes, and in part knows, Creed to be
worth 10000*l*; nay, that now and then he[3] hath 3 or 4000*l* in
his[4] hands, for which he gives the interest that the King gives,

a   repl. 'to'   *b*   repl. 'and there'

1. Pepys presumably means to say
that he took up his wife at Mrs
Turner's house.
2. Cf. Downing to Clarendon, The

Hague, 6 December: Lister, iii.
353–4.   But see below, p. 354 & n. 3.
3. Creed.
4. Povey's.

which is 10 per cent; and that he doth come and demand it every three months, the interest to be paid him[1] – which Povey looks upon as a cunning and mean trick of him; but for all that, he will do, and is very rich. Thence to the office, where we sat and where Mr. Coventry came, the first time after his return from sea; which I was glad of.

So after office to my office, and then home to supper; and to my office again and then late home to bed.

7. Lay long, then up; and among others, Bagwell's wife coming to speak with me put new thoughts of folly into me – which I am troubled at. Thence, after doing business at my[a] office, I by coach to my Lady Sandwiches and there dined with her and found all well – and merry. Thence to White-hall; and we waited on the Duke, who looks better then he did, methinks, before his voyage; and I think a little more stern then he used to do.

Thence to the Temple to my Cosen Roger Pepys, thinking to have met the Doctor to have discoursed our business,[2] but he came not; so I home and there by agreement came my Lord Rutherford, Povy, Gauden, Creed, Alderman Backewell – about Tanger business of account between Rutherford and Gauden.[3] Here they were with me an hour or more. Then after drinking, away; and Povey and Creed stayed and eat with me but I was sorry I had no better cheer for Povey – for the fool may be useful, and is a cunning fellow in his way; which is a strange one, and that that I meet not in any other man nor can describe in him. They late with me; and when gone, my boy and I to music and then to bed.

a repl. 'office' (badly formed)

---

1. The payment of interest at three-monthly intervals was most unusual; both bankers and the Exchequer made up their interest accounts every six months. Moreover, Creed was not entitled to 10%: the legal limit was 6%. The additional 4% which the King gave at this time was a 'gratuity' given of grace and authorised by special warrant.

2. The debt owed by Tom Pepys the tailor at his death to his cousin Dr Thomas Pepys: see above, p. 85 & n. 1.

3. Rutherford was the son and heir of the late Governor of Tangier. He received £7000 in September 1665: below, vi. 221.

8. Up and to my office, where all the morning busy. At noon dined at home, and then to the office, where we sat all the afternoon. In the evening comes my aunt and uncle Wight, Mrs. Norbury and her daughter, and after them Mr Norbury; where no great pleasure, my aunt being out of humour, in her fine clothes and it raining hard. Besides, I was a little too bold with her about her doting on Dr. Venner.[1] Anon they went away; and I till past 12 at night at my office and then home to bed.

9. Up betimes and walked to Mr. Povey's; and there, not without some few troublesome questions of his, I got a note and went and received 117*l*. 05*s*. 00*d*. of Alderman Viner upon my pretended freight of the *William* for Tanger – which overbears me on one side with joy, and on the other to think of my condition if I shall be called into examination about it, and (though in strictness it is due) not be able to give a good account of it.[2]

Home with it, and there comes[a] Captain Taylor to me and he and I did set even the business of the ship *Union*, lately gone for Tanger; wherein I hope to get 50*l* more. For all which, the Lord be praised.

At noon home to dinner, Mr. Hunt and his wife with us, and very pleasant. Then in the afternoon I carried them home by coach; and I to Westminster-hall and thence to Gervas's, and there find I cannot prevail with Jane to go forth with me; but though I took a good occasion of going to the Trumpet, she declined coming – which vexed me (*je ayant grand envie envers elle, avec vrai amour et passion*).

a repl. 'Mr.'

---

1. Probably John Venner, her family physician.
2. The *William* was a merchant-man hired to escort E. India ships as far as St Helena. She sailed in the following January and returned in August: *CSPD 1664–5*, pp. 75, 76 etc. Pepys was presumably using her to transport pieces-of-eight on Vyner's behalf to the Tangier garrison, and covering up the transaction by representing it as a charge for freight – which caused him some concern until payment was authorised on 29 March 1665: below, vi. 70. Plate, coin or bullion was the only form of cargo allowed on ships of the royal navy: PRO, Adm. 2/1725, f. 43*r*. (instruction of 14 January 1662). Abuses of the practice are condemned in Pepys's *Tangier Papers*, pp. 141+, 240+. Cf. *Cat.*, i. 192–5; Pepys, *Memoires* (ed. Tanner), pp. 56+.

Thence home and to my office till one in the morning, setting to rights in writing this day's two accounts of Povey and Taylor; and then quietly to bed.

This day I have several letters, from several places, of our bringing in great numbers of Duch ships.[1]

10. Lay long; at which I am ashamed, because of so many people's observing it that know not how late I sit up, and for fear of Sir W. Batten's speaking of it to others – he having stayed for me a good while. At the office all the morning, where comes my Lord Brunkard with his patent in his hand and delivered it to Sir J. Mennes and myself, we alone being there – all the day.[2] And at noon I in his coach with him to the Change, where he set me down. A modest civil person he seems to be, but wholly ignorant in the business of the Navy as possible, but I hope to make a friend of him, being a worthy man.

Thence, after hearing the great news of so many Duchmen being brought in to Portsmouth and elsewhere,[3] which it is expected shall either put them upon present revenge or despair, I with Sir W Rider and Cutler to dinner all alone to the Great James – where good discourse, and I hope occasion of getting something hereafter.

After dinner to White-hall to the Fishery, where the Duke was with us.

So home and late at my office, writing many letters; then home to supper and to bed. Yesterday came home, and this night I visited, Sir W Pen, who dissembles great respect and love to me, but I understand him very well.

Major Holmes is come from Guiny and is now at Plymouth, with great wealth they say.[4]

---

1. Prizes brought into Dover, Plymouth and Portsmouth: *CSPD 1664-5*, pp. 104, 105, 106; *The Newes*, 8 December, p. 790.

2. For Brouncker and his appointment as a Navy Commissioner, see above, p. 324, n. 3. Pepys kept a copy of the patent (7 December): Rawl. A 216, ff. 113–15.

3. 'We have so many *Dutch* here [Portsmouth] that the *Sea men* talke of learning the *Language* that they may know what a *Hollander* means when he call's for *Quarter*': *The Intelligencer*, 12 December, p. 797.

4. For his voyage, see above, pp. 127, 283 & nn.; for his return, *CSPD 1664-5*, p. 105. He had taken several prizes.

11. *Lords day.* Up and to church alone in the morning. Dined at home mighty pleasantly; in the afternoon I to the French church – where much pleased with the three sisters of the parson,[1] very handsome; especially in their noses – and sing prettily. I hear a good sermon of the old[a] man,[2] touching duty to parents. Here was Sir Samll. Morland and his Lady,[3] very fine, with two footmen in new liverys – the church taking much notice of them – and going into their coach after sermon with great gazing. So I home, and my Cousin Mary Pepys's husband came after me and told me that out of the money he received some months since, he did receive 18*d* too much, and did now come and give it me, which was very pretty.[4] So home, and there found Mr. Andrews and his lady, a well-bred and a tolerable pretty woman, and by and by Mr. Hill; and to singing and then to supper. Then to sing again, and so good-night. To prayers and to bed.[b]

It is a little strange how these psalms of Ravenscroft,[5] after two or three times singing, prove but the same again, though good – no diversity appearing at all almost.

12. Up and with Sir W. Batten by coach to White-hall, where all of us with the Duke. Mr. Coventry privately did tell me the reason of his advice against our pretences to the Priz[e]-office (in his letter from Portsmouth);[6] because he knew that the King and the Duke had resolved to put in some parliament men that have deserved well and that would need be obliged by putting them in.

Thence homeward; called at my booksellers and bespoke some books against the year out. And then to the Change; and so

a followed by blot   *b* MS. 'night'

---

1. ? David Primerose, minister of the French Huguenot church in Threadneedle St.

2. Louis Hérault, minister 1642–3, 1660–75.

3. Morland's wife was French.

4. This was the second instalment of the £50 due to her from the estate of Robert Pepys of Brampton which

had fallen to be paid in August 1664: above, iv. 344. Her husband was Samuel de Santhune, a weaver, who was a brother-in-law of Cisner, the minister.

5. See above, p. 332, n. 1. (E).

6. Coventry to Pepys, 26 November: Rawl. A 174, f. 468. Cf. above, p. 327 & n. 2.

home to dinner and then to the office, where my Lord Brunkard comes and reads over part of our instructions in the Navy;[1] and I expounded it to him, so he is become my disciple. He gone, comes Cutler to tell us that the King of France hath forbid any Canvas to be carried out of his kingdom.[2] And I, to examine, went with him to the East India-house to see a letter, but came too late. So home again and there late, till 12 at night, at my office; and then home to supper and to bed.

This day (to see how things are ordered in the world), I had a command from the Earle of Sandwich (at Portsmouth) not to be forward with Mr. Cholmly and Sir J. Lawson about the Molle at Tanger, because that what I do therein will (because of his friendship to me known) redound against him, as if I had done it upon his scoare.[3] So I wrote to my Lord my mistake, and am contented to promise never to pursue it more – which goes against my mind with all my heart.

13. Lay long in bed; then up, and many people to speak with me. Then to my office, and dined at noon at home; then to the office again, where we sat all the afternoon; then home at night to a little supper; and so after my office again, at 12 at night home to bed.

14. Up; and after a while at the office, I abroad in several places; among other, to my booksellers and there spoke for

1. For the Admiral's Instructions, see above, iii. 24 & n. 1.

2. No such order has been found. Writing to Coventry on this day, Pepys expressed the suspicion that Cutler's news (given to Pepys as a secret) might be the 'forerunner of a tender': *Further Corr.*, p. 32. There was a shortage of canvas and prices rose (Pepys to Coventry, 2 March 1665: *Shorthand Letters*, p. 32), but imports from France continued to get through: *CSPD 1665–6*, p. 132. Pepys himself on 20 July 1665 was charged with the arrangements for importing canvas from St Malo: ib., *1664–5*, p. 483. Pepys was later to

point out (in a parliamentary debate 4 November 1675) the extent of the country's dependence on foreign supplies. Four-fifths, he said, came from abroad, and mostly from France as Vitry and Morlaix canvas: Grey, iii. 408.

3. Cf. above, p. 303, where Pepys reports speaking against the interest of Hugh Cholmley and Lawson, undertakers for the construction of the mole. Sandwich may have had in mind the possibility of being sent to Tangier as Governor: cf. above, p. 313. He was in any case aware that Lawson had the favour of Coventry and probably of the Duke of York.

several books against New Year's day, I resolving to lay out about 7 or 8*l*, God having given me some profit extraordinary of late. And bespoke also some plate, spoons, and forks. I pray God keep me from too great expenses, though*ᵃ* these will still be pretty good money. Then to the Change; and I home to dinner, where Creed (and Mr. Cæsare,[1] my boy's lute master, who plays endeed mighty finely); and after dinner I abroad, parting from Creed, and away to and fro, laying-out or preparing for laying-out more money, but I hope and resolve not to exceed therein. And tonight spoke for some fruit for the country for my father against Christmas; and where should I do it but at the pretty woman's that use to stand at the door in Fanchurch-street – I having a mind to know her.

So home and late at my office, evening reckonings with Shergoll, hoping to get money by that business;[2] and so away home to supper and to bed, not being very well through my taking cold of late and so troubled with some wind.

15. Called up very betimes by Mr. Cholmly, and with him a good while about some of his Tanger accounts. And discoursing of the condition of Tanger, he did give me the whole account of the difference between FitzGerald and Norwood; which were very high on both sides, but most imperious and base on Fitz.Gerald's.[3] And yet, through my Lord Fitzharding's

a repl. 'those'

---

1. Works for the lute by 'Mr. William Smegergill *alias* Caesar' appear in several of Playford's printed song-books. (E).

2. Shergoll was doorkeeper to the Navy Office; the nature of the 'business' has not been discovered. Doorkeepers were often responsible for buying candles, paper, quills etc., for the office, and there is a reference to a new supply of candles below, p. 346.

3. Fitzgerald had recently become Governor after Teviot's death, and was quarrelling with both his chief officers, Norwood and Bridges. They alleged that he had been at fault

in refusing to confirm their arrangements about the Portuguese houses in the town, made in the interregnum before his arrival. He claimed that it was only 'a dispute of some three or four words' which had no relation to the King's service. There were also, at about the same time, reports of quarrels caused by Fitzgerald's Catholicism. Pepys, writing to Sandwich (18 December), mentions these 'jarres' without specifying their causes: NMM, LBK/8, p. 141. Norwood succeeded Fitzgerald in the following February. See Routh, p. 91: John Davis, *Hist. 2nd Queen's Reg.*, i. 77; HMC, *Rawdon Hastings*, ii. 147.

means, the Duke of Yorke is led rather to blame Norwood and to speak that he should be called home, then be sensible of the other. He[1] is a creature of FitzHarding's, as a fellow that may be done with what he will; and himself,[2] certainly pretending to be Generall of the King's Armys when Monke dyeth, desires to have as few great or wise men in imployment as he can now; but such as he can put in and keep under, which he doth this coxcomb Fitz.Gerald.[3]

It seems, of all mankind there is no man so led by another as the Duke is by my Lord Muskerry and this FitzHarding. Insomuch, as when the King would have him to be Privy purse,[4] the Duke wept and said, "But, Sir, I must have your promise, if you will have my dear Charles from me, that if ever you have occasion for an army again, I may have him with me" – believing him to be the best commander of an army in the world. But Mr. Cholmly thinks, as all other men I meet with do, that he is a very ordinary fellow.

It is strange how the Duke also doth love naturally and affect the Irish above the English. He, of the company he carried with him to sea, took above two-thirds Irish and French.[5]

He tells me the King doth hate my Lord Chancellor. And that they, that is the King and my Lord Fitzharding, do laugh at him for a dull fellow;[6] and in all this business of the Duch war doth nothing by his advice, hardly consulting him. Only, he is a good minister in other respects, and the King cannot be without him; but above all, being the Dukes father-in-law, he is kept in; otherwise, Fitzharding were able to fling down two of him. This all the wise and grave lords see, and cannot help it but yield to it.

But he bemoans what the end of it may be, the King's being

1. Fitzgerald. Fitzharding had secured his appointment: above, iv. 116.

2. Fitzharding.

3. Clarendon refers to Fitzharding's 'insatiable ambition': *Life*, i. 388.

4. Fitzharding (then Sir Charles Berkeley) had received this appointment in October 1662: cf. above, iii. 227 & n. 2.

5. An exaggeration: the names of the officers (at the first muster, 16 November 1664) are given in C. Dalton, *Engl. army lists 1661–1714*, i. 42. But the number of Irish officers was inordinately high: cf. *CSPD 1670 Add.*, p. 684.

6. Cf. Clarendon, *Life*, i. 386+.

ruled by these men, as he hath been all along since his coming; to the razing all the strong-holds in Scotland[1] and giving liberty to the Irish in Ireland, whom Cromwell had settled all in one Corner – who are now able, and it is feared every day a massacre again among them.[2]

He being gone, I abroad to the carriers to see some things sent away to my father against Christmas; and I thence to Moore-fields, and there up and down to several houses to drink, to look for a place pour rancontrer la femme de je sais quoy against next Monday, but could meet none; but so to the Coffee-house, where great talk of the Comett seen in several places and among our men[a] at sea and by my Lord Sandwich, to whom I intend to write about it tonight.[3]

Thence home to dinner; and then to the office, where all the afternoon; and in the evening home to supper, and then to the office late, and so to bed.

This night[b] I begun to burn wax candles in my closet at the office, to try the charge and to see whether the smoke offends like that of tallow candles.

a repl. 'ships'   b repl. 'day'

---

1. The Scottish forts erected by Cromwell had been slighted in 1661–2 (following a Council order of 13 July 1661), so that the English garrisons could be withdrawn: *Reg. Privy Counc. Scot. 1661–4*, pp. ix–x, 5–7.

2. I.e. a repetition of the rising of 1641. The 'corner' was Connaught.

3. Since 7 December Sandwich had been making precise observations of the comet from his position at sea off Isle of Wight: Sandwich, pp. 157+. He later sent them to the Royal Society: Birch, ii. 13. A copy of Pepys's letter to him, dated this day, is in NMM, LBK/8, pp. 142–3; printed in *Further Corr.*, pp. 32–3. Pepys himself first saw the comet on 24 December, Evelyn on the 22nd or thereabouts. Mundy (v. 166–8) gives eyewitness descriptions from Cornwall. It was first observed in Spain on 7 November; its perihelion passage was on 24–5 November, and it was last seen on 10 March. (Dates according to the English calendar.) A conference was held in Paris in January 1665 to discuss comets: L. Thorndike, *Hist. Magic*, etc., viii. 323, 324, 327. Lists of contemporary descriptions are in Mundy, App., pp. 190–2; Philipp Carl, *Repertorium der cometen-astronomie*, pp. 72–6; see also BM, Add. 19526, f. 73v. See esp. *Philos Trans.*, iv. (1665–6), pp. 1069, 1071; Edmund Halley, *Synopsis of the astronomy of comets* (1705), pp. 16, 18; Rugge, ii, ff. 124v, 126v–127r; Also below, pp. 348, 352, 355–6, 357. vi. 48.

16. Up and by water to Deptford, thinking to have met la femme de Bagwell, but failed; and having done some business at the yard, I back again, it being a fine fresh morning to walk. Back again, Mr. Wayth walking with me to Halfway-house, talking about Mr. Castles fine knees lately delivered in – in which I am well informed that they are not as they should be to make them knees.[1] And I hope shall make good use of it to the King's service.

Thence home; and having dressed myself, to the Change and thence home to dinner. And so abroad by coach with my wife, and bought a looking-glass by the Old Exchange which costs me 5*l.* 5*s.* – and 6*s* for the hooks. A very fair glass.

So toward my cousin Scotts; but meeting my Lady Sandwiches coach, my wife turned back to fallow them, thinking they might, as they did, go to visit her; and I light, and to Mrs. Harman and there stayed and talked in her shop with her – and much pleased I am with her. We talked about Anth. Joyces giving over trade, and that he entends to live in lodgings, which is a very mad, foolish thing. She tells me she hears and believes it is because he, being now beginning to be called on offices, resolves not to take the new oath, he having formerly taken the Covenant or engagement.[2] But I think he doth very simply, and will endeavour for his wife's sake to advise them therein.

Thence to my cousin Scotts,[3] and there met my Cosen Roger Pepys and Mrs. Turner and The and Joyce – and prated all the while. And so with the Corps to church and heard a very fine sermon of the parson of the parish.[4] And so homeward with

1. These were knee-timbers foisted on the Board by a trick: they were cross-grained, being cut from the roots instead of the branches. See *Shorthand Letters*, pp. 7, 12; NWB, pp. 71, 812; Rawl. A 174, ff. 46–57, passim. Cf. above, p. 312.

2. Joyce (Pepys's cousin by marriage) was a tallow chandler. Pepys reports at 16 January 1666 that he was still planning to retire. Possibly it was the Fire which finally forced him out of business, for by 1666 he had become an innkeeper in Clerkenwell. In January 1668 he died after attempt-

ing to drown himself. The offices he was now trying to evade were probably parochial or livery-company offices. He had taken the oath to parliament in the Civil War (the Covenant, 1643), or the oath to the Commonwealth (the Engagement, 1649).

3. Her husband, Benjamin Scott, citizen and pewterer, of St Sepulchre's, Holborn, had died. In his will (of the 9th) he had left Pepys 20*s.* for a mourning ring.

4. William Bell.

them in their coach; but finding it too late to go home with me, I took another coach; and so home and after a while at my office, home to supper and to bed.

17. Up and to the office, where we sat all the morning. At noon, I to the Change and there, among others, had my first meeting with Mr. Lestrange, who hath endeavoured several times to speak with me – it is to get now and then some news of me, which I shall as I see cause give him.[1] He is a man of fine conversation I think; but I am sure, most courtly and full of compliment.

Thence home to dinner; and then came the looking-glass man to set up the looking-glass I bought yesterday in my dining-room, and very handsome it is.

So abroad by coach to White-hall; and there to the Committee of Tanger, and then the Fishing.

Mr. Povey did in discourse give me a rub about my late bill for money that I did get of him;[2] which vexed me and stuck in my mind all this evening, though I know very well how to cleare myself at the worst.

So home and to my office, where late, and then home to bed.

Mighty talk there is of this Comet that is seen a-nights;[3] and the King and Queen did sit up last night to see it, and did it seems. And tonight I thought to have done so too; but it is cloudy, and so no stars appear. But I will endeavour it.

Mr. Gray did tell me tonight for certain, that the Duch, as high as they seem, do begin to buckle; and that one man in this Kingdom did tell the King that he is offered 40000*l*[a] to make a peace, and others have been offered money also. It seems the taking of their Bourdeaux fleet thus arise from a printed gazette

a repl. '20000*l*'

---

1. Roger L'Estrange between 1663 and 1666 was responsible for the two official newspapers (the only papers published): *The Intelligencer* and *The Newes.* (They were identical, but came out on Mondays and Thursdays respectively.) For his methods of gathering news, see G.

Kitchin, *Sir R. L'Estrange*; P. Fraser, *The intelligence of the secretaries of state ... 1660–88.* Pepys's friend Moore was later the means of giving him news of a naval battle: below, vi. 128.

2. See above, p. 340 & n. 2.
3. See above, p. 346 & n. 3.

of the Duch's boasting of fighting and having beaten the English;[1] in confidence whereof (it coming to Bourdeaux), all the fleet comes out and so falls into our hands.[2]

18. *Lords day.* To church; where God forgive me, I spent most of my time in looking my new *Morena*[3] at the other side of the church, an acquaintance of Pegg Pen's. So home to dinner and then to my chamber to read Ben. Johnsons *Cateline*,[4] a very excellent piece. And so to church again; and thence we met at the office to hire ships, being in great haste and having sent for several maisters of Shipps to come to us. Then home, and there Mr. Andrews and Hill came and we sung finely. And by and by, Mr. Fuller the parson, and supped with me, he and a friend of his; but my music friends would not stay supper. At and after supper, Mr. Fuller and I [told] many stories of apparitions and delusions thereby, and I out with my stories of Tom Mallard.[5] He gone, I a little to my office and then to prayers and to bed.

19. Going to bed betimes last night, we waked betimes. And from our people's being forced to take the key to go out to light a candle, I was very angry and begun to find fault with my wife for not commanding her servants as she ought. Thereupon, she giving me some cross answer, I did strike her over her left eye such a blow, as the poor wretch did cry out and was in great pain; but yet her spirit was such as to endeavour to bite and scratch me. But I cogging with her, made her leave crying, and sent for butter and parsley, and friends presently one with another; and I up, vexed at my heart to think what I had done, for she was forced to lay a poultice or something to her eye all day, and is black – and the people of the house observed it.

But I was forced to rise; and up and with Sir J. Mennes to White-hall, and there we waited on the Duke. And among

---

1. Cf. *Hollandtze Mercurius*, November 1664, p. 177.

2. See above, p. 326 & n. 2.

3. Brunette; she appears to have been Mrs Horsely, the 'pretty black woman' of 29 May 1666.

4. This tragedy was acted and published in 1611; the PL has a copy in the 1692 edition of Jonson's *Works*:

PL 2645. (A). Pepys later set a Catiline soliloquy to recitative music: PL 2803, ff. 108*v*–111*v*. (E).

5. Mallard (Maylard) appears to have been a professional musician, and in 1665 was in Sandwich's service. These stories of his do not appear in the diary.

other things, Mr. Coventry took occasion to vindicate himself before the Duke and us, being all there, about the choosing of Taylor for Harwich.[1] Upon which the Duke did clear him, and did tell us that he did expect that after he had named a man, none of us shall then oppose or find fault with that man. But if we had anything to say, we ought to say it before he had chose him. Sir G. Carteret thought himself concerned, and endeavoured to clear himself. And by and by Sir W. Batten did speak, knowing himself guilty; and did confess that being pressed by the Council, he did say what he did, that he was accounted a fanatique; but did not know that at that time he had been appointed by his Royal Highness – to which the Duke [replied] that it was impossible but he must know that he had appointed him; and so it did appear that the Duke did mean all this while Sir W. Batten. So by and by we parted; and Mr. Coventry did privately tell me that he did this day take this occasion to mention the business, to give the Duke an opportunity of speaking his mind to Sir W. Batten in this business – of which I was heartily glad.

Thence home; and not finding Bagwell's[a] wife as I expected, I to the Change and there walked up and down, and then home; and she being come, I bid her go and stay at Mooregate for me; and after going up to my wife (whose eye is very bad, but she in very good temper to me); and after dinner, I to the place and walked round the fields again and again; but not finding her, I to the Change and there found her waiting for me and took her away and to an alehouse, and there I made much of her; and then away thence and to another, and endeavoured to caress her; but elle ne vouloit pas, which did vex me but I think it was chiefly not having a good easy place to do it upon. So we broke up and parted; and I to the office, where we sat hiring of ships an hour or two; and then to my office and thence (with Captain Taylor home ⟨to my house⟩) to give him instructions and some notice of what, to his great satisfaction, had happened today – which I do because I hope his coming into this office will a little cross Sir W. Batten and may do me good. He gone, I to supper with my wife, very pleasant; and then a little to my office and to

a s.h.

1. See above, p. 326 & n. 1.

bed – my mind, God forgive me, too much running upon what
I can faire avec la femme de Bagwell*ᵃ* demain – having promised
to go to Deptford and à aller à sa maison avec son mari when I
come thither.

20. Up and walked to Deptford, where after doing something at the yard, I walked, without being observed, with Bagwell*ᵇ*
home to his house and there was very kindly used, and the poor
people did get a dinner for me in their fashion – of which I also
eat very well. After dinner I found occasion of sending him
abroad; and then alone avec elle je tentoy à faire ce que je
voudrais, et contre sa force je le faisoy, bien que pas à mon
contentment. By and by, he coming back again, I took leave
and walked home; and then there to dinner, where Dr. Fayr-
brother came to see me, and Luellin; we dined, and I to the
office, leaving them – where we sat all the afternoon, and I late
at the office. To supper and to the office again very late; then
home to bed.

21. Up; and after evening reckonings to this day with Mr.
Bridges the linen-draper for Callicos, I out to Doctors Comons,
where by agreement my cousin Roger and I did meet my Cosen
Dr. Tom Pepys, and there a great many and some high words
on both sides;[1] but I must confess I was troubled: first, to find
my cousin Roger such a simple but well-meaning man as he
is. Next, to think that my father, out of folly and vainglory,
should now and then (as by their words I gather) be speaking
how he had set up his son Tom with his goods and house: and
now these words are brought against him, I fear to the depriving
him of all the profit the poor man intended to make of the lease
of his house and sale of his own goods. I intend to make a
quiet end if I can with the Doctor, being a very foul-tongued
fool,[2] and of great inconvenience to be at difference with such a
one, that will*ᶜ* make that base noise about it that he will.

Thence, very much vexed to find myself*ᵈ* so much troubled

a s.h.   *b* l.h.   *c* followed by blot   *d* repl. 'them'

1. For this dispute, see above, p.   Pepys's father in a letter of 10 July:
85 & n. 1, pp. 249–50 & n.   above, p. 225, n. 2.
2. Cf. the similar phrase used by

about other men's matters, I to Mrs. Turner in Salsbury[a] Court, and with her a little, and carried her (the porter staying for me) our Eagle,[1] which she desired the other day; and we were glad to be rid of her, she fouling our house of office mightily – they are much pleased with her; and thence I home, and after dinner to the office, where Sir W Rider and Cutler came; and in dispute, I very high with them against their demands; I hope to no hurt to myself (for I was very plain with them to the best of my reason): so they gone, I home to supper;[b] then to the office again, and so home to bed.

My Lord Sandwich this day writes me word that he hath seen (at Portsmouth) the Comett, and says it is the most extraordinary thing that ever he saw.

22. Up and betimes to my office and then out to several places. Among others, to Holborne to have spoke with one Mr. Underwood about some English Hemp[2] – he lies against grays Inn. Thereabouts, I to a barbers shop to have my hair cut. And there met with a copy of verses, mightily commended by some gentleman there, of my Lord Mordants in excuse of his going to sea – this late expedition, with the Duke of York. But Lord, they are but sorry things; only, a Lord made them.[3]

Thence to the Change; and there among the merchants, I hear fully the news of our being beaten to dirt at Guiny by De Ruyter with his fleet. The perticulars, as much as by Sir G Carteret afterward I heard, I have said in a letter to my Lord Sandwich this day at Portsmouth[4] – it being most wholly to the utter ruine

a MS. l.h. 'Salbs.'   *b* MS. 'suffer'

---

1. This is the only mention of this pet.

2. For home-grown hemp, see above, iv. 259 & n. 4. Francis Underwood had in 1661 with others taken a lease of several thousands of acres of reclaimed fen in the Bedford Level, where hemp might be grown: *CTB*, i. 224.

3. Mordaunt went to sea in November and returned on 7 December – the dates are established by the dates of the prayers for him which his wife recorded in her diary: *The diarie of Elizabeth Viscountess Mordaunt* (ed. Earl of Roden), pp. 68, 72. The verses have not been traced. Pepys has a scathing reference to him as a good-for-nothing gentleman reformado in *Tangier Papers*, p. 120.

4. Pepys to Sandwich, 22 December: NMM, LBK/8, pp. 143–4 (copy in Hewer's hand); partially printed in *Further Corr.*, pp. 33–4.

of our Royall Company, and reproach and shame to the whole nation, as well as justification to them, in their doing wrong to no man as to his private [property]; only take whatever is found to belong to the Company, and nothing else.¹

Dined at the Dolphin, Sir G. Carteret, Sir J. Mennes, Sir W. Batten, and I, with Sir Wm. Boreman and Sir Theoph. Bidulph and others, Commissioners of the Sewers, about our place below to lay masts in.²

But coming a little too soon, I out again and took boat down to Redriffe, and just*a* in time, within two minutes, and saw the new Vessell of Sir Wm. Petty's lanched, the King and Duke being there. It swims and looks finely, and I believe will do well. The name I think is *Twilight*,³ but I do not know certainly, coming away back immediately to dinner – where a great deal of good discourse and Sir G Carterets discourse of this Guinny business, with great displeasure at the loss of our honour there – and doth now confess that that trade brought all these troubles upon us between the Duch and us.

Thence to the office and there sat late; then I to my office and there till 12 at night; and so home to bed, weary.

23. Up and to my office. Then came by appointment Cosen Tom Trice to me, and I paid him the 20*l* remaining due to him upon the bond of 100*l* given him by agreement, November 1663, to end the difference between us about my aunts, his mother's, money.⁴ And here, being willing to know the worst,

a repl. 'but'

---

1. In October and December de Ruyter had attacked the British forts on the W. African coasts, utterly undoing the work of Holmes's expedition. In the letter Pepys told Sandwich that the company had lost not only its trade but also possessions to the value of £100,000, and was left saddled with debts to the same amount. ''Tis hard to say whether this news be received with more anger, or shame, but there is reason enough for both.'

2. For Commissions of Sewers, see above, iv. 46, n. 1.

3. It was the *Experiment*, the third of Petty's double-keeled ships. In his letter to Sandwich of this date, Pepys described the launch, and added: 'Wagers are layd of all sizes in her defence' (NMM, LBK /8, p. 143). See Evelyn; Marquess of Lansdowne, *The Double-bottom*, pp. 101–2.

4. See above, iv. 351, 384.

I told him, "I hope now there is nothing remaining between you and I of future dispute;" "No," says he, "nothing at all that I know of, but only a small matter of about 20 or 30s that my father Pepys¹ received for me, of rent due to me in the country – which I will in a day or two bring you an account of;" and so we parted.

Dined at home upon a good Turkey which Mr. Sheply² sent us. Then to the office all the afternoon.

Mr. Cutler and others coming to me about business, I hear that the Dutch have prepared a fleet to go the back way to the Streights; where without*a* doubt they will master our fleet.³ This, put to that of Guiny, makes me fear them mightily, and certainly they are a most wise people – and careful of their business. The King of France, they say, doth declare himself obliged to defend them, and lays claim by his Embassador to the wines we have taken from the Duch Bourdeaux-men.⁴ And more, it is doubted whether the Swede will be our friend or no. Pray God deliver us out of these troubles.

This day Sir W. Batten sent, and afterward spoke to me, to have me and my wife come and dine with them on Monday next – which is a mighty condescension in them, and for some great reason I am sure; or else it pleases God, by my late care of business, to make me more considerable even with*b* them then I am sure they would willingly own me to be. God make me thankful and careful to preserve myself so – for I am sure they hate me, and it is hope or fear that makes them flatter me.

It being a bright night, which it hath not been a great while, I purpose to endeavour to be called in the morning to see the Comett; though I fear we shall not see it, because it rises at the highest but 16 degrees, and then the houses will hinder us.

a repl. 'doubtless'   *b* repl. 'them'

---

1. Trice was a step-son of the late Robert Pepys of Brampton.

2. Sandwich's steward at Hinchingbrooke.

3. Rumours were strong that the Dutch would slip through the English guard in the Channel and sail by the north of Scotland to get to either the Mediterranean or India: cf. above, p. 332. In the Mediterranean England had only a handful of ships under Allin. The attempt was not, however, made, the Dutch preferring to spend the winter in advancing their preparations for a spring campaign.

4. See above, p. 348–9.

24. Having sat up all night, to past*a* 2 a-clock this morning, our porter, being appointed, comes and tells us that the Bell-man tells him that the star is seen upon Tower-hill. So I, that had been all night setting in order all my old papers in*b* my chamber, did leave off all; and my boy and I to Tower hill, it being a most fine bright moonshine night and a great frost, but no Comett to be seen; so after running once round the Hill, I and Tom, we home and then to bed.

Rose about 9 a-clock; and then to the office, where sitting all the morning. At noon to the Change to the Coffee-house, and there heard Sir Rd. Ford tell the whole story of our defeat at Guinny – wherein our men are guilty of the most horrid cowardize and perfidiousness, as he says and tells it, that ever Englishmen were. Captain Raynolds, that was the only commander of any of the King's ships there, was shot at by De Ruyter, with a bloody*c* flag flying. He, instead of opposing (which endeed had been to no purpose, but only to maintain honour), did poorly go on board himself to ask what De Ruter*d* would have; and so yielded to whatever Ruyter would desire.[1] The King and Duke are highly vexed at it, it seems, and the business deserves it.

Thence home to dinner and then abroad to buy some things; and among others, to my bookseller's and there saw several books I spoke for, which are finely bound and good books, to my great content.

So home and to my office, where late. This evening, I being informed, did look and saw the Comett, which is now, whether worn away or no I know not, but appears not with a tail; but only is larger and duller then any other star, and is come to rise betimes and to make a great arch, and is gone quite to a new

a MS. 'past a'   *b* repl. 'at'   *c* repl. 'fl'-
        d l.h. repl. s.h. 'he'

---

1. Jacob Reynolds commanded the *Great Gift*, the only warship on the station, at Cape Verde. It appears that instead of unloading their cargoes at the approach of the Dutch – for there was time enough – and making for the shelter of the forts, the merchantmen and the man-of-war (being 'infatuate and disani-mated') sent to ask de Ruyter what he demanded of them. The Dutch were careful to do nothing to the King's ship. Secretary Morice to Winchilsea, 7 February 1665 (HMC, *Finch*, p. 353).

place in the heavens then it was before[1] – but I hope, in a clearer night something more will be seen.   So home to[a] bed.

25.   *Lords day and Christmas=Day.*   Up (my wife's eye being ill still of the blow I did in a passion give her on Monday last) to church alone – where Mr. Mills, a good sermon.   To dinner at home, where very pleasant with my wife and family.[b]   After dinner, I to Sir W. Batten's and there received so much good usage (as I have of late done) from him and my Lady, obliging me and my wife, according to promise, to come and dine with them tomorrow with our neighbours, that I was in pain all the day, and night too after,[c] to know how to order the business of my wife's not going – and by discourse receive fresh instances of Sir J Minnes's folly in complaining to Sir G. Carteret of Sir W. Batten and me for some family offences; such as my having of a stopcock to keep the water from them – which vexes me, but it would more, but that[d] Sir G. Carteret knows him very well. Thence to the French church; but coming too late, I returned and to Mr. Rawlinson's church, where I heard a good sermon of one that I remember was at Pauls with me, his name Maggett.[2] And very great store of fine women there is in this church, more then I know anywhere else about us.

So home and to my chamber, looking over and setting in order my papers and books; and so to supper, and then to prayers and to bed.

26.   Up and with Sir W. Penn to White-hall, and there with the rest did our usual business before the Duke; and then with Sir W. Batten back and to his house, where I by sickness excused my wife's coming to them today.   Thence I to the Coffee-house, where much good discourse; and all the opinion now is that the Duch will avoid fighting with us at home but do all the hurt

a   repl. 'to prayers and'   b   repl. 'my'   c   repl. 'to'
                          d   MS. 'that but'

---

1. See above, p. 346 & n. 3.
2. Richard Meggott (once scholar of St Paul's), Rector of St Olave's,

Southwark; later Canon of Windsor and Dean of Winchester. The church was St Dionis Backchurch.

they can to us abroad – which it may be they may for a while; but that I think cannot support them long.

Thence to Sir W. Batten, where Mr. Coventry and all our families here, women and all, and Sir R. Ford and his. And a great feast – and good discourse and merry. I here all the afternoon and evening till late; only stepped in to see my wife. Then to my office to enter my day's work; and so home to bed, where my people and wife innocently at cards, very merry. And I to bed, leaving them to their sport and blindman's buff.

27. My people came to bed after their sporting, at 4 a-clock in the morning. I up at 7, and to Deptford and Woolwich in a galley, the Duke calling to me out of the barge, in which the King was with him going down the River, to know whither I was going; I told him to Woolwich. But was troubled afterward I should say no farther, being in a galley, lest he think me too profuse in my journys.

Did several businesses; and then back again by 2 a-clock to Sir J. Mennes to dinner by appointment, where all yesterday's company but Mr. Coventry, who could not come. Here merry; and after an hour's chat, I down to the office, where busy late, and then home to supper and to bed. The Comett appeared again tonight, but duskishly.

I went to bed, leaving my wife and all her folks, and Will also, ⟨28.⟩ to come to make Christmas gamballs tonight. I waked in the morning about 6 a-clock, and my wife not come to bed. I lacked a pot but there was none, and bitter cold, so was forced to rise and piss in the chimny, and to bed again. Slept a little longer, and then hear my people coming up and so I rose; and my wife to bed at 8 a-clock in the morning, which vexed me a little, but I believe there was no hurt in it all, but only mirth – therefore took no notice.

I abroad with Sir W. Batten to the Council-Chamber, where all of us to discourse about the way of measuring ships and the freight fit to give for them by the Tun – where it was strange methought, to hear so poor discourses among the Lords themselfs: and most of all, to see how a little empty matter, delivered gravely by Sir W. Penn, was taken mighty well, though nothing in the earth to the purpose.[1]   But clothes, I perceive more and more every day, is a great matter.   Thence home with Sir W. Batten by coach; and I home to dinner, finding my wife still in bed.   After dinner, abroad; and among other things, visited my Lady Sandwich and was there with her and the young ladies playing at Cards till night; then home and to my office late; then home to bed – leaving my wife and people up to more sports, but without any great satisfaction[a] to myself therein.

29.   Up and to the office, where we sat all the morning. Then, whereas I should have gone and dined with Sir W. Penn (and the rest of the officers at his house), I pretended to dine with my Lady Sandwich; and so home, where I dined well and begun to wipe and clean my books in my chamber, in order to the settling of my papers and things there throughly; and then to the office, where all the afternoon sitting; and in the evening home to supper and then to my work again.

30.   Lay very long in bed with wife, it being very cold and my wife very full of a resolution to keep within doors, not so much as to go to church or see my Lady Sandwich before Easter next – which I am willing[b] enough to, though I seem the contrary.   This and other talk kept me a-bed till almost 10 a-clock.   Then up and made an end of looking over all my papers and books and taking everything out of my chamber to have all made clean.   At noon dined; and after dinner, forth to several places to pay away money to clear myself in all the world; and among other, paid my bookseller 6*l* for books I had from him this day, and the silversmiths 22*l*. 18*s*. 00*d* for spoons, forks, and sugar box.   And being well pleased with seeing my

a   repl. 'pleasure'   b   repl. 'unwilling'

---

1. The measuring of ships by tonnage was a difficult matter, on which shipwrights often differed among themselves, as well as from their own Company and from the Navy Board.   Pepys claimed in 1683 that the memorandum he now wrote formed the basis of a Council order of 2 January 1665, effective for over a generation: *Naval Minutes*, pp. 210–11; BM, Add. 36782, ff. 23–4. Cf. below, 9 March 1666; 16 January 1668.

business done to my mind, as to my meeting with people and having my books ready for me – I home and to my office and there did business late; and then home to supper, prayers, and to bed.

31. At the office all the morning, and after dinner there again; despatched first my letters, and then to my accounts, not of the month but of the whole year also, and was at it till past 12 at night – it being bitter cold; but yet I was well satisfied with my work and, above all, to find myself, by the great blessing of God, worth 1349*l* – by which, as I have spent very largely, so I have laid up above 500*l* this year above what I was worth this day twelvemonth. The Lord make me for ever thankful to his holy name for it.

Thence home to eat a little, and so to bed. As soon as ever the clock struck one, I kissed my wife in the kitchen by the fire-side, wishing her a merry New year, observing that I believe I*ᵃ* was the first proper wisher of it this year, for I did it as soon as ever the clock struck one.

So ends the old year, I bless God with great joy to me; not only from my having made so good a year of profit, as having spent 420*l* and laid up 540*l* and upward.

But I bless God, I never have been in so good plight as to my health in so very cold weather as this is, nor indeed in any hot weather these ten years, as I am at this day and have been these four or five months. But am at a great loss to know whether it be my Hare's foote,[1] or taking every morning of a pill of Turpentine, or my having left off the wearing of a gowne.

My family is my wife, in good health, and happy with her –

a repl. 'we'

---

1. A charm worn against colic: see below, vi. 17. The practice may have originated from the use, according to the Paracelsan doctrine of 'signatures', of the herb haresfoot, which, when made into a glyster with honey and salt, 'purgeth the guts of slime and filth': A. Read, *Most excellent . . . medicines* (1652), p. 247. Also used for rheumatism: William G. Black, *Folk Medicine*, p. 154.

her woman Mercer, a pretty modest quiet maid – her chamber-maid Besse – her cook-maid Jane – the little girle Susan, and my boy which I have had about half a year, Tom Edwards, which I took from the King's Chappell. And a pretty and loving quiet family I have as any man in England.

My credit in the world and my office grows daily, and I am in good esteem with everybody I think.

My troubles of my uncles estate pretty well over. But it comes to be but of little profit to us, my father being much supported by my purse.

But great vexations remain upon my father and me from my Brother Tom's death and ill condition, both to our disgrace and discontent – though no great reason for either.

Public matters are all in a hurry about a Duch warr. Our preparations great. Our provocations against them great; and after all our presumption, we are now afeared as much of them as we lately contemned them.

Everything else in the State quiet, blessed be God. My Lord Sandwich at sea with the fleet at Portsmouth – sending some about to cruise for taking of ships, which we have done to a great number.

This Christmas I judged it fit to look over all my papers and books, and to tear all that I found either boyish or not to be worth keeping, or fit to be seen if it should please God to take me away suddenly. Among others, I found these two or three notes which I thought fit to keep –

Age of my Grandfather's Children.[1]

Thomas – 1595.
Mary. March. 16. 1597.
Edith. Octob. 11. 1599.
John, (my father). January. 14. 1601./

My father and mother marryed at Newington in Surry. Octob. 15. 1626.

1. All named here were alive in 1664. Mary Pepys's married name is unknown; Edith was the widow of John Bell. Pepys uses old-style year-dates.

Theyr Children's ages.[1]

Mary.	July. 24. 1627. – – *mort.*	
Paulina.	Sept. 18. 1628. – – *mort.*	
Esther.	March. 27. 1630. – – *mort.*	
John.	January. 10. 1631. – – *mort.*	
Samuel.	Febr. 23. 1632.	

《Went to reside in Magd. Coll. Camb., and
did put on my gown first. March. 5. 165$\frac{0}{1}$.》

Thomas.	June. 18. 1634. – – *mort.*	
Sarah.	August. 25. 1635. – – *mort.*	
Jacob.	May. 1. 1637. – – *mort.*	
Robert.	Nov. 18. 1638. – – *mort.*	
Paulina.	Octobr. 18. 1640.	
John.	Novemb. 26. 1641. – – *mort.*	

Decembr. 31. 1664./

Charmes,[2] *for.*

1. *Stenching of Blood.*/

Sanguis mane in te,
Sicut Christus fecit[a] *in se;*
Sanguis mane in tuâ venâ,

a repl. 'ma'-

---

1. I.e. the children of Pepys's parents. Of those older than Pepys, Mary had died at thirteen years of age, Paulina at three, Esther at one and John at eight. Of those younger, Tom had recently died in 1664; Sarah died at six, Jacob in infancy, Robert some time before the diary opens. Pepys added the word 'mort.' after the close of the diary at least in the case of his brother John, who died in 1677. He did not add it after the names of Paulina and of his father, both of whom died in 1680. All his annotations may therefore have been made between March 1677 and October 1680. In this list Pepys again uses old-style year-dates.

2. For charms and incantations, see Reginald Scot, *Discoverie of witchcraft* (ed. Nicholson), pp. 184+; J. Hastings (ed.), *Encycl. religion and ethics*, iii. 324+; William G. Black, *Folk Medicine*. They were still sold to Irish emigrants as they left Queenstown in the 1880s: Black, p. 83. Pepys's samples are among the commonest. They could be recited as prayers or worn as amulets.

Sicut Christus in suâ pœnâ;
Sanguis mane fixus,
Sicut Christus quando fuit Crucifixus./[1]

2. *A Thorne.*[2]

Jesus, that was of a virgin born
Was pricked both with nail and thorn;
It neither wealed, nor belled, rankled, nor boned;
In the name of Jesus no more shall[a] this.

Or thus[3] –

Christ was of a virgin born,
And he was pricked with a thorn;
And it did neither bell, nor swell;
And I trust in Jesus this never will.

3. *A Cramp.*[4]

Cramp be thou faintless,
As our Lady was sinless,
When she bare Jesus.

4. *A Burning.*[5]

There came three Angells out of the East;
The one brought fire, the other brought frost –
Out fire; in frost.

In the name of the Father and Son and Holy Ghost. Amen./

a   symbol smudged

---

1. In the same words: Scot, op. cit., p. 222; in similar words (from Cornwall); Black, op. cit., p. 80.
2. Black, p. 82 (in similar words).
3. Black, p. 82 (in almost identical words).
4. J. Brand, *Pop. Antiq.* (ed. Hazlitt), i. 153 (in same words, N. country).
5. Black, pp. 80-1 (in similar words).

APPENDIX

[Dr Burnet's prescription and advice[1]]

Dr. Burnetts advice to mee.
The Originall is fyled among my letters.

Take of the Rootes of Marsh=Mallows foure ounces, of Cumfry, of Liquorish of each two ounces, of the Flowers of St. John's Wort two Handsfull, of the Leaves of Plantan, of Ale=hoofe of each three handfulls, of Selfeheale, of Red roses of each one Hand=full, of Cynament, of Nutmegg of each halfe an Ounce; Beate them well, then powre upon them one Quart of old Rhenish wine and about Six houres after strayne it and Clarify it with the white of an Egge; and with a sufficient quantity of Sugar, Boyle it to the Consistence of a Syrrup and reserve it for use.

Dissolve one spoonefull of this Syrrup in every draught of Ale or beere you Drinke.

—————

Morning & evening swallow the Quantity of an hazle=nutt of Cyprus Terebintine.[2]

—————

If you are bound or have a fitt of the Stone eate an ounce of Cassia[3] newly drawne, from the poynt of a Knife.

—————

Old Canary or Malaga wine you may drinke to three or four glasses, but noe new wine, & what wine you drinke lett it bee at Meales./

1. See above, p. 194. This memo-randum is written in Pepys's l.h. on one side of a sheet of paper. The punctuation and capitalisation are his own.

2. A variety of turpentine, often known as Chian.

3. A coarse and cheap variety of cinnamon.

LONDON
IN THE SIXTEEN-SIXTIES
Western half (omitting most minor streets & alleys)

Scale of yards

0   220   440   660   880

Area of Great Fire

To Ham...

Tyburn
Gibbet .... To Oxford ....

Burlington House
Clarendon House
Berkeley House
Piccadilly
St Jam Field (being devel...

Berkshire House

To Knightsbridge & Kensington

St James Palace

Goring House

To Chelsea

Petty F...

1   St Martin-in-the-Fields
2   Wallingford House
3   The Cockpit, Whitehall
4   Axe Yard
5   St Margaret's Ch, Westminster
6   The Gate House, Westminster
7   Westminster Hall
8   The King's House, Drury Lane
9   Maypole in the Strand
10   St Clement Danes Ch, Strand
11   The Duke's Ho., Lincoln's Inn Fields
12   Gaming House in Bell Yard
13   Temple Bar
14   St Dunstan-in-the-West
15   St Andrew's Ch, Holborn

Map prepared by the late Professor T. F. Reddaway

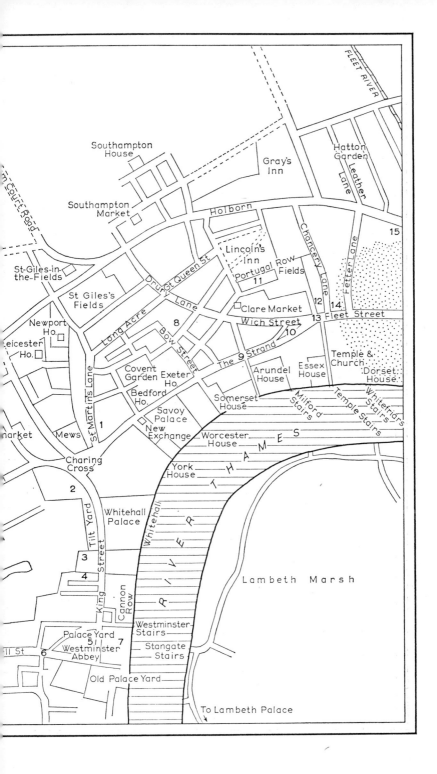

FLEET RIVER

Southampton House

Gray's Inn

Hatton Garden

Leather Lane

Southampton Market

Holborn

Chancery Lane

Lincoln's Inn

Fetter Lane

15

Portugal Row

Fields

11

St-Giles-in-the-Fields

St Giles's Fields

Drury Queen St

Clare Market

12

14

Newport Ho.

Long Acre

8

Wich Street

13 Fleet Street

Leicester Ho.

Bow Street

10

The 9 Strand

Temple & Church

Covent Garden

Exeter Ho.

Arundel House

Essex House

Dorset House

St Martins Lane

Bedford Ho.

Somerset House

Milford Stairs

Temple Stairs

Whitefriars Stairs

1

Savoy Palace

New Exchange

Worcester House

market

Mews

Charing Cross

York House

T   H   A   M   E   S

2

R

Whitehall Palace

Tilt Yard

Whitehall

I

V

3

E

Lambeth Marsh

4

King Street

Cannon Row

R

Palace Yard

Westminster Stairs

5

7

ll St

6

Westminster Abbey

Stangate Stairs

Old Palace Yard

To Lambeth Palace

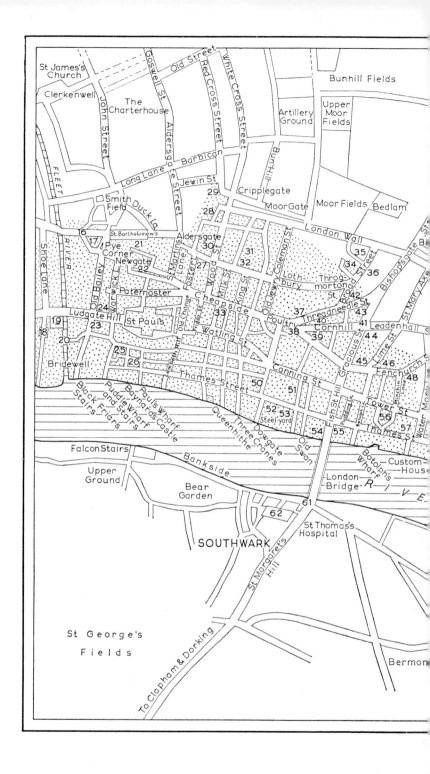

St James's
Church

Clerkenwell

St George's
Fields

St James's Church

John Street
Goswell St
Old Street
Red Cross Street
White Cross Street

The
Charterhouse

Aldersgate Street
Long Lane
Barbican
Jewin St

Bunhill Fields

Artillery
Ground

Upper
Moor
Fields

Cripplegate
29
MoorGate
28

Moor Fields
Bedlam

London Wall

FLEET
RIVER
Shoe Lane
Old Bailey
Fleet Ditch

Smith
Field

Duck La.
St. Bartholomew's

6
17
Pye
Corner
21
Newgate
22
Paternoster
24
Ludgate Hill
23
19
18
20
Bridewell
25
26

Aldersgate
30
27
31
32

Maiden Lane
Foster Lane
Milk St
Wood St
Bread St
Old Change
Cheapside
33
Watling St
St Pauls
Thames Street
Pauls Wharf
Baynards Castle
Puddle Wharf and Stairs
Black Friars Stairs
Bankside

Bunhill

Coleman St
Lothbury
Throgmorton St.
35
34
36

Bishopsgate Street
St Mary Axe

Jewry
Poultry
37
38
39
Cornhill
40
41
42
43
44
45
46
48
Leadenhall St
Lime St
Fenchurch
Minchin Lane

Threadneedle St
Gracious St
Fish St Hill
Pudding La
St Dunstan's La

50
51
52 53
Steel yard
Three Cranes
Queenhithe
Dowgate
54 55
Old Swan
Canning St
56
Tower St
57
Thames St
Water Lane

Falcon Stairs
Upper
Ground
Bear
Garden
Botolph's Wharf
Custom-House
London Bridge
RIVE
61
62
St Thomas's
Hospital
SOUTHWARK
St Margaret's Hill

To Clapham & Dorking

Bermon

LONDON

IN THE SIXTEEN-SIXTIES

Eastern half (omitting most minor streets & alleys)

Scale of yards

```
0      220      440      660      880
```

Area of Great Fire

16 Holborn Conduit
17 St Sepulchre's Ch.
18 Salisbury Court
19 St Bride's Church
20 Bridge in Bridewell
21 Christ Ch. Newgate
22 Newgate Market
23 Ludgate
24 St Martin's Ch.
25 The Wardrobe
26 Doctors' Commons
27 Goldsmiths' Hall
28 Barber Surgeons' Hall
29 St Giles, Cripplegate
30 Haberdashers' Hall
31 Guildhall
32 St Lawrence Jewry
33 St Mary le Bow
34 Dutch Ch. Austin Friars
35 Treasury Office, Navy
36 Gresham College
37 The Post Office, 1666
38 Stocks Market

39 The Great Coffee House
40 Royal Exchange
41 Cornhill Conduit
42 French Church
43 Merchant Taylors' Hall
44 Leadenhall Market
45 St Dionis Backchurch
46 The Mitre, Fenchurch St
47 St Katherine Cree
48 Clothworkers' Hall
49 St Olave's Ch. Hart St
50 Skinners' Hall, Dowgate Hill
51 St Lawrence Poultney
52 All Hallows the Great
53 All Hallows the Less
54 Fishmongers' Hall
55 St Magnus's Church
56 St Dunstan in the East
57 Trinity House
58 All Hallows, Barking
59 Navy Office
60 St Katherine's by the Tower
61 The Bear at the Bridge Foot
62 St Mary Overie (now
    Southwark Cath.)

To Colchester

Whitechapel

To Ratcliff

Petticoat Lane

Ditch

Aldgate

Minories

Goodman's Fields

Victualling Office

The Tower

East Smithfield

60

Iron Gate Stairs

T H A M E S

Pasture Grounds

Wapping Church

To Ratcliff & Limehouse

Sir William Warren's shipyard

To Deptford, Woolwich & Chatham

Rotherhithe Church

Map prepared by the late Professor T. F. Reddaway

SELECT LIST OF PERSONS

ADMIRAL, the: James, Duke of York, Lord High Admiral of England

ALBEMARLE, 1st Duke of (Lord Monke): Captain-General of the Kingdom

ARLINGTON, 1st Earl of (Sir Henry Bennet): Secretary of State

ASHLEY, 1st Baron (Sir Anthony Ashley Cooper, later 1st Earl of Shaftesbury): Chancellor of the Exchequer

ATTORNEY-GENERAL: Sir Geoffrey Palmer

BACKWELL, Edward: goldsmith–banker

BAGWELL, Mrs: Pepys's mistress; wife of ship's carpenter

BALTY: Balthasar St Michel; brother-in-law; minor naval official

BATTEN, Sir William: Surveyor of the Navy

BETTERTON (Baterton), Thomas: actor in the Duke's Company

BIRCH, Jane: maidservant

BOOKSELLER, my: Joseph Kirton (until the Fire)

BOWYER, my father: Robert Bowyer, senior Exchequer colleague

BRISTOL, 2nd Earl of: politician

BROUNCKER (Bruncker, Brunkard, Brunkerd), 2nd Viscount: Commissioner of the Navy

BUCKINGHAM, 2nd Duke of: politician

CARKESSE (Carcasse), James: clerk in the Ticket Office

CARTERET, Sir George: Treasurer of the Navy and Vice-Chamberlain of the King's Household

CASTLEMAINE, Barbara, Countess of: the King's mistress

CHANCELLOR, the: see 'Lord Chancellor'

CHILD, the: usually Edward, eldest son and heir of Sandwich

CHOLMLEY, Sir Hugh: courtier, engineer

COCKE, George: hemp merchant

COFFERER, the: William Ashburnham

COMPTROLLER (Controller), the: the Comptroller of the Navy (Sir Robert Slingsby, 1660–1; Sir John Mennes, 1661–71)

COVENTRY, Sir William: Secretary to the Lord High Admiral, 1660–7; Commissioner of the Navy

CREED, John: household and naval servant of Sandwich

CREW, 1st Baron: Sandwich's father-in-law; Presbyterian politician

CUTTANCE, Sir Roger: naval captain

DEANE, Anthony: shipwright

DEB: *see* 'Willet, Deborah'

DOWNING, Sir George: Exchequer official, Envoy-Extraordinary to the United Provinces and secretary to the Treasury Commission

DUKE, the: usually James, Duke of York, the King's brother; occasionally George (Monck), Duke of Albemarle

DUKE OF YORK: *see* 'James, Duke of York'

EDWARD, Mr: Edward, eldest son and heir of Sandwich

EDWARDS, Tom: servant

EVELYN, John: friend, *savant*; Commissioner of Sick and Wounded

FENNER, Thomas (m. Katherine Kite, sister of Pepys's mother): uncle; ironmonger

FERRER(s), Capt. Robert: army captain; Sandwich's Master of Horse

FORD, Sir Richard: Spanish merchant

FOX, Sir Stephen: Paymaster of the Army

GAUDEN, Sir Denis: Navy victualler

GENERAL(s), the: Albemarle, Captain-General of the Kingdom, 1660–70; Prince Rupert and Albemarle, Generals-at-Sea in command of the Fleet, 1666

GIBSON, Richard: clerk to Pepys in the Navy Office

GWYN, Nell: actress (in the King's Company) and King's mistress

HARRIS, Henry: actor in the Duke's Company

HAYTER, Tom: clerk to Pepys in the Navy Office

HEWER, Will: clerk to Pepys in the Navy Office

HILL, Thomas: friend, musician, Portuguese merchant

HINCHINGBROOKE, Viscount (also 'Mr Edward', 'the child'): eldest son of Sandwich

HOLLIER (Holliard), Thomas: surgeon

HOLMES, Sir Robert: naval commander

HOWE, Will: household and naval servant of Sandwich

JAMES, DUKE OF YORK: the King's brother and heir presumptive (later James II); Lord High Admiral

JANE: usually Jane Birch, maidservant

JOYCE, Anthony (m. Kate Fenner, 1st cousin): innkeeper

JOYCE, William (m. Mary Fenner, 1st cousin): tallow-chandler

JUDGE-ADVOCATE, the: John Fowler, Judge-Advocate of the Fleet

KNIPP (Knepp) Mrs: actress in the King's Company

LADIES, the young, the two, the: often Sandwich's daughters

LAWSON, Sir John: naval commander

LIEUTENANT OF THE TOWER: Sir John Robinson

L'IMPERTINENT, Mons.: [?Daniel] Butler, friend, ? clergyman

LORD CHAMBERLAIN: Edward Mountagu, 2nd Earl of Manchester; Sandwich's cousin

LORD CHANCELLOR: Edward Hyde, 1st Earl of Clarendon (often called Chancellor after his dismissal, 1667)

LORD KEEPER: Sir Orlando Bridgeman

LORD PRIVY SEAL: John Robartes, 2nd Baron Robartes (later 1st Earl of Radnor)

LORD TREASURER: Thomas Wriothesley, 4th Earl of Southampton

MARTIN, Betty (née Lane): Pepys's mistress; shopgirl

MENNES (Minnes), Sir John: Comptroller of the Navy

MERCER, Mary: maid to Mrs Pepys

MILL(E)S, Rev. Dr John: Rector of St Olave's, Hart St; Pepys's parish priest

MONCK (Monke), George (Lord): soldier. See 'Albemarle, 1st Duke of'

MONMOUTH, Duke of: illegitimate son of Charles II

MOORE, Henry: lawyer; officer of Sandwich's household

MY LADY: usually Jemima, wife of Sandwich

MY LORD: usually Sandwich

NELL, NELLY: usually Nell Gywn

PALL: Paulina Pepys; sister (sometimes spelt 'pall')

PEARSE (Pierce), James: courtier, surgeon to Duke of York, and naval surgeon

PENN, Sir William: Commissioner of the Navy and naval commander (father of the Quaker leader)

PEPYS, Elizabeth (née St Michel): wife

PEPYS, John and Margaret: parents

PEPYS, John (unm.): brother; unbeneficed clergyman

PEPYS, Tom (unm.): brother; tailor

PEPYS, Paulina (m. John Jackson): sister

PEPYS, Capt. Robert: uncle, of Brampton, Hunts.

PEPYS, Roger: 1st cousin once removed; barrister and M.P.

PEPYS, Thomas: uncle, of St Alphege's, London

PETT, Peter: Commissioner of the Navy and shipwright

PICKERING, Mr (Ned): courtier, 1662–3; Sandwich's brother-in-law and servant

POVEY, Thomas: Treasurer of the Tangier Committee

PRINCE, the: usually Prince Rupert

QUEEN, the: (until May 1662) the Queen Mother, Henrietta-Maria, widow of Charles I; Catherine of Braganza, wife of Charles II (m. 21 May 1662)

RIDER, Sir William: merchant

ROBERT, Prince: Prince Rupert

RUPERT, Prince: 1st cousin of Charles II; naval commander

St MICHEL, Alexandre and Mary: parents-in-law

St MICHEL, Balthasar ('Balty'; m. Esther Watts): brother-in-law; minor naval official

SANDWICH, 1st Earl of: 1st cousin once removed, and patron; politician, naval commander and diplomat

SHIPLEY, Edward: steward of Sandwich's household

SIDNY, Mr: Sidney Mountagu, second son of Sandwich

SOLICITOR, the: the Solicitor-General, Sir Heneage Finch

SOUTHAMPTON, 4th Earl of: Lord Treasurer

SURVEYOR, the: the Surveyor of the Navy (Sir William Batten, 1660–7; Col. Thomas Middleton, 1667–72)

TEDDIMAN, Sir Thomas: naval commander

THE: Theophila Turner

TREASURER, the: usually the Treasurer of the Navy (Sir George Carteret, 1660–7; 1st Earl of Anglesey, 1667–8); sometimes the Lord Treasurer of the Kingdom, the Earl of Southampton, 1660–7

TRICE, Tom: half-brother; civil lawyer

TURNER, John (m. Jane Pepys, distant cousin): barrister

TURNER, Betty and Theophila: daughters of John and Jane Turner

TURNER, Thomas: senior clerk in the Navy Office

VICE-CHAMBERLAIN, the: Sir George Carteret, Vice-Chamberlain of the King's Household and Treasurer of the Navy

VYNER, Sir Robert: goldsmith–banker

WARREN, Sir William: timber merchant

WARWICK, Sir Philip: Secretary to the Lord Treasurer

WIGHT, William: uncle (half-brother of Pepys's father); fishmonger

WILL: usually Will Hewer

WILLET, Deborah: maid to Mrs Pepys

WILLIAMS ('Sir Wms. both'): Sir William Batten and Sir William Penn, colleagues on the Navy Board

WREN, Matthew: Secretary to the Lord High Admiral, 1667–72

SELECT GLOSSARY

A Large Glossary (of words, phrases and proverbs in all languages) will be found in the *Companion*. This Select Glossary is restricted to usages, many of them recurrent, which might puzzle the reader. It includes words and constructions which are now obsolete, archaic, slang or dialect; words which are used with meanings now obsolete or otherwise unfamiliar; and place names frequently recurrent or used in colloquial styles or in non-standard forms. The definitions given here are minimal: meanings now familiar and contemporary meanings not implied in the text are not noted, and many items are explained more fully in *Companion* articles ('Language', 'Food', 'Drink', 'Music', 'Theatre' etc.), and in the Large Glossary. A few foreign words are included. The spellings are taken from those used in the text: they do not, for brevity's sake, include all variants.

ABLE: wealthy
ABROAD: away, out of doors
ACCENT (of speech): the accentuation and the rising and falling of speech in pronunciation
ACCOUNTANT: official accountable for expenditure etc.
ACHIEVEMENT: hatchment, representation of heraldic arms
ACTION: acting, performance
ACTOR: male or female theatrical performer
ADDES: adze
ADMIRAL SHIP: flagship carrying admiral
ADMIRATION; ADMIRE: wonder, alarm; to wonder at
ADVENTURER: investor, speculator
ADVICE: consideration
AFFECT: to be fond of, to be concerned
AFFECTION: attention
AIR: generic term for all gases
ALL MY CAKE WILL BE DOE: all my plans will miscarry
ALPHABET: index, alphabetical list
AMBAGE: deceit, deviousness

AMUSED, AMUZED: bemused, astonished
ANCIENT: elderly, senior
ANGEL: gold coin worth *c.* 10s.
ANGELIQUE: small archlute
ANNOY: molest, hurt
ANOTHER GATE'S BUSINESS: different altogether
ANSWERABLE: similar, conformably
ANTIC, ANTIQUE: fantastic
APERN: apron
APPRENSION: apprehension
APPROVE OF: criticise
AQUA FORTIS (FARTIS): nitric acid
ARTICLE: to indict
ARTIST: workman, craftsman, technician, practitioner
ASPECT (astrol.): position of stars as seen from earth
ASTED: Ashtead, Surrey
AYERY: airy, sprightly, stylish

BAGNARD: bagnio, prison, lock-up
BAILEY, BAYLY: bailiff
BAIT, BAŸTE: refreshment on journey (for horses or travellers). *Also* v.

BALDWICK: Baldock, Herts.

BALK: roughly-squared beam of Baltic timber

BALLET: broadside ballad

BAND: neckband

BANDORE: musical instrument resembling guitar

BANQUET: course of fruits, sweets and wine; slight repast

BANQUET-, BANQUETING-HOUSE: summer-house

BARBE (s.): Arab (Barbary) horse

BARBE (v.): to shave

BARN ELMS: riverside area near Barnes, Surrey

BARRICADOES (naval): fenders

BASE, BASS: bass viol; thorough-bass

BASTE HIS COAT: to beat, chastise

BAVINS: kindling wood, brushwood

BAYLY: see 'Bailey'

BAYT(E): see 'Bait'

BEARD: facial hair, moustache

BEFOREHAND, to get: to have money in hand

BEHALF: to behave

BEHINDHAND: insolvent

BELL: to throb

BELOW: downstream from London Bridge

BELOW STAIRS: part of the Royal Household governed by Lord Steward

BEST HAND, at the: the best bargain

BEVER: beaver, fur hat

BEWPERS: bunting, fabric used for flags

BEZAN, BIZAN (Du. *bezaan*): small yacht

BIGGLESWORTH: Biggleswade, Beds.

BILL: (legal) warrant, writ; bill of exchange; Bill of Mortality (weekly list of burials; *see* iii. 225, n. 2)

BILLANDER (Du. *bijlander*): bilander, small two-masted merchantman

BIRD'S EYE: spotted fabric

BIZAN: see 'Bezan'

BLACK (adj.): brunette, dark in hair or complexion

BLACK(E)WALL: dock on n. shore of Thames below Greenwich used by E. Indiamen

BLANCH (of coins): to silver

BLIND: out of the way, private, obscure

BLOAT HERRING: bloater

BLUR: innuendo, charge

BOATE: boot or luggage compartment on side of coach

BODYS: foundations, basic rules; structure; (of ship) sectional drawings

BOLTHEAD: globular glass vessel with long straight neck

BOMBAIM: Bombay

BORDER: *toupée*

BOTARGO: dried fish-roe

BOTTOMARYNE, BOTTUMARY, BUMMARY: mortgage on ship

BOWPOTT: flower pot

BRAINFORD: Brentford, Mdx.

BRAMPTON: village near Huntingdon in which Pepys inherited property

BRANSLE: branle, brawl, group dance in duple or triple measure

BRAVE (adj.): fine, enjoyable

BRAVE (v.): to threaten, challenge

BREAK BULK: to remove part of cargo

BREDHEMSON, BRIGHTHEMSON: Brighton, Sussex

BRIDEWELL-BIRD: jailbird

BRIDGE: usually London Bridge; also jetty; landing stairs

BRIEF: collection authorised by Lord Chancellor for charity

BRIG, BRIGANTINE: small vessel equipped both for sailing and rowing

BRIGHTHEMSON: *see* 'Bredhemson'

BROTHER: brother-in-law; colleague

BRUMLY: Bromley, Kent

BRUSH (s.): graze

BUBO: tumour

BULLEN: Boulogne

BULLET: cannon-ball

BUMMARY: *see* 'Bottomaryne'

BURNTWOOD: Brentwood, Essex

BURY (of money): pour in, salt away, invest

BUSSE: two- or three-masted fishing boat

CABALL: inner group of ministers; knot

CABARETT (Fr. *cabaret*): tavern

CALES: Cadiz

CALICE, CALLIS: Calais

CALL: to call on/for; to drive

CAMELOTT, CAMLET, CAMLOTT: light cloth usually made from goat hair

CANAILLE, CHANNEL, KENNEL: drainage gutter (in street); canal (in St James's Park)

CANCRE: canker, ulcer, sore

CANNING ST: Cannon St

CANONS: boot-hose tops

CANTON (heraldic): small division of shield

CAPER (ship): privateer

CARBONADO: to grill, broil

CARESSE: to make much of

CARRY (a person): to conduct, escort

CAST OF OFFICE: taste of quality

CATAPLASM: poultice

CATCH: round song; (ship) ketch

CATT-CALL: whistle

CAUDLE: thin gruel

CELLAR: box for bottles

CERE CLOTH: cloth impregnated with wax and medicaments

CESTORNE: cistern

CHAFE: heat, anger

CHALDRON: $1\frac{1}{3}$ tons (London measure)

CHAMBER: small piece of ordnance for firing salutes

CHANGE, the: the Royal (Old) Exchange

CHANGELING: idiot

CHANNELL: *see* 'Canaille'

CHANNELL ROW: Cannon Row, Westminster

CHAPEL, the: usually the Chapel Royal, Whitehall Palace

CHAPTER: usually of Bible

CHARACTER: code, cipher; verbal portrait

CHEAP (s.): bargain

CHEAPEN: to ask the price of, bargain

CHEQUER, the: usually the Exchequer

CHEST, the: the Chatham Chest, the pension fund for seamen

CHILD, with: eager, anxious

CHIMNEY/CHIMNEY-PIECE: structure over and around fireplace

CHIMNEY-PIECE: picture over fireplace

CHINA-ALE: ale flavoured with china root

CHINE: rib (beef), saddle (mutton)

CHOQUE: attack

CHOUSE: to swindle, trick

CHURCH: after July 1660, usually St Olave's, Hart St

CLAP: gonorrhoea

CLERK OF THE CHEQUE: principal clerical officer of a dockyard

CLOATH (of meat): skin

CLOSE: shutter; (of music) cadence

CLOUTERLY: clumsily

CLOWNE: countryman, clodhopper

CLUB (s.): share of expenses, meeting at which expenses are shared. *Also* v.

CLYSTER, GLISTER, GLYSTER: enema

COACH: captain's state-room in large ship

COCK ALE: ale mixed with minced chicken

COCKPIT(T), the: usually the theatre in the Cockpit buildings, Whitehall Palace; the buildings themselves

COD: small bag; testicle

CODLIN TART: apple (codling) tart

COFFEE: coffee-house

COG: to cheat, banter, wheedle

COLEWORTS: cabbage

COLLAR DAY: day on which knights of chivalric orders wore insignia at court

COLLECT: to deduce

COLLIER: coal merchant; coal ship

COLLOPS: fried bacon

COLLY-FEAST: feast of collies (cullies, good companions) at which each pays his share

COMEDIAN: actor

COMEDY: play

COMFITURE (Fr. *confiture*): jam, marmalade

COMMEN, COMMON GUARDEN: Covent Garden

COMMONLY: together

COMPASS TIMBER: curved timber

COMPLEXION: character, humour

COMPOSE: to put music to words. *Also* 'Composition'

CONCEIT (s.): idea, notion

CONCLUDE: to include

CONDITION (s.): disposition; social position, state of wealth

CONDITION (v.): to make conditions

CONDITIONED: having a (specified) disposition or social position

CONGEE: bow at parting

CONJURE: to plead with

CONJUROR: wizard who operates by conjuration of spirits

CONSIDERABLE: worthy of consideration

CONSTER: to construe, translate

CONSUMPTION: (any) wasting disease. *Also* 'Consumptive'

CONTENT, by/in: by agreement, without examination, at a rough guess

CONVENIENCE: advantage

CONVENIENT: morally proper

CONVERSATION: demeanour, behaviour; acquaintance, society

COOLE: cowl

CORANT(O): dance involving a running or gliding step

COSEN, COUSIN: almost any collateral relative

COUNT: to recount

COUNTENANCE: recognition, acknowledgement

COUNTRY: county, district

COURSE, in: in sequence

COURSE, of: as usual

COURT BARON: manorial court (civil)

COURT-DISH: dish with a cut from every meat

COURT LEET: local criminal court

COUSIN: *see* 'Cosen'

COY: disdainful; quiet

COYING: stroking, caressing

CRADLE: fire-basket

CRAMBO: rhyming game

CRAZY: infirm

CREATURE (of persons): puppet, instrument

CRUSADO: Portuguese coin worth 3s.

CUDDY: room in a large ship in which the officers took their meals

CULLY: dupe; friend

CUNNING: knowledgeable; knowledge

CURIOUS: careful, painstaking, discriminating; fine, delicate

CURRANT: out and about

CUSTOMER: customs officer

CUT (v.): to carve meat

CUTT (s.): an engraving

DAUGHTER-IN-LAW: stepdaughter

DEAD COLOUR: preparatory layer of colour in a painting

DEAD PAYS: sailors or soldiers kept on pay roll after death

DEALS: sawn timber used for decks, etc.

DEDIMUS: writ empowering J.P.

DEFALK: to subtract

DEFEND: to prevent

DEFY (Fr.): to mistrust. *Also* Defyance

DELICATE: pleasant

DELINQUENT: active royalist in Civil War and Interregnum

DEMORAGE: demurrage, compensation from the freighter due to a shipowner for delaying vessel beyond time specified in charter-party

DEPEND: to wait, hang

DEVISE: to decide; discern

DIALECT: jargon

DIALL, double horizontal: instrument telling hour of day

DIRECTION: supervision of making; arrangement
DISCOVER: to disclose, reveal
DISCREET: discerning, judicious
DISGUST: to dislike
DISPENSE: provisions, supplies
DISTASTE (s.): difference, quarrel, offence. *Also* v.
DISTINCT: discerning, discriminating
DISTRINGAS: writ of distraint
DOATE: to nod off to sleep
DOCTOR: clergyman, don
DOE: dough. *See* 'All my cake . . .'
DOGGED: awkward
DOLLER: *see* 'Rix Doller'
DORTOIRE: dorter, monastic dormitory
DOTY: darling
DOWNS, the: roadstead off Deal, Kent
DOXY: whore, mistress
DRAM: timber from Drammen, Norway
DRAWER: tapster, barman
DRESS: to cook, prepare food
DROLL: comic song
DROLLING, DROLLY: comical, comically
DRUDGER: dredger, container for sweetmeats
DRUGGERMAN: dragoman, interpreter
DRY BEATEN: beaten without drawing blood
DRY MONEY: hard cash
DUANA: divan, council
DUCCATON: ducatoon, large silver coin of the Netherlands worth 5s. 9d.
DUCKET(T): ducat, foreign gold coin (here probably Dutch) worth 9s.
DUKE'S [PLAY] HOUSE, the: playhouse in Lincoln's Inn Fields used by the Duke of York's Company from June 1660 until 9 November 1671; often called 'the Opera'. Also known as the Lincoln's Inn Fields Theatre (LIF)
DULL: limp, spiritless

EARTH: earthenware

EASILY AND EASILY: more and more slowly
EAST INDIES: the territory covered by the E. India Company, including the modern sub-continent of India
EAST COUNTRY, EASTLAND: the territory (in Europe) covered by the Eastland Company
EFFEMINACY: love of women
ELABORATORY: laboratory
ELECTUARY: medicinal salve with a honey base
EMERODS: haemorrhoids
ENTENDIMIENTO (Sp.): understanding
ENTER (of horse): to break in
ENTERTAIN: to retain, employ
EPICURE: glutton
ERIFFE: Erith, Kent
ESPINETTE(S): spinet, small harpsichord
ESSAY: to assay
EVEN (adv.): surely
EVEN (of accounts): to balance
EVEN (of the diary): to bring up to date
EXCEPT: to accept
EXPECT: to see, await

FACTION: the government's parliamentary critics
FACTIOUS: able to command a following
FACTOR: mercantile agent
FACTORY: trading station
FAIRING: small present (as from a fair)
FAIRLY: gently, quietly
FALCHON: falchion, curved sword
FAMILY: household (including servants)
FANCY (music): fantasia
FANFARROON: fanfaron, braggart
FARANDINE, FARRINDIN: *see* 'Ferrandin'
FASHION (of metal, furniture): design, fashioning
FAT: vat
FATHER: father-in-law (similarly with 'mother' etc.)
FELLET (of trees): a cutting, felling

FELLOW COMMONER: undergraduate paying high fees and enjoying privileges

FENCE: defence

FERRANDIN, FARRINDIN, FARANDINE: cloth of silk mixed with wool or hair

FIDDLE: viol; violin

FINE (s.): payment for lease

FINE FOR OFFICE (v.): to avoid office by payment of fine

FIRESHIP: ship filled with combustibles used to ram and set fire to enemy

FITS OF THE MOTHER: hysterics

FLAG, FLAGGMAN: flag officer

FLAGEOLET: end-blown, six-holed instrument

FLESHED: relentless, proud

FLOOD: rising tide

FLUXED (of the pox): salivated

FLYING ARMY/FLEET: small mobile force

FOND, FONDNESS: foolish; folly

FOND: fund

FORCE OUT: to escape

FORSOOTH: to speak ceremoniously

FORTY: many, scores of

FOXED: intoxicated

FOX HALL: Vauxhall (pleasure gardens)

FOY: departure feast or gift

FREQUENT: to busy oneself

FRIENDS: parents, relatives

FROST-BITE: to invigorate by exposure to cold

FULL: anxious

FULL MOUTH, with: eagerly; openly, loudly

GALL: harass

GALLIOTT: small swift galley

GALLOPER, the: shoal off Essex coast

GAMBO: Gambia, W. Africa

GAMMER: old woman

GENERAL-AT-SEA: naval commander (a post, not a rank)

GENIUS: inborn character, natural ability; mood

GENT: graceful, polite

GENTILELY: obligingly

GEORGE: jewel forming part of insignia of Order of Garter

GERMANY: territory of the Holy Roman Empire

GET UP ONE'S CRUMB: to improve one's status

GET WITHOUT BOOK: to memorise

GIBB-CAT: tom-cat

GILDER, GUILDER: Dutch money of account worth 2s.

GIMP: twisted thread of material with wire or cord running through it

GITTERNE: musical instrument of the guitar family

GIVE: to answer

GLASS: telescope

GLEEKE: three-handed card game

GLISTER, GLYSTER: see 'Clyster'

GLOSSE, by a fine: by a plausible pretext

GO TO ONE'S NAKED BED: to go to bed without night-clothes

GO(O)D BWYE: God be with ye, good-bye

GODLYMAN: Godalming, Surrey

GOODFELLOW: convivial person, good timer

GOODMAN, GOODWIFE ('Goody'): used of men and women of humble station

GOOD-SPEAKER: one who speaks well of others

GORGET: neckerchief for women

GOSSIP (v.): to act as godparent, to attend a new mother; to chatter. *Also* s.

GOVERNMENT: office or function of governor

GRACIOUS-STREET(E): Gracechurch St

GRAIN (? of gold): sum of money

GRAVE: to engrave

GREEN (of meat): uncured

GRESHAM COLLEGE: meeting-place of Royal Society; the Society itself

GRIEF: bodily pain

GRUDGEING, GRUTCHING: trifling complaint, grumble

GUEST: nominee; friend; stranger

GUIDE: postboy

GUILDER: *see* 'Gilder'

GUN: flagon of ale; cannon, salute

GUNDALO, GUNDILOW: gondola

GUNFLEET, the: shoal off Essex coast

HACKNEY: hack, workhorse, drudge

HAIR, against the: against the grain

HALF-A-PIECE: gold coin worth *c.* 10*s.*

HALF-SHIRT: sham shirt front

HALFE-WAY-HOUSE: Rotherhithe tavern halfway between London Bridge and Deptford

HALL, the: usually Westminster Hall

HANDSEL: to try out, use for first time

HAND-TO-FIST: hastily

HANDYCAPP: handicap, a card game

HANG IN THE HEDGE: to be delayed

HANGER: loop holding a sword; small sword

HANGING JACK: turnspit for roasting meat

HANK: hold, grip

HAPPILY: haply, perchance

HARE: to harry, rebuke

HARPSICHON, HARPSICHORD: keyboard instrument of one or two manuals, with strings plucked by quills or leather jacks, and with stops which vary the tone

HARSLET: haslet, pigmeat (esp. offal)

HAVE A GOOD COAT OF [HIS] FLEECE: to have a good share

HAVE A HAND: to have leisure, freedom

HAVE A MONTH'S MIND: to have a great desire

HAWSE, thwart their: across their bows

HEAD-PIECE: helmet

HEART: courage

HEAVE AT: to oppose

HECTOR: street-bully, swashbuckler

HERBALL: botanical encyclopaedia; *hortus siccus* (book of dried and pressed plants)

HERE (Du. *heer*): Lord

HIGH: arrogant, proud, high-handed

HINCHINGBROOKE: Sandwich's house near Huntingdon

HOMAGE: jury of presentment at a manorial court

HONEST (of a woman): virtuous

HOOKS, off the: angry, mad

HOPE, the: reach of Thames downstream from Tilbury

HOPEFUL: promising

HOUSE: playhouse; parliament; (royal) household or palace building

HOUSE OF OFFICE: latrine

HOY: small passenger and cargo ship, sloop-rigged

HOYSE: to hoist

HUMOUR (s.): mood; character, characteristic; good or ill temper

HUMOUR (v.): to set words suitably to music

HUSBAND: one who gets good/bad value for money; supervisor, steward

HYPOCRAS: hippocras, spiced white wine

ILL-TEMPERED: out of sorts, ill-adjusted (to weather etc.; cf. 'Temper')

IMPERTINENCE: irrelevance, garrulity, folly. *Also* 'Impertinent'

IMPOSTUME: abscess

IMPREST: money paid in advance by government to public servant

INDIAN GOWN: loose gown of glazed cotton

INGENIOUS, INGENUOUS: clever, intelligent

INGENUITY: wit, intelligence; freedom

INGENUOUS: *see* 'Ingenious'

INSIPID: stupid, dull

INSTITUCIONS: instructions

INSTRUMENT: agent, clerk

INSULT: to exult over

INTELLIGENCE: information

INTRATUR: warrant authorising payment by Exchequer

IRISIPULUS: erysipelas

IRONMONGER: often a large-scale merchant, not necessarily a retailer

JACK(E): flag used as signal or mark of distinction; rogue, knave. *See also* 'Hanging jack'

JACKANAPES COAT: monkey jacket, sailor's short close-fitting jacket

JACOB(US): gold sovereign coined under James I

JAPAN: lacquer, lacquered

JARR, JARRING: quarrel

JEALOUS: fearful, suspicious, mistrustful. *Also* 'Jealousy'

JERK(E): captious remark

JES(S)IMY: jasmine

JEW'S TRUMP: Jew's harp

JOCKY: horse-dealer

JOLE (of fish): jowl, a cut consisting of the head and shoulders. *See also* 'Pole'

JOYNT-STOOL: stout stool held together by joints

JULIPP: julep, a sweet drink made from syrup

JUMBLE: to take for an airing

JUMP WITH: to agree, harmonise

JUNK (naval): old rope

JURATE (of Cinque Ports): jurat, alderman

JUSTE-AU-CORPS: close-fitting long coat

KATCH: (ship) ketch

KEEP A QUARTER: to make a disturbance

KENNEL: *see* 'Canaille'

KERCHER: kerchief, head-covering

KETCH (s.): catch, song in canon

KETCH (v.): to catch

KING'S [PLAY] HOUSE, the: playhouse in Vere St, Clare Market, Lincoln's Inn Fields, used by the King's Company from 8 November 1660 until 7 May 1663; the playhouse in Bridges St, Drury Lane, used by the same company from 7 May 1663 until the fire of 25 January 1672. Also known as the Theatre Royal (TR).

KITLIN: kitling, kitten, cub

KNEES: timbers of naturally angular shape used in ship-building

KNOT (s.): flower bed; difficulty; clique, band

KNOT (v.): to join, band together

KNOWN: famous

LACE: usually braid made with gold- or silver-thread

LAMB'S-WOOL: hot ale with apples and spice

LAMP-GLASS: magnifying lens used to concentrate lamp-light

LAST: load, measure of tar

LASTOFFE: Lowestoft, Suff.

LATITUDINARIAN: liberal Anglican

LAVER: fountain

LEADS: flat space on roof top, sometimes boarded over

LEAN: to lie down

LEARN: to teach

LEAVE: to end

LECTURE: weekday religious service consisting mostly of a sermon

LESSON: piece of music

LETTERS OF MART: letters of marque

LEVETT: reveille, reveille music

LIBEL(L): leaflet, broadside; (in legal proceedings) written charge

LIE UPON: to press, insist

LIFE: life interest

LIFE, for my: on my life

LIGHT: window

LIGNUM VITAE: hard W. Indian wood with medicinal qualities, often used for drinking vessels

LIMB: to limn, paint

LIME (of dogs): to mate

LINK(E): torch

LINNING: linen

LIPPOCK: Liphook, Hants.

LIST: pleasure, desire

LOCK: waterway between arches of bridge

LOMBRE: *see* 'Ombre'

LONDON: the city of London (to be distinguished from Westminster)

LOOK: to look at/for

LOOK AFTER: to have eyes on

LUMBERSTREETE: Lombard St

LUTE: pear-shaped instrument with six courses of gut strings and a turned-back peg-box; made in various sizes, the larger instruments having additional bass strings

LUTESTRING: lustring, a glossy silk

LYRA-VIALL: small bass viol tuned for playing chords

MAD: whimsical, wild, extravagant

MADAM(E): prefix used mainly of widows, elderly/foreign ladies

MAIN (adj.): strong, bulky

MAIN (s.): chief purpose or object

MAISTER: expert; professional; sailing master

MAKE (s.): (of fighting cocks) match, pair of opponents

MAKE (v.): to do; to copulate

MAKE LEGS: to bow, curtsey

MAKE SURE TO: to plight troth

MALLOWS: St Malo

MAN OF BUSINESS: executive agent, administrator

MANAGED-HORSE (cf. Fr. *manège*): horse trained in riding school

MANDAMUS: royal mandate under seal

MARGARET, MARGETTS: Margate, Kent

MARGENTING: putting margin-lines on paper

MARK: 13s. 4d.

MARMOTTE (Fr., term of affection): young girl

MARROWBONE: Marylebone, Mdx

MASTY: burly

MATCH: tinderbox and wick

MATHEMATICIAN: mathematical instrument-maker

MEAT: food

MEDIUM: mean, average

METHEGLIN: strong mead flavoured with herbs

MINCHIN-LANE: Mincing Lane

MINE: mien

MINIKIN: thin string or gut used for treble string of lute or viol

MISTRESS (prefix): used of unmarried girls and women as well as of young married women

MISTRESS: sweetheart

MITHRYDATE: drug used as an antidote

MODEST (of woman): virtuous

MOHER (Sp. *mujer*): woman, wife

MOIS, MOYS: menstrual periods

MOLD, MOLDE, MOLLE (archit.): mole

MOLEST: to annoy

MOND: orb (royal jewel in form of globe)

MONTEERE, MOUNTEERE: huntsman's cap; close-fitting hood

MOPED: bemused

MORECLACK(E): Mortlake, Surrey

MORENA (Sp.): brunette

MORNING DRAUGHT: drink (sometimes with snack) taken instead of breakfast

MOTHER-IN-LAW: stepmother (similarly with 'father-in-law' etc.)

MOTT: sighting line in an optical tube

MOUNTEERE: *see* 'Monteere'

MOYRE: moire, watered silk

MUM: strong spiced ale

MURLACE: Morlaix, Brittany

MUSCADINE, MUSCATT: muscatel wine

MUSIC: band, choir, performers

MUSTY: peevish

NAKED BED: *see* 'Go to one's n.b.'

NARROWLY: anxiously, carefully

NAUGHT, NOUGHT: worthless, bad in condition or quality, sexually wicked

NAVY: Navy Office

NAVY OFFICERS: Principal Officers of the Navy – i.e. the Comptroller, Treasurer, Surveyor, Clerk of the Acts, together with a variable number of Commissioners; members of the Navy Board. Cf. 'Sea-Officers'

NEARLY: deeply

NEAT (adj.): handsome

NEAT(s.): ox, cattle

NEITHER MEDDLE NOR MAKE: to have nothing to do with

NEWSBOOK: newspaper (weekly, octavo)

NIBBLE AT: to carp at

NICOTIQUES: narcotics, medicines

NIGHTGOWN(E): dressing gown

NOISE: group of musical instruments playing together

NORE, the: anchorage in mouth of Thames

NORTHDOWNE ALE: Margate ale

NOSE: to insult, affront

NOTE: business

NOTORIOUS: famous, well-known

NOUGHT: *see* 'Naught'

OBNOXIOUS: liable to

OBSERVABLE (adj.): noteworthy, notorious

OBSERVABLE (s.): thing or matter worthy of observation

OF: to have

OFFICE DAY: day on which a meeting of the Navy Board was held

OFFICERS OF THE NAVY: *see* 'Navy Officers'

OLEO (Sp. *olla*): stew

OMBRE (Sp. *hombre*): card game

ONLY: main, principal, best

OPEN: unsettled

OPERA: spectacular entertainment (involving use of painted scenery and stage machinery), often with music

OPERA, the: the theatre in Lincoln's Inn Fields. *See* 'Duke's House, the'

OPINIASTRE, OPINIASTREMENT (Fr.): stubborn, stubbornly

OPPONE: to oppose, hinder

ORDER: to put in order; to punish

ORDINARY (adj.): established

ORDINARY (s.): eating place serv-

ing fixed-price meals; peace-time establishment (of navy, dockyard, etc.)

OUTPORTS: ports other than London

OVERSEEN: omitted, neglected; guilty of oversight

OWE: to own

PADRON (?Sp., ?It. *patrone*): master

PAGEANT: decorated symbolic float in procession

PAINFUL: painstaking

PAIR OF OARS: large river-boat rowed by two watermen, each using a pair of oars. Cf. 'Scull'

PAIR OF ORGANS/VIRGINALS: a single instrument

PALACE: New Palace Yard

PALER: parlour

PANNYARD: pannier, basket

PARAGON: heavy rich cloth, partly of mohair

PARALLELOGRAM: pantograph

PARCEL: share, part; isolated group

PARK, the: normally St James's Park (Hyde Park is usually named)

PARTY: charter-party

PASQUIL: a lampoon

PASSION: feeling, mood

PASSIONATE: touching, affecting

PATTEN: overshoe

PAY: to berate, beat

PAY A COAT: to beat, chastise

PAYSAN (Fr.): country style

PAY SICE: to pay dearly (sixfold)

PENDANCES, PENDENTS: lockets; earrings

PERPLEX: to vex

PERSPECTIVE, PERSPECTIVE GLASSES: binoculars

PESLEMESLE: pell-mell, early form of croquet

PETTY BAG: petty cash

PHILOSOPHY: natural science

PHYSIC: laxative, purge

PHYSICALLY: without sheets, uncovered

PICK: pique

PICK A HOLE IN A COAT: to pick a quarrel, complain

PICKAROON (Sp. *picarón*): pirate, privateer

PIECE: gold coin worth *c*. 20*s*.

PIECE (PEECE) OF EIGHT: Spanish silver coin worth 4*s*. 6*d*.

PIGEON: coward

PINK(E): small broad-beamed ship; poniard, pointed weapon

PINNER: coif with two long flaps; fill-in above low *décolletage*

PIPE: measure of wine (*c*. 120 galls.)

PIPE (musical): recorder or flageolet; between 4 June and 19 September 1667, flageolet

PISTOLE: French gold coin worth 16*s*.

PLACKET: petticoat

PLAIN: unaffected

PLAT(T): plate, plan, chart, map; arrangement; level; [flower] plot

PLATERER: one who works silver plate

PLAY (v.): to play for stakes

POINT, POYNT: piece of lace

POINT DE GESNE: Genoa lace

POLE: head; head-and-shoulder (of fish); poll tax

POLICY: government; cunning; self-interest

POLLARD: cut-back, stunted tree

POMPOUS: ceremonious, dignified

POOR JACK: dried salt fish

POOR WRETCH: poor dear

POSSET: drink made of hot milk, spices, and wine (or beer)

POST (v.): to expose, pillory

POST WARRANT: authority to employ posthorses

POSY: verse or phrase engraved on inside of ring

POWDERED (of meat): salted

PRACTICE: trick

PRAGMATIC, PRAGMATICAL: interfering, conceited, dogmatic

PRATIQUE: ship's licence for port facilities given on its presenting clean bill of health

PRESBYTER JOHN: puritan parson

PRESENT (s.): shot, volley

PRESENT, PRESENTLY: immediate, immediately

PRESS BED: bed folding into or built inside a cupboard

PREST MONEY (milit., naval): earnest money paid in advance

PRETTY (of men): fine, elegant, foppish

PREVENT: to anticipate

PRICK: to write out music; to list

PRICK OUT: to strike out, delete

PRINCE: ruler

PRINCIPLES (of music): natural ability, rudimentary knowledge

PRISE, PRIZE: worth, value, price

PRIVATE: small, secret, quiet

PRIZE FIGHT: fencing match fought for money

PROPRIETY: property, ownership

PROTEST (a bill of exchange): to record non-payment

PROUD (of animals): on heat

PROVOKE: to urge

PULL A CROW: to quarrel

PURCHASE: advantage; profit; booty

PURELY: excellently

PURL(E): hot spiced beer

PUSS: ill-favoured woman

PUT OFF: to sell, dispose of

PYONEER: pioneer (ditch digger, labourer)

QU: cue

QUARREFOUR: crossroads

QUARTERAGE: charge for lodgings or quarters; quarterly allowance

QUARTRE: position in dancing or fencing

QUEST HOUSE: house used for inquests, parish meetings

QUINBROUGH: Queenborough, Kent

QUINSBOROUGH: Königsberg, E. Prussia

RACE: to rase, destroy

RAKE-SHAMED: disreputable, disgraceful

RARE: fine, splendid
RATE: to berate, scold
RATTLE: to scold
RATTOON: rattan cane
READY: dressed
REAKE: trick
RECEPI: writ of receipt issued by Chancery
RECITATIVO (*stilo r.*): the earliest type of recitative singing
RECONCILE: to settle a dispute, to determine the truth
RECORDER: family of end-blown, eight-holed instruments (descant, treble, tenor, bass)
RECOVER: to reconcile
RECOVERY (legal): process for re-establishment of ownership
REDRIFFE: Rotherhithe, Surrey
REFERRING: indebted, beholden to
REFORM: to disband
REFORMADO: naval/military officer serving without commission
REFRESH (of a sword): to sharpen
RELIGIOUS: monk, nun
REPLICACION (legal): replication, plaintiff's answer to defendant's plea
RESEMBLE: to represent, figure
RESENT: to receive
RESPECT: to mean, refer to
RESPECTFUL: respectable
REST: wrest, tuning key
RETAIN (a writ): to maintain a court action from term to term
REVOLUTION: sudden change (not necessarily violent)
RHODOMONTADO: boast, brag
RIDE POST: to travel by posthorse, to ride fast
RIGHT-HAND-MAN: soldier on whom drill manoeuvres turn
RIGHTS, to: immediately, directly
RIS (v.): rose
RISE: origin
RIX DOLLER: Dutch or N. German silver coin (*Rijksdaalder, Reichsthaler*) worth c. 4s. 9d.

ROCKE: distaff
ROMANTIQUE: having the characteristics of a tale (romance)
ROUNDHOUSE: uppermost cabin in stern of ship
ROYALL THEATRE, the: *see* 'Theatre, the'
RUB(B): check, stop, obstacle
RUFFIAN: pimp
RUMP: remnant of the Long Parliament
RUMPER: member or supporter of the Rump
RUNLETT: cask
RUNNING: temporary

SACK: white wine from Spain or Canaries
SALT: salt-cellar
SALT-EELE: rope's end used for punishment
SALVE UP: to smooth over
SALVO: excuse, explanation
SARCENET: thin taffeta, fine silk cloth
SASSE (Du. *sas*): sluice, lock
SAVE: to be in time for
SAY: fine woollen cloth
SCALE (of music): key; gamut
SCALLOP: scalloped lace collar
SCALLOP-WHISK: *see* 'Whiske'
SCAPE (s.): adventure
SCAPE (v.): to escape
SCARE-FIRE: sudden conflagration
SCHOOL: to scold, rebuke
SCHUIT (Du.): Dutch canal boat, barge
SCONCE: bracket, candlestick
SCOTOSCOPE: portable *camera obscura*
SCOWRE: to beat, punish
SCREW: key, screw-bolt
SCRUPLE: to dispute
SCULL, SCULLER: small river-boat rowed by a single waterman using one pair of oars. Cf. 'Pair of oars'
SEA-CARD: chart
SEA-COAL: coal carried by sea

SEA-OFFICERS: commissioned officers of the navy. Cf. 'Navy Officers'
SECOND MOURNING: half-mourning
SEEL (of a ship): to lurch
SEEM: to pretend
SENNIT: sevennight, a week
SENSIBLY: perceptibly, painfully
SERPENT: firework
SERVANT: suitor, lover
SET: sit
SET UP/OFF ONE'S REST: to be certain, to be content, to make an end, to make one's whole aim
SEWER: stream, ditch
SHAG(G): worsted or silk cloth with a velvet nap on one side
SHEATH (of a ship): to encase the hull as a protection against worm
SHIFT (s.): trial; dressing room
SHIFT (v.): to change clothes; to dodge a round in paying for drinks (or to get rid of the effects of drink)
SHOEMAKER'S STOCKS: new shoes
SHOVE AT: to apply one's energies to
SHROUD (shrew'd): shrewdish, peevish
SHUFFLEBOARD: shovelboard, shove-ha'penny
SHUTS: shutters
SILLABUB, SULLYBUB, SYLLABUB: milk mixed with wine
SIMPLE: foolish
SIT: to hold a meeting
SIT CLOSE: to hold a meeting from which clerks are excluded
SITHE: sigh
SKELLUM: rascal, thief
SLENDERLY: slightingly
SLICE: flat plate
SLIGHT, SLIGHTLY: contemptuous; slightingly, without ceremony
SLIP A CALF/FILLY: to abort
SLOP(P)S: seamen's ready-made clothes
SLUG(G): slow heavy boat; rough metal projectile
SLUT (not always opprobrious): drudge, wench

SMALL (of drink): light
SNAP(P) (s.): bite, snack, small meal; attack
SNAP (v.): to ambush, cut down/out/off
SNUFF: to speak scornfully
SNUFFE, take/go in: to take offence
SOKER: old hand; pal; toper
SOLD(E)BAY: Solebay, off Southwold, Suff.
SOL(L)ICITOR: agent; one who solicits business
SON: son-in-law (similarly with 'daughter' etc.)
SON-IN-LAW: stepson
SOUND: fish-bladder
SOUND, the: strictly the navigable passage between Denmark and Sweden where tolls were levied, but more generally (and usually in Pepys) the Baltic
SPARROWGRASS: asparagus
SPEAK BROAD: to speak fully, frankly
SPECIALITY: bond under seal
SPECIES (optical): image
SPEED: to succeed
SPIKET: spigot, tap, faucet
SPILT, SPOILT: ruined
SPINET: single-manual wing-shaped keyboard instrument with harpsichord action
SPOIL: to deflower; injure
SPOTS: patches (cosmetic)
SPRANKLE: sparkling remark, *bon mot*
SPUDD: trenching tool
STAIRS: landing stage
STAND IN: to cost
STANDING WATER: between tides
STANDISH: stand for ink, pens, etc.
STATE-DISH: richly decorated dish; dish with a round lid or canopy
STATESMAN: Commonwealth's-man
STATIONER: bookseller (often also publisher)
STEEPLE: tower
STEMPEECE: timber of ship's bow
STICK: blockhead

STILLYARD, the: the Steelyard
STIR(R): rumour
STOMACH: courage, pride; appetite
STOMACHFULLY: proudly
STONE-HORSE: stallion
STOUND: astonishment
STOUT: brave, courageous
STOWAGE: storage, payment for storage
STRAIGHTS, STREIGHTS, the: strictly the Straits of Gibraltar; more usually the Mediterranean
STRANG: strong
STRANGERS: foreigners
STRIKE (nautical): to lower the top-sail in salute; (of Exchequer tallies) to make, cut
STRONG WATER: distilled spirits
SUBSIDY MAN: man of substance (liable to pay subsidy-tax)
SUCCESS(E): outcome (good or bad)
SUDDENLY: in a short while
SULLYBUB: see 'Sillabub'
SUPERNUMERARY: seaman extra to ship's complement
SURLY: imperious, lordly
SWINE-POX: chicken-pox
SWOUND: to swoon, faint
SYLLABUB: see 'Sillabub'
SYMPHONY: instrumental introduction, interlude etc., in a vocal composition

TAB(B)Y: watered silk
TABLE: legend attached to a picture
TABLE BOOK: memorandum book
TABLES: backgammon and similar games
TAILLE, TALLE (Fr. taille): figure, shape (of person)
TAKE EGGS FOR MONEY: to cut one's losses, to accept something worthless
TAKE OUT: to learn; perform
TAKE UP: to agree on
TAKING (s.): condition
TALE: reckoning, number
TALL: fine, elegant
TALLE: see 'Taille'

TALLY: wooden stick used by the Exchequer in accounting
TAMKIN: tampion, wooden gun plug
TANSY, TANZY: egg pudding flavoured with tansy
TARGET: shield
TARPAULIN: 'tar', a sea-bred captain as opposed to a gentleman-captain
TAXOR: financial official of university
TEAR: to rant
TELL: to count
TEMPER (s.): moderation; temperament, mood; physical condition
TEMPER (v.): to moderate, control
TENDER: chary of
TENT: roll of absorbent material used for wounds; (Sp. tinto) red wine
TERCE, TIERCE: measure of wine (42 galls.; one-third of a pipe)
TERELLA: terrella, spherical magnet, terrestrial globe containing magnet
TERM(E)S: menstrual periods
THEATRE, the: before May 1663 usually Theatre Royal, Vere St; afterwards usually Theatre Royal, Drury Lane (TR)
THEM: see 'Those'
THEORBO: large double-necked tenor lute
THOSE: menstrual periods
THRUSH: inflammation of throat and mouth
TICKELED: annoyed, irritated
TICKET(T): seaman's pay-ticket
TIERCE: see 'Terce'
TILT: awning over river-boat
TIMBER: wood for the skeleton of a ship (as distinct from plank or deals used for the decks, cabins, gun-platforms etc.)
TIRE: tier
TOKEN, by the same: so, then, and
TONGUE: reputation, fame
TOPS: turnovers of stockings
TOUCHED: annoyed
TOUR, the: coach parade of beau monde in Hyde Park

TOUSE: to tousle/tumble a woman

TOWN(E): manor

TOY: small gift

TOYLE: foil, net into which game is driven

TRADE: manufacture, industry

TRANSIRE: warrant allowing goods through customs

TRAPAN, TREPAN: to perform brain surgery; cheat, trick, trap, inveigle

TREASURY, the: the Navy Treasury or the national Treasury

TREAT: to handle (literally)

TREAT, TREATY: negotiate, negotiation

TREBLE: treble viol

TREPAN: *see* 'Trapan'

TRIANGLE, TRYANGLE: triangular virginals

TRILL(O): vocal ornament consisting of the accelerated repetition of the same note

TRIM: to shave

TRUCKLE/TRUNDLE-BED: low bed on castors which could be put under main bed

TRYANGLE: *see* 'Triangle'

TRY A PULL: to have a go

TUITION: guardianship

TUNE: pitch

TURK, the: used of all denizens of the Turkish Empire, but usually here of the Berbers of the N. African coast, especially Algiers

TURKEY WORK: red tapestry in Turkish style

TURKY-STONE: turquoise

TUTTLE FIELDS: Tothill Fields

TWIST: strong thread

UGLY: awkward

UMBLES (of deer): edible entrails, giblets

UNBESPEAK: countermand

UNCOUTH: out of sorts or order, uneasy, at a loss

UNDERSTAND: to conduct oneself properly; (s.) understanding

UNDERTAKER: contractor; parliamentary manager

UNHAPPY, UNHAPPILY: unlucky; unluckily

UNREADY: undressed

UNTRUSS: to undo one's breeches, defecate

UPPER BENCH: name given in Interregnum to King's Bench

USE: usury, interest

USE UPON USE: compound interest

VAPOURISH: pretentious, foolish

VAUNT: to vend, sell

VENETIAN CAP: peaked cap as worn by Venetian Doge

VESTS: robes, vestments

VIALL, VIOL: family of fretted, bowed instruments with six gut strings; the bowing hand is held beneath the bow and the instrument held on or between the knees; now mostly superseded by violin family

VIRGINALS: rectangular English keyboard instrument resembling spinet; usually in case without legs

VIRTUOSO: man of wide learning

WAISTCOAT, WASTECOATE: warm undergarment

WAIT, WAYT (at court etc.): to serve a turn of duty (usually a month) as an official

WARDROBE, the: the office of the King's Great Wardrobe, of which Lord Sandwich was Keeper; the building at Puddle Wharf containing the office; a cloak room, dressing room

WARM: comfortable, well-off

WASSAIL, WASSELL: entertainment (e.g. a play)

WASTCOATE: *see* 'Waistcoat'

WASTECLOATH: cloth hung on ship as decoration between quarter-deck and forecastle

WATCH: clock

WATER: strong water, spirits

WAY, in/out of the: accessible/inaccessible; in a suitable/unsuitable condition

WAYTES: waits; municipal musicians

WEATHER-GLASS(E): thermometer (or, less likely, barometer)

WEIGH (of ships): to raise

WELLING: Welwyn, Herts.

WESTERN BARGEMAN (BARGEE): bargee serving western reaches of Thames

WESTMINSTER: the area around Whitehall and the Abbey; not the modern city of Westminster

WHISKE: woman's neckerchief

WHITE-HALL: royal palace, largely burnt down in 1698

WHITSTER: bleacher, launderer

WIGG: wig, cake, bun

WILDE: wile

WIND (s.): wine

WIND LIKE A CHICKEN: to wind round one's little finger

WINDFUCKER: talkative braggart

WIPE: sarcasm, insult

WISTELY: with close attention

WIT, WITTY: cleverness, clever

WONDER: to marvel at

WOODMONGER: fuel merchant

WORD: utterance, phrase

WOREMOODE: wormwood

WORK: needlework. *Also* v.

WRETCH: *see* 'Poor wretch'

YARD: penis

YARE: ready, skilful

YILDHALL: Guildhall

YOWELL: Ewell, Surrey